T0295739

Roman Inequality

Roman Inequality

Affluent Slaves, Businesswomen, Legal Fictions

EDWARD E. COHEN

OXFORD
UNIVERSITY PRESS

Oxford University Press is a department of the University of Oxford. It furthers the University's objective of excellence in research, scholarship, and education by publishing worldwide. Oxford is a registered trade mark of Oxford University Press in the UK and certain other countries.

Published in the United States of America by Oxford University Press
198 Madison Avenue, New York, NY 10016, United States of America.

Library of Congress Cataloging-in-Publication Data
Names: Cohen, Edward E., author.
Title: Roman inequality : affluent slaves, businesswomen, legal fictions / Edward E. Cohen.
Description: New York : Oxford University Press, [2023] | Includes bibliographical references and index.
Identifiers: LCCN 2023003836 (print) | LCCN 2023003837 (ebook) | ISBN 9780197687345 (hardback) | ISBN 9780197687352 (epub)
Subjects: LCSH: Social stratification—Rome—History. | Slaves—Rome—Social conditions. | Equality—Economic aspects—Rome—History. | Rome—Social conditions. | Rome—Economic conditions.
Classification: LCC HN10 .R7 C64 2023 (print) | LCC HN10 .R7 (ebook) | DDC 305.5086/250937—dc23/eng/20230206
LC record available at https://lccn.loc.gov/2023003836
LC ebook record available at https://lccn.loc.gov/2023003837

DOI: 10.1093/oso/9780197687345.001.0001

To my sons, Daniel Gideon Cohen and Jonathan Zubrow Cohen.

For whom the unexamined life has never been worth living.

Contents

Acknowledgments

DESPITE THE WIDESPREAD belief that until relatively recently Roman law was not a serious field of study for native-born American scholars,[1] I was fortunate as a graduate student in Classics at Princeton University to have first studied Roman Law more than sixty years ago with Profs. P. R. Coleman-Norton and Frank Bourne, and subsequently to have worked with Prof. Bourne as a Visiting Lecturer in Roman Law at Princeton. Princeton's early devotion to this "unique law of objective and humane magnificence" (as I termed it in the third sentence of my first book) was for me the catalyst for a lifetime immersed in law. Strangely, however, the contributions of Bourne and Coleman-Norton to the study of *ius Romanum* (especially their *Ancient Roman Statutes* [with Alan Johnson]) remain largely unappreciated (and almost unacknowledged), but not by me.

While obtaining my J.D. at the University of Pennsylvania Law School, I was further inspired by Prof. George L. Haskins, legal historian of the first rank. Those familiar with his work will, I think, see his influence still vital in this book.

Beyond my teachers of yesteryear, I am grateful to all those who have now aided me in the preparation and production of this volume. Gilles Bransbourg, now heading the American Numismatic Society, was kind enough to read the entire manuscript, and has aided me greatly with his unique command of economic knowledge of the Roman world. For valuable input I thank a number of other Romanists and historians: Profs. Clifford Ando (Chicago), Barbara Biscotti (Milan), Kim Bowes (Penn), Richard Gamauf (Vienna), William Harris (Columbia), Marco Maiuro (Rome "La Sapienza"), Philipp Scheibelreiter (Vienna), Walter Scheidel (Stanford), and Jakub Urbanik

1. See Schiller 1971.

(Warsaw). None of these scholars necessarily endorses any of my views. I remain solely responsible for remaining errors and insufficiencies.

I have also benefited from the comments and reactions of academic audiences in the United States and Europe who attended my lectures covering in incipient form a portion of the material included in this volume.

Johanna Kaiser has prepared the Indices and the list of Abbreviations.

At Oxford University Press, Stefan Vranka has once again furnished much-appreciated encouragement and good judgment. Rada Radojicic has provided insights and suggestions that have materially enhanced this volume. Dorothy Bauhoff has provided skilled copy-editing. Oxford's anonymous readers have offered many valuable suggestions. In my experience, one of the great rewards of working with OUP in ancient studies is the consistently high level of its manuscript reviewers.

Above all, my deepest and ever-continuing appreciation is to my wife, Betsy.

This book is dedicated to my sons: Daniel Gideon Cohen and Jonathan Zubrow Cohen, humanists of the highest order, *menschen* who exemplify the joinder of breath-taking economic accomplishment with deep involvement and achievement in humanistic endeavors and pleasures.

Abbreviations

AE:	L'Année épigraphique
CIL:	*Corpus Inscriptionum Latinarum*. Consilio et auctoritate Academiae Litterarum Regiae Borussicae editum. (Berlin, 1863–).
CPL:	Corpus papyrorum Latinarum
Dig.:	Digest of Justinian
IG:	*Inscriptiones Graecae* (1873–
ILS:	Dessau, H. *Inscriptiones Latinae Selectae*. 3 vols. (Berlin, 1892–1916).
FIRA:	Fontes iuris Romani Anteiustininiani
ORF:	*Oratorum Romanorum Fragmenta*
PIR^2:	*Prosopographia Imperii Romani*. 1933. 2nd ed. Berlin and Leipzig.
RE:	*Paulys Realencyclopädie der classischen Altertumswissenschaft. With many supplements. 1893–.*
TLL:	*Thesaurus Linguae Latinae*. 1900–. Leipzig.
TPSulp:	Tabula(e) Pompeiana(e) Sulpiciorum

Ancient authors and works are abbreviated according to the recommendations of the *Oxford Classical Dictionary*, 3rd edn.

Abbreviations

Introduction

AT ROME DURING the Early and High Empires, a scanty sliver of men and women in both the free and the slave populations—a tiny elite of affluent slaves and wealthy free persons—prospered amidst a mass of impoverished free inhabitants and of impecunious enslaved inhabitants,[1] confirming that the legal status of a slave (juridically inferior to that of every free person) or of a woman (juridically inferior in many respects to that of a man) was not dispositive, ipso facto, of all other dimensions of his or her life, nor of every aspect of his or her place in society. In fact, the Early Empire was run to a considerable extent by an imperial administration consisting almost entirely of privileged slaves and former slaves.[2]

Ancient Western literature in general stereotypically attributes to women and slaves similar negative attributes;[3] ancient European legal systems, products of patriarchal societies, tend to deny judicial entitlement and juridical standing to both women and slaves. In Athens, for example, women and slaves (*douloi*) were similarly without rights and similarly victimized.[4] At Rome, according to the jurisprudent Papinian, "in many aspects of Roman

1. For the Roman elite, equality was not an iconic ideal: ipsa aequitas iniquissima est (Cic. *Rep.* 1.53); Pliny *Ep.* 9.5.3: nihil est ipsa aequalitate inaequalius ("nothing could possibly be more distressingly inequitable than unflinching equality for all": Peachin 2011: 22–23).

2. See Chapter 5.

3. See Just 1985. Aristotle, for example, treated women and slaves together: the woman's inferiority was to be contrasted with the slave's utter worthlessness (*Poetics* 1454a21–22).

4. See Vidal-Naquet 1986: 206–207; Cantarella 1987: 38; Keuls 1985: 6; Schuller 1985: passim; Wright [1923] 1969.

Roman Inequality. Edward E. Cohen, Oxford University Press. © Oxford University Press 2023.
DOI: 10.1093/oso/9780197687345.003.0001

law the situation of women (was) inferior to that of men,"[5] especially in situations governed primarily by custom (*mores*). Yet, despite a multitude of manifestations of juridical bias against females, Roman commercial law was in principle gender-blind,[6] and the accomplishments of Roman businesswomen, both free and enslaved, attest to the opportunities offered by egalitarian legal practices that often trumped gender-discriminatory customs.

Slaves' acquisition of wealth was actually aided by the preferential orientation of the legal system: Roman law—to modern Western eyes counterintuitively[7]—privileged servile enterprise to the detriment of free enterprise.[8] The economic success of slaves engaged entrepreneurially in business activity bares an anomaly to which only minimal academic attention has been directed: the paradox of a Roman economy dependent on slave entrepreneurs operating within a legal system that supposedly deprived slaves of all legal capacity, a system absolutely closed to any legal recognition of unfree persons.[9] Juridical theory and commercial reality were thus existentially in conflict. Extensive evidence and multiple studies, however, have demonstrated that legal systems invariably develop mechanisms to close significant gaps that may arise between actuality and traditional juridical principles[10]—although these mechanisms may not be transparently reflected in the most formal, and conservative, doctrinal presentations of "the law."[11] Rome was no exception.

---

5. *Dig.* 1.5.9: "In multis iuris nostri articulis deterior est condicio feminarum quam masculorum." Cf. Cic. *De Rep.* 3.10.17: lex utilitatis uirorum gratia rogata in mulieres plena est iniuriae. cur enim pecuniam non habeat mulier?

6. See Chapter 4, pp. 136–139.

7. Prevailing scholarship assumes that "the Roman legal system privileged those of higher status over those with degraded ones" (Bond 2016: 10, citing Garnsey 1970: 275). "The outlook, values and interests of the upper classes, including the jurists, were of fundamental importance" (McGinn 2017: 159; cf. 133). In agreement (for example): Knapp 2016: 365; Kelly 1966: esp. 1–84; North, Wallis, and Weingast 2009: 44–45, 48–49, 159–160, 195. A more nuanced view: Volterra 1993; Doria 2012: 118–119.

8. Although the word "enterprise" is attested in Latin only in the medieval period (*interprisa* in the sense of French *entreprise*, Italian *impresa*, German *Unternehmen* [Latham 1965, s.v.]), "it is justifiable to speak about enterprises in the sense of 'business organization' in ancient Rome" (Földi 1996, who analyzes the variegated legal structures of Roman "enterprises"). Cf. Petrucci 1991 who devotes an entire monograph to "studi sull'impresa finanziaria Romana."

9. See Chapter 1, n. 12 and related text; Chapter 2, pp. 59–60.

10. See Black and Bell 2011 (Asian jurisdictions); Smith 2007 (United States); Urbanik 2014: 959–960 (praetors' adaptation of Roman legal procedures to societal change). Cf. R. Grillo et al. 2009 (Europe and Africa); Nelken and Feest, eds. 2001 (Latin America, Japan, S.E. Asia).

11. See Chapter 1, n. 10; Chapter 2, pp. 59–65.

This book explores the casuistry through which Roman jurists created legal methodologies and interpretations facilitating a commercial reality utterly incompatible with the fundamental precepts that the jurists continued explicitly to insist upon. Because of the importance to the Roman economy of servile enterprise and servile wealth, and of female commercial activity and success, the law had to find a mechanism to deal with business actuality, and so it did—through the Roman legal fiction (*fictio*), a modality inhabiting a parallel universe, so to speak, where juridical theory and commercial factuality accommodate each other in a utilitarian dimension in which "truth" is that which is socially or economically requisite—and where unhelpful judicial dogma is allowed no overt presence in legal process or analysis.[12] "A slave cannot really owe or be owed anything: when we [(Roman jurists discuss a 'slave's debts' and)] misuse this term, we are recognizing reality rather than referencing a formal obligation under civil law."[13]

Similarly, provisions establishing male supervision of women's economic and other activities remained in formalistic existence—even as juridical authorities conceded that in fact at Rome "adult women handle their business matters for themselves."[14] In this book, especially in Chapter 4, we will chronicle the widespread involvement of women, both free and slave, in a broad spectrum of Roman mercantile pursuits and commercial businesses, and the legal and economic significance, implications, and complications of this phenomenon.

In preparing this book, I have had to deal with a number of conceptual or methodological issues. Some—such as the Roman concept of "ownership,"[15] the Roman use of legal fictions,[16] and the Roman failure to develop a systematized "commercial law"[17]—are discussed at appropriate places in the

12. On the absolute incompatibility, for example, between commercial reality and legal theory relating to slaves' "ownership" of property—and its resolution through legal fiction—see Chapter 2, section on "Owning Assets through the *Peculium*."

13. *Dig.* 15.1.41 (Ulp.): nec seruus quicquam debere potest nec seruo potest deberi, sed cum eo uerbo abutimur, factum magis demonstramus quam ad ius ciuile referimus obligationem. For the law's recurrent recognition of slaves as debtors, see Chapter 2, pp. 62–63.

14. Mulieres enim quae perfectae aetatis sunt, ipsae sibi negotia tractant (Gaius, *Institutes*, 1.190–191). See Chapter 4, section on "Male Guardianship over Women."

15. See Chapter 1, n. 87 and related text; Chapter 2, pp. 59–60.

16. See Chapter 2, pp. 60–63.

17. See Chapter 2, pp. 63–65.

text. Other matters, less specific in context or requiring more extensive treatment, are considered in this Introduction.

Time and Place

For the vast number of books written about Rome, "the term 'Roman' is central, and yet, paradoxically, it is rarely defined or given meaning."[18] For me, in writing of Rome, its society, its economy, its law, the term "Roman" is set within these considerations:

By conventional criteria, a "society refers to a particular group of people within a specific territory."[19] The Roman Empire encompassed innumerable such local groupings—municipalities, kingdoms, provinces, villages[20]—distributed over a vast area but "rigidly isolated from one another, both by habit and by law,"[21] a detachment and expanse that primitive transportation and nascent modalities of communication magnified beyond modern conceptualization.[22] These groups often tenaciously preserved separate societal values, institutions, and languages, and were expected to perform many governmental tasks entirely without supervision by the central government at Rome.[23] Many of their members, however, had already assumed, or were in the process of assuming, a parallel self-identification as "Romans."[24] Roman culture—"Roman Society"—in effect became a unifying mechanism for the residents of an extensive and diverse Empire of non-Roman, Roman, and assimilating persons.

Moreover, during the first centuries BCE and CE, Roman conquests had brought an "astronomical . . . influx of resources . . . wealth, bullion, land,

---

18. Revell 2009: xi.

19. Scupin and DeCorse 1992: 46. For expansive and nuanced definition, see Mayhew 1968.

20. See Strabo, *Geog.* 17.3.24. Cf. Mattingly 2011: 76; Meyer-Zwiffelhoffer 2002: 9.

21. Peachin 2002: 3. Cf. Humfress 2013: 77: "different models of imperial and local civic interaction developed in distinct geographical regions. . . ." For the relative penetration of Roman law and the retention of indigenous law in various parts of the Empire, see below, pp. 17–25.

22. See Tuori 2007(b): 48; Ando 2016(a): 17, who observes "how constrained [the empire's] politics were by the material effects of its size and the inefficiency of communications and transportation technology regimes."

23. See Chapter 5, pp. 167–169.

24. For Greek-speaking elites' obtaining of Roman citizenship, and resultant bifurcated self-identification, see Gleason 2006: 228–229; Swain 1996.

slaves [and/] or various other tangibles or intangibles"[25] to an economy increasingly monetized[26] and employing increasingly sophisticated financial mechanisms.[27] In large portions of the Empire, far-flung trade relationships had come into existence.[28] Recent scholarship has even demonstrated a remarkably extended and extensive labor market in which forces of supply and demand allocated workers through grids sometimes spread over more than a single province (occasionally even throughout the entire Empire).[29] Roman manufacturing came to be organized through intricate legal and organizational arrangements.[30] In effect, a "Roman economy" had emerged as a unified entity encompassing interrelated parts and processes, rather than as merely a series of independent markets subject to a single sovereignty.

Accordingly, a study of Roman inequality might theoretically encompass all territories under the rule of Rome and relate to all the peoples residing in these lands. Nonetheless, the composition of surviving evidence, and the centrality and sovereignty of the capital in and over virtually every aspect of the High Empire, mandate a focus on the city of Rome, and on the peninsula of Italy. Still, I treat as relevant all evidence, regardless of provenance, that illuminates inequality in a Roman context, and that explicates the servile and female beneficiaries of that disparity.[31] Chronologically, I deal primarily with the High Empire of the second and third centuries CE, but in exegesis of that High Empire I do not exclude information and insights involving the later

25. Tan 2017: 14, xvi. See Tan 2017: 3–39; Shatzman 1975; Frank 1933; Kay 2014, esp. 194–195 and 288–294.

26. von Reden 2012: 267–272; Verboven 2011: 95; Kessler and Temin 2008; Lo Cascio 2008; Harris 2008, 2019(a).

27. von Reden 2012: 276–283; Hollander 2007, passim; Malmendier 2009; Temin 2013: 172–173. Cf. Besnier 1976.

28. On the "impressive commercial networks in the Mediterranan area" arising during "the late Republican period and the early Principate," see Kehoe 2012(a): 205.

29. Bernard 2017: 63–64; Holleran 2017: 88–90; Temin 2013: 114–138, and 2004; Allen 2009; Rathbone 2009; Scheidel 2009, 2010.

30. See Kay 2014: 227–229; Reynolds 2018: 360–380 (interprovincial trade in the Principate and High Empire). Cf. Foy 2018: 265–267 (glass); Harris 1980a (lamps); Steinby 1993 (bricks); Fülle 1997 (*terra sigillata*); Harris 2018: 229–232 (distribution of wood); Russell 2018: 240–253 (stone).

31. Such broad demarcation and targeted focus are not atypical. Cf. Scheidel, 2012 (b): 109, n. 6: "'Roman' is defined very broadly, with emphasis on Italy and citizen society but encompassing all areas under Roman rule."

years of the Republic, the earlier years (the "Principate") of the Empire, and the centuries ("Late Antiquity") that followed the Empire's military acme.

An "Ignominious Truth": Ancient Studies' Lack of Statistics

Although this book deals with affluent slaves and businesswomen, it is impossible to determine with exactitude (or even with approximation) the number of Roman slaves who gained access to economic opportunity or the number of women who were involved in commerce. Indeed, modern scholarship is unable to establish even the approximate number of the Empire's inhabitants who were unfree,[32] or the percentage of Italy's population that was enslaved,[33] or what portion of the inhabitants of Rome were *servi*.[34] Economic historians of Rome have long acknowledged this "problem of non-existent quantitative data,"[35] the "ignominious truth" that "there are no ancient statistics,"[36] the absence even of surviving archival material[37] that would make it possible to establish the numerical prevalence or numerical paucity of phenomena discussed in this book. In fact, we know of no effort, in the whole of classical

32. Scheidel projects slaves as constituting perhaps 10 percent of the overall population of the Roman Empire (2011: 289). Others are satisfied with the conclusion that the percentage of slaves in the Empire was lower than their portion of the population in Italy: Hopkins 1978: 99, n. 99. Cf. Chapter 3, nn. 168–169, and related text.

33. A good guess is that slaves constituted probably only about 20 percent of the peninsula's inhabitants. See Kay 2014: 178–183; Temin 2013: 136; Scheidel 2011: 289; 2012(b): 92; Launaro 2011: Table 1.1 at 16. A few scholars argue for a higher ratio, up to 35 percent: Morley 2011: 265; Hopkins 1978: 101 (Table II.1) (cf. Beloch 1902: 418, 435–436).

34. In the time of Augustus, the percentage of enslaved inhabitants of the capital has recently been estimated at less than 10 percent: Morley 2013: 42 (50,000 slaves in a total population of perhaps 650,000). Hermann-Otto estimates that slaves might have constituted only 5 percent of the Roman population (2013: 63).

35. Garnsey and Saller 2009: 75. Classical antiquity, however, is not the only important area sans statistics: see, for example, Williamson 2009 (*History without Evidence: Latin American Inequality since 1491*).

36. A. H. M. Jones, Introduction to his Inaugural Lecture (1950). Cf. the similar observation by Momigliano in his own Inaugural Lecture (1952). On this absence of statistics in the ancient Mediterranean world, see Picard, 2008: 27–30; Bowman and Wilson 2009: v; Morris and Manning 2005: 33–34; Andreau, Briant, and Descat 1997: 5–6; Cohen 1992: 27.

37. On the fragmentary evidence that has survived from public and private archives in Roman territories, see Geens 2008: 135–138; Messeri 2001: 62–63; Posner 1972: 136–159. "A large-scale study of public archives across the empire remains a *desideratum*" (Czajkowski and Eckhardt 2020: 8, n. 41).

antiquity, to assemble, classify, and tabulate arithmetical data in a systematic fashion in order to present significant information about a specific ancient subject.[38]

In contrast, present-day studies in economic history almost always feature a plethora of statistics, mathematical models generated from this numerical data, and quantitative insights resulting from those models.[39] Yet the absence of statistical material has not proven entirely irreparable for Roman economic history. In recent years, scholars have increasingly sought to fill this lacuna through surrogate material or "proxies." Accordingly, some scholars have sought to employ the substantial, and ever growing, numerical information preserved through epigraphy, papyrology, numismatics, and literature to generate the statistical information that the ancients did not leave us.[40] Technical analyses of residential material remains from antiquity,[41] especially house size, have sought to quantify the blatant economic inequality seemingly explicit in this material.[42] Other scholars have undertaken comparative studies, turning to societies that appear similar to the Roman, but from which statistical material *is* available.[43] Efforts have even been made to provide quantitative insight into the entire Roman economy through the application of traditional economic analyses (such as supply-and-demand curves) augmented by comparative material.[44] Academic reception of these studies, however, has been "lukewarm" (Elliott 2020: 62–63), in large part because of their apparent

38. Our sources do, of course, report numbers, perhaps as many as a million for all aspects of classical antiquity and for a period exceeding 1,000 years (Finley 1986: 27–28). As a result of archaeological and other discoveries in the years since Finley's estimate, arithmetical material preserved from the ancient world has increased exponentially, "but they are spread out over nearly a millennium and scattered over more than four million square kilometres in cities, towns, and villages, kingdoms, provinces, and districts" (Verboven 2018: 346).

39. For example, Piketty's historically oriented "Capital in the Twenty-first Century" (2014), dealing as my book does with "Financial Inequality," offers almost 100 statistical tables in a text of 753 pages.

40. A sampling: Epigraphy: Groen-Vallinga and Tacoma 2017; Allen 2009. Papyrology: Blouin 2014; Bagnall, Keenan, and MacCoull 2011 (P.Lond.Copt. 1075); Bagnall and Frier 1994. Literature: Szaivert and Wolters 2005; Tomber 2018: 531. Numismatics: Bransbourg 2022; Howgego 2009; Scheidel 2009; Butcher and Ponting 2015; Metcalf 2016.

41. Fochesato, Bogaard, and Bowles 2019; Jongman 2009.

42. Stephan 2013; Kron 2014; Flohr 2016.

43. See Bang 2002 (Rome and India); Scheidel 2015 (China), 2019: 42–48 (various empires), 2020 (early modern European countries). Cf. Milanovic, Lindert, and Williamson 2007: Tables 1 and 2 (and related text).

44. See, for example, Maddison 2007: 33–62, and, more thoroughly, Temin 2013 ("The Roman Market Economy"). See also the various essays in Bowman and Wilson ("Quantifying the

excessive subjective speculation.[45] In contrast, scholarly consensus has sometimes arisen from studies based not on mathematical projections but on a unanimity of Roman anecdotal evidence, for example on the gross economic inequality resulting from the striking poverty of the overwhelming majority of both the free and enslaved inhabitants of Italy—in counterpoise to the reported vast wealth of the few.

Economic history, however, is not inherently an ancillary division of the fields of Statistics or Mathematics. Partially obviating the need for arithmetical data, still-emerging "Behavioral Economics"[46] and some of the methodologies of neoclassical economics (but not unbounded "economic rationality"[47]) offer helpful non-numerical approaches.[48] Most importantly, New Institutional Economics (NIE), which has enjoyed growing prestige and importance in recent years,[49] emphasizes not numbers but the "institutional rules of the game" and "background constraints" that are generated by legal precepts and practices and by informal societal values and controls which together determine transaction costs, and thereby tend to channel the

---

Roman Economy") and de Callataÿ, ed., 2014 ("Quantifying the Greco-Roman Economy and Beyond").

45. "Analysis (through) empirical studies . . . (sometimes) involves what might seem an unhealthy dose of conjecture" (Scheidel 2020: 341). "(S)canty surviving evidence is pressed to its limits, and at times doubtless a bit beyond" (Bagnall and Frier 1994: xvii). Similarly: Kay 2014: 274–278. Cf. Verboven who characterizes the results of efforts to quantify the Roman economy as "flimsy," "fuzzy" (2018: 347, 351). For a devastating critique of efforts to "integrate Roman economies in long-term cliometrics," see Bowes 2021 ("the macro-economic data is largely a fiction produced by a set of circular calculations") (quotations at pages 9, 27). Similarly: Lemercier 2015.

46. See Dhami 2017; Thaler 2016; Cartwright 2014.

47. The often limited, sometimes nonexistent, information available to participants in the Roman economy renders nugatory in the Roman context neoclassical economics' omniscient, entirely profit-motivated *homo economicus*. See Elliott 2020: 11–13; Davies 2007: 130.

48. "(T)he economic historian benefits from the wide array of tools, concepts, and hypotheses . . . from the works of the founding fathers (Smith, Ricardo, Marx, Keynes) to the most recent research, hypotheses—and controversies" (Bresson 2016: xxii).

49. For the dominant view—laudatory and appreciative of NIE's contribution to ancient economic history—see, for example, Elliott 2020: 11 ("new institutionalism appears best equipped to handle the persistent problem of limited empirical evidence"); Lo Cascio 2020: 111–112 ("NIE's impact has been felt both on the overall reconstruction of structure and performance of these economies, and on the detailed analysis of specific issues"). Cf. the Introduction and various essays in Scheidel, Morris, and Saller 2007, especially Frier and Kehoe 2007: 113–114; Bresson 2016: 15–27; Jones 2014. For the enormous, in his opinion deleterious, present influence of NIE on the study of ancient economies, see Boldizzoni 2011, esp. 39–53.

organization of commerce.[50] When standard social science identifies a phenomenon within a society, a quantitative response is virtually automatic: as determined numerically, how important was the practice? Was the phenomenon dominant within its culture, did it occur frequently, was it real but rare? Questions that are sometimes difficult to answer even in contemporary Western nations submerged by data[51] Questions almost always impossible to answer in past societies deficient in original and/or surviving data.

Yet, by its very definitional formulation, our investigation of "elite slaves" eschews attention to the "typical" unfree (and relatively unskilled) person whose presence and importance might be reliably triangulated only through statistics. Since the contours and content of a society are determined, at least in part, by its institutions, the importance of phenomena present in that society may be revealed through study of its legal rules and practices, even in the absence of quantitative confirmation or arithmetical specificity. Because the formal precepts of Roman law (in Latin, *ius Romanum*), mandate the absolute legal nullity of slaves, even isolated examples of affluent and/or powerful *servi* are immediately revelatory. Because women were supposedly denied participation in certain Roman occupations, even a few surviving *testimonia* of women active in such pursuits refute erroneous assertions of female exclusion.[52] In fact, we possess far more than isolated examples: in distinct counterpoint to the exclusively elitist orientation of most Roman authors of *belles lettres*, the focus of Roman legal analysis is often directed to problematic situations involving slaves and women.[53]

This juridical material has survived in unique profusion: slaves are discussed in about a quarter of all texts in the *Digest* and in 28 percent of the surviving Imperial Constitutions.[54] Indeed, "there is scarcely a title of

50. On the NIE paradigm, see Williamson 1979, 1985: 30; Ménard and Shirley 2005; Greif 2006: 29–53; Brousseau and Glachant 2008.

51. A prominent example: statistical analysis underpins the entirety of Piketty's analysis of contemporary economic inequality (2014)—widely praised for its accurate mustering of insightful numerical proof ("invaluable documentation": Krugman 2014), and widely condemned for its inaccurate portrayal of the same phenomenon through incorrect statistical analysis ("unpersuasive . . . weak empirical, analytical, and ethical arguments": Blume and Durlauf 2015: 751).

52. See Chapter 4, sections on "Women in Commerce," "Gender Equality and Inequality."

53. See Pölönen 2016: 9; Matthews 2006: 483.

54. Morabito 1981: 33–34. These figures probably understate the ubiquity of slave-related legal issues in the High Empire: "it is reasonable to think that the Byzantine compilers [of the *Digest*] tended to attenuate rather than emphasize the original preponderance of references to slavery" (Schiavone 2020: 21–22).

the *Digest* in which he (the slave) does not figure."[55] Accordingly, juridical sources are replete, for example, with discussions of, and references to, slaves' liberation through self-purchase, and to slaves' actual control, at least partly for their own benefit, of substantial funds and property (*peculia*)—and to the social and juridical manifestations and ramifications of these assets and purchases.[56]

Law and Legal Evidence

This book does make significant use of evidence from Roman law, preserved principally in Justinian's *Digest*, a compilation that contains discussions in detail of legal problems grouped broadly by juridical category and excerpted from apparently far more complete (and far earlier) original treatments of the subjects under discussion. This paring and pruning often severs substance from context and "sometimes obscures the very essence of some of these rules" (Du Plessis 2012: 131). Yet the large number of cases relating to slavery suggests, ipso facto, the importance of servitude within Roman law, and by extension, within Roman society, and conversely the potential importance of legal sources to an understanding of slavery within that society. Indeed, in virtually every book of the *Digest*, slaves are centrally discussed: at Rome "there is scarcely a problem which can present itself, in any branch of the law, the solution of which may not be affected by the fact that one of the parties to the transaction is a slave."[57] Similarly, of some 2,500 rescripts on private legal matters dating from 117 to 305 CE and preserved in the *Codex*, approximately a quarter (about 650) are addressed to female petitioners, suggesting the significant presence of businesswomen in Roman commerce.[58]

For scholars, however, the value of Roman legal sources has been somewhat limited by the relative academic segregation of juridical and nonjuridical disciplines dealing with ancient Rome.[59] Romanists—usually connected with

55. Crook 1967: 55. In agreement: Schiavone 2020: 22; Buckland [1908] 1970: v; Gardner 2011: 415; Crook 1967: 55; Watson 1987, passim.

56. These subjects are discussed in detail in Chapters 2 and 3 hereafter.

57. Buckland [1908] 1970: v. Cf. Gardner 2011: 415; Crook 1967: 55; Watson 1987, passim; Schiavone 2020: 22.

58. See Chapter 4, n. 41 and related text.

59. On "the underlying assumptions about law and practice that separate lawyers' and historians' histories," see Pölönen 2016: 8–14; Könczöl 2017. Sirks 2002: 169 ff. offers thoughts on how "ancient historians and legal historians approach ancient sources distinctively." Cf. Günther

law faculties and focused on explicating juridical issues—generally have paid minimal attention to historical and literary materials.[60] This reflects legal scholars' focus on elucidating and (if possible) resolving juridically significant issues—in contrast to historians' and classicists' focus on social and economic issues relating to Roman society. In fact, lacking professional training in ancient history, "most scholars of Roman law . . . tend to treat their material as ahistorical."[61] In turn, lacking legal training, ancient historians and classicists have tended to treat jurisprudential material cursorily—or even to ignore it.[62] Classicists even manifest "skepticism" (Harper 2012: 909) as to the value of legal evidence for Roman historical studies. But juridical sources are replete with discussions of, and references to, slaves' liberation through self-purchase, and to slaves' actual control, at least partly for their own benefit, of substantial funds and property (*peculia*)—and to the social and juridical manifestations and ramifications of such assets and purchases.[63] Likewise, legal sources establish clearly the important involvement of many women in economic activity at Rome.[64]

2018: 267: "Throughout the 20th century, Roman Law was mainly an enigma for historians and classical philologists alike." This has recently changed somewhat: see, for example, Sirks 2018 and the work of Bruce Frier and his sometime students, including Thomas McGinn and Dennis Kehoe—classicists who have acquired, and have made use of, a good knowledge of law and legal materials. Oxford University Press has now introduced a new series of monographs "devoted to the interaction between legal history and ancient history" ("Oxford Studies in Roman Society & Law"), and Brill has just issued (2023) a volume on *Law and Economic Performance in the Roman World.*

60. Fleckner 2014: 218; Günther 2018. Cf. the essays in Haferkamp and Repgen eds. 2017. A relatively recent exhaustive consideration of *redemptio suis nummis*, for example, based on a dissertation submitted to the law faculty at the University of Mainz, contains more than a thousand citations to Roman juridical sources and only 37 references to literary and inscriptional material (Heinemeyer 2013: 372–381 [Quellenverzeichnis]: cf. Liebs 2015).

61. Cairns and du Plessis 2007: 3. In legal writing, "it is sometimes difficult to discern the difference between ancient Romans and dead Germans. . . . Romanists have tended to see Rome as . . . a *Rechtsstaat*" (Tuori 2007[b]: 39). According to Gardner: "Most detailed studies of Roman law . . . are unreadable, and most are unread, save under stress of necessity, by historians" (1986: 1, 2). Meyer notes that "[t]he Roman Empire of the Romanist" remains a frozen conceptualization originally formulated by historians of the nineteenth century CE, and now largely discarded by contemporary ancient historians (2004: 3).

62. Wiedemann [1987] 1997: 19: "Classical scholars and ancient historians have generally been less aware of the wealth of material about slavery provided by Roman legal texts than they might have been."

63. These subjects are discussed in detail in Chapters 2 and 3 hereafter.

64. See Chapter 4, section on "Gender Equality and Inequality."

Nevertheless, an academic exploring legal material primarily for historical insight confronts a number of fundamental challenges: (1) Although scholars increasingly assume the close correlation of social practices and legal rules within a given society, at Rome there is often considerable deviation between theoretical juridical rules and the law actually applied to innovative commercial operations involving slaves and/or women. (2) In contrast, for example, to the forensic speeches surviving from the Athenian law courts in which societal information and legal rules are generally set forth within the perspective and background of actual disagreements generating antagonistic litigation,[65] it is unknown to what extent "cases" discussed in Roman digests are derived from true conflicts or represent only hypothetical situations not sourced from real disputes. (3) Do materials selected and edited in the sixth century CE accurately convey the legal, social and economic realities of the period, centuries earlier, when the redacted materials were actually created? To what extent have "interpolations" mutilated the information originally set forth? (4) How did Roman law interact with the various indigenous juridical arrangements functioning within imperial territory?

Law and Society

In the opinion of most legal scholars,[66] law is typically "embedded" within the society that it regulates,[67] and accordingly does not function or develop autonomously. Moreover, extensive evidence and multiple studies have demonstrated that legal systems invariably develop mechanisms to close significant gaps that may arise between changing societal reality and traditional

65. Although some scholars view Athenian private litigation as largely "theatre" (Humphreys 2007; Oulhen 2004: 254) or as a venue for the venting of elite social animosities (D. Cohen 1995: 70, 82; Osborne 1985), with litigants sometimes seeking actually to lose their cases (Todd 2002: 246, 1994: 131, n. 180), I view Athenian litigation as essentially the effort of real people to prevail in real conflicts by persuading a majority of jurors to vote in their favor (thus E. Harris 2013: 12–13; 2018[b]: 2; E. Cohen 2018[c]: 30).

66. Law is generally seen as "coextensive with society," "a mirror of society" (Friedman [1985] 2005: 12, 195). Similarly: Pölönen 2016: 15; Tamanaha 2001; Horwitz 1977; Hurst 1956.

67. Hence, the title of the introductory Chapter 1 in McGinn 1998: "Law in Society." Greece provides a clear historical example. "(F)or the ancient Greeks, laws (were) embedded within the societies of which they were a part" (Lanni and Wallace 2018: 2). Cf. Millett and Todd 1990: 15 ("Law and legal process in Athens were embedded in society"). But even for the Greeks, many scholars believe that "legal issues . . . must be investigated from a legal point of view," "not as a manifestation of political and social confrontation": Maffi 2018: 72. Cf. Wolff 1975.

juridical principles.[68] But some Romanists have asserted that "law in the Roman legal sources very frequently does not reflect the values and interests of society at large,"[69] a claim that provides some justification for classicists' tendency to ignore or disdain evidence from *ius Romanum*. Although a purported total separation of Roman law from Roman society is very much a minority opinion even among Romanists,[70] many scholars *have* thought that ongoing commerce at Rome and throughout the Empire largely ignored Roman law, which has been denigrated as only "an extraordinarily complex and difficult system [lacking] practical utility,"[71] applicable only to the elite levels of Roman life.[72]

Considerable evidence, however, shows that the use of Roman law extended through all levels of Roman economic and social life. Continuing finds and new editions of ancient Roman documentation of business matters, for example, have demonstrated that routine banking and other transactions closely followed, and were memorialized in accordance with, Roman law principles,[73] refuting suggestions that ongoing commerce largely ignored *ius Romanum*. In recent years, books and chapters in volumes have illuminated many aspects of Roman civilization through the prism of its law.[74] Roman law

68. See n. 10 above.

69. Watson 2007: 34. For earlier suggestions of the separation of Roman law from its societal context, see von Jhering 1852–1865 and Schulz 1934.

70. See Tuori 2007(a): Chapter 3.

71. Wolf 2015: 61 (who disagrees with this characterization) summarizing earlier "suspicion" of the real-life relevance of Roman law principles to the overall economy.

72. "The outlook, values and interests of the upper classes, including the jurists, were of fundamental importance in giving shape to Roman private law" (McGinn 2017: 159; cf. 133). Knapp asserts that only 1 or 2 persons per thousand Romans "were regularly engaged in legal processes. Everyone else was marginalized—that is, their social, economic and political concerns were dealt with only as they were conguent with or impinged on some interest of these few adult citizen males" (2016: 365).

73. This fresh material includes the first adequate edition of the Tabulae Herculanenses (Camodeca 2017), which overcomes "le sue gravi insufficienze e lacune" (2017: 5) of Pugliese Carratelli and Arangio-Ruiz 1946–1961: cf. Wolf 2010(a); Camodeca 1994. Also very important are the wax tablets from Murécine (the "Archive of the Sulpicii") discovered in 1959 and published in an exhaustive edition by Camodeca (1999). Cf. Wolf 2010(b). See also the archives of Lucius Caecilius Iucundus (Andreau 1974). For an overview of this material, Gröschler 1997; Meyer 2004.

74. Examples include Cairns and Du Plessis, eds., 2007; essays by Lewis, Du Plessis, Johnston, Aubert, Sirks, and Metzger in Johnston, ed., 2015; all of the chapters in Aubert and Sirks, eds., 2002; Johnston 1999 ("Roman law in its social and economic context": ix); essays on "Law and Life of Rome" by Henderson, Cloud, and Rawson in McKechnie, ed., 2002: 191–288.

is now seen as a "reflection" of actual life,[75] to such an extent that even the prime advocate of the "autonomy" of *ius Romanum*[76] has acknowledged that "Roman law is the perfect laboratory for a study of law in society" (Watson 2007: 35).[77]

"Hypothetical" Cases

Justinian's *Digest* contains discussions of multitudinous legal problems. These items have been characterized by some modern scholars as "cases" and have even been gathered into "casebooks"—on property law, contracts, delict, family law, etc.[78]—akin to the "casebooks" that for many years have been ubiquitous in contemporary legal education in the United States,[79] presenting American court decisions relating to actual disputes involving real people. Analogously, scholars have tended to treat the material preserved in the *Digest* as though at least reflective of actual legal situations—"cases," as it were—and have used this material extensively, especially in recent years, in seeking to illuminate numerous aspects of Roman society and economy. In this book I, too, frequently make reference to and argue from this material.

Although Romanists have long debated whether the catalysts for these "cases" were actual disputes or fictitious generalizing hypotheses of academic origin intended to present abstract principles of law,[80] I believe that even the premises underlying fictionalized legal problems of the High Empire can themselves provide considerable insight into Roman life, even if at least some of this material is merely hypothesis not sourced from actual life. For example, in setting these problems, jurisprudents often employ stock names—the litigants Aulus Agerius and Numerius Negidius, the slave Stichus—"all

---

75. "Roman Law as a Reflection of Social and Economic Life in Antiquity" is the actual subtitle of Aubert and Sirks, eds., 2002.

76. "Isolation from the rest of life is a strong characteristic of Roman private law": Watson 1995: 64.

77. For Watson's highly nuanced "view of the relationship between law and society," set forth most clearly in Watson 1993 and 2001, see Ewald 1995.

78. Frier 1989, 1993; Hausmaninger and Gamauf 2012; Frier and McGinn 2004.

79. Some critics have seen reliance on the "case" method and on "casebooks" (instead of systematic presentation of the main principles of law, as in Blackstone or Gaius) as "the shame of American legal education": see especially Watson 2006, who deems "the casebook method . . . an exercise in futility" (79), a "fatal flaw" in American legal education (13).

80. See, for example, Johnston 1999: 24–26; Peachin 2002: 3–4; Daube 1965; Cherry 1996; Crook 1967: 15; 1973.

fictitious characters in made-up cases."[81] Sometimes, however, the same factual pattern appears more than once in the *Digest*, with stock names appearing in one rendition and apparently real names used in another, suggesting that even seemingly hypothetical situations had in fact their origin in real life.[82] Monetary sums in discussions in the *Digest* are with regularity startlingly low, leading commentators to conclude that the amounts cited are merely illustrative, and not the actual amounts that would have been encountered in real-life commercial transactions.[83] Yet it has been suggested that the figures appear reductive because sixth-century compilers of the *Digest* altered numbers set forth in the sources (written centuries earlier) to reflect a sixth-century CE equivalence of 1,000 *sesterces* per *aureus*, a ratio far higher than that prevailing in the second and third centuries CE at the time of the creation of the legal materials later gathered, truncated, and edited to produce the *Digest*.[84] The use of exemplary (rather than actual) monetary units, however, does not establish the fictitious nature of the legal situations under discussion: jurisprudents, for example, might have felt that retention of actual sums from specific cases was incompatible with the establishment of generalized juridical principles.

Even if we cannot confirm the truth of specific information set forth in "cases" discussed in the *Digest*, "it would be surprising if the jurists designed hypothetical cases which were entirely remote from the realities of life in Rome."[85] Thus, the jurisprudent Ulpian discusses a situation in which a slave had been appointed (*praepositus*) to manage a business at Arelate in southern Gaul dealing in olive oil.[86] This slave also dealt in loans for cash. Ulpian reports that a customer had provided a loan intended for the olive oil business but was unable to prove that the money had actually been "accepted" in connection with that business. Ulpian notes that an earlier jurisprudent had allowed an equitable action (*utilis actio*) on the purported basis[87] that the slave had also

81. Aubert 2002:184.

82. See *Dig.* 32.38.4 and *Dig.* 32.93.pr.; *Dig.* 34.3.28.4 and 34.3.31.2; *Dig.* 35.2.25.1 and *Dig.* 33.1.21.1. Cf. *Dig.* 14.3.20.

83. Volterra [1967] 1993. Cf. McGinn 2017: 142–145.

84. Maragno 2017.

85. Johnston 1999: 24.

86. On slaves' appointment autonomously to operate businesses, see Chapter 1, pp. 43–48. On this case, see Chapter 1, pp. 46–47.

87. "just as if," *quasi*.

been "appointed" to deal in loans.[88] Although Ulpian seeks presumably only to illustrate legal issues relating to equitable actions, and is not seeking to provide twenty-first-century historians with useful information on the economic situation and functioning of Roman provincial slaves and their businesses, it seems reasonable to infer that some slaves may have been engaged simultaneously in commercial multitasking, and that finance and mercantile activities may have been controlled by the same unfree individual, that masters may have been liable under certain circumstances for the complex dealings of such slaves, that enterprises dealing in olive oil may have received and extended credit, that slaves appointed to manage such enterprises may have achieved a high degree of financial sophistication and may have commanded significant resources, and so forth. While much of this transaction was mystifying even for the best legal minds in Rome, and a fortiori is unclear to us, the factual pattern underlying the legal issues was necessarily plausible to a Roman audience of legal practitioners and students. Even if the case under discussion were in whole or in part a hypothetical construction by Ulpian, even esoteric juridical promulgations would have been meaningless and useless if the proffered factual context did not reflect actual Roman life.

Anachronism and Interpolation

This book deals primarily with the High Empire—the apex of Roman juridical thought and scholarship. From the authors of this period, the second and third centuries CE, a prodigious production of legal material survives. But the primary mechanism for the preservation of these testimonia, Justinian's *Digest*, was compiled only in the sixth century CE. Although the *Digest* consists of abbreviated selections from legal analyses created at a much earlier period, Justinian specifically directed the compilers not to retain provisions that, by the sixth century, were outdated ("had fallen into disuse"). He enjoined them to make changes—additions, excisions, and improvements—in order to produce a coherent and consistent juridical totality, a seamlessly amended text that would read as if it had been so written ab initio.[89] And so modern

88. *Dig.* 14.3.13.pr (Ulp.): habebat quis seruum merci oleariae praepositum Arelate, eundem et mutuis pecuniis accipiendis: acceperat mutuam pecuniam: putans creditor ad merces eum accepisse egit proposita actione: probare non potuit mercis gratia eum accepisse. licet consumpta est actio nec amplius agere poterit, quasi pecuniis quoque mutuis accipiendis esset praepositus, tamen Iulianus utilem ei actionem competere.

89. *De Conceptione Digestorum* 7, 10: si quid in ueteribus non bene positum libris inueniatis uel aliquod superfluum uel minus perfectum, super uacua longitudine semota et quod

scholars must consider the possibility that something attributed in the *Digest* to an author of a much earlier period may in fact reflect at least in part the law or the life of Justinian's time.

These alterations to the original texts of second- and third-century discussions have been termed *interpolations*,[90] and through much of the twentieth century Romanists "spent much energy hunting for interpolations and found far too many."[91] In recent decades, Romanists have rued the excesses of earlier scholarship: "nowadays the trend in Roman law studies has swung back from a hypercritical approach to a more nuanced one, whereby the substance of legal texts, if not their form, is considered genuine unless proved otherwise with overwhelming arguments or evidence."[92] Romanists now generally recognize that "in Justinian's *Digest* interpolations as to substance are restricted to a small number of easily recognizable categories."[93] And so in this work, material purporting to be from the high classical period is accepted as such—unless the text as transmitted presents transparent difficulties and/or there is convincing paleographical or other tangible basis for rejecting the content proffered by the text.[94]

Indigenous Law and Roman Law

Roman law *was* pervasive throughout the Empire, as was indigenous law (*ius gentis*)[95]—both before and after promulgation in 212 CE of the *Constitutio*

---

imperfectum est repleatis et omne opus moderatum et quam pulcherrimum ostendatis. . . . si aliquid in ueteribus legibus vel constitutionibus, quas antiqui in suis libris posuerunt, non recte scriptum inueniatis, et hoc reformetis et ordini moderato traditis . . . ut hoc uideatur esse uerum, et optimum et quasi ab initio scriptum . . . quae leges in ueteribus libris positae iam in desuetudinem abierunt, nullo modo uobis easdem ponere permittimus. . . .

90. On the compilers' methodology for, and on the general substance of, these interpolations, see Wenger 1953: 854–865; Wieacker 1988: I.154–182.

91. Aubert and Sirks 2002: v. In fact, "clarity about the alterations and omissions made by the compilers can be achieved only in those cases in which the same text has not only survived in the *Digest* but is also attested elsewhere" (Kaiser 2015: 128).

92. Aubert and Sirks 2002: v.

93. Watson 2007: 27. Cf. Lokin 1995: 271; Watson 1994: 113.

94. For example, *Dig*. 3.5.30 (31) where the reading "liberto uel amico" is independently known to be legally impossible at the time of Papinian: see Chapter 2, n. 168.

95. See Wibier 2020: 480–482 (Gaul); Fournier 2010 (Hellenophone East); Mélèze (Modrzejewski) 2006, 2005, 1993, 1970 (Egypt); Yiftach-Firanko 2009 (Egypt); Kantor 2013 (Phrygia), 2016 (Asia Minor); Stolte 2001 (Mesopotamia); Czajkowski 2020: 93–98 (Judea); Hezser, ed., 2003 (Jewish law); Maehler 2005 (Greek law); Cotton 2009 (Nabatean law).

Antoniniana (Decree of Caracalla) extending citizenship to virtually all residents of Roman territory.[96] Upon entry into the Empire, local communities (*civitates peregrinae*) typically had been allowed to continue using their own indigenous law[97]—a practice consistent with the Empire's general delegation of administrative functions to local entities without direct imperial supervision,[98] consonant with the imperial strategy of perpetuating Roman dominance by discouraging unity among subject populations,[99] and compatible with Roman juridical theory which envisioned Roman law as merely the law of Rome in a universe of many other legitimate judicial structures.[100] Citizens had the option to make use of Roman or local law: no governmental edict *required* the use of either, but practical considerations sometimes favored or mandated the use of one, sometimes of the other, sometimes of a mélange.[101] Nonetheless, Roman legal provisions and procedures were continually encroaching: many local persons, and many indigenous communities, themselves preferred Roman legal fora[102]—and for good reason(s).

---

96. Some scholars believe that the Constitutio Antoniniana did subject virtually all provincial residents to the precepts of Roman law: Yiftach 2009: 543. In agreement: Talamanca 1971; Honoré 2004: 113; Rowlandson and Takahashi 2009: 117. Substantial evidence, however, demonstrates the continued (although non-exclusive) use of indigenous law, especially in Egypt (Alonso 2020: 46–47 ["it is striking how many practices that challenged the most basic principles of Roman law continued to be common and accepted after 212"]); Tuori 2007(b): 43 (papyrological evidence shows "that no such wholesale adoption (of Roman law) occurred"); Carrié 2005: 274–275; Meyer 2004: 183; Garnsey 2004: 146–147; Lintott 1993: 154–160; Galsterer 1986: 24; Seidl 1973). For the false suggestion that Roman law was not actually in general use, at Rome or in the Empire, except among a small elite, see above, this Introduction, pp. 13–14.

97. Gell. *Noc. Att.* 16.13.4 (cum suis moribus legibusque uti possent); Cic. *Epist. Att.* 6.1.15 (Graeci inter se disceptent suis legibus). Cf. Gell. *Noc. Att.* 16.13.8–9. See Schiavone 2020: 15; Richardson 2015: 49–50; Ando 2006: 184; Crawford, *Rom. Stat.* 19, esp. 31–36.

98. See Chapter 5, pp. 167–169.

99. See Ando 2011(a): 25; 2012: 75–85; 2013.

100. Gaius *Inst.* 1.1: omnes populi, qui legibus et moribus reguntur, partim suo proprio, partim communi omnium hominum iure utuntur: nam quod quisque populus ipse sibi ius constituit, id ipsius proprium est uocaturque ius civile, quasi ius proprium ciuitatis: . . . populus itaque Romanus partim suo proprio, partim communi omnium hominum iure utitur. Cf. *Dig.* 1.1.9 (Gaius). See Ando 2011(a): 3–4; 2014(a); Humfress 2011.

101. Mélèze (Modrzejewski) 1993: 988; Humfress 2011: 36–37; 2013: 80–81; Maehler 2005.

102. "Local inhabitants . . . recognized the value of judgments which carried the weight of Rome's military dominance" (Richardson 2015: 45).

Despite their survival under imperial rule,[103] indigenous courts were inherently inferior to Roman tribunals. The provincial governor's juridical authority and that of the Roman courts functioning under his power were restricted only by the governor's own discretion[104] and by the provisions of the Provincial Edict (*edictum provinciale*) which the governor had himself promulgated.[105] Roman provincial authorities could accept for resolution any legal matter presented to them by any free resident (even those lacking Roman citizenship).[106] As a result, "the sources are full of provincial non-Romans appealing to Roman officials," availing themselves of "access to Roman authorities as final adjudicators."[107] Moreover, numerous provincial entities, on their own initiative, abrogated their community's use of indigenous law by seeking and obtaining the "honor"[108] of becoming a Roman *municipium* or *colonia*[109]—whereupon they received an imperial charter,[110]

103. Except for Egypt, all the *poleis* in the Eastern Empire continued to maintain their own autonomous courts (Alonso 2013: 352). Despite a priori characterizations of the Western Empire as a "wasteland" (Humfress 2011: 44), there is no evidentiary basis for asserting the absence of indigenous courts in the West (Czajkowski and Eckhardt 2020: 11).

104. This was true even under the Republic. See Cic. *Ep. Quint.* 1.1.22.

105. By the reign of Hadrian, the content of the provincial edict had been largely standardized, but (as with the Praetor's Edict in Rome proper) on re-issuance each governor could make changes, probably in an appendix varying with local conditions. See the preserved fragments of Gaius's treatise, in thirty books, *On the Provincial Edict.*

106. Jördens 2012(a): 62–64; 2012(b): 252; Bryen 2008: 200 ("[T]he Roman legal system in the provinces was fundamentally . . . a system which could be accessible to all free individuals"); Humfress 2011: 37. Cf. Haensch 1997: 334–342; Meyer-Zwiffelhoffer 2002; Lewis 1981 (Egypt); Robert 1949 (Asia); Habicht 1975 (Asia).

107. Knapp 2016: 364. Plutarch notes the frequency of provincials' unforced preference for Roman judgment over local jurisdictional authority (*Praecepta ger. rei pub.* 814e–815b). Spagnuolo Vigorita has gathered numerous examples of this phenomenon: 1993: 23–28.

108. "Honor": Boatwright 2000: 172. Cf. Gell. *Noc. Att.* 16.13.1–9.

109. Hadrian alone granted this status to at least thirty-two entities: *Hist. Aug.* (Hadrian 21.7). See Roselaar 2016: 125. (By the High Empire, the nuanced factors distinguishing Roman *municipia* and *coloniae* had largely disappeared. Compare, for example, the similar juridical structure and legal provisions of the *municipium* Irni and the *colonia* Urso. See Scheid 1999 [*municipia*], Rüpke 2006 [*coloniae*]).

110. Still largely extant, *mirabile dictu*, are a number of these charters granted in Spain by the Flavian emperors (see Richardson 1996: 188–210; Eck 2020: 315–317), including the famous Lex Flavia Irnitana Municipalis relating to the previously unknown polity of Irni (text: González and Crawford 1986: 182; exegesis: Gardner 2001). See also the leges Salpensana and Malacitana (Riccobono 1964: 30a, 30b), likewise dating from the Flavian period). Other Spanish charters have been preserved in fragments (lex Uillonensis [Sevilla] and charters from Duratón and Italica). On these Spanish inscriptions, see Ortiz de Urbina 2013; González 1986: 242–243. Fragments of charters from other parts of the Empire have also survived: codes

providing in effect for the use of Roman law in all dealings involving members of the community.[111]

Although some local persons might have preferred to litigate in their own municipal tribunals functioning with rules and values reflecting local, not Roman, culture, for the many business and personal matters involving individuals from more than a single town Roman law was a natural and neutral choice.[112] Even within the same community, use of indigenous law was constrained by the fact that many "local" residents were in fact "foreigners" (*incolae*).[113] These outsiders were often free persons who by birth were citizens elsewhere, including Roman citizens (who might either be immigrants to the local area, or indigenous persons who had ultimately succeeded in attaining Roman citizenship [*civitas*]). Many residents (slaves, women, minors) held inferior, if any, rights in the local community. From varied motivation(s), all these people might have sought to avoid being judged under indigenous law: some as "foreigners" might fear possible prejudice in local courts if in contention with a native citizen; others might be unfamiliar with indigenous law and processes; still others might covet possible litigational advantage(s) in a Roman venue.[114] Women would have preferred the relative gender equality afforded by Roman juridical rules governing property and obligations.[115]

In the event, so many persons chose to use Roman law that the provincial authorities in many jurisdictions came to function as tribunals of first instance, rather than as merely potential sites of appeal.[116] Roman governors

---

from Troesmis in Moesia Inferior (177–180 CE: Eck 2013: 211–212; Eckhardt 2020: 428–432) and from Lauricum in Noricum (212–217 CE), and elsewhere. All these documents contain similar provisions (Roselaar 2016: 125; Eck 2020: 316). Cf. also the earlier Republican charters (lex Ursonensis and Tabula Heracleensis).

111. Lex Irnitana: §§ 84–93. Section 93 is specific: quibus de rebus in h(ac) l(ege) nominatim cautum scriptumue non est, quo iure inter se municipes municipi Irnitani agant, de iis rebus omnibus ii inte[r se] agunto, quo ciues Romani inter se iure ciuili agunt agent.

112. On factors affecting (at least theoretically) availability and choice of forum when parties were not "citizens of the same town," see Sirks 2018: 56–60. Cf. Liebs 2009: 456–460.

113. See Roselaar 2016: 132–133; Gagliardi 2006: 263–328.

114. For local inhabitants' reasons for preferring Roman rather than indigenous tribunals, see Meyer 2007: 62–63; Cotton 2002: 18; Satlow 2005: 65. Generally, in imperial and colonial situations in which multiple jurisdictions are available, individuals tend not to limit themselves to a single system but opt for varied venues in accordance with their own perceived advantages: see Benton 2002: 8, 2007.

115. See Chapter 4, pp. 136–137, 36–37. Cf. Benke 2012: 221; Goodman 1991; Ando 2014(b).

116. Ando 2016(b): 283, 290; Jördens 2020: 23–25.

and their Roman subordinates in practice had a natural affinity for their own law—to which they attributed exceptional excellence: already during the Republic, Cicero had judged "every indigenous law (*ius civile*), with the exception of our own, disordered and almost absurd."[117] Nonetheless, Roman provincial authorities, pursuant to imperial policy, encouraged and even facilitated continued use of substantive local law[118]—even in proceedings before Roman tribunals. Acceptance of local law in Roman courts was so pronounced that indigenous law remained dominantly in use in Egypt,[119] the sole Eastern province known to have entirely lacked indigenous courts.[120] Already in the first century CE, the Emperor Claudius was confirming the preservation of legal and other rights which the citizens of Alexandria had enjoyed in the centuries before their entry into the Empire.[121] Similarly, Hadrian in the second century CE opines approvingly on the Narkyians' retention of their own indigenous law.[122] A papyrus document from the early second century CE memorializing legal proceedings opens with the admonition that "it is best to litigate in accordance with local law,"[123] meaning that "peregrines are to be judged in these matters not according to Roman law but *suis legibus*."[124] In a letter to Pliny the Younger, the Emperor Trajan adds

---

117. omne ius civile, praeter hoc nostrum, inconditum ac paene ridiculum: *de orat.* 1.44.197. Modern commentators likewise laud Roman law as a unique achievement, even claiming that "law was an invention of the Romans" (Schiavone 2020: 13).

118. Alonso 2020: 45–50, Schönbauer 1952, 1960, and others have "disprove(n) Arangio-Ruiz's notion of a mere *de facto* tolerance" of local law (Alonso 2020: 49). Cf. Arangio-Ruiz 1950.

119. See Wolff and Rupprecht 2002: 120, passim; Anagnostou-Canas 1991: 253–268; Taubenschlag 1959. But insights gained from Egypt "are not at all limited to this province alone but can lay claim to much more general validity" (Jördens 2020: 18–19).

120. Because of the absence of indigenous tribunals, "peregrine private law would not have kept its hold in Egypt without the consistent endorsement of the Roman jurisdiction" (Alonso 2013: 352). Lack of autonomous local courts: ibid.; Mélèze (Modrzejewski) 1966: 534, *pace* Seidl 1965.

121. P. London 6.1912 (lines 57–59) (= Trismegistos: 16850): καὶ τὰ ἄλλα δὲ οὐχ ἧσσον εἶναι βούλομαι βέβαια πάνθ᾽ ὅσα ὑμῖν ἐχαρίσθη ὑπό τε τῶν πρὸ ἐμοῦ ἡγεμόνων καὶ τῶν βασιλέων καὶ τῶν ἐπάρχων. . . .

122. IG^{2} IX.I.5, l. 15 (Narykians retaining "the laws of the Opuntians").

123. In this context, literally "the law of the Egyptians." P. Oxy. 42.3015:

> κάλλιστόν ἐστιν αὐτοὺς
> [δικ]αιοδοτεῖν π[ρὸς] τοὺς Αἰγυπτίων νόμους
> [ἐ]φ᾽ οἷς ἔξεστι κ[α]ὶ μεταδιατίθεσθαι.

See Ando 2015(c): 117.

124. Alonso 2020: n. 63. (suis legibus: "under their own laws")

imperial imprimatur to the same sentiment: "the law of each individual polity (*civitas*) must be followed" (which Trajan terms the "safest" choice).[125] On questions relating to the collection of public debts by entities (*civitates*) in Bithynia and Pontus, Trajan likewise concludes that issues should be resolved according to the indigenous law of the entity seeking payment—but Roman authorities, in judicial hearings, should see that private parties are not thereby improperly victimized.[126] In fact, the grants bestowing Roman citizenship on provincial residents (who thereby gained access to Roman law) generally provided for the recipients' parallel continuing involvement with local law (*ius gentium*[127]). The Decree of Caracalla similarly confirmed provincial citizens' continuing rights and obligations at local law.[128]

Such amalgamating interaction of Roman and local law was a recurrent phenomenon in the High Empire. Latin technical terms (in translation or transliteration) appear frequently in commercial instruments and legal documents drawn in local languages.[129] In documents prepared in accordance with indigenous legal traditions or requirements, especially in Egypt, over an extended period, Roman "*stipulatio* clauses" increasingly are added, in Greek and/or in Latin,[130] thus rendering the agreements actionable under either indigenous or Roman law.[131] Even had *stipulatio* language not been added, many local agreements were being drafted to comply, in any event, with Roman

---

125. Pliny *Ep.* 10.113: id ergo, quod semper tutissimum est, sequendam cuiusque ciuitatis legem puto.

126. Pliny *Ep.* 10.109: quo iure uti debeant Bithynae uel Ponticae ciuitates in iis pecuniis, quae ex quaque causa rei publicae debebuntur, ex lege cuiusque animaduertendum est. . . . in iniuriam priuatorum id dari a me non oportebit.

127. saluo iuris gentis: "all prior rights and obligations at local law being preserved." "Tabula Banasitana," Morocco (*Inscriptions antiques du Maroc*: Euzennat and Marion 1982, no. 94). The term appears to have been standard wording accompanying grants of citizenship to elite peregrines. See Ando 2016(a): 174 ("the brevity [of the provision] bespeaks a common understanding"); Ando 2016(b); Gardner 2001: 216 ("those receiving Roman citizenship . . . must also retain their local citizenship"); Mélèze (Modrzejewski) 2014: 319–323.

128. saluo iuris gentis = μένοντος [τοῦ νόμου τῶν πολιτευμ]άτων (P.Giss 40 [Kuhlmann 1994]): recipients retained "diritti, ma anche obblighi e doveri" (Marotta 2016: 487). See Sirks 2018: 59; Buraselis 2007: 137–138; Wolff 1956: 367–371; Oliver 1989: 504; Alonso 2020: 50–51.

129. Stolte 2009; Sirks 2018: 60 (with reference to "Greek equivalents or translations of Latin legal-technical terms").

130. "et interrogatus spopondit," in Greek "ἐπηρωτηθεὶς ὡμολόγησε." See Yiftach-Firanko 2009: 554; Rupprecht 1994: 96–97.

131. Use of *stipulatio* "does not mean that the person declaring this wanted to apply Roman law . . . he wanted to be sure that if litigation was conducted before a Roman court, the

legal requirements for enforcement.[132] Roman law even came to allow the use of languages other than Latin in satisfaction of at least some Roman juridical requirements[133]—and to treat certain non-Roman agreements as construable within Roman contractual categories (such as *locatio/conductio*), enabling such peregrine arrangements to be enforced in Roman courts.[134] Similarly in the second century CE, the archives of Babatha, a Jewish woman from Roman Arabia, provide for guardianship arrangements in accordance with the indigenous laws of Judaea but do so through documents in *Greek*[135] drafted with provisions satisfying Roman requirements for an *actio tutelae*.[136] On occasion, Roman law even adopted provisions of local law, especially those regarding family relations: the Senate, for example, abolished in 49 CE the prohibition against marriage between an uncle and a fraternal niece—a relaxation of incestual prohibitions in order to authorize the Emperor Claudius's marriage to Agrippina,[137] a change arguably introduced into Roman law by provincial governors, now senators, aware through their acquired knowledge of indigenous law that although prohibited by Rome's *ius civile* such marriages had long been lawful under the local laws of various provinces (*iura gentium peregrinarum*).[138]

---

document would not be declared invalid" (Sirks 2018: 59). For the range of relations that might become enforceable in Roman venues through *stipulatio* recitations, see Simon 1964.

132. Alonso 2020: 58–59.

133. See, for example, *Dig.* 32.11.pr. (Ulp.): fideicommissa quocumque sermone relinqui possunt, non solum Latina uel Graeca, sed etiam Punica uel Gallicana uel alterius cuiuscumque gentis; *Dig.* 45.1.10 (Ulp.): omnis sermo contineat uerborum obligationem. Cf. Matthews 2006: 482; Stolte 2001: 177 (Syriac).

134. For the "legal institutions of Roman law that were at the same time *ius gentium*," see Sirks 2018: 66–72.

135. "Greek was the language used by the Romans to communicate with their Eastern subjects" (Meyer 2007: 60, n. 33). See Rosén 1980: 220–222.

136. P Yadin 28–30. For the Babatha archives, see Chiusi 2020; Czajkowski 2017; Meyer 2007: 53–56; Cotton 2002: 18.

137. Gaius 1.62: fratris filium uxorem ducere licet, idque primum in usum uenit cum diuus Claudius Agrippinam fratris sui filiam uxorem duxisset. Cf. Frier and McGinn 2004: 36–37 ("Endogamy and Exogamy").

138. See Buongiorno 2015: 32: "questi membri del *consilium* possano aver riportato le proprie esperienze di governatori provinciali, fornendo *rechtsvergleichende Argumente* in ordine alle unioni endogamiche: argomenti che sono da riconnettersi ad un comune sostrato . . . l'oriente fenicio, egizio e poi ellenistico. É su tali argomenti che si sarebbe fondata la giustificazione della modicazione del *ius civile vetus:* ossia nella recezione informale, nell'ordinamento giuridico romano, di un istituto di *ius gentium peregrinarum*." Cf. Buongiorno 2013.

How had Romans and provincials come to have knowledge of the others' legal culture? In providing hearings to local litigants,[139] the small number of Roman provincial officials[140] would have depended on indigenous functionaries for assistance. Of necessity, these local persons would have developed some knowledge of Roman procedures and of the substance of Roman law—thus expanding and intensifying Roman societal impact on indigenous culture. In turn, to satisfy imperial policy favorable to indigenous law, Roman officials employed local "legal experts" (termed in Greek *nomikoi*[141] or *pragmatikoi*[142]) through whom they obtained knowledge of indigenous law.[143] Local legal substance, however, often was customary, unwritten, unclear, and/or disputed.[144] A Roman magistrate accordingly might find himself, through adversarial proceedings, establishing original interpretations of indigenous law—albeit precedents filtered through the "contamination" of Roman social values, juridical orientation, and legal procedures. In addition to enlightening Roman officials, local experts on indigenous law are known to have assisted peregrine litigants in Roman legal proceedings,[145] and to have prepared documents complying with Roman legal requirements.[146] Probably as a result of the efforts of *nomikoi*, Pliny the Younger, while a provincial governor, repeatedly complains to Trajan that local litigants have knowledge of, and are citing to him, imperial juridical *responsa* and edicts of which he himself has no knowledge.[147]

Ancient evidence thus reveals: a Roman jurisprudence dominantly omnipresent throughout the Empire but functioning through officials who were

---

139. On the multitude of requests from provincial persons that might be addressed to a governor, see P. Yale I 61 (22 May 208–210 [209?]); Haensch 1994.

140. On the limited number of Romans involved in provincial administration, see Chapter 5, pp. 136–139.

141. On νομικοί, see Huttner 2020: 147–149; Alonso 2013: 354; Liebs 2002; Christophilopoulos 1973; Taubenschlag 1951; Kunkel 1967: 267–270, 354; Mason 1974: 70.

142. On πραγματικοί, see Nörr 1965; Robert 1960: 416.

143. Kantor 2009: 263; 2015: 2. See, for example, P. Oxy. 2.237, col. VII, lines 29–38 and Col. VIII, ll. 2–7.

144. Alonso 2013: 357–394; Ando 2015(c), 2016(b): 290–291. For the fullest insight into the relationship between Roman law and customary law in the provinces (esp. Egypt), see Mélèze (Modrzejewski) 2014; Humfress 2011: 40–47.

145. Kantor 2013; Jones 2007.

146. See above, pp. 22–23.

147. Pliny, *Ep.* 10.56–57, 10.65.3, 10.72–73. See Kantor 2020: 187.

often learning about, interacting with, implementing, preserving, and even determining local law; indigenous *ius* locally vital and importantly influential; both forms of law strongly affected by their interaction.

Textual Matters

I have purposely handled the letter "vee" (v) inconsistently. In the text, it appears as "v," the form with which educated anglophone readers are familiar. In my notes, when Latin is reproduced, the form "u" appears, consistent with the absence of "v" from the Latin alphabet.

Unless otherwise indicated, all translations and paraphrases of ancient sources are my own.

My manuscript was delivered to Oxford University Press in December 2021, and it has accordingly been impossible to consider systematically secondary literature that has appeared thereafter.

I

Inequality

IN RECENT YEARS, economic inequality has been the focus of numerous studies that have demonstrated the gross disparities—the great chasms in wealth and income—that in numerous civilizations have differentiated a few ultra-rich individuals from the multitudinous remainder of society.[1] At Rome, too, a stark economic gap separated the very few wealthiest individuals ("top 1 percent"[2]) from all others ("the have-nots, the vast majority of citizens"[3]). Roman slaves (Latin *servi*, singular *servus*), in their masses, of course, appear among the have-nots, as impoverished and exploited denizens of the lowest rung of society.[4] "The Roman slavery system was by nature oppressive and was maintained for the benefit of the privileged only;"[5] slavery at Rome was effectively "a state of living death."[6] "Many [slaves] were violently mistreated: chain-gangs and vicious punishments, including execution on

---

1. See, for example, Alfani and Frigeni 2016 (Middle Ages and thereafter); Flannery and Marcus 2012 (prehistory); Osberg and Smeeding 2006 (modern US treated comparatively); Scheidel 2017 (Stone Age to 21st century). Regional studies have ranged, for example, from Europe (Alfani and Di Tullio 2019 [Venice]; Alfani 2010, 2015 [Italy]; Prados de la Escosura 2008 [Spain]; Reis 2017 [Portugal]; Bengtsson et al. 2018 [Sweden]; Malinowski and Van Zanden 2017 [Poland]) to the Ottoman Empire (Cosgel and Boğaç 2012; Canbakal 2013), Japan (Saito 2015), and the United States (Lindert and Williamson 2016).

2. "In the Roman empire [this 1 percent] would have encompassed the three orders alongside the uppermost slice of non-categorized elite households" (Scheidel 2020: 343 [see also 347]). Cf. Scheidel and Friesen 2009: 76, Table 6.

3. Humfress 2006: 183, quoting Daube 1969: 72.

4. See Temin 2013: 121–123; various essays in Atkins and Osborne 2006, esp. Osborne, 3–5, and Perkins, 60ff.; Harris 2011a. Cf. Rowan 2017.

5. Bradley 1987: 19–20.

6. Bradley 1994: 25.

Roman Inequality. Edward E. Cohen, Oxford University Press. © Oxford University Press 2023.
DOI: 10.1093/oso/9780197687345.003.0002

the mere say-so of the owner, were commonplace" (Harris 2007: 527). "The terrible coercion that relentlessly accompanied the existence of millions of slaves was never substantively eased, nor was the ferocious discipline to which they were subjected" (Schiavone 2020: 20). But servile poverty and ruthless exploitation are not the entire story: in this book I seek to show that a disparity similar to that afflicting free persons also occurred among the unfree population: some *servi*, while still enslaved to private individuals, themselves commanded significant wealth and power, sometimes even owning their own subordinate slaves. This financial inequality—wealthy slaves, impoverished free persons—was exasperated by a legal inequality—the juridical privileging of servile over free enterprise.

Financial Inequality: Affluent Slaves, Impoverished Free Persons

The Roman Law of Persons is based on a single fundamental distinction: all people are either free or slave.[7] But within this existential dichotomy, there *is* a further differentiation: by Roman legal dogma—the unyielding, theoretical "law in the books," opposed to quotidian juridical reality (or "law in action"[8])—free persons' juridical status encompassed many variations (*multae differentiae*), but servitude was inherently indivisible:[9] *servi* individually and as a class were supposedly homogeneous and undifferentiated, mere items of property totally lacking rights.[10] In reality, however, Roman slaves differed

7. Gaius 1.9: summa diuisio de iure personarum haec est, quod omnes homines aut liberi sunt aut serui. Cf. *Dig.* 1.5.3 (Gaius).

8. "Law in action refers to the law as it is applied by the legal decision-makers" (Pölönen 2016: 13). Cf. Ehrlich 2002: 486–506; Nelken 1984; Pound 1910. Legal dogma "can be a poor guide to what courts and people actually do, and vice versa" (Pölönen 2016: 16). See Jakab 2013: 125–126; Korporowicz 2011: 212–213; Legrand 2001: 396; Zweigert-Kötz 1996: 10; Galanter 1989.

9. Just. *Inst.* I.3.5: in seruorum condicione nulla differentia est. in liberis multae differentiae sunt. Cf. *Dig.* 1.5.5.pr. (Marc.): *Dig.* 4.5.3.1 (Paul): seruorum quidem una est condicio; seruile caput nullum ius habet ideoque nec minui potest.

10. "It is the subjection to that particular cluster of powers, usually applied to things, that makes the slave a slave" (Harper and Scheidel 2018: 92). Because "seruile caput nullum ius habet," slaves could be dealt with as animals . . . mistreated at will" (Lewis 2015: 152). Cf. Mouritsen 2011: 13: "in strict legal terms a slave was defined as property, subject to *ius mancipii* similar to land and livestock." Similarly Gardner 2011: 415. Variations in the social situation of slaves, however, have long been recognized: Schumacher 2011; Gamauf 2016: 387, n. 9.

enormously in their personal status, standing, and wealth.[11] There were "superior slaves" (*ordinarii*), "underslaves" (*vicarii*), "public slaves" (*servi publici*),[12] "private slaves" (*servi privati*), "manumitted" slaves (*servi statuliberi*),[13] "voluntary slaves," imperial slaves (*Caesaris servi*), slaves operating autonomously, slaves occupying positions of authority and emolument, including those working as *institores*, *dispensatores*, *procuratores*, *vilici*, and *actores*.[14]

In contrast, much of the non-enslaved population was unified by its poverty:[15] free people, in *their* masses, survived, often at a level of bare subsistence, from self-employment in small-scale agricultural and artisanal work, and from working for others for compensation. Poverty was so pervasive and oppressive that to some Romans, "the life of a slave appeared better than that of a free man."[16] Free "wage laborers" (*mercennarii*), who were almost equated with slaves by upper-class authors, were often still worse off economically.[17]

---

11. These distinctions are consonant with the "spectrum of statuses" that Finley proposed as an analytical framework for understanding the pattern of differences among "slaves" in ancient Greece—placing at "one end of the spectrum . . . the pure chattel, the slave who was only a thing" (1982: 147). In contrast, Marxist thinking traditionally "conceived all (slaves) as a single class" (Vlassopoulos 2016: 85). Cf. Finley 1964, 1965; Alföldy 2011: 196.

12. Public slaves were owned by local political and administrative units throughout the Empire. Although this category of *servi* was until recently "largely ignored" (Lenski 2005: paragraph 1), publication of important new material on Roman municipalities, especially the Lex Irnitana (see González and Crawford 1986; Metzger 2016), has stimulated fresh interest in *servi publici*: studies such as Sudi 2013 and Weiss 2004 have now finally supplanted Halkin 1897. On the status, standing, and perquisites of public slaves, see Bruun 2008: 551–553. On public slaves in the City of Rome during the Republic, see Eder 1980; for public slaves in late antiquity, Lenski 2006; for female public slaves, Cimarosti 2005. For a survey of significant recent scholarship on issues relating to *servi publici*, especially in the provinces, see Luciani 2017: 45, nn. 7–8.

13. These were slaves "manumitted" subject to a yet unfulfilled condition. See Koops 2020: 51–52, 55–56.

14. On *ordinarii* and *vicarii*, see this chapter, pp. 36–38; on "voluntary slaves," Chapter 3, section on "Entrepreneurial Self-Enslavement"; on imperial slaves, Chapter 5; on slaves operating autonomously, this chapter, "Legal Inequality: The Privileging of Servile Enterprise"; on slaves holding important positions in private enterprises, this chapter, pp. 42–48, and Chapter 2, p. 8.

15. On Roman poverty, see Harris 2011(a); Atkins and Osborne, eds. 2006; Holman 2001; Garnsey 1999; Prell 1997; Hamel 1989; Bolkestein 1939.

16. Temin 2013: 132. The free population overall was so impoverished that Silver (discussing "self-enslavement") claims that "for many Romans slavery was a step up, not a disastrous step down" (2011: 112). For volunteered self-enslavement by free persons, see Chapter 3, section on "Entrepreneurial Self-Enslavement."

17. Harris 2007: 528. Cf. Treggiari 1980; de Ste. Croix 1981: 179–204; Marcone 2016: 31 ("la differenza fra un salariato e uno schiavo era minima").

An academic consensus (although not a unanimity) concludes that "the mass of the population lived at or near subsistence levels."[18]

Some free persons, however, *were* able to enjoy at least a modicum of prosperity. The offspring of emancipated slaves—so-called *ingenui*—likely inherited property and financial assets from their parents or from others. Many artisans and shop-owners probably enjoyed what might be termed a "middle-class" existence.[19] In various parts of the Empire, especially in Egypt and North Africa, considerable evidence attests to the existence of many apparently self-sufficient independent land-owners and tenants.[20] A few *equites* appear to have engaged in entrepreneurial activities for their own accounts.[21] Self-employed free individuals would likely have imparted to their children knowledge of their trades and professions, providing a springboard for potential prosperity. Financial operations are a good example. Although many banks were organized through complex structures operated (and sometimes owned) by slaves and former slaves,[22] free bankers operating their own self-proprietorships appear often in juridical sources. Thus, for example, the banker Quintus Caecilius Candidus seems to have had absolute discretion to invest clients' funds in interest-generating situations,[23] and the banker "Gaius Seius" (in dealing with a client who appears to be a freedman) similarly had the power to handle a client's monies at the banker's discretion, subject to an eventual reconciliation of amounts received and expended.[24]

---

18. Garnsey and Saller 2009: 71. Cf. Hawkins 2016: 57: "something on the order of 84–90 percent of the Roman world's inhabitants lived either just above, at, or below subsistence level." Similarly: Taylor 2016: 353; Rathbone 2009; Allen 2009.

19. Mayer 2012; Bowes 2021(a); Flohr 2016: 80; Bransbourg 2022a, 2022b and personal correspondence (July 4, 2022).

20. See Maiuro 2012. Roman taxation, however, seems especially to have oppressed free farmers, causing many to abandon their meager holdings, already beset—before taxes—by the difficulty of competing with large estates worked by *serui* (see De Ligt 2002c: 48; Shaw 1983: 149–150; Brunt 1988).

21. Shaw 2020: 173–193; Welch 1995: 145; Torelli 1980.

22. See Cerami, Di Porto, and Petrucci 2004: 149–174; Petrucci 1991: 313–392; Petrucci 2002: 103–137. Cf. below, this chapter, pp. 47–48.

23. Quintus Caecilius Candidus ad Paccium Rogatianum epistulam scripsit in uerba infra scripta . . . "Uiginti quinque nummorum, quos apud me esse uoluisti, notum tibi ista hac epistula facio, ad ratiunculam meam ea peruenisse: quibus ut primum prospiciam, ne uacua tibi sint: id est usuras eorum accipias, curae habebo" (*Dig.* 16.3.28 [Scaeuola]).

24. Lucius Titius Gaium Seium mensularium, cum quo rationem implicitam habebat propter accepta et data, debitorem sibi constituit et ab eo epistulam accepit in haec uerba: "ex ratione mensae, quam mecum habuisti, in hunc diem ex contractibus plurimis remanserunt apud me ad

The impecuniousness of a large portion of the free population, moreover, should not be exaggerated. "Survival at subsistence level" ("having barely adequate access to the resources required for life"[25]) should not be equated with destitution—the total lack of income or resources that is "usually rapidly fatal."[26] Recent archaeological studies have demonstrated that even impoverished Roman communities may have enjoyed access to a variety of foods and material goods. For example, the "Roman Peasant Project," a series of archaeological field surveys targeting the "smaller/poorer" structures near modern Cinigiano in southern Tuscany (the majority dating from the late Republican/early imperial periods), has shown that inhabitants' diets included occasional supplements of meat from the pigs and pastoral animals (sheep, goats, and cattle) which they kept.[27] Even at Mons Claudianus, in a remote desert portion of Egypt, about 500 kilometers south of Cairo, archaeological evidence suggests the availability of "a healthy, balanced diet."[28] A few scholars have even concluded that an increase in Roman economic capacity in the early imperial period provided some ordinary individuals with access to enhanced consumer items.[29]

In contrast, however, a free elite—minuscule in number[30]—lived palatially. Econometric studies suggest that during the late Republic and Early Empire the top 1 percent received a highly disproportionate share of total income.[31] Similarly, the wealthiest 1 percent of the population controlled a massive portion of total assets: one scholar has even opined that "less than

---

mensam meam trecenta octaginta sex et usurae quae competierint; summam aureorum, quam apud me tacitam habes, refundam tibi. Si quod instrumentum a te emissum, id est scriptum, cuiuscumque summae ex quacumque causa apud me remansit, uanum et pro cancellato habebitur." (*Dig.* 2.14.47.1 ([Scavola]). For detailed discussion of this somewhat convoluted relationship, see Andreau 1987: 558–560.

25. Osborne 2006: 1. "To be poor was to be vulnerable, above all to food shortage" (Morley 2006: 33). Cf. Scheidel 2006: 40.

26. Purcell 1994: 657.

27. Bowes, ed. 2021(b). Cf. Bowes et al. 2017: 167, 193.

28. Van der Veen 1998: 108. Cf. Rowan 2017.

29. Erdkamp 2015; Lo Cascio 2009; Kehoe 2015a; Kron (forthcoming).

30. See Humfress 2006: 183 ("the poor . . . the vast majority of citizens"); Jongman 2008 ("only a small elite escaped life near subsistence"); Temin 2013: 257 ("the expansion of Roman rule had yielded great profits . . . captured by a few people"). Similarly: Kay 2014, passim; Hobson 2015a, 2015b.

31. Scheidel 2020: 344, n. 12; Lo Cascio 2008: 620; Storey 2000. Cf. Milanovic, Lindert, and Williamson 2007: 65–69 ("subsistence was the norm, and high inequality skewed the distribution of any gains from development"). Goldsmith 1987: 36 calculates that the top 3 percent

half a percent of the empire's population . . . probably held 80 percent or more of the total wealth."[32] "The largest Roman private fortunes equaled about 1.5 million times the average annual per capita income in the empire. . . ."[33] Indeed, inequality of wealth in the Early Empire has been calculated as almost equaling that of the contemporary United States (Gini coefficient at Rome 0.42–0.44; US 0.45).[34] At the apex of this plutocracy stood the few hundred persons who were senators,[35] possessors of the huge fortunes required for enrollment in this prestigious body, but themselves precluded by senatorial membership itself from open participation in economic activity.[36] Because of legal impediments to the hiring of free labor and for other reasons (discussed below), Roman senators were virtually compelled to interact with "slaves and freedmen in commerce, manufacture, and financial life" (Andreau 1999: 157). This interconnection offered some slaves and former slaves enormous economic opportunity.

Of course, not all *servi* controlling property (*peculia*) were wealthy: one individual describes himself on his funeral epitaph, as impoverished in his *peculium*, but wealthy in spirit.[37] Yet substantial evidence testifies to the many unfree persons who enjoyed affluence. Numerous *servi* spent large sums to erect costly inscriptions honoring themselves and others, sometimes attesting to their capacity for substantial expenditures from their own resources (*de suo*): the slave Arphocras, for spectacular example, reports spending 175 *denarii* to obtain a burial spot in an ossuary and expending a further 80

controlled as much as 50 percent of personal wealth. Maiuro 2012: 117–134 suggests that the wealthiest 1 percent held only about 30 percent of total wealth (127).

32. Knapp 2011: 5–6. On the lifestyle and investments of "wealthiest Romans, less than 1 percent of the population," see Ellickson 2020: 164 ff.

33. Scheidel 2017: 4.

34. Scheidel and Friesen 2009. On "rising inequality" among the free population for a "quarter-millenium" under the Empire, see Scheidel 2012(a): 14–15. Cf. Vivenza 2012: 34.

35. On the small (and proportionately declining) size of the Senate during the Roman Empire, see Shaw 2020: 162; Eck 1973: 385.

36. On the vast wealth of Roman senators, see Verboven 2008a: xliv–xlv; Coffee 2017: 39; Talbert 1984: 47–66; Duncan-Jones 1982: 17–32, 343–344; Nicolet 1976; Shatzman 1975. On considerations precluding senators' direct involvement in commerce (and methodologies sometimes employed to circumvent such restrictions), see Verboven 2008b; Hoyer 2018: 49–50; Temin 2004.

37. Peculio pauper, animo diuitissimus (ILS 8436 = CIL VI 8012). The holder of the *peculium* was a former slave, now free: see Chapter 2, sections on "Owning Assets through the *Peculium*" and "The Manumission of Skilled Slaves: Facilitating Commerce through Legal Fiction."

denarii to purchase space in a *columbarium*.[38] Cases in the *Digest* posit private slaves owning buildings,[39] cattle,[40] precious metals,[41] and monies.[42] Roman comedy frequently alludes to slaves who have accumulated assets, occasionally in significant amounts.[43] *Servi* operated banks, sometimes entirely for the slaves' own benefit, sometimes paying their owner (*dominus*) a portion of the profits generated.[44]

Some slaves are even said to have squandered money on girlfriends.[45] Thus Juvenal claims satirically that a rich man's slave himself could enjoy the favors of courtesans of class at enormous cost—while free men hesitated to engage even common whores.[46] Slaves even took wives or concubines who were themselves free: of some 462 wives of imperial slaves, only about a quarter of these spouses appear to have been slaves.[47] (A response to this phenomenon of wealthy *servi* enticing higher-status women into cohabitation apparently was the *senatus consultum* Claudianum [52 CE], which provided for the enslavement of free women who persisted in living with slaves without their masters'

38. AE 1980: 150 (c. 50 CE). Cf. CIL II.6338 ff.; CIL II² 7.981; CIL XI 6314 = ILS 3581; AE 1903: 140. Arphocras's expenditure amounted to the approximate cost of a slave (see prices set forth at Ruffing and Drexhage 2008: 321–336) or about a year of legionary wages (Liebs 2000: 121).

39. *Dig.* 15.1.22 (Pomp.); *Dig.* 33.8.6.pr (Ulp.).

40. *Dig.* 15.3.16 (Alf.).

41. *Dig.* 14.4.5.13 (Ulp.).

42. *Dig.* 19.1.38.pr. (Cels.).

43. See, for example, Plaut. *Rud.* 112, 929 ff.; *Trin.* 433; *Asin.* 498, 539–541. Cf. Spranger 1961: 67–68; Fabre 1981: 274. For slaves' ownership of assets in their *peculia* (which are seemingly alluded to even in the XII Tables [VII.12], dating perhaps from the fifth century BCE), see Chapter 2, section on "Owning Assets through the *Peculium*."

44. See below, this chapter, pp. 47–48.

45. *Dig.* 11.3.16 (Alf. Uerus): dominus seruum dispensatorem manumisit, postea rationes ab eo accepit et cum eis non constaret, conperit apud quandam mulierculam pecuniam eum consumpsisse. . . .

46. I.3.131–136: diuitis hic seruo cludit latus ingenuorum | filius; alter enim quantum in legione tribuni | accipiunt donat Caluinae uel Catienae, | ut semel aut iterum super illam palpitet; at tu, | cum tibi uestiti facies scorti placet, haeres | et dubitas alta Chionen deducere sella.

47. Weaver 1972: 114: "a startling and important fact—only 23% of the wives of Imperial slaves from all areas can possibly have been slaves . . . and from Rome, whence come over three-quarters of all these inscriptions, the proportion is as low as 17%." Cf. Penner 2013: 160–167; Milailescu-Birliba 2006: 71; Chantraine 1980; Weaver 2001: 109; Saller 2000: 831.

consent.[48]) Rich slaves were sometimes able even to command dowries from the fathers of free women who gave their daughters in "matrimony" to these unfree men.[49] The father of Claudius Etruscus, for prominent example, while still enslaved,[50] had married Etrusca, the aristocratic scion of a wealthy family, adding to an enslaved imperial administrator the prestige of high marital pedigree.[51] Some female slaves were even able to provide dowries for themselves when entering into "marriage" with male slaves.[52] So wealthy were some *servi* that Roman legal experts struggled to distinguish between legitimate gifts from slaves to their masters and transfers of capital returned to those masters:[53] largess by slaves even evoked regulation under the *lex* Cincia (which explicitly authorized gifts from slave to owner).[54]

Despite the unreliability of the specific sums reported in literary sources as having been accumulated by slaves occupying high position in the emperor's service,[55] it is clear that individual imperial slaves did acquire huge fortunes: one of Nero's *servi* reportedly paid for his own manumission the princely (and

48. Taylor 2016: 356; Kehoe 2011: 148. This legislation was supposedly advanced by Claudius on the advice of Pallas, a close advisor who had originally been owned by Augustus's sister (Tac. *Ann.* 12.53). On the *s. c.* Claudianum, see Sirks 2005; Harper 2010. On Pallas, see Chapter 5, esp. pp. 172–173.

49. *Dig.* 16.3.27 (Paul): Lucius Titius cum haberet filiam in potestate Seiam, Pamphilo seruo alieno in matrimonium collocauit, cui etiam dotem dedit, quam sub titulo depositi in cautionem contulit. . . .

50. iura tamen geniali cordi | . . . iungere festa | conubia et fidos domino genuisse clientes (Stat. *Silvae* 3.3.108–110). On the father of Etruscus, see Chapter 5, pp. 171–172.

51. quis sublime genus formamque insignis Etruscae | nesciat? . . . . |nec uulgare genus; fasces summamque curulem frater et Ausonios enses mandataque fidus | signa tulit. . . . | (119) *sic* quicquid patrio cessatum a sanguine, mater | reddidit (Stat. *Silvae* 3.3.111–120).

52. *Dig.* 23.3.39.pr. (Ulp.): si serua seruo quasi dotem dederit, deinde constante coniunctione ad libertatem ambo peruenerint peculio eis non adempto et in eadem coniunctione permanserint, ita res moderetur, ut, si quae ex rebus corporalibus uelut in dotem tempore seruitutis datis exstiterint, uideantur ea tacite in dotem conuersa, ut earum aestimatio mulieri debeatur.

53. *Dig.* 15.3.7.pr. (Ulp.). On slaves' gifts to their masters, see Buchwitz 2010; Gamauf 2016: 395.

54. *Frag. Vat.* 307: (lex Cincia) item excipit "si quis a seruis quique pro seruis seruitutem seruierunt accipit duit." See Dumont 1987: 115; Fabre 1981: 287; Mommsen 1878. On the context and purpose of the *lex Cincia* overall, see Coffee 2017: 40–43; Zimmerman 1990: 482–484; David 1992: 128–137.

55. Roman historians and biographers, often lacking precise knowledge of wealth rumored to have been obtained by powerful imperial slaves, may have opted for massive exaggeration and embellishment of these assets because of their strong antagonism toward regimes in conflict with their own romanticized republicanism. Tacitus explains: Tiberii Gaique et Claudii ac Neronis res florentibus ipsis ob metum falsae, postquam occiderant recentibus odiis compositae sunt (*Ann.* 1.1). On the heuristic reliability of literary sources regarding imperial

improbably high) sum of 13 million *sesterces*[56] (perhaps US$100 million on a purchasing power parity basis); a slave of Galba bought the position of imperial *dispensator* at a reported price of one million *sesterces.*[57] Another imperial slave, Phosphorus Lepidianus, acting on his own account, is attested as having advanced to the Bank of the Sulpicii some 94,000 *sesterces.*[58] Pallas, ultimately "minister of finance" (*a rationibus*) in the imperial government, while apparently still a mere personal slave of Antonia (niece of Augustus), is reported to have owned an estate in Egypt, presumably as part of his *peculium.*[59] Pallas also appears to have been the owner of the *horti Pallantiani*, iconic parkland property in Rome.[60] Drusilianus (nicknamed the "Chunky"), serving in Spain as an imperial slave of Claudius, supposedly owned a silver dining service weighing some 500 pounds![61] According to Ammianus Marcellinus, at the beginning of Julian's reign (about 361 CE) cooks and other palace slaves received a substantial yearly salary (*annuum stipendium grave*) and other valuable emoluments; in addition to his salary, for example, a palace barber is reported to have received a *daily* benefit equivalent to 20 times a day's food requirement for himself and his pack animals.[62]

Private slaves also are known sometimes to have received periodic stipends. Lucian, writing in Greek in the second century CE, confirms that monthly payments to *servi* were widespread in the great Roman houses.[63] Seneca, for

---

slaves and the difficulty of differentiating imperial slaves (*servi*) from freedmen (*liberti*), see Chapter 5, pp. 174–179.

56. Pliny *H.N.* 7.129. Cf. Millar 1992: 136.

57. Dio Cass. 57.10.4. On *dispensatores*, see Chapter 2, pp. 69–70.

58. TPSulp. 69. For the use of their own monies by imperial slaves and freedmen in commercial dealings, and the absence of imperial funds from private transactions, see Rathbone and Temin 2008: 388.

59. CIL XIV, Supp. 4535, ll. 20–21; *P London* 195. On servile *peculia*, see Chapter 2.

60. Frontin. *Aq.* 19, 20, 69; *Plin, Ep.* 7.29, 8.6. See Richardson 1992: s. v.

61. Pliny, *N.H.* 33.52 (145): Claudii principatu seruus eius Drusilianus nomine Rotundus, dispensator Hispaniae citerioris, quingenariam lancem habuit, cui fabricandae officina prius exaedificata fuerat.

62. Amm. Marc. 22.4 9–10. On the slave status of these imperial functionaries, see Bradley 1987: 108–109.

63. ὁπόταν, ὦ βέλτιστε, τῆς νουμηνίας ἐπιστάσης ἀναμιχθεὶς τῷ Πυρρίᾳ καὶ τῷ Ζωπυρίωνι προτείνης τὴν χεῖρα ὁμοίως τοῖς ἄλλοις οἰκέταις καὶ λάβης ἐκεῖνο ὀτιδήποτε ἦν τὸ γιγνόμενον, τοῦτο ἡ πρᾶσίς ἐστιν. Lucian (περὶ τῶν ἐπὶ Μισθῷ συνόντων) 36.23.

example, suggests that at least some of his urban servants received a monthly stipend of five *modii* of wheat and five *denarii* in cash.[64]

Slaves could even be public benefactors. At Llerena in Spain, an inscription records a grave altar paid for by an imperial slave from his own *peculium*.[65] At Mheimes in Africa, an imperial slave paid from his own funds for the rebuilding of the local *teloneum* (customs office).[66] A public slave from "his own money" is reported to have provided the Aequiculi with a sanctuary, including a temple, attendant work areas, and statues of Serapis and of Isis.[67] We know of a slave who provided a temple and statuary, and of another *servus* who aided a municipality in financing religious statues.[68] Similar servile benefactions are memorialized in a number of other locations.[69]

At Rome, *servi* even represented a high percentage of the city's intellectual elite, some of whom are reported to have attained considerable wealth.[70] The slave educator Epaphroditos, for example, an inveterate collector of manuscripts, had acquired two houses and a large library at Rome.[71] Other slaves are attested as maintaining separate domiciliary establishments, sometimes in provinces and locations distant from their masters' residences, enriching themselves and impoverishing their absentee masters.[72] A freedman

---

64. *Epist. Mor.* 80.8: seruus est, quinque modios accipit et quinque denarios. Five modii were equivalent to about 33 kilograms. Cf. Hor. *Ep.* 1.14.40; Petr. *Satyr.* 75.4.

65. CIL II^2 7.981: de suo. Cf. CIL II 6338ff.; AE 1903.140.

66. CIL VIII.12314 = ILS 1654. On the financing and building of public buildings in Africa in the Roman period, sometimes a joint public/private undertaking, see Hoyer 2018: 88–96.

67. CIL IX 4112 (= ILS 4381): pro salute ordinis et populi signa / Serapis et Isidis cum ergasteris suis / et aediculam in scholam permit / tente ordine / Apronianus r(ei) p(ublicae) Aequicul(orum) ser(uus) ark(arius) / cum Aequicula Bassilla et Aequi /culo Aproniano fil(io) pec(unia) sua fecit / l(ocus) d(atus) d(ecreto) d(ecurionum). On public slaves (serui publici), see above, this chapter, n. 12.

68. ILS 3581 (= CIL I^2 3391, CIL XI 6314): Faustus Uersenni Publii seruus Priapum et templum de suo peculio faciendum curauit. Ibid. 3611 (= CIL X 1582): Lares Augustos . . . Sodalis C. Modi Cimbri seruus, Aeschinus Octavi M. seruus magistr. de suo faciendum curauit. On slaves' participation in Roman religious life, see Schumacher 2001a: 269.

69. See, for example, CIL II^2 7.954 (Emerita [Mérida]) in Spain; AE 1980.150.

70. Suet. *Gram. Rhet.* Cf. Kolendo 1979; Christes 1979.

71. Suda 2.334/2004 (Adler): ὠνήθη ὑπὸ Μοδέστου . . . ὠνούμενος δὲ ἀεὶ βιβλία ἐκτήσατο μυριάδας τρεῖς . . . ᾤκει τε ἐν τοῖς καλουμένοις Φαινιανοκορίοις δύο οἰκίας αὐτόθι κτησάμενος. On a surviving statue, he is denominated a "grammaticus Graecus" (CIL VI 9454).

72. *Dig.* 40.9.10 (Gaius), 5.1.19.3 (Ulp.). Cf. *Dig.* 41.2.1.14 (Paul.: Cassius and Julian); *Corpus Papyrorum Judaicarum* II, nos. 419 a and c. Roman slaves' maintenance of living quarters separate from that of their masters parallels the Athenian institution of "slaves living independently"

in Petronius's *Satyricon* claims to have bought his liberty for 1,000 *denarii*.[73] An inscription testifies to a doctor (one P. Decimius Merula) who was able to pay 50,000 *sesterces* for his freedom.[74]

Under the Roman system of superior slaves (*ordinarii*) and subordinate slaves (*vicarii*), some *servi* effectively "owned" their own slaves, sometimes in large numbers. Juridical texts routinely deal with issues relating to these relationships:[75] the subordinate slave is treated as the property of the *servus ordinarius*[76] in the same way that a free owner (*dominus*) is the master of his own slaves.[77] Many passages in Roman literature allude in passing to this arrangement.[78] Epigraphic evidence confirms the phenomenon.[79] Thus, although information on personal status is provided for only a minority of the deceased non-free persons memorialized in a trove of more than 400 inscriptions found within the *columbarium* of the Statilii, a senatorial family prominent during the Principate,[80] individuals themselves enslaved appear as the "owners" (*ordinarii*) of more than half the 169 slaves whose situation *is* attested. In fact, most of the identified slave-owning slaves controlled more than a single underslave: Faustus and Suavis, for example, are identified as *vicarii* under the control of Eros, who is himself owned by a freedman whom he serves as *dispensator*, an important financial or accounting office at that

---

(*douloi khôris oikountes*), an arrangement that permitted unfree persons to conduct their own businesses, establish their own households, and sometimes even to own their own slaves.

73. 57.6: mille denarios pro capite solui.

74. ILS 7812: medicus clinicus, chirurgus, ocularius; VIuir., hic pro libertate dedit quinquaginta milia.

75. See *Dig.* 14.1.1.22 (Ulp., citing Pomponius); *Dig.* 14.4.5.1 (Ulp.); *Dig.* 15.1.37.1 (Iul.); *Dig.* 10.3.25 (Iul.); *Dig.* 33.7.12.44 (Ulp.); *Dig.* 33.8.4 (Gaius); *Dig.* 33.8.21 (Scaeu.); *Dig.* 33.8.22.1 (Lab. Frag.); *Dig.* 33.8.25 (Cels.); *Dig.* 21.2.5 (Paul.). No less than 64 cases in the Digest deal with *uicarii* (Morabito 1981:111, n. 65). Cf. Melillo 1981: 340 ff.

76. See, for example, *Dig.* 15.1.17 (Ulp.): si seruus meus ordinarius uicarios habeat id quod uicarii mihi debent an deducam ex peculio serui ordinarii?

77. *Dig.* 15.1.17 (Ulp.): dominus eorum, id est ordinarius seruus.

78. See Plaut. *Asin.* 432–439, *Persa* 33, 474–745; Poen. 221–223, *Pseud.* 604–611, *Stich.* 188, 453, *Truc.* 95–98, *Mil.* 823–25; Ter. *Ad.* 376–381; Cic. *Uerr.* II.1.36.93, II.3.38.86, *Par. Stoic.* 5.2.36–37; Cato, *De Re Rust.* 5–7, 142; Uarro, *De Re Rust.* 1.17.4–6; Columella, *De Re Rust.* 1.9.3; Hor. *Sat.* 2.7.79–83; Plin. *N.H.* 33.52.145; Sen. *Tranq.* 8.5.

79. Reduzzi Merola 1990: 189–201 catalogues some 134 allusions to *serui uicarii* recorded on surviving epigraphical material (citations which she discusses in detail at 1990: 131–187).

80. CIL VI 6223, 6413, 6482, 6485, 6487, 6495, 6516, 6517, 6520, 6583, 6597, 6598, 6605, 6608, 6621, 6622, 6623, 6626, 6629, 6631, 6637, 6639. See Mouritsen 2013; Hasegawa 2005.

time available only to slaves.[81] Inscriptions found in the *columbarium* of the Volusii Saturnini show a similar pattern: twenty-four *ordinarii* are there reported as superordinate over some 48 *vicarii*.[82] The imperial slave Musicus Scurranus held no less than sixteen underslaves, including a doctor (*medicus*) and a businessman (*negotiator*);[83] another enslaved member of the emperor's household, a certain Felix, *dispensator* at Hispalis, owned at least five *vicarii*.[84] In all, there survive some sixty-five examples of imperial slaves owning underslaves.[85] *Vicarii* might even own their own slaves. Vegetus, for example, *vicarius* of Montanus, an imperial slave, is reported on a wax tablet found in 1994 in the City of London, to have "purchased and received" the female slave Fortunata.[86] According to Plutarch, slaves of the elder Cato even reportedly borrowed money from their master to purchase *servi* whom they trained and then resold at a profit.[87]

For us[88]—but apparently not for the Romans[89]—a slave's ownership of other slaves does present serious conceptual challenges. How can an enslaved

---

81. CIL VI 6275, 6276. Cf. Schumacher 2010: 31; Ramin and Veyne [1981] 2001: 268. See Chapter 2, pp. 69–70, with n. 115.

82. See Buonocore 1984. Cf. Eck 1972.

83. CIL VI 5197 = ILS 1514. The *uicarii*, all but one male, set up a commemorative inscription setting forth their various functions (see Bruun 2014: 617). For other epigraphically preserved testimonia to the wealth and power of imperial slaves, see Schumacher 2001a: 270–274. For the disproportionately high representation of males among the imperial slaves commemorated on the epigraphical epitaphs constituting the bulk of surviving information on the imperial household, see the data in Chantraine 1980 ("the emperor had very limited use for female slaves" [Bruun 2014: 617]).

84. CIL II.1198 = ILS 1659, a post-Hadrianic inscription.

85. See Weaver 1972: 201.

86. Uegetus Montani Imperatoris Aug(usti) ser(ui) Iucun/diani uic(arius) emit mancipioque accepit pu/ellam Fortunatam. . . . See Tomlin 2003; Camodeca 2006; Reduzzi Merola 2007; Korporowicz 2011; du Plessis 2020: 449–450.

87. *Cato Mai.* 21.7: ἐδίδου δὲ καὶ τῶν οἰκετῶν τοῖς βουλομένοις ἀργύριον· οἱ δ᾿ ἐωνοῦντο παῖδας, εἶτα τούτους ἀσκήσαντες καὶ διδάξαντες ἀναλώμασι τοῦ Κάτωνος μετ᾿ ἐνιαυτὸν ἀπεδίδοντο. Cf. Plut. *Cato Mai.* 10.6.

88. Entire books have been written about the multitudinous legal issues raised, directly and tangentially, by a slave-owning slave (*servus ordinarius*) and his human enslaved property. See Reduzzi Merola 1990 (primarily a juridical treatment: Magalhães 2009: 131), summarized in Reduzzi Merola 2010: 21–31. Erman 1896 remains the iconic study of *uicarii*. Cf. Weaver 1972: 200–206.

89. Roman legal concepts of "ownership" always remained pragmatically elastic and definitionally imprecise. "Ownership (*dominium*) in Roman law is difficult to define, and the Romans themselves did not trouble to do this" (Johnston 1999: 53). For a fuller discussion of the conflict

slave-master be identified as a "slave" *tout court*? But how can (s)he be excluded? Such Janus-like overlordship makes clear that at Rome a slave's legal status—juridically inferior to that of every free person—was not dispositive, ipso facto, of every other dimension of his or her life, nor of every aspect of his or her place in society. A slave generating for his own benefit considerable cash or other disposable assets gains the power that money bestows—an economic strength supplemental to or even eliminatory of purported personal impotence. An imperial slave wielding authority over free citizens attains an ascendancy inconceivable to the hapless enslaved agricultural worker or lowly household assistant.[90] A free person entering into slavery voluntarily under contractual provisions negotiated with a future master is not without legal rights.[91] Even servile "knowledge" could constitute a form of power.[92] Money, skills, insights, personal relations with important individuals ("patrons"), positions in government, contractual rights—by Foucauldian conceptualization all constitute potential or actual nexuses of ascendancy: "Power is everywhere . . . and comes from everywhere."[93] "How important was the question of free birth really to the common Roman, when confronted with other factors such as wealth and influence?"[94]

Legal Inequality: The Privileging of Servile Enterprise

The financial conservatism of the Roman upper classes during the late Republic and the Early Empire has been often noted.[95] Wealthy Romans

between commercial reality and legal theory relating to slaves' "ownership" of property—and its resolution through "legal fiction"—see Chapter 2, pp. 59–65.

90. See Chapter 5, pp. 169–173.

91. See Chapter 3 for the phenomenon of free persons entering voluntarily into slavery, in order to pursue commercial opportunities unavailable to the unenslaved—and who, after garnering economic success through the Roman institution of the *peculium*, regain their freedom through "self-purchase" with "their own funds" (*suis nummis*), emerging economically and socially enhanced as "freedmen." Cf. Chapter 2, section "The Manumission of Skilled Slaves: Facilitating Commerce through Legal Fiction."

92. For "the power of knowledge and technology" in the Roman Republic, see Harris 2016: 69–70.

93. Foucault [1976] 1998: 63. Cf. 100–101.

94. Bruun 1990: 284.

95. For example, by Shaw 2020: 169; Bang 2008: 153, n. 71; Johnston 2007, 1999: 108–109: Verboven 2014: 77, 2007: 872; Temin and Rathbone 2008; Zwalve 2002: 118; Kehoe 1997.

tended to invest only in real estate and agriculture, largely avoiding commercial undertakings, for many reasons (including ideological-based disdain for commerce[96]) but in part because the legal structure of Roman business was inhospitable to, and in early times entirely incompatible with, profit-seeking enterprises of scale and complexity, and in part because judicial rules mandated unlimited personal financial liability for free persons involved in commerce. In adaptive response, Roman law came to develop elaborate mechanisms to facilitate enterprises of size and sophistication, and to mitigate investors' economic exposure—modalities that in practice favored servile over free enterprise.

Business Organization

Roman business was family business[97]—functioning through the *pater familias* and/or his relatives and dependents, including slaves and former slaves, who were considered, juridically and socially, to be members of the family.[98] There was no alternative. Roman law never recognized corporations (commercial entities operating as "legal persons").[99] It treated associations or partnerships as mere aggregations of individuals, never as a single entity

96. This disdain, however, was complexly nuanced ("non si possa individuare un sistema di valori coerente riguardo la valutazione sociale delle attività lavorative": Cristofori 2016: 161).

97. *Familia* ("family"): "The Roman *familia* was much broader than today's simple 'nuclear' family, extending from the oldest living male . . . to include his minor children, his slaves, and all his adult male descendants and their households" (Hansmann et al. 2020: 201). Cf. Glossary to Watson, ed.: 1985, 1999, *s.v.*: "As well as a family in the modern sense this term sometimes also covers a person's whole household, including freedmen and slaves as relations." Roman authorities are clear in considering slaves as members of the Roman *familia*: see, for example, *Dig.* 50.16.195.3 (Ulp.): seruitutium quoque solemus appellare familias ("we also customarily describe slaves as *familiae*": translation Frier and McGinn 2004: 19); Sen. *Epist.* 47.14: (Romani) dominum patrem familiae appellauerunt, servos . . . familiares." See also Osgood 2011(b): 70–74.

98. *Dig.* 50.16.195 (Ulp.); *Dig.* 14.1.1.4 (Ulp.); *Dig.* 14.3.7.1 (Ulp.). "The use of slaves and social dependants in key business functions was . . . characteristic of Roman society. . . . The *familia* structure was so ingrained in Roman society that it provided a ready made structure around which to organize business activities" (Frier and Kehoe 2007: 130). Cf. Hansmann et al. 2020: 226; Jones 2006: 218–243; Edmonson 2011: 338; Bürge 1987: 500–508; Kirschenbaum 1987: 122–123; Kaser 1970: 333 ff., 343 ff. For manumitted slaves as continuing members of the *pater familias*' family, see Tac. *Ann.* 13.32.1; Fabre 1981:131–140; below, Chapter 2, "The Manumission of Skilled Slaves: Facilitating Commerce through Legal Fiction."

99. Cerami et. al. 2004: 61–63; D'Arms 1981: 41; Fleckner 2020: 234–236. Di Porto characterizes the transformation from Roman to modern commerce as a transition from (1) businesses functioning through actual persons who lacked legal standing to (2) businesses that were themselves artificial persons who did possess legal standing ("dalla persona fisica non giuridica alla

entitled to its own legal standing.[100] Roman law rejected even the conduct of business through individuals (employees or representatives) having the power to bind principals while remaining personally free of liability: it never accepted "agents" in the Common Law sense of the term in which "*B*, authorized by *A*, may go through a transaction on behalf of *A*, with *C*, with the result that all the effects of the transaction, all the rights and liabilities created by it, will take effect between *A* and *C*, *B* having no concern whatever with them and acting merely as a conduit pipe."[101] The absence of a general provision for "agency" effectively precluded free men from legally acting on behalf of other free men.[102]

As persons not *sui iuris*,[103] family members—including slaves and even sons—had no legal standing and therefore could not be juridically responsible for commercial commitments. Because Rome did not recognize agency,

---

persona giuridica non fisica") (1997: 450 ff.). Cf. di Porto 1984: 169–204. Malmendier's belief in the existence of Roman stock corporations (2002, 2005, 2009, 2013) "is partly the result of differing interpretations, partly the result of factual mistakes" (Fleckner 2020: 235, n. 12).

100. Schulz 1951: 86–89; Buckland and McNair 1965: 56–59; Johnston 1999: 106–107; Zwalve 2002: 119–120. Citing *Dig.* 3.4.1.pr. (Gaius), Badian suggests that in exceptional cases the government might have offered temporary recognition as an entity to groupings of *publicani*, but admits that "there seems to be no evidence on this" (1983: 136–137). Cf. Malmendier 2005: 38; Hansmann, Kraakman, and Squire 2006: 1360–1361.

101. Buckland and McNair: 1965: 217. Less technically correct, but more accessibly, Nicholas sets forth the Common Law doctrine: "if an agent enters into a contract on behalf of his principal with a third party, he creates rights and duties directly between principal and third party, and himself incurs neither" (1962: 201). See also Aubert 2015: 228; Bodel 2011: 316; Kehoe 2011: 146–147; Miceli 2008; Finkenauer 2008; Gordon 2007; Plescia 1984; Thomas 1976: 308; Kaser 1975: Vol. 2: 99.

102. However, free men could involve themselves in the affairs of others, undertaking limited or extended activities—but at the peril of unlimited personal liability, without the power to bind the person on whose behalf they were purportedly acting, and always provided that they received no compensation (*lucrum*) therefor. See *Dig.* 17.1.4 (Paul.): mandatum nisi gratuitum nullum est. (Cf. Kehoe 2017: 116–127; 2020: 317–320; Dimopoulou 1999: 479–486; Verboven 2002: 227–230). Elaborate rules came to govern such *mandata* and/or *gestiones negotiorum*, leading ultimately to the "mandate" and "commercial agency" conceptualizations adopted in modern times by jurisdictions that have "received" the Civil Law—adaptations intended to ameliorate the absence in Roman Law of the Anglo-American conception of agency. See North 1997; Holmes and Symenoides 1999.

103. A seminal characteristic of Roman law is the enormous power of the father (*patria potestas*) as chief of the family (*pater familias*). Only the head of a Roman household is *sui iuris* ("under his [or her] own legal power"): all other household members—principally slaves and children—are subject to his power, and in theory entirely, and in practice largely, have no legal personality of their own. See Gaius, *Inst.* 1.48, 52, 55; Pahud 2013: 119–147; Kehoe 2011: 144–147; Johnston 1999: 30–31; Frier and McGinn 2004: 18–22. Yet Roman commitment to juridical gender neutrality resulted in the anomaly of some women exercising as *mater familias* power similar to the male patriarch's *patria potestas*. See Perry 2016: 437; Benke 2012: 222,

the *pater familias* originally was not liable for his subordinates' actions,[104] nor was a slave responsible for business transactions,[105] leaving without remedy aggrieved parties who had dealt commercially with dependents—a result perceived by the jurisprudents as unfair.[106] Accordingly, the law came to hold principals responsible under the *actiones institoria* and *exercitoria* for liabilities incurred (and advantages obtained) through their dependents.[107] As members of the family, slaves were therefore subsumed under the father's juristic *persona* and became capable of binding the *pater familias*.[108]

Dependents' capacity to act for a *pater familias* became critical to the economy as the Roman polity transformed itself into a heavily monetized, world-encompassing *imperium*, as Roman wealth and enterprise increased apace, generating unprecedented commercial complexity.[109] A single principal could not be in more than one place at a given moment, and could directly enter into only a single arrangement at a single time. But no sizable or complex business could function through exclusive dependence on a sole

---

n. 38. Cf. Chapter 4, section on "Gender Equality and Inequality: Fathers' and (Sometimes Mothers') Power over Family Members."

104. *Dig.* 50.17.133 (Gaius): Melior condicio nostra per seruos fieri potest, deterior fieri non potest.

105. Although a slave involved in commerce might theoretically become legally obligated under "natural law" (Zimmerman 1990: 7–10), practically he was not liable under Roman law (*ius ciuile*): his legal incapacity prevented his being sued in court (*Dig.* 50.17.107 [Gaius]: cum seruo nulla actio est). See Metzger 2014.

106. See *Dig.* 14.3.1 (*Ulp.*): "Aequum praetori uisum est, sicut commoda sentimus ex actu institorum, ita etiam obligari nos ex contractibus ipsorum et conueniri." See also Paul. *Sent.* 2.8.1. Cf. Wacke 1994.

107. As Aubert explains, "in the early history of the *actio institoria*, only dependent people (slaves and persons-in-power) could be appointed as business managers" (1994: 417). Although it is clear that these so-called *actiones adiecticiae qualitatis* were developed not prior to the transformation of the economy that followed the enormous expansion of Roman power during the late Republic, Romanists have long, and in my opinion inconclusively, disputed the exact chronology of this development: see Aubert 2013: 192–193; 1994: 70–100; de Ligt 2020: 91–93; Miceli 2008: I.49; Guarino 1997: 336–337; Solazzi 1963, esp. 243, n. 1; Zeber 1981: 13–23.

108. Dependents acting on behalf of a *pater familias* were not, however, "agents" as conceptualized by the Common Law. In Roman law, "the subordinate who administered a *peculium* and concluded contracts based thereupon . . . never receded into the background. . . . Jurisprudentially, he and his principal were regarded as co-real *debitores*" (Kirschenbaum 1987: 68–69). See *Dig.* 15.1.3.3 (Ulp.). For appropriate use of the term "agent" in the context of classical civilizations, see Kehoe 2015(b): 244–248; Cohen 2017.

109. In comparison to modern multinational corporations, however, Roman enterprises were "relatively small" (Abatino and Dari-Mattiacci 2011: 6). Similarly: Fleckner 2010: 654; Andreau 2004: 124. Cf. Labruna 1994.

proprietor.[110] Roman business accordingly compensated for Roman law's rejection of free persons acting on behalf of other free persons by coming to operate largely through presently and formerly enslaved persons, who, as family members, had the legal capacity to act for the head of the family.[111]

Limiting Liability by Empowering Slaves

Slaves involved in commerce were not uniformly mere low-level functionaries working under the supervision of their present or former *dominus*. In fact, Roman slaves were frequently skilled in trade, craft, or commerce,[112] while masters—compliant with elite attitudes of contempt for commercial activity[113]—seldom had acquired business expertise through personal experience, and therefore were in no position to train or to oversee servile labor. Moreover, the law strongly discouraged masters' personal involvement in business: limitations on owners' financial liability under the *actio tributaria*, for example, were effective only when a *dominus* was not directly engaged in, or even knowledgeable of,[114] mercantile operations—a strong disincentive to masters' gaining commercial expertise by working in their own enterprises. Although the owner of an entity operated by another person as manager (*institor*) was normally liable only for losses occurring pursuant to the terms of the manager's appointment (*praepositio*),[115] personal involvement in, or

110. On this need for "de-personalization" of Roman commercial businesses, see Abatino, Dari-Mattiacci, and Perotti 2011.

111. Pesaresi 2008: 9–11; di Porto 1984: 31 ff.; Serrao 1989: 17 ff.

112. Slaves often received extensive practical education: see Plut. *Cat. Mai.* 21.6, *Crass.* 2.5–6; Petron. *Satyr.* 46.3–8; *Dig.* 19.2.13.3 (Ulp.). Cf. Tran 2017: 258; Bodel 2011: 330–334; Laes 2008; 262–263; Temin 2004: 535; Teitler 1985: 31; Forbes 1955: 342; Booth 1979.

113. Cic. *Off.* 1.150–51; Livy 21.63.4 (quaestus omnis patribus indecorus). See Verboven and Laes 2017: 2; Cristofori 2016: 150–162; Merola 2016: 314; Andreau 2004(a): 84; Aubert 2015: 228; Andermahr 1998: 1; D'Arms 1981: 20–47. Working-class ("plebeian") values, however, conferred considerable prestige on skilled artisans, even on freedmen: see Tran 2017; Veyne 2000: 1192–1194; Joshel 1992: 4–7 and 79–85; De Robertis 1963: 21–97.

114. Ulpian notes that a master's assets loaned to a slave's *peculium* were relegated to the status of general (external) creditor, instead of enjoying priority over all third-party claimants, if the master merely "knew that a slave was using the stock of the *peculium* in conducting business" (si scierit seruum peculiari merce negotiari: *Dig.* 14.4.1.pr. [Ulp.]). Cf. Hansmann, Kraakman, and Squire 2020: 219–220.

115. See *Dig.* 14.1.1.12 (Ulp.); Gaius 4.71. Cf. Tchernia 2011: 42–47; De Martino 1958 [1981]: 276, 1941 [1981].

supervision of, a manager's activity subjected a principal to an action *quod iussu*,[116] which carried unlimited liability and was available whenever a subordinate acted at the direction (*voluntas*) of a *dominus*.[117] Absent personal involvement, an owner was fully liable only for the manager's activities that *were* authorized under the *praepositio*. Complete limitation of liability, however, was available to *domini* only through the Roman institution of the *peculium*.[118] Because debtors' inability to meet obligations empowered creditors under Roman insolvency procedures to seize and sell all of the obligors' assets (even if this aggregate value far exceeded the amount owed—with no obligation to return excess proceeds to the debtor),[119] wealthy Romans, especially those seeking extraordinary profits in inherently risky pursuits,[120] were strongly motivated to limit their liability by entrusting such ventures entirely to skilled slaves operating absolutely autonomously of their owners.

Although there was no explicit legal prohibition of the use of free persons as managers or supervisors,[121] as a practical matter slave status was requisite for Roman positions "involving the handling of owners' money."[122] In any case, Roman businesses, based on a family structure that included only slaves and relatives, had no use for a free outsider (*extraneus*). Such an interloper would have functioned poorly, if at all, amidst the social and legal strictures (the "institutional rules of the game"[123]) through which the family—and a

116. *Dig.* 15.4 (Ulp., Paul.). See Schleppinghoff 1996; de Ligt 2002a; Bisazza 2003.

117. See *Dig.* 14.1.1.19–20 (Ulp.). Cf. Chiussi 2007a; Aubert 2015: 229–231; Sirks 2018: 87.

118. See Fleckner 2010: 301–310; 2014: 217; and discussion in Chapter 2, pp. 57–58.

119. The basic—and harsh—Roman procedure in insolvency was *bonorum venditio* (see Gaius 3.78–79; cf. 2.97). During the imperial period, the rigor of this procedure was slightly mitigated by the introduction of *bonorum cessio* which continued to provide for confiscation of goods in value potentially above, sometimes far more than, the amount owed: *Dig.* 42.3 (Ulp., Paul., Modestinus, Marcianus); Pakter 1994.

120. On the interplay between the severe Roman rules of personal liability and the financial conservatism of the Roman upper classes, see above, this chapter, pp. 38–39.

121. *Dig.* 14.3.1 (Ulp.): . . . si quidem seruum proprium institorem habuit . . . si autem uel alienum seruum uel etiam hominem liberum. . . . Until late antiquity, however, the general legal principle applied that "per extraneam personam nihil nobis adquiri posse" (Gaius 2.95).

122. "(T)he carrying of slave status was not just typical for those exercising roles as either *vilicus*, *actor* or *dispensator*, but in principle necessary" (Schumacher 2010: 31). Cf. Ramin and Veyne [1981] 2001: 268 ("la servitude était la condition sine qua non de toute profession où l'on maniait l'argent de son employeur").

123. "Institutional Rules of the Games" are a critical focus of the New Institutional Economics: see above Introduction, pp. 8–9.

business firm based on the family—operated. Accordingly, almost all Roman business managers (*institores*) were slaves;[124] *procuratores*, the most-elevated supervisors of family operations, were invariably slaves;[125] administrators of agricultural operations, *vilici* ("stewards/bailiffs"), were always (or virtually always) enslaved.[126] Furthermore, the law's rejection of free men serving as agents meant that a free labor staff could not achieve the economies of scale available to centralized organizations deploying a multitude of slave operatives who as members of the family *were* empowered to act legally on behalf of the ultimate *pater familias*. Slave-operated enterprises need not fear future competition from, or the purloining of customers or contacts by, ambitious or disaffected staff. Reliance on a proprietor's own dependents (instead of free contractors) eliminated, or largely mitigated, the costs that might otherwise be incurred in seeking to equalize the asymmetrical informational advantages enjoyed by contractors whose superior knowledge, arising from personal involvement in a business function, might be employed against the economic interests of a *pater familias* not personally participating in the enterprise and therefore largely ignorant of its detailed operations and of the proverbial "secrets of the trade."[127] Continuity of operation was protected through the employment in key positions of slaves, whose tenure was at the pleasure of a master, instead of through the use of free persons who might at any time, even for entirely personal motivations, choose to pursue other activity.[128] Because an extended and extensive labor market had developed already in the early

---

124. Aubert, in his magisterial study of Roman *institores*, concluded that "the overwhelming majority of business managers were slaves" (1994: 417). "Legal and literary sources tend to assume that *institores* . . . were slaves rather than free" (Mouritsen 2011: 220). Cf. Morabito 1985.

125. In imperial times, *procuratores* appear sometimes (and increasingly under the High Empire) to be slaves who have been manumitted. See Chapter 2, nn. 174–175 and related text.

126. See Schumacher 2010: 31, 2011: *passim*; Silver 2016(a); Carlsen 1995; Beare 1978. Scheidel (1990: 593) notes that some *uilici* are known to have continued in their positions after manumission: cf. Chapter 2, section on "The Manumission of Skilled Slaves: Facilitating Commerce through Legal Fiction," and Gsell 1932.

127. For informational asymmetry even between master and slave, and its negative implications, see *Dig.* 14.4.5.1 (Ulp.), *Dig.* 2.13.4.3 (Ulp.), *Dig.* 3.5.41 (Paul.); between co-masters, see *Dig.* 14.4.3.pr. (Ulp.). For other examples of the influence of Roman legal provisions and procedures on transaction costs, Terpstra 2008: 356–369; 2013, passim; Kehoe, Ratzan, and Yiftach 2015: 15–27; Andreau 2020: 106.

128. Slaves' appointment to high imperial positions has similarly been attributed to a desire to avoid the discontinuities inherent in the employment of free persons: "unlike nobles, slaves' tenure of office was not restricted to short periods" (Hopkins 1978: 124). Cf. Chapter 5, pp. 178–179.

Principate,[129] in which slaves seem to have predominated among those entering into work contracts (*locatio/conductio operarum*),[130] persons needing additional workers could employ hired *servi* to augment those unfree persons already functioning in the business.[131] Slave managers could also make use of unlimited numbers of unfree sub-representatives (*vicarii*), who could, like the *institor* himself, act on behalf of the ultimate *pater familias*.[132] "No wonder, therefore, that many Roman business enterprises—banks, factories, shops and even schools—were run by slaves" (Zwalve 2002: 122).

By agreement with their masters,[133] slaves often operated their businesses at least partially for their own direct benefit.[134] Artemidôros, in his second-century-CE treatise on interpreting dreams, explains that the appearance of a creditor in a slave's dream signifies a "master seeking an *apophora*,"[135] a sharing arrangement long attested in the Mediterranean world, through which an owner received from his *servus* a portion of the revenue generated by the slave.[136] In the fourth century BCE, for example, Athenian slaves, as principals, operated the largest and most successful bank (*trapeza*) in Attica,[137] making

---

129. For the allocation of workers, free and slave, within the City of Rome and elsewhere, through grids sometimes spread over more than a single province, responsive to forces of supply and demand, see Bernard 2017: 63–64; Holleran 2017: 88–90; Temin 2013: 114–138, and 2004; Allen 2009; Rathbone 2009; Scheidel 2009, 2010.

130. Bürge 1993; Zuiderhoek 2017: 29, and 2013. Cf. Plaut. *Uid.* 25; Sen. *Ben.* 7.5.3. Rathbone 1991, however, documents the hiring of substantial numbers of temporary free workers on Egyptian estates.

131. See *Dig.* 19.2.42–43 (Paul.), 45.1 (Paul.), and 48.1 (Modestinus); 32.73.3 (Ulp.); 47.5.1.5 (Ulp.); *P. Wisc.* 16.5.

132. See, for example, *Dig.* 15.1.6 (Celsus), 15.1.7.4 (Ulp.). Cf. Buckland [1908] 1970: 246 ff., 640 ff.; Brinkhoff 1978: 133 ff.; Zeber 1981: 72; Schumacher 2001: 270–274. On *vicarii*, see pp. 36–37 above.

133. On the practical significance and juridical effectiveness of agreements between slaves and masters, see Chapter 3, pp. 107–114.

134. Even in North America in the nineteenth century, slave-masters frequently leased out Black slave craftsmen who lived and worked autonomously, sharing with their owners a portion of their revenues (which were generally roughly equivalent to the earnings of free Black and White artisans): see Goldin 1976.

135. 3.41: Δανειστὴς οἰκέτῃ δεσπότην σημαίνει ἀποφορὰν ἀπαιτοῦντα.

136. See Xen. *Ath. Pol.* 1.10–11; Aiskhin. 1.97; Dem. 27 (Milyas); Hyper. *Athen.* 9. Cf. Chapter 3, pp. 109–110; Cohen 2000: 134–136.

137. Dem. 36.13–14: ἐμίσθωσεν Ξένωνι καὶ Εὐφραίῳ καὶ Εὔφρονι καὶ Καλλιστράτῳ . . . . τὰς παρακαταθήκας καὶ τὴν ἀπὸ τούτων ἐργασίαν αὐτὴν ἐμισθώσαντο. . . καὶ ἐλευθέρους ἀφεῖσαν ὡς μεγάλ' εὖ πεπονθότες. On this passage, see Chapter 3, p. 109.

an annual payment of a sizable fixed rental: the slaves retained the remainder of the net income generated from the bank.[138] Roman legal sources preserve numerous examples of owners similarly receiving a portion of the revenues generated by slaves.[139] Labeo, for example, posits a case where a *servus*, taking the initiative to hire himself out, was entitled to divide with his *dominus* the resultant income.[140] Paulus describes a slave skilled in construction craftwork who was paying an annual fixed fee (*annuam mercedem*) to his master (and was accordingly entitled to retain the remainder of his income for himself).[141] Papinian considers the legal consequences of a slave's payment to a person who seems to be but is not actually the slave's *dominus*.[142] Ulpian concludes that a slave is entitled to redress if his master has wrongfully appropriated earnings to which the *servus* was entitled.[143]

Beyond their primary pursuits on behalf of their owners, slaves might engage in additional lines of business for their own benefit. Paulus, for example, describes the financing of commercial purchases of barley and the rental of warehouses, apparently for his own account, by a slave *institor* who also was engaged in lending money on behalf of his master.[144] The slave Hesychus is attested in the Murecine tablets as making loans on behalf of his master (tablet 51) and separately on behalf of himself (tablets 52, 67).[145] The jurisprudent Julian discusses a slave who had been appointed by his master to manage

138. Dem. 36.37. Cf. Cohen 2018(a): 57.

139. See *Dig.* 15.3.16 (Alf.); *Dig.* 18.1.40.5 (Paul.); *Dig.* 20.1.32 (Scaeu.); *Dig.* 26.7.32.3 (Mod.); *Dig.* 33.7.12.3 (Ulp.); *Dig.* 33.7.18.4 (Paul.); *Dig.* 33.7.20.1 (Scaeu.); *Dig.* 40.7.14.pr (Alf.); *Cod.* 4.14.5 (Gord., 243 CE).

140. *Dig.* 19.2.60.7: seruum meum mulionem conduxisti: neglegentia eius mulus tuus perit. Si ipse se locasset, ex peculio dumtaxat et in rem uersum damnum tibi praestaturum dico: sin autem ipse eum locassem, non ultra me tibi praestaturum, quam dolum malum et culpam meam abesse: quod si sine definitione personae mulionem a me conduxisti et ego eum tibi dedissem, cuius neglegentia iumentum perierit, illam quoque culpam me tibi praestaturum aio, quod eum elegissem, qui eiusmodi damno te adficeret.

141. *Dig.* 33.7.19.1 (Paul.): seruum uero arte fabrica peritum, qui annuam mercedem praestabat.

142. *Dig.* 12.6.55: si seruus non locatus mercedem ut domino praedoni rettulit, non fiet accipientis pecunia.

143. *Dig.* 40.7.3.8 (Ulp.): si, quod ex mercedibus suis coegit heredi dederit, an ad libertatem perueniat? Et puto, si quidem ex operis dederit . . . ad libertatem peruenturum.

144. *Dig.* 14.5.8: Titianus Primus praeposuerat seruum mutuis pecuniis dandis et pignoribus accipiendis: is seruus et iam negotiatoribus hordei solebat pro emptore suscipere debitum et soluere . . . cum autem et alia quaedam gessisse et horrea conduxisse et multis soluisse idem seruus probaretur. . . .

145. Camodecca 1999. On Hesychus, see Gardner 2011: 422–423; Serrao 1984.

an oil business, but had apparently also been authorized to engage in lending activity: the gravamen of the case involves the issue, never resolved in Julian's analysis, as to whether the slave had been operating the financial business also for his master, or solely for himself.[146] Julian's phrasing of the issue, however, necessarily presupposes that a slave might actually engage in his own business activity for his own account (in addition to working as his master's employee-manager in another area of commerce).

According to Ulpian, slaves could even enter into legally recognized partnerships (*societates*),[147] and were authorized and able to operate banks, even without a master's knowledge (*inscio domino*).[148] Enslaved bankers were sometimes entitled not merely to a portion but to all of the business's ongoing profits—with the owner benefiting from compensation at the time of the slaves' manumission or from prior periodic payments similar to those otherwise due a lender.[149] Papinian describes such a slave-controlled operation, opining that delivery of a banking business (*mensae negotium*) pursuant to a testator's binding request (*fideicommissum*), but secured for the heirs by a guarantee (*cautio*) of the assets, is the equivalent of a sale (and no further inquiry is allowed as to the ratio of debt and assets).[150] But Romanists have

146. *Dig.* 14.3.13.pr. (Ulp.): habebat quis seruum merci oleariae praepositum Arelate, eundem et mutuis pecuniis accipiendis: acceperat mutuam pecuniam: putans creditor ad merces eum accepisse egit proposita actione: probare non potuit mercis gratia eum accepisse. licet consumpta est actio nec amplius agere poterit, quasi pecuniis quoque mutuis accipiendis esset praepositus, tamen Iulianus utilem ei actionem competere ait. On this case, cf. Chapter 2, n. 135 (and related text).

147. *Dig.* 17.2.63.2: Patri autem uel domino socii, si iussu eorum societas contracta sit, non esse hanc exceptionem dandam. . . .

148. *Dig.* 2.13.4.3: sed si seruus argentariam faciat (potest enim) . . . si inscio domino fecit, satis dominum iurare eas se rationes non habere. On slaves operating banks at Rome for their own accounts, see Petrucci 2002: 103–137, esp. 118–127; Andreau 2001: 129–131; Crook 1967: 188, 313 (n. 44); Juglar 1894: 15.

149. *Dig.* 2.13.4.2. A *pater familias* can be compelled to produce banking records when he draws profits from the banking business (*cum quaestum refert*), necessarily implying the existence of cases where the master does not share in operating cash flow. Andreau speculates that Roman owners in lieu of a share in ongoing profits, preferred to receive a fixed payment, "une partie de l'argent gagné plus importante que ce qu'aurait versé un emprunteur à son creancier" (1987: 614) or to receive compensation only when banking slaves were manumitted (1999: 68). For slaves' possible purchase of their own freedom with "their own funds" generated during servitude, see Chapter 2, section "Owning Assets through the *Peculium*"; Chapter 3, section "Manumission Pursuant to Contract."

150. *Dig.* 31.77.16: mensae negotium ex causa fideicommissi cum indemnitate heredum per cautionem susceptum emptioni simile uidetur et ideo non erit quaerendum, an plus in aere alieno sit quam in quaestu.

shown that such a *fideicommissum* relating to the sale of a business required as a counterparty a slave acting through his *peculium*.[151] Implicit in Papinian's example is the presence of a slave operating a bank for his own account through his *peculium*.[152]

A further example of servile operation of a bank through a *peculium* is offered by Scaevola in his discussion of a testator's direction that there be no accounting required from a slave for the slave's administration of the testator's assets, whether the slave dealt with the assets through or outside the slave's bank (*mensa eius*).[153]

Finally, the tale of the slave Callistus who in the late second century CE, for example, operated a bank in the Piscina Publica area of Rome, generating considerable deposits, enjoying for himself the full cash flow from the bank, entirely without the involvement of his master, Marcus Aurelius Carpophorus (himself an imperial slave who, only after the bank ultimately incurred financial difficulties, assured creditors that he would try to learn something about his slave's business activities).[154] Because jurisprudents recognized that even banks originated by free persons might come under the control of *servi*, they imposed the same duties on operators without regard to whether they were slaves, sons, or heirs of the original owner.[155]

---

151. Serrao 1989: 36 ff. On the legally binding effect of a testator's fideicommissum already in the Early Empire, see Burdese 1993: 710, 722; Petrucci 1991: 389; Talamanca 1993/1994: 844.

152. Petrucci 2002: 124: "si deve considerare implicita l'esistenza di uno schiavo che esercita la *mensa peculiaris* che forma oggetto del fedecommesso."

153. *Dig.* 34.3.28.9: rationes actus rei meae quae per mensam eius siue extra mensam in diem mortis meae gesta est, exigatis eoque nomine eum liberetis. On this passage, see Petrucci 1991: 30, 239, and 361; Garcia Garrido 2001: 53 ff.

154. Hippolytos, Ἔλεγχος κατὰ πασῶν αἱρέσεων (Refutatio omnium haeresium) 12.1 (ed. Marcovich). Οἰκέτης ἐτύγχανε Καρποφόρου τινός, ἀνδρὸς πιστοῦ ὄντος ἐκ τῆς Καίσαρος οἰκίας. τούτῳ ὁ Καρποφόρος . . . χρῆμα οὐκ ὀλίγον κατεπίστευσεν, ἐπαγγειλάμενος κέρδος προσοίσειν ἐκ πραγματείας τραπεζιτικῆς· ὃς λαβὼν τράπεζαν ἐπεχείρησεν ἐν τῇ λεγομένῃ Πισκίνῃ πουπλικῇ. ᾧ οὐκ ὀλίγαι παραθῆκαι τῷ χρόνῳ ἐπιστεύθησαν ὑπὸ χηρῶν καὶ ἀδελφῶν προσχήματι τοῦ Καρποφόρου· ὁ δὲ ἐξαφανίσας τὰ πάντα ἠπόρει. οὗ ταῦτα πράξαντος οὐκ ἔλιπεν ὃς ἀπαγγείλῃ τῷ Καρποφόρῳ, ὁ δὲ ἔφη ἀπαιτήσειν λόγους παρ᾽ αὐτοῦ. See Ligios 2015; Andreau 2010: 166–167; Bogaert 1973: 252–255.

155. *Dig.* 2.13.9.1 (Paul.): nihil interest, si successores aut pater aut dominus argentarii eiusdem fuerunt professionis: quia cum in locum et in ius succedant argentarii, partibus eius fungi debent.

2

Fiction

RECONCILING ECONOMIC REALITY AND JURIDICAL PRINCIPLES

THE ABJECT, HORRENDOUS, and lamentable situation of the vast majority of Roman slaves is, of course, widely recognized.[1] But in recent years there has been growing academic acknowledgment of a tangential phenomenon: the rich former slaves ("freedmen"), "some richer than any member of the Roman elite,"[2] who dominated commerce as the prosperous entrepreneurial *glitterati* of a sybaritic empire.[3] Like legendary Venus, for prevailing scholarship the business-capable, wealthy *libertus* seems to emerge miraculously born without antecedent gestation.[4] In my opinion, however, business operation by prosperous manumitted slaves is an unsurprising

---

1. See Chapter 1, pp. 26–27.

2. Morley 2011: 283.

3. See, for example, Mouritsen on freedmen's "participation in the economy, especially the urban commercial sector, which they seem to dominate completely" (2011: 206). Cf. Verboven 2014: 77; Osgood 2011: 2: "freedmen often wildly successful economically." Freedmen's legendary riches were much bruited. Pliny, *H. N.* 33.134–135 claims that many ex-slaves were wealthier than the tycoon Crassus: one freedman in 8 BCE, even after substantial losses from civil war, supposedly owned 4,116 slaves, 3,600 pairs of oxen, 257,000 other animals, and 60 million *sesterces* in cash—many times the minimum wealth required of a senator. Cf. *H. N.* 22.92, 33.145, 35.201, 36.60. See similarly Sen. *Epist. Mor.* 27.5, 86.7; Mart. *Epig.* 5.13; Petron. *Satyr.*, 26–78. Cf. Verboven 2011; Silver 2011: 102–106; Bodel 2005: 190; Fabiani 2002: 101; Torelli 1994: 184.

4. Andreau, for example, attributes the spectacular success of rich freedmen to chance, "au sort, au hasard et au culte de la Fortune" (1992: 241); Verboven ascribes their wealth "sometimes to their professional talent" (2011: 92). Efforts to explain this efflorescence are few and usually cursory, and generally divide between those who see freedmen's prosperity as largely dependent on (1) financial assistance from their former masters (e.g., Mouritsen 2011: 227–228; Brunt

Roman Inequality. Edward E. Cohen, Oxford University Press. © Oxford University Press 2023.
DOI: 10.1093/oso/9780197687345.003.0003

sequel to the rich *non*-manumitted slaves who, even while still legally enslaved, had been operating businesses on their own and at least partly for their own benefit—a phenomenon widespread in both Republican and early imperial Rome.[5]

In this chapter, I will consider how, through the *peculium* (paradigmatically a fund that a slave held for use in his own commercial pursuits), some skilled Roman slaves were able to accumulate assets that even the law implicitly recognized as effectively their own, and were able to continue to hold these assets as they emerged after manumission as free and affluent businessmen. This is an element of economic reality that Roman law, as a consequence of the existential centrality of its doctrinal commitment to the legal nullity of slaves, could not explicitly embrace. But because of the importance to the Roman economy of servile enterprise and servile wealth,[6] a jurisprudential mechanism had to be found to accommodate this dependence.[7] Voilà: the Roman legal fiction (*fictio*), which reconciled legal dogma and commercial actuality by attributing to an enslaved individual practical ownership of his *peculium* while continuing to deny slaves' capacity to "own" anything. And so, in discussions relating to the *peculium*, surviving Roman legal texts reveal, *sotto voce*, a continuing clash, a conflict setting the most formal, and conservative, doctrinal presentation of "the law" against the law's practical application in commerce—a dualism that has been largely ignored in modern scholarly literature, but attesting yet again that at Rome, "law in action was fundamentally different from the law in the books."[8]

1983[b]: 314; Meiggs 1973: 224), or to the contrary (2) a decisive break with their ex-owners and resultant *de novo* emergence as independent entrepreneurs (D'Arms 1981; Bodel 1999: 42).

5. For example, virtually every slave in Plautus's comedies appears to possess a *peculium* (Ligt 2007, 1999: 223 ff.). Cicero assumes that a slave in a responsible position holds a *peculium* (*Uerr.* 2.3.86).

6. "(B)y the early Empire, *peculia*, often of very large size, had become a ubiquitous feature of Roman economic life: a *peculium* could include an entire farm or a business operation" (Frier and McGinn 2004: 263).

7. On legal systems' development of mechanisms to close significant gaps that may arise between actuality and traditional juridical principles, see Introduction, n. 10 and related text.

8. Watson 2007: 35. Cf. Chapter 1, n. 8.

Generating the Peculium

Present over a vast range of business activities,[9] often oriented toward the production of profits,[10] the *peculium* was "a sum of money, a commercial or industrial business, or a small separate property . . . (for a) slave's use, free disposal, and fructification through commercial or other transactions."[11] *Peculia* might contain virtually anything (*res omnes*)—tangible personalty, real estate, underslaves and *their peculia*, livestock, even debt obligations.[12] Prevailing scholarly opinion insists that a *peculium* originated from the transfer of a portion of the master's own assets,[13] "a kind of personal property granted to a slave from his master" (Jakab 2013: 138), "a fund of money and other things which was given to a slave or a son for his use (although) belong(ing) to the owner or the father" (Watson 1987: 154).[14] In Republican Rome, the *peculium* is said to have "resembled the allowance that modern parents give to children" (Frier and McGinn 2004: 263)—and like a parental allowance, a *peculium* supposedly could be withdrawn at the mere whimsy of a *pater familias*![15]

---

9. *Peculia* extended to every facet of mercantile activity: Pedius libro quinto decimo scribit ad omnes negotiationes porrigendum edictum (*Dig.* 14.4.1.1 [Ulp.]).

10. in quantum locupletior dominus factus esset . . . actionem de peculio dandam (*Dig.* 15.1.3.12 [Ulp.]). "Creditors of the *peculium* could bring an action called *actio de in rem verso*" for the owner's "enrichment" by, or "special profit" received from, the *peculium*: Berger 1953: 624.

11. Ibid.

12. *Dig.* 15.1.7.4 (Ulp.): in peculio autem res esse possunt omnes et mobiles et soli: uicarios quoque in peculium potest habere et uicariorum peculium: hoc amplius et nomina debitorum. Cattle: Varro, *De Re Rust.* 1.17.7, 1.19.3.

13. Gamauf dissents: "modern scholars generally tend to overlook or underestimate the fact that it was not necessarily the master who provided the funds of a *peculium*" (2009: 334). Zeber (1981: 24–25) believes that at its origin a slave's *peculium* could come only from the owner's property (*ex re patris*) but that thereafter additional contributions might come from the master and/or from independent sources (*ex re aliena*). Cf. Brinkhoff 1978.

14. Similarly: Hawkins 2016: 132 ("funds or productive capital which a Roman paterfamilias could place under the control of one of his dependents"); Fleckner 2014: 214 ("a great 'gift' "); Abatino and Dari-Mattiacci 2020: 273; 2011: 3 ("assets entrusted to him by his masters [the *peculium*]"); Tchernia 2011: 42 ("façon d'utiliser les esclaves pour le commerce . . . leur donner un pécule"); Gardner 2011: 421 ("a fund made available to the slave for the conduct of business"); Johnston 1999: 100 ("a fund of property granted by a paterfamilias to a person in his power"); Kirschenbaum 1987: 33–34 ("granted by a master to his slave for the latter's utilization"); Verboven 2011: 99; Buti 1976: 15; Knoch 2005: 178; Wacke 2006: 254; Zwalve 2002: 121. Ligt (2007: 13) envisions masters establishing *peculia* by granting specific amounts of investment funds to selected slaves.

15. Master's absolute right to terminate *peculium*: Fleckner 2014: 217, 225. Cf., for example, Gamauf's assertion that "the fear that [the *peculium*] might be renounced (*ademptio peculii*)

This opinion mirrors a formalistic Roman juridical tradition that treated only the master's actions, not the slave's, as relevant to the establishment of a *peculium*: the *dominus* alone was supposedly "able to increase, to decrease, or to take away completely the slave's *peculium*."[16] In fact, however, the origins of the *peculium*, and the primacy of the master in its continuance, were long disputed in legal literature at Rome. From a relatively early time, some jurists did accede to economic reality, ignoring concepts of servile nullity, instead focusing on a slave's actual role in establishing a *peculium*. These commentators attributed the origins of this fund (*ita igitur nascitur peculium*) solely to a *servus*'s ability on his own to generate assets beyond the master's minimal (but obligatory) contribution to servile sustenance.[17] In fact, a citation in the *Digest* explicitly defines the servile *peculium* as "that which someone has generated by his own thrift or has by his services merited receiving from any source whatsoever and which a master shall have wanted his slave to hold just as if it were his own (the slave's) personal property."[18] The jurisprudent here clearly attributes an active role to the slave in producing assets for his *peculium*. The master's contribution, however, is unclear: on one interpretation, the *peculium* may be derived from three possible sources, including a possible contribution from the *dominus* ("what a person has earned by his own thrift or has been given by a third party in return for services, plus that which he [the owner] wished his slave to have as his own property"[19]); by another interpretation, there is no contribution from the master, who to the contrary might actually increase his own estate by appropriating part of the assets generated by the slave ("anything a slave has been able to save by his own economies or has been given by a third party in return for meritorious

---

motivated slaves holding responsible positions within the *domus*" (2009: 339). In practice, however, the difficulties of terminating a functioning commercial *peculium* were often insurmountable: see below, section on "Retaining Peculium Assets after Manumission," pp. 36–38.

16. *Dig.* 15.1.4.pr. (Pomp.): cum serui peculium totum adimere uel augere uel minuere dominus possit, animaduertendum est non quid seruus, sed quid dominus constituendi seruilis peculii gratia fecerit.

17. *Dig.* 15.1.40.1 (Marcian): Quomodo autem peculium nascitur, quaesitum est, et ita ueteres distinguunt si id adquisiit seruus quod dominus necesse non habet praestare, id esse peculium. si uero tunicas aut aliquid simile quod ei dominus necesse habet praestare, non esse peculium. . . . ita igitur nascitur peculium. There is considerable dispute as to whether *ueteres* necessarily refers to lawyers active in the Republican period: see Zeber 1981: 34, n. 11; Guarino 1963: 279.

18. *Dig.* 15.1.39 (Florentinus): Peculium et eo consistit, quod parsimonia sua quis parauit uel officio meruerit a quolibet sibi donari idque uelut proprium patrimonium seruum suum habere quis uoluerit.

19. Translation: Frier and McGinn 2004: 265. Cf. *Dig.* 15.1.57.2 (Tryph.).

services or has been allowed by his master to keep as his own"[20]). Indeed, a master might claim to have made a contribution merely by treating property already in the slave's possession as if it had been handed over.[21]

A slave might establish a *peculium* even without explicit authorization by his master: acquiescence might be implied or conjectural or even constructively hypothesized from an absence of prohibition. Thus, Marcellus insists that although "some [Roman jurisprudents] think" that a slave cannot hold a *peculium* without his master's acquiescence, "for a slave to have a *peculium* there's no need for authorization by his *dominus*, but only that it not be forbidden that he have it."[22] Accordingly, Ulpian opines that a slave of an insane owner is legally capable of having a *peculium*, even if the *dominus* should be legally incapable of assenting to its establishment, since such an impaired master also would lack the capacity to forbid it.[23] Pomponius notes that a slave might generate assets for his own *peculium* even without his master's knowledge (although not if the master would have forbidden the *peculium* had he known about it—a necessarily hypothetical form of veto).[24] In fact, much of Book 15—the section of the *Digest* dealing with the *peculium*—is devoted to the indicia by which and the circumstances under which a master

20. Translation: Watson ed. 1985, 1999: I.

21. *Dig.* 15.1.8 (Paul.): peculium fecit . . . si tradidit aut, cum apud eum esset, pro tradito habuit." Cf. *Dig.* 15.1.4.pr. (Pomponius): peculii est . . . . quod dominus ipse separauerit suam a serui rationem discernens.

22. *Dig.* 15.1.7.1 (Marcellus): ut quidam putant peculium seruus habere non potest nisi concedente domino. ego autem puto non esse opus concedi peculium a domino seruum habere, sed non adimi, ut habeat. Micolier (1932: 289, 482 ff.) even concludes that as a matter of law the master's "acquiescence" came to be so attenuated that a *peculium* might be created by a slave acting as an independent businessman even without any actual or inferred assent by his master.

23. In furiosi quoque curatorem dicimus dandam de peculio actionem: nam et huius seruus peculium habere potest, non si fuerit concessum, ut habeat, sed si non fuerit prohibitum, ne habeat: "A madman's slave is able to hold a *peculium* not if it shall have been allowed that he hold it, but if it shall not have been prohibited that he hold it" [*Dig.* 15.1.3.4].) By the same rationale (that is, lack of prohibition), the slave of a minor would have been able to administer a *peculium* even though the law prohibited a ward from establishing a *peculium* for the slave even with the consent of the ward's guardian: Etiam impuberes dominos de peculio obligari ait: non enim cum ipsis impuberibus contrahitur, ut tutoris auctoritatem spectes. Idem adicit pupillum non posse seruo peculium constituere nec tutoris auctoritate (*Dig.* 15.1.3 .3 [Pedius]). It sufficed that "it shall not have been prohibited that (the slave) hold it."

24. *Dig.* 15.1.49.pr.: Non solum id peculium est, quod dominus seruo concessit, uerum id quoque, quod ignorante quidem eo adquisitum sit, tamen, si rescisset, passurus erat esse in peculio. Cf. Pesaresi 2008: 16.

could be found to have acquiesced (*concessisse*) actively or passively or theoretically in the establishment (or augmentation) of a *peculium*.[25] This entire line of discussion would be meaningless if the quintessential source of a *peculium* was an actual transfer of some of a master's assets to a slave's account—an easily determinable issue of fact, but a standard inherently inconsistent with the concept of acquiescence.

Surviving inscriptional and literary evidence illustrates how slaves were able to produce income for themselves—money and property to establish (or increase) a *peculium* without an owner's contribution. Vergil's enslaved Tityrus alludes to the possibility of generating a *peculium* (and ultimately gaining freedom) through cash that he could obtain for himself by selling sacrificial animals and cheeses.[26] According to Seneca (the Younger) and Terence, slaves sometimes developed their *peculia* by eating frugally and selling the residue saved from the slaves' own alimentary allocations.[27] Apuleius describes fraternal strife occasioned by one brother's alleged selling of delicacies purloined from a master's banquets "to increase (that brother's) *peculium*."[28] Some *servi*, working for third parties under arrangements negotiated by their masters, received salaries that they retained.[29] Even agricultural slaves are known to have maintained their own cattle and sometimes a small plot from which they might generate funds to create or increase a *peculium*.[30] And slaves working in a great variety of occupations—including managers, entertainers, doctors, courtesans, even doorkeepers—might receive and retain supplemental

---

25. The subject is also alluded to elsewhere in the *Digest*. See, for example, *Dig.* 41.2.1.5 (Paul.). For a guide to the long history of Romanist disputation concerning the nature of master's acquiescence (*permissus domini, concessio peculii*), see Zeber 1981: 24–37.

26. *Eclogues* 1.31–35: dum me Galatea tenebat | nec spes libertatis erat nec cura peculi: | quamuis multa meis exiret uictima saeptis, | pinguis et ingratae premeretur caseus urbi, | non umquam grauis aere domum mihi dextra redibat.

27. Sen. *Letters* 80.4; mancipia quoque condicionis extremae . . . peculium suum, quod comparauerunt uentre fraudato, pro capite numerant. Cf. Ter. *Phorm.* 43–44.

28. *Metamorph.* 10.14: cotidie ac partes electiores surripere atque iis diuenditis peculium latenter augere.

29. P. Oxy. 14.1647 (slave learning weavers' craft receives maintenance from her owner and salary from local weaver: θρέψειν καὶ ἱματεῖν τὴν παῖδα καὶ παρέξεσθαι αὐτὴν τῷ διδασκάλῳ . . . μισθοῦ ἐπὶ μὲν τὸν πρῶτον ἐνιαυτὸν κατὰ μῆνα δραχμῶν ὀκτώ). Other examples: Biezunska-Malowist 1977: 85 ff.

30. Varro *De Re Rust.* 1.17.5 (dandaque opera ut habeant peculium), 1.19.3 (de pecore . . . quae solent esse peculiaria pauca habenda), 2.10.5 (in horum emptione solet accedere peculium aut excipi).

compensation ("tips") from their clients which in turn could be directed toward the funding of a *peculium*.[31] The jurisprudent Pomponius explicitly insists that the earnings of even a free man serving "in good faith" as a slave belong to his putative owner (as well as any income generated from the *dominus*'s own capital), but that any transactional profits and all gifts received belong to the nominal slave.[32] Such emoluments could ultimately amount to considerable sums: a slave boasts on a surviving funereal stone that from his thriftiness he was able to accumulate the funds needed for a monumental epitaph.[33]

While masters did on occasion transfer their own property to a slave's *peculium*,[34] several passages in the *Digest* are premised on the *peculium* containing assets originating not from the slave owner's property (*res*), but from a slave's own contribution (*parsimonia sua vel officio*[35]). Thus Tryphonius, providing an opinion during the Severan period, alludes to the portion of a slave's *peculium* that had been generated by the *servus*'s own efforts or that had been given to the slave personally.[36] Ulpian sets forth a multitude of sources from which a slave might generate funds: "from a fortuitous gain, or from the benevolence or generosity of a friend, or by the slave's delayed payment or by the slave's making a commitment or providing for a third-party payment (*se delegante*) or recognizing a personal obligation."[37] Tubero and Celsus accordingly define a *peculium* as that which a slave, with the acquiescence of his

---

31. Managers and doorkeepers: Petron. *Satyr.* 26–78, *passim*, esp. §§30–31. Entertainers: Pliny, *H.N.* 7.128; Tac. *Ann.* 13.27; *Dig.* 12.4.3.5 (Ulp.). Doctors: CIL XI 5400 = ILS 7812. Prostitutes: Dion. Hal. 4.24.1–6; Plaut. *Pseud.* 224–229. Maids: Ter. *Heaut.* 300 ff. Cf. Plaut. *Most.* 253 (dabo aliquid hodie peculi tibi, Philematium mea), *Persa* 192 (aliqui te peculiabo); Juv. 3.188–89 (clientes | cogimur et cultis augere peculia servis). On prostitutes' capacity to obtain financial and other benefits from their clients, see, in Athenian context, Cohen 2015(a): 54–56, 64–65.

32. *Dig.* 41.1.19: Liber homo, qui bona fide mihi seruit, id quod ex operis suis aut ex re mea pararet, ad me pertinere sine dubio Aristo ait: quod uero quis ei donauerit aut ex negotio gesto acquisierit, ad ipsum pertinere. Cf. *Dig.* 41.3.44.pr (Pap.).

33. Hoc monumentum ex mea frugalitate feci (ILS 8265 = CIL VI 7582).

34. *Dig.* 15.1.8 (Paul.): Non statim quod dominus uoluit ex re sua peculii esse, peculium fecit, sed si tradidit. . . .

35. *Dig.* 15.1.39; n. 14 above and related text.

36. *Dig.* 15.1.57.2 (Tryph.): quae autem seruo donata fuerint siue quid ex operis suis adquisierit, ad legatarium non pertinere.

37. siue ex aduenticio lucro, siue etiam amici beneficio uel liberalitate uel proregante eo uel repromittente uel se delegante uel in se recipiente debitum redemptus sit (*Dig.* 40.1.4).

master, holds independently of his owner's assets (literally "separated from his owner's accounts"), after deduction of whatever is owed to the master.[38]

This "separation of accounts" and determination of the amount, if any, owed to the master, required detailed accounting records, and in fact, during the imperial centuries at least, "every economic unit"—households, families, even farms (*villae rusticae*)—"carefully recorded all transactions, especially financial ones," in account books,[39] compiled pursuant to sophisticated business conceptualization (albeit an acumen unrelated to modern systems of double-entry and GAAP accounting).[40] Nonetheless, Roman jurists recognized the potential for manipulation inherent in the operation of businesses through servile *peculia*.[41] In an economy heavily dependent on credit and even on "credit money,"[42] in which loans were often extended to servile *peculia* by third parties, and advances and repayment of money were commonplace between *servus* and *dominus*, the financial rights of slave, owner, and creditor might often have been affected by the characterization placed on related-party transactions, especially in the determination of a servile *peculium*'s true debt to a slave's owner. Records might be unreliable. *Servi*, for example, might be indebted to masters for items the slaves had never formally noted in their books of account;[43] masters might have removed assets that arguably should have been retained in *peculia*;[44] other problems might

38. *Dig.* 15.1.5.4 (Ulp.): Peculium autem Tubero quidem *sic* definit, ut Celsus libro sexto digestorum refert, quod seruus domini permissu separatum a rationibus dominicis habet, deducto inde si quid domino debetur. For the juridical significance of arrangements between master and slave(s), see Chapter 3, section on "Agreements between Slave and Master."

39. Jakab 2013: 139. Cf. Jakab 2009: 39–46. Labeo describes these accounts: rationem autem esse Labeo ait ultro citro dandi accipiendi, credendi, obligandi soluendi sui causa negotiationem (*Dig.* 2.13.6.3 [Ulp.]).

40. On the sophistication of Roman accounting, see Minaud 2005: 69–115 and Migeotte 2008: 61; on the limits of Roman accounting, Abatino and Dari-Mattiacci 2011: 22–23; Giliberti 1984. Cf. Bresson and Aubert (forthcoming).

41. Pomponius alludes to the "incerta causa rationis et genere negotii huiusmodi" (*Dig.* 40.7.5.pr.). Cf. *Dig.* 35.1.32 (Africanus): rationes reddere nihil aliud sit quam reliqua soluere.

42. "(D)ebt was in fact the life-blood of the Roman economy, at all levels" (Harris 2006: 9). See Harris 2019(a) passim; Stelzenberger 2008: 168–178; von Reden 2012: 278–279; Kay 2014: 114–127; Howgego 1992: 13.

43. Hi servi domino debitores fuerunt tam ex aliis causis quam ex ratione kalendarii (*Dig.* 15.1.58 [Scaeuola]).

44. Summa cum ratione etiam hoc peculio praetor imputauit, quod dolo malo domini factum est, quo minus in peculio esset (*Dig.* 15.1.21.pr. [Ulp.]). Cf. *Dig.* 35.1.40.3 (Iauolenus): dominus seruo aureos quinque legauerat: "aureos quinque quos in tabulis debeo."

surface upon examination.[45] In the event of financial insolvency or difficulty, *domini* would have benefited from inflating the amount of funds which they claimed to have lent to the *peculium*; outside creditors would have gained from minimizing the amounts owed to the master; the interests of the slave operator of a *peculium* might diverge from those of either creditors or owner, or both.[46] To protect outsiders from possibly misleading manipulation of *peculium* accounts, Roman jurisprudents held that it was actionably unjust (*malum dolum*) for a master even to permit, to the harm (*necem*) of creditors, the complication (literally, "entanglement") of the structured activities of a *peculium*.[47]

A fund entirely self-produced by a *servus* would have protected against such "entanglement" and otherwise would have been quite advantageous for the *dominus* who would have gained the right to share in the fund's profits while avoiding any potential losses (since the slave owner's liability was limited to the value of the *peculium* itself which [when self-generated] would have contained no contribution from the master). If, however, a slave could not accumulate resources sufficient for business needs without obtaining assets from his owner, the master's interest was best served by advancing funds as a loan, thereby not increasing the net value of the *peculium*.[48] Because the master was liable to claimants against the *peculium* only up to (*dumtaxat*) the net value of the *peculium*, his potential liability did not increase by his making loans to the *peculium*, and he thereby gained the added advantage that debt owed to the *dominus* received priority over claims of other creditors.[49] (Because of this priority, lenders and customers, in evaluating creditworthiness, might tend to disregard monies advanced to a *peculium* as a loan by the *pater familias*: allusions are made in legal sources to fictitious or fraudulent

45. *Dig.* 33.8.6.4 (Ulp.): cum peculium seruo legatur, non etiam id conceditur, ut petitionem habeat pecuniae, quam se in rationem domini impendisse dicit. See Johnston 2002: 1–11; Thilo 1980: 137–139.

46. See Bürge 2010: 380–381.

47. *Dig.* 15.1.21.pr. (Ulp.): sed et si eum intricare peculium in necem creditorum passus est, Mela scribit dolo malo eius factum.

48. See Gaius *Inst.* 4.73 (cum autem quaeritur, quantum in peculio sit, ante deducitur, quod patri dominoue quique in eius potestate sit, a filio seruoue debetur, et quod superest, hoc solum peculium esse intellegitur).

49. *Dig.* 15.1.9.4 (Ulp,): nam ut eleganter Pedius ait, ideo hoc minus in peculio est, quod domino uel patri debetur, quoniam non est uerisimile dominum id concedere seruo in peculium habere, quod sibi debetur. On this *privilegium deductionis*, see Chiusi 2007(b); Abatino and Dari-Mattiacci 2020: 283.

expenses that might be claimed by an owner through entries into the relevant accounts seeking to reduce the value of the *peculium*, and thus his related maximum liability.)[50]

Full protection against unlimited responsibility for losses, however, was legally conditioned on owners' truly entrusting total control of relevant operations to their slaves:[51] if a *servus* purportedly operating through a *peculium* was in fact only a manager (*institor*) working under a personally involved master who actually owned the business, the *dominus* became liable ipso facto for unlimited damages (*in solidum*) under the *actiones institoria* and *exercitoria*.[52] In Ulpian's opinion, mere knowledge of a slave's business activity resulted under the *actio tributaria* in the owner's forfeiting his right to a preferential position as creditor for any funds that he had lent to the slave's *peculium* unless he had actively voiced objection to the slave's commercial actions.[53] Active involvement, however, would have subjected him to potentially unlimited liability under the *actio institoria*. "The *paterfamilias* could enjoy limited liability for what his slave or child did only as long as he remained at arm's length from the business, appointed them to do nothing, authorized nothing and did nothing."[54] But in choosing to have no relationship to income-producing assets controlled and operated by one's slave, a *dominus* effectively transferred "ownership" of the assets in the *peculium* to his *servus*—and Roman law adapted to this reality.

---

50. *Dig.* 15.1.49.2 (Pomponius): si dominus in rationes suas referat se debere seruo suo, cum omnino neque mutuum acceperit neque ulla causa praecesserat debendi, nuda ratio non facit eum debitorem.

51. An affirmative "Grant of Unrestricted Management" (*concessio liberae administrationis*) may have been required for a slave to administer a *peculium*, and its related business(es), entirely without a master's involvement. See Ulpian, quoting Marcellus (as reported by Iulianus): alia causa est peculii liberae administrationis: nam haec specialiter concedenda est) (*Dig.* 15.1.7.1). The contours and parameters of this *libera administratio peculii*, if it exists as a distinct institution (which I doubt), remain unclear, and indeed much disputed, despite substantial attention from Romanists over an extended period: see Pahud 2013: 300–306; Aubert 2013: 195, n. 12 and related text; Martini 1980: 105; Apathy 1979: 400; Buti 1976: 36.

52. *Dig.* 19.2.60.7 (Labeo); *Dig.* 14.1.6.pr. (Paul.). See Verboven 2002: 28; Zwalve 2002; Roth 2010: 110; Johnston 1999: 103–105 (*contra* Bang 2008: 277–278, 280).

53. *Dig.* 14.4.1.2–3 (Ulp.): peculiarem autem mercem non *sic* uti peculium accipimus, quippe peculium deducto, quod domino debetur accipitur, merx peculiaris etiamsi nihil sit in peculio, dominum tributoria obligat, ita (3) demum si sciente eo negotiabitur. scientiam hic eam accipimus, quae habet et uoluntatem, sed ut ego puto, non uoluntatem, sed patientiam: non enim uelle debet dominus, sed non nolle. si igitur scit et non protestatur et contra dicit, tenebitur actione tributoria. See Chiusi 1993: 288 ff.; di Porto 1984: 218 ff. Cf. Chapter 1, n. 49.

54. Johnston 2007: 181.

Owning Assets through the Peculium

A fundamental principle of Roman law was the absolute legal nullity of slaves.[55] *Servi*, denied juridical recognition as human beings,[56] had no recognized rights[57] (other than perhaps a theoretical entitlement not to be murdered[58]). A Roman slave was thus supposedly unable to enter into a contract or to be a party to a civil lawsuit.[59] By the letter of the law, he lacked the capacity to own (in Latin, "hold" [*habere*]) property of any kind.[60] In economic reality, nevertheless, the Roman slave did "hold" (*tenere*) enormous amounts of property, for "the *peculium* was regarded in the market-place as de facto property of slaves. . . ."[61] *Servi* accordingly treated funds in their *peculia* as their own: maintaining deposit accounts in banks, making loans to third parties, sending funds overseas.[62] Indeed, "many will have had secret funds hidden away."[63] Legal theory and commercial reality were thus existentially in conflict—a clash arising not from any dogmatic (even if moribund) Roman

---

55. *Dig.* 50.17.32 (Ulp.): quod attinet ad ius ciuile, serui pro nullis habentur. See also *Dig.* 4.5.3.1 (Paul.); *Dig.* 28.1.20.7 (Ulp.).

56. See Chapter 1, n. 10 and related text.

57. Gai. *Inst.* 2.87, 3.104; *Dig.* 15.1.41 (Ulp.). Cf. Crook [1967] 1984: 56; Gofas 1973: 44–45.

58. Right not to be murdered: *Dig.* 1.6.2 (Ulp.); *Dig.* 34.1 (Ulp.). For possible protection against excessive cruelty: Buckland [1908] 1970: 36; Greenridge 1894: 63 ff.; Thomas 1976: 393.

59. See Metzger 2014; Burdese 1981; Biscardi 1975.

60. Ipse enim, qui in potestate alterius est, nihil suum habere potest (*Dig.* 41.10.1 [Gaius]). Papinian explains: qui in aliena potestate sunt, rem peculiarem tenere possunt, habere possidere non possunt, quia possessio non tantum corporis, sed et iuris est (*Dig.* 41.2.49.1). Cf. Modestinus (*Dig.* 41.1.52): rem in bonis nostris habere intellegimur, quotiens possidentes exceptionem aut amittentes ad reciperandam eam actionem habemus" ("we are considered to 'hold' (*habere*) something among our assets whenever possessing it we have a (valid) defense (against efforts to alienate it), or having lost it we have a (valid) action for recovering it." See also *Dig.* 17.1.12.2 (Ulp.); *Dig.* 39.5.19.4 (Ulp.); *Dig.* 39.6.23 (Africanus); *Dig.* 39.6.44 (Paul). In short, "ownership *(dominium)* in Roman Law is difficult to define, and the Romans themselves did not trouble to do this" (Johnston 1999: 53).

61. Zeber cites the *peculium* as "a very good example of a large divergence between legal construction and social practice" (1981: 39). Modern legal scholars continue to treat the *peculium* as "owned" by the *dominus* (e.g., Fleckner 2020: 255: "the masters, not the *peculium* holders, were the owners of the *peculium* items"; Gamauf 2016: 390: "it was of course always owned by the master"; Abatino and Dari-Mattiacci 2011: 9: "both the slave and his *peculium* remained property of the master"; Mouritsen 2011: 170, n. 237: "the master's permission was needed before the slave could alienate his *peculium*").

62. See *Dig.* 16.3.1.33 (Ulp.); *Dig.* 40.7.40.6 (Scaeu.); *Dig.* 44.7.14 (Ulp.).

63. Koops 2020: 57.

legal definition of "ownership,"[64] but from Roman juridical inability explicitly to allow the attribution of rights (especially rights of "ownership") to slaves. But legal systems invariably adapt to altered social and economic actualities.[65] Rome was no exception—and for Rome the mediating mechanism was the legal fiction[66]—in Latin *fictio* (*credendum est*)[67]—reconciling legal dogma and commercial reality by attributing practical ownership of the *peculium* to its enslaved operator.

In fact, virtually every area of Roman law, public and private, is replete with legal fiction.[68] Romanists have identified scores of juridical fabrications set forth in surviving classical Roman law sources.[69] The praetor, for example,

---

64. Roman law in fact never did develop "a unified doctrine of possession" (Baldus 2016: 538): "terms relating to possession and those relating to ownership were confused" (Capogrossi Colognesi 2016: 534). Cf. Amirante 1983: 3 ff. Traditionally, "ownership in Roman law was expressed through factual control of a corporeal object more than by the idea of an abstract right over it" (Capogrossi Colognesi 2016: 525). For useful introductions to the continuing effort to achieve a working explanation of an elusive concept: Biscotti 2004: 3–6, 21, n. 2; Kaser 1986; Diosdi 1971: 133 ff. Cf. Albanese 1979: 151; Apathy 1979: 399.

65. See Introduction, n. 10 and related text.

66. On scholars' and analysts' vertiginous inability to resolve fundamental issues precluding a clear definition of "legal fiction," see below, this chapter, section on "The Manumission of Skilled Slaves: Facilitating Commerce through Legal Fiction." Regarding legal fictions generally in Roman law, see Bianchi 1997; Robbe 1978; Bretone 2011; García Garrido 1957–1958. For the fullest discussion of "le rapport qui unit fondamentalement droit et fiction" in Roman law, see Thomas [1995] 2011: 137 and ff. (cf. Dekkers 1935). Birks 1986 compares the use of fictions in Roman and English common law; Moskovitz 2003, the use of fictions in Roman and Rabbinic law. For fictions in ancient Greek law, see Pringsheim 1950: 244–247; 1956. On the role of fictions in European medieval legal theory, see Jones 1940: 166–173. For proponents of "critical legal theory," the juridical system itself is often in its entirety seen as a "fiction": see Unger 2015: Part I; Ward 2004.

67. The Romans explicitly applied the term *fictio* to legal suppositions which were factually untrue but compatible with the desired solution. See Gaius's discussion of *fictiones* at *Inst.* 4.32 (contra in ea forma, quae publicano proponitur, talis fictio est, ut etc.), 34–38. Cf. Quintilian *Orat.* 5.10.95 (duci argumenta non a confessis tantum sed etiam a fictione, quod Graeci cat' hypothesin uocant). See Ando 2015(b): 296–299. "Credendum est": see below n. 81 and related text.

68. "Le droit romain offre un champ d'étude incomparable à la fiction. . . . il n'est pratiquement pas de domaine du droit privé et du droit public qui échappe à ce procédé de l'élaboration juridique" (Thomas [1995] 2011: 137). "Fictions are ubiquitous in Roman law . . . (but) they have received remarkably little attention from Romanists." Ando 2015(b): 295. "The subject cries out for monographic study" (Ando 2016[b]: 286). Some Romanists, including the highly respected Polish scholar Jakub Urbanik (personal communication to author), reject Ando's assertion, noting the profusion of publications over many years on legal fictions in Roman law. But these treatments generally are focused on juridical science, not on the historical issues that might be illuminated by attention to Roman legal fictions.

69. See Thomas [1995] 2011: 171–186.

made extensive use of "legal fictions" to grant actions otherwise unavailable (*actiones ficticiae*), including suits opened to foreigners "as if they were Roman citizens," and actions allowed to or against a *bonorum possessor* "as if he were *heres*."[70]

Accordingly, Roman legal experts never were forced explicitly to abandon the atavistic but (by the High Empire) manifestly fictitious principle that a slave cannot own property.[71] Yet Roman legal experts likewise never ceased to treat assets in a slave's *peculium* as though they were the private property (*velut proprium patrimonium*) of the slave controlling the *peculium*.[72] By definition,[73] a slave was entitled to treat a *peculium* just as if it were "his own." Paulus confirms this explicitly: "the *peculium* is understood to be the property of the slave, analogous (*quasi*) to the owned property (*patrimonium*) of the free man (*liber homo*)."[74] Ulpian and Marcellus both equate a slave's *peculium* to the free person's *patrimonium*.[75] Ulpian rules out even the possibility of a *pater familias* owning a *peculium*.[76] A slave's *peculium* was consistently treated as property entirely separate from the master's assets (*res domini*).[77] The jurist Marcellus even postulates a situation in which an owner, intending to sell a slave, instead had freed him in return for money received directly from the slave, for the master a loss of the funds he would have received from the

70. On the *actiones ficticiae*, see Mercogliano 2001(a), Berger 1953, *s.v.* Cf. the *actio publicana* which allowed a claim posited on the fiction that *usucapio* had been completed. On the importance of fictions in Roman procedure generally, see Ando 2016(b): 285–289. Cf. Ando 2011(b).

71. *Dig.* 41.2.49.1 (Papinian) (Latin text above, n. 55); *Dig.* 50.16.182 (Ulp.): pater familias liber "peculium" non potest habere, quemadmodum nec seruus "bona." See also *Dig.* 17.1.12.2 (Ulp.); *Dig.* 39.5.19.4 (Ulp.); *Dig.* 39.6.23 (Africanus); *Dig.* 39.6.44 (Paul.).

72. For a survey of the Roman concept of "private property" (*patrimonium*), see most recently Pahud 2013: 111 ff., 248–257, who concludes that "il n'existe pas de notion clairement définie du patrimoine dans le droit romain de l'époque classique" (248). For Roman efforts to account for *patrimonium*, see Minaud 2005: 232–245.

73. Isid. *Etym.* 5.25.5: peculium est quod pater uel dominus filium suum uel seruum pro suo tractare patitur.

74. *Dig.* 15.1.47.6: quasi patrimonium liberi hominis peculium serui intellegitur. Free people even came to speak informally of their *patrimonium* as their *peculium*: plerique ὑποκοριστικῶς patrimonium suum peculium dicunt (*Dig.* 36.1.17.pr [Ulp.]).

75. *Dig.* 15.1.32.pr. (Ulp.): qui cum seruo contrahit, uniuersum peculium eius quod ubicumque est ueluti patrimonium intuetur. *Dig.* 15.1.19.1: Marcellus scribit . . . eum enim qui contrahit totum serui peculium uelut patrimonium intuitum. Cf. *Dig.* 15.1.5.3 (Ulp.).

76. *Dig.* 50.16.182: Latin text above, n. 71.

77. See *Dig.* 15.1.4.pr. (Pomp.); *Dig.* 15.1.5.4 (Ulp.); *Dig.* 15.1.7.6; *Dig.* 15.1.9.6 (Ulp.); *Dig.* 15.1.37.1–2 (Iulianus); *Dig.* 40.1.6 (Alfenus/Varus); *Dig.* 41.1.37.1 (Iul.).

third-party purchaser if on sale of the slave the *dominus* had actually been entitled both to receive the purchase price from the outside buyer and to retain the assets constituting the slave's *peculium*.[78] Even where a *dominus* in writing had explicitly and publicly forbidden third parties to do business with his slave who controlled a *peculium*, in business transactions the slave still could utilize his own assets, that is, the resources of the *peculium*, as he wished: only the master's own assets (that is, those separated from the *peculium*) were protected from suit by a person who—notwithstanding the master's dictum—had interacted commercially with the slave; assets in the servile *peculium* remained fully exposed to customers' legal actions.[79]

In order to reconcile the irreconcilable, the Roman jurisprudents explicitly acknowledged that "one must close one's eyes" (*oculis coniventibus*) to the clear incompatibility between legal recognition of a slave's ownership of assets in his *peculium* and legal insistence that slaves, qua slaves, had no capacity to own anything. Thus the Roman "legal fiction" with which this chapter deals is the factual falsity of the juridical framework governing slaves' business activity, and the casuistry through which Roman jurisprudents skillfully preserved a legal framework seemingly confirming a fictitious world in which slaves are absolute nullities, while simultaneously creating legal methodologies and rules facilitating a commercial reality utterly in conflict with the fundamental juridical precepts that should have governed servile business activity.

Accordingly, in dealing with manumissions in which a slave purchases his own freedom with "his own cash," using funds in his *peculium*, Ulpian says that it's not really correct to use the expression "purchased with his own cash" since a slave cannot have cash of his own—but we "close our eyes" to juridical doctrine, yielding to, and giving legal effect to, economic reality (*credendum est*).[80] Popular usage reflected this reality: in an inscription of the second century CE, a public slave is said to have used "his own money" (*sua*

---

78. On slaves' purchase of their freedom with their own money (*suis nummis*), see Chapter 3, section on "Self-Purchase: Complement to Self-Sale."

79. Quotiens in taberna ita scriptum fuisset "cum Ianuario seruo meo geri negotium ueto," hoc solum consecutum esse dominum constat, ne institoria teneatur, non etiam de peculio (*Dig.* 15.1.47.pr [Paul.]). Cf. *Dig.* 14.3.17.4 (Paul.); *Dig.* 15.1.29.1 (Gaius): etiamsi prohibuerit contrahi cum seruo dominus, erit in eum de peculio actio. See Burdese 1982.

80. Is qui suis nummis emitur epistula diuorum fratrum ad Urbium Maximum in eam condicionem redigitur, ut libertatem adipiscatur. Et primo quidem nummis suis non proprie uidetur emptus dici, cum suos nummos seruus habere non possit: uerum coniuentibus oculis credendum est suis nummis eum redemptum, cum non nummis eius, qui eum redemit, comparatur. proinde siue ex peculio . . . redemptus sit, credendum est suis nummis eum redemptum. *Dig.* 40.1.4 pr.-1. On this passage, see Chapter 3, pp. 100–101.

pecunia) to finance a temple, attendant work areas, and statuary.[81] Roman legal experts similarly had little difficulty in formulating an appropriate juridical treatment for slaves' debts, although—the jurists again noted—*stricto sensu* a slave cannot incur debts: for the jurists, "when we misuse this term, we are recognizing reality rather than relating to a formal obligation under civil law."[82] This recognition was pervasive: legal materials frequently speak of slaves' "creditors."[83] Javolenus, jurisprudent of the High Empire, rejects the opinion of Servius, denying legal effectiveness to a testator's direction to his heir to pay five aureos "which I owe to my slave (as recorded) in the accounting records (*in tabulis*)." For Servius, "a master could owe nothing to his slave!" But by the time of Javolenus, the law was following not the dogma of the "civil" law (*ius civile*) but the reality of "natural" debts from owner to slave, and "that (*ius naturale*) is the law which we observe" (translation: Watson 1985, 1999).[84]

Rome's failure to develop a systematized "commercial law" may accordingly perhaps best be understood as a response to, and a reflection of, the tension inherent in the collision between the reality of enslaved persons' unfettered control of many aspects of Roman business, and the legal dogma decreeing those unfree persons' absolute legal incapacity (and hence juridical invisibility). With a generally far less systematized judicial process, Athens had earlier developed a specialized commercial law,[85] and pre-modern European jurisdictions thereafter had little or no difficulty in constructing a legal edifice with specialized rules ("commercial law") governing newly developed mercantile instrumentalities such as the "draft" and the "commenda" financing mechanism. But Roman law—even though noted for its high abstraction of

81. CIL IX 4112 (= ILS 4381): pro salute ordinis et populi signa / Serapis et Isidis cum ergasteris suis / et aediculam in scholam permit / tente ordine / Apronianus r(ei) p(ublicae) Aequicul(orum) ser(uus) ark(arius) / cum Aequicula Bassilla et Aequi /culo Aproniano fil(io) pec(unia) sua fecit / l(ocus) d(atus) d(ecreto) d(ecurionum). For other references to a slave's "own money" see Chapter 1, pp. 35, 38.

82. *Dig.* 15.1.41 (Ulp.): nec seruus quicquam debere potest nec seruo potest deberi, sed cum eo uerbo abutimur, factum magis demonstramus quam ad ius ciuile referimus obligationem.

83. See, for example, *Dig.* 15.1.9.5 (Ulp.) (creditor serui); *Dig.* 15.1.27.7 (Gaius) (quod ipse crediderim seruo meo); *Dig.* 15.1.47.3 (Paul.) (creditor serui).

84. *Dig.* 35.1.40.3 (Iauolenus): dominus seruo aureos quinque legauerat: "heres meus Sticho, seruo meo, quem testamento liberum esse iussi, aureos quinque quos in tabulis debeo, dato." nihil seruo legatum esse Namusa Seruium respondisse scribit, quia dominus seruo nihil debere potuisset: ego puto secundum mentem testatoris naturale magis quam ciuile debitum spectandum esse, et eo iure utimur.

85. Sirks 2018: 53. Cf. Cohen 2005.

precepts and the promulgation of broad doctrines universally applicable to individual situations—never developed a specialized law especially applicable to mercantile subjects and to persons engaged in trade.[86] Although modern scholars have written works entitled *Roman Commercial Law* ("Diritto commerciale romano," "Droit commercial romain," and such), they invariably merely discuss, subject by subject, disparate topics of business activity,[87] unable to find in Roman jurisprudential material any overarching system of rules able to regulate the full economic spectrum.[88] Since the persons to be specially treated in an autonomous system of mercantile law would have been at Rome juridically "non-persons," how could they and their activities be the explicit and segregated subject of the kind of abstracted and systematic clarity that is elsewhere a frequent hallmark of Roman jurisprudence?

Consider, for example, the absence in Roman law of a systematized doctrine of agency. Because of *ius Romanum*'s bedrock rejection of any person *sui iuris* acting as agent for another such person,[89] an action *de peculio* was available only with regard to family members ("persons in [the *pater familias*'s] power")—a principle inherent in Roman law on which no theoretical concession was possible. But here too reality prevailed. As Ulpian and Labeo explain, "although an action *de peculio* is available only with regard to a person 'in power,' nonetheless an action *de peculio* is available even in the case of persons *not* 'in power.'" A good example, according to Ulpian, is a former slave who is now free through testamentary process, but *was* in power at the time of a transaction normally giving rise to litigation *de peculio*. The law will treat such a free person as still enslaved, and on the basis of this fiction will allow a suit *de peculio* to proceed.[90] *Ius romanum* similarly disregards the actual status of a free man who has in good faith been laboring for someone as a slave—and accordingly will grant an action *de peculio* against his putative "master,"

86. "Ein besonderes Handelsrecht haben die Römer daneben nicht ausgebildet" (Kaser 1971: 474). In agreement: Aubert 2015; Bianchi 2007. Cf. Andreau 2020: 103; Fadda 1903 [1987]; Goldschmidt 1891.

87. See Cerami, Dio Porto, and Pettrucci 2004; Cienfuegos 2007; Fleckner 2010. Cf. Sirks 2012.

88. Sirks 2018: 53–54.

89. See Chapter 1, pp. 40–42.

90. *Dig.* 15.1.3.pr.-1 (Ulp.): licet tamen praetor, si cum eo qui in potestate sit gestum sit, polliceratur actionem, tamen sciendum est et si in nullius sit potestate, dari de peculio actionem, ut puta si cum seruo hereditario contractum sit ante aditam hereditatem. (1) unde Labeo scribit et si secundo tertioue gradu substitutus sit seruus et deliberantibus primis heredibus cum eo contractum sit, mox repudiantibus eis ipse liber heresque exstiterit, posse dici de peculio eum conueniri.

who in fact is not the subject's owner, without regard to whether the laborer is actually free or someone else's slave.[91] Jurisprudents insist that actual ownership of a slave (the theoretical basis for an action) is—in this Roman world of legal fiction—less relevant than the reality of actual control over an individual whatever his "true" status.[92] Again, where a master has not actually established *peculia* for underslaves (*vicarii*), he will be considered to have done that which he has not done.[93] In the context of such accommodations—frequently brilliant displays of casuistry—there could be no expounding of pedantic, routinized rules which might serve as beacons of consistency, constituting a clearly enunciated "commercial law." By avoiding excessive clarity on commercial topics, Roman jurisprudents were able to accommodate the fictions that actually lubricated the Roman entrepreneurial system—without abandoning or contradicting the internal consistency to which legal science, in Roman antiquity and in modern context, has aspired.

Retaining Peculium *Assets after Manumission*

Upon manumission, slaves generally retained the assets in their *peculia*—again for the jurists a concession to economic reality, achieved partly through legal fictions that effectively avoided explicit confirmation of servile ownership rights.

Modern scholars have long recognized that "even when slaves were sold, it was common to let them take the *peculium* with them."[94] Similarly—and

91. *Dig.* 15.1.1.6 (Ulp.): non enim solum seruorum propriorum nomine conueniemur, item communium, uerum eorum quoque qui bona fide nobis seruiunt, siue liberi sint siue serui alieni.

92. Ibid.: nec magis dominium seruorum esse spectandum quam facultatem habendi eos.

93. *Dig.* 15.1.1.6 (Celsus): definitio peculii quam Tubero exposuit, ut Labeo ait, ad uicariorum peculia non pertinet, quod falsum est: nam eo ipso, quod dominus seruo peculium constituit, etiam uicario constituisse existimandus est. On the relationship between the *peculia* of *ordinarii* and *uicarii*, see *Dig.* 15.1.38.2 (Africanus); *Dig.* 15.1.17 (Ulp.); above, Chapter 1, pp. 36–38.

94. Mouritsen 2011: 176. *Dig.* 4.3.7.pr. (Ulp., Julian): eum uendidit cum peculio. The Murecine Tablets confirm this practice: the slave Hesychus, owned by E-uenus Prianus, had made a loan of 3,000 *sesterces* to a certain C. Nouius Eunus, through his *peculium*. Fourteen months later Hesychus had a new owner (the Emperor Gaius), but he nonetheless had retained the debt owed by Eunus. Camodecca 1999: Tablets 52, 67, 68. Cf. Dumont 1987: 110. In the late Republic, the *peculium* did not in all cases follow the slave: Varro, *De Re Rust.* 2.10.5 (in horum emptione solet accedere peculium aut excipi). Upon the death of a *seruus* holding a *peculium*, the fund automatically was reincorporated into the estate of the master: *Dig.* 15.2.3 (Pomp.); *Dig.* 4.9.7.6 (Ulp.); *Dig.* 15.2.1.3 (Ulp.).

without regard to the form of manumission[95]—upon a master's liberation of a slave during the master's own lifetime (*inter vivos*), the former slave took his *peculium* along with his freedom.[96] After *inter vivos* manumission, freed slaves even retained in their *peculia* underslaves (*vicarii*) who did not thereby become or remain the property of the overslave's master.[97] The jurists further opined that unless a *peculium* had been affirmatively terminated at the time that a slave was granted his freedom, he is *assumed* on manumission to have retained his *peculium*, to the extent of the assets actually present in the fund or collectible in the normal course of business.[98] The authorities were thus artfully implying that the master was making a gift to a former slave no longer unable to own property,[99] a formulation that avoided explicit recognition of a slave's prior ownership rights to the assets in his *peculium*. This response enabled the jurisprudents to maintain the fiction that a slave's commercial *peculium* belongs to his master—while effectively conveying the *peculium*'s assets to the slave upon his obtaining "freedom." Ulpian, for example, concludes that "unless their *peculia* had been terminated," on the manumission of a male and a female slave who until their freedom had maintained a continuing relationship, any property previously given by the woman to the man as if it were a dowry is converted into true dotal assets automatically (*tacite*): the woman accordingly is entitled to a valuation for any assets remaining from her earlier delivery of property.[100] But this formulation is again fictitious, because in reality, in any significant commercial situation involving a functioning business,

95. Buckland [1908] 1970: 189–190: slave's entitlement to retain *peculium* not affected by form of manumission (formal [*uindicta*] or informal [*inter amicos, per epistulam*, adoption, appointment, etc.]).

96. "Dans le cas de l'affranchissement entre vifs, il [le pécule] est censé rester à l'esclave" (Pahud 2013: 292). "If a slave was sold or freed, he kept his peculium" (Temin 2013: 124). In agreement: Buckland [1908] 1970: 189; Apathy 1979: 405; Micolier 1932: 205; Mandry 1876: 197; Mouritsen 2011: 177; Gamauf 2016: 390–391, n. 40. Cf. Barja de Quiroga 2007: 91; Jones 2006: 59; Roth 2010: 96 ("manumission during the lifetime of the master appears to have attracted an uncomplicated, if not an automatic transfer of the slave's peculium").

97. This result is confirmed, for spectacular example, by the enormous trove of inscriptions found within the *columbarium* of the Statilii (see Chapter 1, pp. 36–37). Cf. Mouritsen 2011: 151.

98. *Dig.* 15.1.53: si Sticho peculium cum manumitteretur ademptum non est, uidetur concessum. In contrast, according to Paulus, the right to pursue through the courts claims against debtors had to be explicitly entrusted to former slaves upon manumission (ibid.: debitores autem conuenire nisi mandatis sibi actionibus non potest).

99. See *Vat. Fr.* 261 (Pap.) (peculium uindicta manumisso uel inter amicos si non adimatur, donari uidetur); Just. *Instit.* 2.20.20; *Codex* 7.28.

100. *Dig.* 23.3.39.pr.: Si serua seruo quasi dotem dederit, deinde constante coniunctione ad libertatem ambo peruenerint peculio eis non adempto et in eadem coniunctione permanserint,

creditors' rights as a practical matter precluded termination of a slave's *peculium*: Roman legal opinion suggests that diminution or abrogation of a *peculium* was as to creditors inherently fraudulent (*dolum malum*).[101]

Testamentary manumissions—which appear to have occurred less frequently than *inter vivos* emancipations[102]—likewise were often, but not always, explicitly accompanied by bequest to the former slave of the assets in his *peculium*.[103] Prevailing opinion formally insisted that the *peculium* passed to the former slave only if the testator explicitly affirmed its continuation (in Buckland's formulation, "it did not pass unless it was expressly given"[104]). This requirement of affirmative direction was in form strongly variant from the standard that governed *inter vivos* manumissions—mere absence of termination of the *peculium*—a differentiation that has been judged by at least one recent commentator as "the root for wide-reaching historical interpretation."[105] But in practice it made little difference, for even when a testator provided no explicit direction in his will regarding conveyance of the *peculium* to his manumitted slave, but *had* arguably left vague indications not inconsistent with such conveyance, jurisprudents of the High Empire assigned the *peculium* to the manumitted slave, availing themselves of the legal fiction of testator's conveyance—thus meeting commercial expectations and satisfying societal views which attributed ownership of *peculia* to slaves active in business, while still preserving the façade of juridical dogma that denied slaves' capacity to own assets. Ulpian openly confides that "sometimes even if a *peculium* has not

---

ita res moderetur, ut, si quae ex rebus corporalibus uelut in dotem tempore seruitutis datis exstiterint, uideantur ea tacite in dotem conuersa, ut earum aestimatio mulieri debeatur.

101. *Dig.* 15.1.21.pr. (Ulp.): summa cum ratione etiam hoc peculio praetor imputauit, quod dolo malo domini factum est, quo minus in peculio esset. sed dolum malum accipere debemus, si ei ademit peculium. Mela, writing during the early Empire, believed that a master committed *dolum malum* even by "allowing" a *peculium* to lack transparency (ibid.: sed et si eum intricare peculium in necem creditorum passus est, Mela scribit dolo malo eius factum). Surviving Roman law materials do not elucidate how a *dominus* might prove absence of *dolum malum* (Johnston 2007: 178).

102. Koops 2020: 50–52; Roth 2010: 98–99; Mouritsen 2011: 180–183.

103. See Buckland [1908] 1970: 190–196; Pahud 2013: 292–296. Freedom through testament evoked considerations different from those relating to transactions during the master's lifetime. Since on the owner's death his entire estate often had to be revisited and prevailing arrangements possibly modified, abrogation of the slave's business (and his *peculium*) at this point might be less disruptive and less evocative of controversy than continuing the operation.

104. Buckland [1908] 1970: 189–190. Buckland's interpretation has been the worldwide *communis opinio* for more than a century (Roth 2010: 96).

105. Roth 2010: 99.

been bequeathed, it is treated as if it had been."[106] Ulpian offers an example of the lengths to which *ius Romanum* might stretch in order to ignore factuality. "A testator had manumitted a slave on condition that he render his accounts and pay 100 to the heirs. The Emperors Severus and Caracalla ruled that indeed a *peculium* is not owed unless actually bequeathed: however, if the slave has complied with the terms set forth, it is our interpretation that the testator wanted him to *retain* (*emphasis added*) the *peculium* if he truly met the conditions set forth. The testator's desire is clear from the testator's having ordered the former slave to pay 100 from the *peculium*."[107]

The underlying rationale for this casuistry is that a reduction or an elimination of a *peculium* would have run strongly contrary to the master's own self-interest and to communal social mores that recognized *peculia* as the property of enslaved businessmen.

Financially, assets in a *peculium* were under the actual control of the slave holding the *peculium* who alone would typically fully understand the nature, value, and context of these resources and might alone have ongoing relationships with creditors and customers. A master typically would have little or no knowledge of what was actually in the fund.[108] An effort to seize control of these assets, and to eliminate the slave's interest therein, would concomitantly have eliminated or reduced the worth of the ongoing business that was functioning through the *peculium*—to the master's harm: the *dominus* would have remained liable to financial and trade creditors (under the *actiones annalis* and *de in rem verso*[109]), but concerns about the continuity of the business, generated by an attempted termination of the *peculium*, would likely have immediately driven away customers, might have deterred ongoing and fresh financing, and might even have been the catalyst for immediate

106. *Dig.* 33.8.8.7: interdum etsi non sit legatum peculium, uelut legatum *sic* accipitur.

107. Ibid.: quidam seruo libertatem, si rationes reddidisset, dederat, et si heredibus centum intulisset. imperator igitur noster cum patre rescripsit, peculium quidem non nisi legatum deberi: 'uerum,' inquit, 'si condicionibus praescriptis paruit seruus, testatorem uoluisse eum retinere peculium interpretamur: uidelicet ex eo, quod ex peculio eum iusserat centum inferre.

108. See Aubert 2013, especially 197, 195: "no one except the slave in charge of the *peculium* may actually know with precision and accuracy what it is made of," "the master . . . may be unclear about its contents and components." In agreement: Koops 2020: 57; Johnston 2002.

109. The *actio de in rem uerso*, analogously to the *actio de peculio*, was "perpetual" (*perpetua*), that is "quamdiu seruus in potestate est" (see Chiusi 2001, passim). The *actio annalis* was available for a year after a slave was freed or died: post mortem eius qui in alterius potestate fuerit, posteaue quam is emancipatus manumissus alienatusue fuerit, dumtaxat de peculio et si quid dolo malo eius in cuius potestate est factum erit, quo minus peculii esset, in anno, quo primum de ea re experiundi potestas erit, iudicium dabo (*Dig.* 15.2.1.pr.).

litigation. Any resultant disposition of the assets of the resulting emaciated operation would likely have been at "fire-sale" prices.

Juridically, an attempt to deprive a commercially active slave of his *peculium* would have raised substantial legal issues, both equitable and factual, including claims of fraud (*dolum malum*) that might be advanced by creditors adversely affected by such a maneuver.[110] Popular and even legal opinion recognized the *peculium* as the property of its slave operator;[111] Roman sources repetitively attest to a *servus*'s purchase of his own freedom "with his own money."[112] Not surprisingly, therefore, there is not a single known example of a *dominus* ever attempting to withdraw a *peculium* as to which an action at law was pending.[113] This silent evidence speaks loudly, for few commercial enterprises—in the Roman period or at present—can operate without generating significant litigation in the ordinary course of business.

In summary, a slave's *peculium* (1) was generated by the slave himself—although his owner might make contribution; (2) was held by the slave, and recognized implicitly as though it were his own property (*velut proprium patrimonium habere*); and (3) was after manumission an immediately available source of capital for the wealthy freedmen so prominent in Roman society and commerce. The skilled slave who had accumulated assets for himself while initially working in his owner's business(es) could thus metamorphose into a prosperous (albeit still enslaved) operator of a commercial *peculium* before emerging finally (after manumission) as a freedman, commencing his life of "liberty" well capitalized with at least some of the assets from his servile *peculium*. Petronius's fictional Trimalchio illustrates this progression.[114] As a slave, Trimalchio acquires skill in financial matters, receiving instruction in accounting and administration. Taking as his guiding deity Minerva, goddess inter alia of business people, Trimalchio advances to the position of *dispensator*

110. Cf. Buchwitz 2012: 29.

111. See above, this chapter, section on "Owning Assets through the *Peculium*."

112. See Chapter 3, section on "Self-Purchase: Complement to Self-Sale."

113. See Knoch 2005: 179–180 and 182; Watson 1987: 43; Buti 1976: 13–70.

114. The fabricated world of Trimalchio is "recognizably rooted in reality" (Verboven 2013: 125), indeed "the most illuminating example of the wealth of those freedmen in the first century AD who 'made it,'" presented in a fashion conveying an "effet de reel" (Andreau 2013: 114–115). Care is needed, however, in utilizing comic material (the essence of the *Satyricon*): see Carlsen 2010: 78; Cohen 2015(a): 15–18.

("chief accountant" or "financial manager"),[115] for slaves in wealthy families a senior post involving the receipt and disbursement of cash, requiring the management of important financial transactions—and offering opportunity to generate the funds that might seed a substantial servile *peculium*.[116] Relevant sources suggest that all *dispensatores* were slaves,[117] and that many ultimately came to control their own *peculia*, sometimes gathering assets on a magnificent scale, ultimately after manumission emerging as wealthy freedmen.[118] Commercial slaves' economic opportunities were so much greater than those conventionally available to free persons that some free men appear voluntarily to have sold themselves into slavery in order to share in the purchase price (akin perhaps to a "signing bonus") and to obtain the business income and wealth potentially available to slaves, but not to free men.[119]

The Manumission of Skilled Slaves: Facilitating Commerce through Legal Fiction

All people are either free or slaves. Slavery is an undifferentiated condition. . . . But free men are either born free (ingenui) or made free (libertini).

—Justinian, Gaius, *Principles of Roman Law*[120]

115. Mineruaque ducente Romam intrabat. Hinc quemadmodum rationicari didicisset, denique dispensator factus esset, omnia diligenter curiosus pictor cum inscriptione reddiderat (Petron. *Satyr*. 29.3). Cf. ibid. 30.1–2, 45.8, 53.10. On *dispensatores*, see Minaud 2005: 174–177; Muñiz Coello 1989: 109; Boulvert 1970: 429; Ruggiero 1961: 1920, s.v. *dispensator*.

116. Gaius *Inst*. 1.122: unde serui quibus permittitur administratio pecuniae dispensatores appellati sunt. For Cicero's dependence on his *dispensator* in financial matters, see Cic. *Att*. XV.15.3, XVI.2.1. Cf. Verboven 2013: 129–130; Crook 1967: 187–188.

117. Schumacher 2010; Aubert 1994: 197. But cf. CIL X 5081, CIL III 14427, a badly damaged inscription from Lower Moesia which has been restored, unconvincingly in my opinion, to read "lib(erto) . . . di(spensatoris?)."

118. *Dig*. 46.3.62: "dispensatorem meum testamento liberum esse iussi et peculium ei legaui . . . ." Undertakings pursued by such *dispensatores* subjected their masters to actions *de peculio* (*Dig*. 14.3.12 [Iulianus]). The most spectacular example of a *dispensator* accumulating enormous wealth is Musicus Scurranus (see Chapter 1, p. 37) For other wealthy *dispensatores*, see Pliny *H.N*. 7.39.128, 33.52.145; Petron. *Satyr*. 30.

119. The phenomenon of "self-enslavement" is discussed in Chapter 3, section on "Entrepreneurial Self-Enslavement." On the privileging of servile enterprise, see Chapter 1, section on "Legal Inequality: The Privileging of Servile Enterprise."

120. (Just. *Inst*. I.3.5:) In seruorum condicione nulla differentia est. (Gaius *Inst*. 1.9:) omnes homines aut liberi sunt aut serui . . . liberorum hominum, alii ingenui sunt, alii libertini. Cf. Mélèze (Modrzejewski) 1976.

Despite multitudinous analyses by legal theorists and legal historians, definition of a "legal fiction" has defied consensus, raising "fundamental philosophical issues about fact, fiction, truth and knowledge" (Twining 2015: vii): contradictory approaches and the "epistemological and ontological context in which discussion of fictions inevitably must occur" have made "the entire experience of thinking about fictions a seriously vertiginous business" (Del Mar 2015: ix). Nonetheless, legal fictions have been prolific in many societies.[121] At Rome, inter alia, they were remarkably effective at facilitating commerce by permitting skilled slaves after manumission to continue functioning on behalf of their former masters. But by creating an "alternative" juridical reality, Roman legal fiction relating to manumission generated a narrative potentially confusing to modern scholarship and purposefully not entirely clear in antiquity. Slaves freed after manumission were not as "free" as their descendants, who had never endured the *macula servitutis* ("stain of enslavement"). But manumission was still for slaves highly desirable and for Roman society highly significant.

Mouritsen has observed that Rome freed its private slaves "more often and in greater numbers than any other slave-based society in history."[122] The possibility of manumission thus provided an important incentive for slaves to work diligently and productively, and supplied an outlet for masters to act on affectionate and appreciative feelings that they might develop toward their dependents. Although emancipation of the typical private slave did not necessarily create any special difficulty, manumission of skilled and often affluent enslaved individuals posed a potentially existential challenge for Roman commerce: the absence in Roman law of a general provision for "agency" effectively precluded free men from legally acting on behalf of other free men.[123] Members of a free man's family (which included his slaves), in contrast, could act on that individual's behalf. By the letter of the law—legal dogma—emancipated slaves ceased to be family members of their former owner, and therefore lost this modality of agency. "Roman law in action,"[124] however, ignored this reality and instead acquiesced in the legal fiction that former slaves engaged in commerce were still family members of their former owner,

---

121. See above, this chapter, pp. 59–63.

122. Mouritsen 2016: 402. Cf. Mouritsen 2011: 120–131. On the frequency of manumission at Rome, see Chapter 3, section on "Generally High Rates of Manumission?"

123. See Chapter 1, section on "Legal Inequality: The Privileging of Servile Enterprise."

124. For "law in action" as distinct from "law in the books," see Chapter 1, n. 8 and related text.

and therefore still capable of acting for their former master, a significant capacity because of the importance of servile agency to the overall economy.[125] Economic reality prevailed over possible alternative constructions of "fact, fiction, truth, and knowledge."

In interpreting evidence for this phenomenon, recent scholarship has tended to minimize the immediate importance of emancipation, arguing (in Mouritsen's words) that fundamentally "release from servitude merely entailed the transition from one familial role to another": it was a "process designed to negate that any transition had taken place at all."[126] As a result, "the fully independent freedman was considered anomalous"[127]—although his offspring, never having been enslaved, would themselves enjoy the benefits of full freedom.[128] Gaius actually separates "free men" (*liberi*) into two separate groupings, those born free (*ingenui*) and those not originally free (*libertini*). For Gaius, just as there was a clear distinction between *liberi* and *servi*, there was also a differentiation between *ingenui* and *libertini*. Both were "free," but not identically so. Despite Roman law's fundamental division of mankind into two absolutely separated categories—free persons and enslaved individuals—manumitted slaves "were not wholly free . . . their semi-freedom or semi-slavery placed them in a twilight zone between the completely free and the completely non-free."[129] "Within [Roman law's] construction of slavery and freedom manumission posed a problem . . . call[ing] into question the given character of both statuses" (Mouritsen 2011: 11).

To be sure, some commercially important slaves, after manumission, might have exercised their right to live as they wish—severing all (or virtually all) their relationship with their former owners.[130] Yet because of the responsibilities and dependence inherent in the continuing relationship

125. See Chapter 1, pp. 23–33.

126. Mouritsen 2011: 147, 11.

127. Mouritsen 2011: 174.

128. MacLean 2018: 2. Cf. Vermote 2016.

129. Zelnick-Abramovitz 2005: 6 (with respect to the Greek world, including the eastern part of the Roman empire). "Manumitted slaves in the Greek world were often tied to their former masters . . . by bonds of reciprocal asymmetrical exchange. These bonds . . . rendered their status somewhat servile" (7). Cf. Darmezin 1999: 211–212. Sosin, however, argues that "in the Greek world" "the intermediate or hybrid juridical state of conditional freedom is a modern invention" (2015: 325).

130. For Mouritsen (2011: 158), a slave's separation (supposedly rare) from his master's family after manumission was a punishment, not a reward.

between the former *dominus* (as *patronus*) and the erstwhile *servus*,[131] in actual practice the freedman's situation was in important respects not absolutely differentiable from the manumitted individual's earlier status as a "slave."[132] The *libertus* was no longer a slave *tout court*, but he was not entirely a free man either.

Although Roman law provides a variety of mechanisms for freeing a slave, some "formal" and some "informal," the type of manumission had no effect on freedmen's subsequent obligations to, or dependence on, the former *dominus*.[133] After "liberation," the *libertus* still owed to his former master and the master's family many of the same duties and obligations as before; he was still entitled to many of the same benefits; he continued, generally and essentially, to be a member of the master's family[134]—and was treated as such juridically. As a result, he was still able to act on his former owner's behalf as though he were still enslaved, and thus was able to participate in the advantages—for himself and his former owner—available to businesses operated by slaves, but proscribed for free enterprise.[135]

131. Significantly, the original owner's position as *patronus* was protected even when manumission occurred not by the owner's action but by force of law. For example, manumission was mandatory in the event of the breach of a sales covenant prohibiting the use of a female slave in the commercial provision of sexual services—even where the violator was a later purchaser not in privity with the original owner and therefore presumably "had not been warned of the existence of the covenant" (McGinn 1998: 293). See *Dig*. 37.14.7.pr. (Mod.): Diuus Uespasianus decreuit ut, si qua hac lege uenierit, ne prostitueretur et, si prostituta esset, ut esset libera, si postea ab emptore alii sine condicione ueniit, ex lege uenditionis liberam esse et libertam prioris uenditoris. On the grant of freedom by force of law, see Wagner 1967: 172; Mitteis 1908: 182, n. 62 ("nach Analogie des Statusliber"). On covenants forbidding prostitution of female slaves, see Chapter 3, n. 130 and related text.

132. A few scholars have argued that all (or virtually all) relationship between the former master and the manumitted slave was eliminated if manumission had been effectuated through "self-purchase" (*seruus suis nummis emptus*). See Mouritsen 2011: 173–174. But no evidence has been adduced in support of this assertion other than the argument that it would have been "illogical . . . if a slave who had used his *peculium* with sufficient enterprise to enable him to purchase his freedom, should have found himself in his new status, subject to more rather than less constraint" (Garnsey [1981] 1998: 33; cf. 1996: 39; 1981). For contextual analysis of the institution of self-purchase, see Chapter 3, section on "Self-Purchase: Complement to Self-Sale."

133. Hawkins 2016: 133 (comparing informal manumission with formal procedures). On forms of manumission, see Chapter 3, n. 187. Obligations of freedmen to their former masters were slightly eased during the late Republic and early Empire (cf. the lex Iunia Norbana adopted under Tiberius), but no fundamental changes were enacted during the long imperial period (Fabre 1981: 217226, 317–331; Waldstein 1986: 131–208).

134. See Scheidel 2012(b): 101; Los 1995.

135. See Chapter 1, section on "Legal Inequality: The Privileging of Servile Enterprise."

Freedmen often continued to reside in the former master's home,[136] where they continued to be subject to the master's domestic discipline in the same way and to the same extent as slaves still formally in servitude.[137] Many were even buried in the erstwhile owner's family tomb (which was frequently designed with space for inhumation of freedmen); some *liberti* not interred in the family crypt were buried nearby.[138] The freedman even carried the gentilical (that is, family) name of his patron.[139] To his former owner and present patron, instead of the burdens of servitude, the freedman now owed onerous obligations of *obsequium* ("respect," a vague but belittling and restrictive responsibility),[140] of *operae* (continuing services that had to be provided even after manumission),[141] and of *bona* (potential property benefits accruing to the patron on the freedman's death).[142] The result was, according to Quintilian, "a freedman bound (to his patron) through the 'boon' of liberation."[143] One former master notes approvingly on a freedman's funeral inscription that "he did nothing except on the express command (*voluntas*)" of

136. See *Dig.* 7.8.2.1 (Ulp.); *Dig.* 14.3.19.1 (Pap.); *Dig.* 21.1.17.15 (Caelius); *Dig.* 26.7.37.1 (Pap.); *Dig.* 26.7.58.pr. (Scaeuola); Pliny, *Ep.* 2.17.9, 7.27.12; Tac. *Hist.* 1.22, *Ann.* 2.31. Cf. Fabre 1981: 131–162; Mouritsen 2011: 220–21.

137. *Dig.* 48.19.11.1 (Marcianus): furta domestica si uiliora sunt, publice uindicanda non sunt, nec admittenda est huiusmodi accusatio, cum seruus a domino uel libertus a patrono, in cuius domo moratur . . . offeratur quaestioni.

138. Fabre 1981: 141–162. Note, for example, the burial of the freedmen of L. Fabricius L. f. Caesennius Gallus (CIL XIV.354): see D'Arms 1976: 391–393.

139. See Fabre 1981: 93–124. Cf. Solin 1974, 1996; Panciera 1977.

140. No legal definition delineated the comportment that might constitute a freedman's failure to behave properly to his patron. Violation of this opaquely abstract commitment exposed the *libertus* to a charge of "ingratitude" (*accusatio liberti ingrati*), carrying harsh penalties including a possible return to formal enslavement. See *Dig.* 37.15 (de obsequiis parentibus et patronis praestandis), *Cod.* 6.6. Cf. Perry 2014: 71–78; Gardner 1993: 23–25; Watson 1987: 39–40; Waldstein 1986: 51–69.

141. *Dig.* 38.1 (de operis libertorum); *Cod.* 6.3; Tac. *Ann.* 13.26–27. See Kaser 1938; Koops 2020: 66–71; Masi-Doria 2011; Wildstein 1986 for a "juristisch-dogmatisch" approach to *operae*. Cf. Pescani 1967; Schiller 1971: 28–30; Hermann-Otto 2013: 69, 2009, *passim*. According to Verboven (2011: 96), freedmen who had purchased their liberty "with their own money" were not subject to the obligation to provide *operae*; Waldstein (1986: 123–130) argues the opposite, viz. that the provision of *operae* was regularly used by slaves as a means of purchasing their freedom on a credit rather than a cash basis. See, however, Chapter 3, sections on "Self-Purchase: Complement to Self-Sale" and "Manumission Pursuant to Contract."

142. Gaius *Inst.* 3.40–54 (de Zulueta 1953: 128–31); *Tit. Ulp.* 29.1–3; *Dig.* 50.16.195.1 (Ulp.). See Watson 1987: 35–39; Sirks 1981.

143. libertus tam beneficio obligatus manumittentis: Quint. *Decl. Min.* 259.9. Cf. Cic. *Uerr.* 2.1.124.

his manumittor.[144] Even when a freedman worked on his own affairs independently of his former master, he did so with the former master's permission and with a continuing relationship to the ex-owner's family.[145] Some Romans even asserted that the aggregate burden accompanying so-called manumission actually amounted to continued slavery: in words attributed to Quintilian, a speaker declares that "the man accepting manumission imposes servitude on himself."[146] Verres, according to Cicero, never thought that "freedmen" were truly free.[147] As Publilius Syrus, himself a former slave, observed, "to accept (this) benefit (of manumission) is to sell (one's) freedom."[148] "By accepting freedom, (freedmen) also surrendered a major part of it."[149]

Frequent references in Latin to freedmen as "slaves" (*servi*) confirm the prevalent Roman perception of manumission as a mere transfiguration of prior servitude into a fresh vassalage.[150] Although such allusions are sometimes dismissed as *ad hominem* rhetorical disparagements of little or no heuristic significance,[151] a juridical comment preserved in the *Fragmenta Vaticana* (early fourth century CE) insists that the term "slave" encompasses "freedmen"[152]—a conflation confirmed by surviving Roman inscriptions.[153]

---

144. CIL VI.9222: sine uoluntate patroni nihil fecit.

145. *Dig.* 34.19.1 (Scaeuola): testamento ita cautum fuit: 'libertis meis cibaria quaeque alia praestabam ab heredibus meis praestari uolo': unus ex libertis ex uoluntate patroni negotii sui gratia quadriennio ante diem mortis afuit.... quaesitum est, an isti quoque cibaria et reliquia, quae ceteris libertis legata sunt, debeantur. Respondit (Scaeuola): cur non? Cf. *Dig.* 34.2.4 (Paul.).

146. Quint. *Decl. Min.* 388.23: seruitutem sibi manumissus imponit. 'Huic' inquit 'debeo manus, operas, testamentum.'

147. Cic. ii. *Uerr.* 1.127: quos numquam liberos putauit, libertinos homines solitus sit appellare.

148. *Sent.* B5 (48): beneficium accipere libertatem est uendere. Cf. Cic. *Uerr.* 2.1.124.

149. Mouritsen 2011: 146–147. Morabito (1981: 9) offers a similar judgment: "la condition de l'esclave et celle de l'affranchi doivent être analysés comme deux formes d'une même domination." For MacLean (2018: 76), "manumission created not a fully autonomous citizen but a *libertus* under the supervision of his patron." Cf. Visky 1970.

150. Mommsen 1878: 22 (on the basis of inscriptional evidence): "quod libertini in multis deterioris iuris sunt, ita ipsum serui uocabulum de libertino quoque usurpatur." Cf. Casavola 1960: 80 (dissenting).

151. Treggiari 1969: 265.

152. Seruis liberti continentur. *Fr. Vat.* 307 (alluding to the Lex Cincia, which had been confirmed by Augustus, and referred to by Cicero [*de Orat.* II.71, *ad Att.* 1.20]).

153. See CIL X.8054, 8: CIL I² 413; CIL I² 412, X.8054.7; CIL I² 416; CIL I² 466; CIL XV.6149; CIL I² 1758; CIL IX.2782; and CIL I² 2273 (next note).

A Republican sepulchral inscription, for example, alludes to a freedwoman's patron (and patroness) and yet concomitantly refers to the deceased woman as an *ancilla* (maid-servant or female slave).[154] Tacitus reports that Agrippina raged against Nero's girlfriend Acte, indiscriminately impugning her as a "freedwoman" and as a "slave" (*ancilla*).[155] Cicero similarly describes his freedman Marcus Tullius Tiro as a slave—not negatively but in the context of lauding his integrity and reliability.[156] Describing Sextus Pompey, Velleius uses the two terms (*servi*, *liberti*) interchangeably.[157] In discussing a proposal by Clodius, Cicero refers to his own freedmen as "slaves."[158] Roman authors recurrently identify sometimes as freedmen, sometimes as slaves, persons who had originally served as imperial *servi* and had now been "freed"[159]: Pliny the Younger, for example, complains about the wealthy and powerful freedman Pallas—but refers to him indiscriminately as *servus* and as *libertus*.[160] Again, in discussing a provision of traditional Roman law (*lex maiorum*) providing for harsh punishment for all enslaved members of the household of a master murdered by his own slave(s), a Roman senator conflates slaves and *liberti* who had continued to reside in the family home, arguing that freedmen of the household should also be punished.[161] Roman manumission accordingly may be best understood as a halfway house to true liberation: scholars have frequently commented on the total freedom enjoyed by the offspring of

154. CIL I^2 2273(= Dessau 8417): Plotia L. et Fufiae l. Prune haec uocitatast ancilla hic sitast. Haec qualis fuerit contra patronum patronam parentem coniugem monumentum indicat.

155. *Ann.* 14.13: Agrippina libertam aemulam, nurum ancillam . . . fremere.

156. *Fam.* 5.20.1–2: M. Tullius, scriba meus . . . ita accepi librum a meo seruo scriba, ut eundem acceperim a fratre tuo.

157. Vell. 2.73.1: libertorum suorum libertus seruorumque seruus. Treggiari correctly sees that "the second part of the phrase probably does not expand the information given by the first half: freedmen are meant again" (1969: 266).

158. Seruos nostros libertos suos effecisset (*Milo* 89).

159. See Chapter 5, pp. 176–179.

160. *Epist.* 8.6: (4) Pallanti seruo, (12) liberti, libertus, (14) mancipi, (16) quod dari liberto promitti seruis uidebant.

161. Tac. *Annal.* 14.45: censuerat Cingonius Uarro ut liberti quoque qui sub eodem tecto fuissent Italia deportarentur. On the murder of Pedanius Secundus, Prefect of the City, see Chapter 3, pp. 117–118. Cf. the conflation of *liberti* with *serui* in the proposed collective punishment of the household of Afranius Dexter, a consular Roman who died mysteriously (Pliny *Ep.* 8.14.12–15).

freedmen and freedwomen—in contrast to the continuing confining bonds between *liberti* and their "former" *domini.*[162]

In economic reality, for skilled and prosperous slaves, little changed upon manumission. The assets formerly held in servile *peculia* often remained intact, now owned by freedmen. The *Monumentum Statiliorum* and a number of passages in the *Digest* attest to the large numbers of "underslaves" (*vicarii*), previously owned through servile *peculia,*[163] who after manumission of the superior slave (*servus ordinarius*) continued to be owned by that former *servus ordinarius*, now their newly freed master. They too continued to live in the home of the *pater familias* who had manumitted the superior slave.[164] "The slave-shopkeeper and the slave-shipmaster upon manumission would remain in the same position as he had been before manumission" (Kirschenbaum 1987: 142).[165] Individuals who had managed a business as slaves were expected as freedmen to continue to administer the operation in the same fashion as previously.[166] Slaves who had been working on financial matters continued, now "liberated," to do the same work as in their servile past.[167] Managers of farm properties (*vilici*, "bailiffs") are attested as expected to continue in their positions after manumission.[168] The *Digest* offers many examples of freedmen continuing to act on behalf of their former masters—a *libertus* running a money-lending business belonging to a *pater familias* (*Digest* 14.3.20

162. "(T)he freeborn son was viewed as entirely different from the freed father" (Mouritsen 2011: 269). Cf. Treggiari 1969: 229–236; Duff [1928] 1958: 50–51. Strikingly, in the Western Empire the male offspring of freedmen were eligible to hold, and did hold in large numbers, local magistracies, an honor legally prohibited to freedmen themselves. See D'Arms 1981: 134–140; Pleket 1971, esp. 244; Garnsey 1975.

163. Cf. Chapter 1, pp. 36–37.

164. CIL VI.9102. Cf. *Dig.* 15.1.4.6 (Pomponius); 15.1.6 (Celsus); 15.1.7.4 (Ulp.).

165. Cf. Schiller 1971: 25: "The freedman is found carrying on the same enterprises as when he was a slave."

166. *Dig.* 26.7.58.pr. (Scaeuola): qui negotiationem per Pamphilum et Diphilum prius seruos, postea libertos exercebat, suo testamento eos tutores reliquit et cauit, ut negotium eodem more exerceretur, quo se uiuo exercebatur.

167. *Dig.* 34.3.12 (Iulian): manumitted accountant (Erotem manumisit in eodem actu habuit rationesque subscripsit etc.). *Dig.* 14.3.19.1 (Pap.): manumitted banker (si dominus, qui seruum institorem apud mensam pecuniis accipiendis habuit, post libertatem quoque datam idem per libertum negotium exercuit, uaritate status non mutabitur periculi causa).

168. *Dig.* 40.5.41.15 (Scaeu.): herede filio suo ex asse instituto libertatem dedit in haec uerba: 'December dispensator meus, Seuerus uilicus et Uictorina uilica Seueri contubernalis in annos octo liberi sunto: quos in ministerio filii mei esse uolo. Cf. *Dig.* 32.97 (Paul.); 32.41.2 (Scaeu.).

[Scaevola]), a *libertus* buying purple in Asia for his principal (*Digest* 3.5.30[31] pr. [Papinian]), a freedman undertaking to arrange a loan on behalf of a principal, seemingly on a "one-off" basis.[169] Even the fictional Trimalchio, on withdrawing from personal business activity, began to make loans through his freedmen.[170] A passage in the *Digest* alludes to the frequency with which overseas businesses and operations in locations distant from the principals' residence are operated independently *per servos atque libertos* ("through slaves and freedmen").[171] Freedmen and slaves together are now known to have operated the bank of C. Sulpicius Faustus.[172] Even earlier, Cicero alludes to partnerships (*societates)* in which principals' slaves and freedmen (and other free people) worked together in commercial undertaking.[173] Slaves and former slaves function as *procuratores*, that is, as supervisors of family operations "at the top of the domestic hierarchy."[174] These positions were originally held exclusively by slaves of the establishment's owner, but by imperial times the highest positions in the greatest houses were usually filled by *liberti*.[175] Even during the Republican period, Cicero's slave Marcus Tullius Tiro famously after manumission continued to represent his former master

169. *Dig.* 3.5.30[31] pr. (Pap.). Cf. Aubert 1994: 109, n. 282.

170. Manum de tabula. Sustuli me de negotiatione et coepi <per> libertos faenare. et sane nolentem me negotium meum agere.... Petron. *Satyr.* 76.9–10. On the emendation *per*, see Buecheler 1862; Friedländer 1891; Müller 1995; all *ad loc.* Tran (who terms the emendation *per* "contestable") suggests that the mechanism for such lending might have been through loans to a principal's freedmen who would then relend the funds to others [2013/14: Part III]).

171. *Dig.* 40.9.10 (Gaius): quod frequenter accidit his, qui transmarinas negotiationes et aliis regionibus, quam in quibus ipsi morantur, per seruos atque libertos exercent: quod saepe, adtritis istis negotiationibus longo tempore, id ignorant. . . . (discussing the multitude of insolvencies caused through manumission of slaves by owners unaware of the precariousness of their own financial situation).

172. TPSulp. 87, 48. Cf. Verboven 2000: 164.

173. Cic. *Parad. Stoic.* 46: cum seruis, cum libertis, cum clientibus societates. Cf. ibid.: dimissiones libertorum ad defaenerandas diripiendasque prouincias.

174. Mouritsen 2011: 217. On *procuratores* and their vital role in the Roman economy, see Aubert 1994: 183–186; Schäfer 1998, esp. 181–193; Verboven 2002: 338–339. Cf. Pflaum 1950.

175. Serrao 1947: 1–9; Watson 1961: 6–9; Kaser 1970: 348–349; Angelini 1971; Behrends 1971; Aubert 1994: 107; Guarino 1997: 336. Often, according to Hermann-Otto (2001), slave *procuratores* had originally been free men (*ingenui*) who had sold themselves into servitude. (On such self-sale, see Chapter 3, section on "Entrepreneurial Self-Enslavement.") Verboven (2002: 239–260) argues that under the Republic at least some procurators were free men acting pursuant to reciprocal obligations undertaken because of friendship (*amicitia*), although he does recognize that even at this time "most private *procuratores* that are attested epigraphically were freedmen" (2002: 254). See, for example, CIL VI. 7370, 9449, 9831, 9833, 9834. Cf. Gaius, *Inst.* 1.19: iusta causa manumissionis . . . seruum procuratoris habendi gratia . . . manumittat.

in commercial dealings and continued to dominate household operation.[176] Petronius's Trimalchio, former slave now wealthy freedman, co-heir to his former master's personal senatorial-level estate (*patrimonium laticlavium*), explicitly refers to his new fortune as the "maturation" (*fermentum*) of his *peculium*.[177]

How mechanically did legal fiction enable such *liberti* lawfully to act as agents for principals in a system that limited juridically effective representation of a free man exclusively to the *pater familias*'s slaves and sons[178] who, under the *actiones institoria*, *exercitoria*, and *de peculio*, were alone granted the power to incur liabilities and to obtain rights on behalf of their principal?[179] If sons and slaves alone could legally represent the *pater familias*, then the freedman—no longer a slave—must be seen as a son. Accordingly, "(t)he former slave became a son 'sine natura,' while the (former) owner took the place of the (absent) father . . . the release from servitude merely entailed the transition from one familial role to another."[180] The patron became "so to speak, a legal father."[181] And in a remarkable development, the law came to recognize a so-called action "quasi-*institoria*" to give this new "quasi-son" the capacity to enter into arrangements legally binding on the *pater familias*.

Harper (2011: 121) finds that in the late imperial period "procurators were freedmen or still slaves."

176. See Cic. *Fam*. 16.4.3, 16.19, 16.24.

177. Petron. *Satyr*. 76: coheredem me Caesari fecit, et accepi patrimonium laticlauium . . . .hoc loco Fortunata rem piam fecit: omne enim aurum suum, omnia uestimenta uendidit et mi centum aureos in manu posuit. hoc fuit peculii mei fermentum. Significantly, he does not refer to his wealth as his *peculium*. While our sources, as discussed above, sometimes include freedmen inexactly within the grouping of *serui*, wealthy slaves uniformly hold their assets within, and are identified through, their *peculia*—a fund by definition and by practice available only to slaves. See, for example, CIL I² 3391, CIL XI 6314 (= ILS 3581): Faustus Uersenni Publii seruus Priapum et templum de suo peculio faciendum curauit. Cf. above, this chapter, pp. 51–56; Chapter 1, pp. 27–28.

178. Even without the ability legally to bind a principal, free persons could, in limited contexts, undertake matters on behalf of others. Juridical issues arising from such activity tended to be treated within the law of "mandate" (*mandatum*). See Chapter 1, p. 40, n. 102.

179. See Chapter 1, pp. 40–41.

180. Mouritsen 2011: 147. *Dig*. 37.15.9 (Ulp.): liberto et filio semper honesta et sancta persona patris ac patroni uideri debet. "The relation of patron to freedman approximated to that of father to son" (Duff [1928] 1958: 36). Cf. Veyne 1961: 221–223; Verboven 2011: 96 ("when a childless freedman died intestate, his patron took the place of a father").

181. Duff [1928] 1958: 49. Fabre (1981: 94) alludes to "les rapports avec l'ancien maître, dont l'affranchi est comme la créature, sur le plan socio-juridique, de la même manière que le *filius familias* est celle de son père."

During the Republican period the *actio institoria* had been created as one of the "Supplemental Procedures" (*actiones adiecticiae qualitatis)* that had innovatively made *patres familias* legally responsible for liabilities incurred (and advantages obtained) through their dependents, facilitating the representation of principals by sons and slaves in response to the then nascent commercial reality of complex businesses operated by family members.[182] But in the imperial period the *actio institoria*—inaugurated at a time when all *institores* were actual family members[183]—did not address or resolve the legal issues arising from the phenomenon of the *procurator*, generally a freedman, functioning during the Principate as the overall director of a master's sometimes vast domains or of a master's complex of affiliated businesses, rather than as the manager (*institor*) of a business owned by the master. Not an *institor*, the *procurator* was therefore irrelevant to the *actio institoria*,[184] because as *liberti*—neither slaves of, nor biological relatives of the *pater familias*—these *procuratores* were ontologically not family members. Yet—as we have seen—realistically they were quasi-family members (and were sometimes even conflated with the family's slaves who under Roman law and social understanding were members of the family [*familia*][185]). The great Papinian (who flourished in the early third century CE) was the first jurisprudent, to our knowledge, to have seen that a fictitious (that is, "virtual," in Latin *quasi*) process offered a solution to the legal and ethical issues raised by the quasi-familial position of a *libertus* acting as chief steward of family wealth and enterprise. And so Papinian proceeded to fashion the *actio quasi-institoria* (sometimes referred to as an *actio ad exemplum institoriae,* or simply as an *actio utilis*).[186]

In Book 31 of his treatise on the Praetor's Edict, Papinian posits a situation in which a *dominus* had authorized (*mandaverat*) his *procurator* to borrow money, with repayment guaranteed by a third party. This third-party surety subsequently had been found liable (to the creditor). Under strict application of prior law, the *dominus* would often not have been obligated to reimburse

---

182. See Chapter 1, pp. 40–42.

183. See Chapter 1, n. 107.

184. In fact, *procuratores* might even appoint *institores* to manage businesses owned by a *dominus*: see *Dig.* 14.3.5.18 (Ulp.); 14.3.6 (Paul.).

185. For slaves as members of the *familia* (family or household), see Chapter 1, n. 97.

186. On the *actio quasi-institoria*, see especially Rabel 1913; Benke 1988. Cf. Burdese 1971; Hamza 1980: 212, 227, n. 238; Fercia 2008: 244–245.

the guarantor because a free *procurator* could not legally bind another free man (here the *dominus*). Furthermore such a *procurator* (stricto sensu not usually a family member because, by the third century CE, generally not a slave) could not subject a master to one of the *actiones adiecticiae qualitatis*, nor was the master liable to an *actio institoria* (since the *dominus* had not commissioned [*praeposuerat*] the *procurator* as an operating manager [*institor*] of a business owned by the master). For this quasi-family member, however, Papinian devises an action *quasi-institoria*, reasoning that the master seems *virtually* to have commissioned (*quasi praeposuisse*) the *procurato*r to enter into the loan: therefore an action *quasi-institoria* (*virtually* an *actio institoria*) must be granted to the guarantor against the *dominus*.[187] Papinian insisted, in a separate case, that this action should be available against the *dominus* even if the *procurator* was able from his own funds to repay a guarantor and had promised to do so.[188] Similarly, in Papinian's opinion, this quasi-action was available against a *dominus* whose *procurator* had sold a property, and had given to the buyer a warranty (*cautio*) against eviction, but only if the owner had actually authorized (*mandavit)* the sale.[189] The action *quasi-institoria* could be invoked to resolve various situations where a *dominus* might otherwise inequitably avoid responsibility because of his employment of a *procurator* who as a free man was not able legally to bind his principal (the *dominus*). By analogy to the *actio quasi-institoria*, a creditor or a guarantor could sue the principal himself whenever a freedman acting as *procurator* had been authorized to borrow funds and to obtain a guarantor—even if the *dominus* had never actually received the money that had been borrowed and/or guaranteed.[190]

187. *Dig.* 17.1.10.5 (Ulp.): Idem Papinianus libro eodem refert fideiussori condemnato, qui ideo fideiussit, quia dominus procuratori mandauerat, ut pecuniam mutuam acciperet, utilem actionem dandam quasi institoriam, quia et hic quasi praeposuisse eum mutuae pecuniae accipiendae uideatur.

188. *Dig.* 14.3.19.pr.: in eum, qui mutuis accipiendis pecuniis procuratorem praeposuit, utilis ad exemplum institoriae dabitur actio: quod aeque faciendum erit et si procurator soluendo sit, qui stipulanti pecuniam promisit. Burdese (1971: 64) asserts, unconvincingly in my opinion, that quod aeque etc. is a post-classical interpolation.

189. *Dig.* 19.1.13.25 (Ulp.): si procurator uendiderit et cauerit emptori, quaeritur, an domino uel aduersus dominum actio dari debeat. et Papinianus libro tertio responsorum putat cum domino ex empto agi posse utili actione ad exemplum institoriae actionis, si modo rem uendendam mandauit. On the authenticity of this passage, see Kaser 1974: 196, n. 187.

190. *Dig.* 3.5.30 pr. (Pap.): liberto procuratori mandauit pecuniam accipere mutuam: cuius litteras creditor secutus contraxit et fideiussor interuenit: etiamsi pecunia non sit in rem eius uersa, tamen dabitur in eum negotiorum gestorum actio creditori uel fideiussori, scilicet ad exemplum institoriae actionis. For the reading "liberto procuratori," see Burdese 1971: 75 and Serrao 1971: 831, n. 17.

The *actio quasi-institoria* came to be far-reaching in its commercial applications and far-removed from factual underpinning—available to achieve an equitable result even in the case of enslaved employees clearly not functioning in a managerial role. Thus, Ulpian reports on Labeo's making the *actio quasi-institoria* available against an undertaker whose slave, assigned to clean corpses, had robbed a dead body, even though Labeo recognized that actions for both theft and insult were available.[191] Similarly, equitable principles could be invoked, and actual facts ignored, in the case of slaves confusingly operating more than one business. For example, a creditor had advanced funds to a slave whose master had appointed him to operate an oil business. The *servus* separately was conducting a financial business for which he also was receiving financing. Although the creditor allegedly had advanced funds because of his belief that this loan was to be used in the oil business, the creditor was ultimately unable to establish such utilization and therefore, having exhausted the procedures available to him, could not bring against the slave's owner a further *actio institoria*, which might have asserted that the slave had also been appointed as *institor* for a loan business. In the real legal world, the plaintiff had no remedy. But in the universe of legal fiction (a domain of justice), all was well. The jurisprudent Julian, writing before Papinian's deployment of the all-purpose *actio quasi-institoria*, is forced to invoke an "equitable action" (*actio utilis*) to grant a fresh opportunity at pursuing his case to the creditor who, in the dimension of legal dogma, had exhausted all opportunity.[192] Legal fact is excised; legal fiction prevails.

---

191. *Dig.* 14.3.5.8: (Labeo) ait, si libitinarius seruum pollinctorem habuerit isque mortuum spoliauerit, dandam in eum quasi institoriam actionem, quamuis et furti et iniuriarum actio competeret. Scholars have discussed at length the reasons why a jurisprudent might invoke an action *quasi-institoria*. Was the *actio institoria* unavailable because the errant servant had been assigned the single task of cleaning corpses rather than the management of the totality of the undertaking business? Or was the improper act beyond the scope of the slave's *praepositio* (see Chapter 1, pp. 42–43)? Or did the slave's responsibility not actually involve a business that required management? For further discussion with reference to prior literature, see Benke 1988: 605; Johnston 1995.

192. *Dig.* 14.3.13.pr. (Ulp.): habebat quis seruum merci oleariae praepositum Arelate, eundem et mutuis pecuniis accipiendis: acceperat mutuam pecuniam: putans creditor ad merces eum accepisse egit proposita actione: probare non potuit mercis gratia eum accepisse. licet consumpta est actio nec amplius agere poterit, quasi pecuniis quoque mutuis accipiendis esset praepositus, tamen Iulianus utilem ei actionem competere ait. On this case, see Tran 2014; Johnston 1995: 1518–1519.

3

Opportunity

FROM FREEDOM TO SLAVERY—FROM SLAVERY TO FREEDOM

OFTEN LIVING IN relative poverty, confronting an economic system "rigged" to favor servile enterprise, unavoidably knowledgeable of the flamboyant wealth and flaunted prosperity of those freed slaves who in servitude had accumulated property through their *peculia*—and after manumission had retained those servile assets—a free Roman might well have envied, and sought to emulate, the skilled *servi* who, through gaining lucrative positions open only to slaves,[1] had "gamed" the system and achieved prosperity otherwise largely unobtainable by free Romans.[2] This chapter discusses the phenomenon of free persons entering voluntarily into slavery, in order to pursue commercial opportunities unavailable to the non-enslaved—and who, after garnering economic success through the Roman institution of the *peculium*, regain their freedom through "self-purchase" with "their own funds" (*suis nummis*), emerging economically and socially enhanced as "freedmen." The cycle is complete: from impoverished freedom to slavery—from slavery to a prosperous freedom.

1. See Chapter 1, pp. 42–45.

2. For the privileging of slave enterprise and the impoverishment of much of the free population, see Chapter 1. For assets taken and retained through their *peculia* by successful slaves, see Chapter 2.

Roman Inequality. Edward E. Cohen, Oxford University Press. © Oxford University Press 2023.
DOI: 10.1093/oso/9780197687345.003.0004

Entrepreneurial Self-Enslavement

Once freed, a freedman immediately lacks even food, and suffers most horrendously. He has been liberated into a slavery far worse than his prior servitude.[3]

—Epictetus, *Dissertations* 35–36

Many actions quite beneficial for others lose their altruistic character because a price is extracted. The merchant benefits cities; the doctor, those who are ill; the slave-dealer, those who are for sale. But these benefactors receive no gratitude, because in helping others, they are also helping themselves.[4]

—Seneca, *De Beneficiis* IV. 13.3

Roman sources abundantly attest to the process through which free men (citizens or not) were able voluntarily to sell themselves into slavery.[5] Yet scholars of Roman history have largely glossed over or even ignored self-sale, even in discussions of the sources of supply of slaves.[6] Scholars of Roman law have been reluctant to lend credence to the juridical evidence for self-sale. The only English-language monographs on the "Roman Law of Slavery"—Buckland's magisterial tome of 1908 and Watson's more selective analysis of 1987—both discuss some of the multitudinous testimonia

---

3. εἶτα ἀπηλευθέρωται ... καὶ εὐθὺς μὲν οὐκ ἔχων ποῖ φάγῃ ... πάσχει τὰ δεινότατα ... ἐμπέπτωκεν εἰς δουλείαν πολὺ τῆς προτέρας χαλεπωτέραν.

4. Multa quae summam utilitatem aliis adferunt, pretio gratiam perdunt. Mercator urbibus prodest, medicus aegris, mango uenalibus; sed omnes isti, quia ad alienum commodum pro suo ueniunt, non obligant eos, quibus prosunt. On Roman slave dealers and their business activities, see Boese 1973; Harris 1980b.

5. A sampling: Dio Khrys. 15.23; Petron. *Satyr.* 57.4; Clement, *Corinth.* 1.55; Gaius *Inst.* 1.119–121; *Just. Inst.* 1.3.4; *Dig.* 1.5.5.1; *Dig.* 1.5.21; *Dig.* 4.4.9.4; *Dig.* 21.1.17.12; *Dig.* 28.3.6.5; *Dig.* 40.12.4; *Dig.* 40.12.7; *Dig.* 40.12.23.pr.; *Dig.* 40.12.40; *Dig.* 40.13.1.pr.; *Dig.* 40.13.3; *Dig.* 40.14.2.pr.; *Dig.* 48.19.14; *CTh.* 4.8.6; *Cod.* 7.16.16; *Cod.* 7.18.1; *Cod.*18.1.pr.

6. "Most scholars play [self-sale] down as a source of slaves" (Hunt 2018: 46). Veyne 2001: 247–280 (reprint of Ramin and Veyne 1981) is the first and (to this date) only detailed philological and juridical treatment of self-sale: "eine detaillierte Auseinandersetzung mit deren Quellenbasis fehlt" (Gamauf 2017). For other references to self-sale, see Hermann-Otto 2013: 65; 2001: 171–184; Harris 1999: 73; Söllner 2005: 60, 2012. Cf. Silver 2011 and 2016(a), below n. 12. A few other scholars, although acknowledging the existence of evidence for self-sale of free people into slavery, treat the practice as aberrational (errantly entered into by a few persons "ignorant of the law" [Mouritsen 2011: 10]). Hunt 2018: 47: "such self-sales cannot have been significant numerically." Similarly: Glancy 2002: 80–85.

confirming the practice of voluntary enslavement, but both deny that Roman law recognized the right of free persons willfully to enter into servitude.[7] Buckland concedes that "the general rule is that any *liber homo* over twenty years of age who knowingly allows himself to be sold as a slave, in order to share the price, is enslaved," but such enslavement, for Buckland, is merely a penalty for fraud: "it is essential that the buyer have been deceived: if he knew, then there is no bar to the claim of liberty."[8] Although Watson accepts "the rule, stated to be peculiarly Roman, that a free person who allowed himself to be sold as a slave in order to share in the price does become a slave," he too adopts Buckland's interpretation that "the Roman rule is (merely) an economical way of inhibiting frauds" that might be perpetrated on buyers (1987: 9). Watson even provides a vignette—unsupported by Roman evidence (which does not exist)—vivifying the purported scam: "A free man would act as if he were held as a slave and be sold by a friend who would disappear from the scene. A short time later the supposed slave would be 'recognized' by another who would claim his liberty, and the friends, including the supposed slave, would share in the price" (Watson 1987: 9). Accepting the conclusion of Buckland and Watson, the prevailing view among Romanists is that "technically at least a Roman citizen could not sell himself into slavery."[9] Crook, however, noticing Buckland's uncharacteristic uncertainty about his own conclusion denying legal validity to

---

7. Buckland [1908] 1970: 427–436; Watson 1987: 9–10 (cf. Watson 1974: 31 ff.).

8. Buckland [1908] 1970: 428, citing *Cod.* 7.18.1 and *Cod.* 7.16.5.1(Latin text, below nn. 72 and 73), passages that actually focus not on fraud but on payment as requisite for a legally effective entry into voluntary servitude. Although in 7.18 the person not compensated (and who was therefore entitled to regain his freedom) had not been forthcoming about his free status when he permitted himself to be enslaved (dissimulata condicione sua distrahi se passus est), a number of passages in Title 40 of the *Digest* show that slavery is not vitiated by a buyer's actual knowledge or ignorance of a putative slave's free status: see *Dig.* 40.12.7.pr.-2; *Dig.*40.12.14; *Dig.*40.12.33 (all Ulp.), discussed below in nn. 74–75 and related text, and at pp. 98–99 below.

9. Knapp 2011: 132. Cf. Melluso 2000: 27–29. Some Romanists (including Veyne 2001: 262; Gamauf 2017) reject self-sale as violative of the rule that "a private agreement cannot make a person someone else's slave or freedman" (conuentio priuata neque seruum quemquam neque libertum alicuius facere potest: *Dig.* 40.12.37 [Callistratus]). But this provision should be understood only as nullifying private pacts that purport to contravene public bestowal of freedom on an individual, as in the case of manumission lawfully realized (see Hermann-Otto 2004: 177 and n. 24 thereto; Silver 2011: 78–79; 2018: 18). Self-sale, in fact, was itself unequivocally authorized by Roman law (see discussion below, pp. 10–11). On provisions in modern, Roman, and Greek public law invalidating aspects of private arrangements ("invalidity clauses"), see Dimopoulou 2014: 249–250; Cohen 2014(a); Velissaropoulos 2011: 220–222; Quadrato 1983: 79–107.

self-sale,[10] concludes that "one cannot be sure" whether a free Roman might "legitimately sell himself so as make himself irrevocably a slave."[11]

This paradox of academic negation (or minimization) of affirmative evidence for self-enslavement reflects, in my opinion, an implicit assumption that no free person would willingly choose servitude.[12] But in the context of an economy that impoverished many free persons and of a legal system that privileged servile enterprise, and within a social system that offered urban slaves "a high rate of social advancement, which was often much greater than that of the freeborn proleteriate,"[13] it should not be inconceivable, or even surprising, that some free individuals possessing skill and/or ambition appear willingly to have opted for a slavery that offered the possibility of accumulating wealth, the expectation of future manumission, and the retention after liberation of a substantial portion of the assets that individuals had accumulated during servitude. In contrast, persons moving from slavery to freedom did have to worry about survival itself. A philosopher, resident at Rome in the late first and early second centuries CE, himself originally a slave, asserted that "once freed, a freedman immediately lacks even food, and suffers most horrendously. He has been liberated into a slavery far worse than his prior servitude."[14] Similar sentiments are expressed in Roman comedy, and even in epigrammatic poetry: a slave in Plautus's *Epidicus*, for example, worries about proffered freedom, fearing inability even to feed himself;[15] Martial extolls slaves' freedom from the financial worries of their masters.[16]

---

10. "Buckland discussed the problem with less than his usual magisterial confidence" (Crook 1967: 299, n. 114).

11. Crook 1967: 61. In conflict with other economic historians (including Engerman 1973), Silver advances economic arguments in support of voluntary servitude (2011: especially 74, 89–95; cf. Silver 2016[a]: 72–75). McGinn, in his study of "the economy of prostitution in the Roman World," accepts an individual's right "under Roman law (to) sell oneself into slavery with attendant prostitution" (2004: 57).

12. Cf. Rio 2012: 661: "[Contemporary scholars] find it incomprehensible that anyone should ever wish to part with personal freedom, whatever the price . . . modern ways of thinking about self-sale (have) had a deeply distorting effect on modern scholarship on this topic." Scheidel, who concedes that "genuine self-sales may arguably have occurred," nonetheless assumes that "the quantitative weight of such events was presumably minimal" (2011: 300).

13. Weaver 1972: 1.

14. Epictetus, *Dissertations* 35–36: see above in this chapter, n. 3, for the original Greek text.

15. 721–730, 726: "nouo liberto opus est quod pappet." Cf. Plaut. *Men.* 1149; *Capt.* 119–120 and 270–273; *Rud.* 1218–1222. Similarly, *Cas.* 293: liber si sim, meo periclo uiuam; nunc uiuo tuo.

16. *Epigrams* 9.92, line 1: Quae mala sunt domini, quae serui commoda . . . etc.

To allay this anticipated harsh poverty of free inhabitants, a number of masters on manumitting slaves provided them with a continuing "annuity"—but usually at levels barely providing subsistence, intended to deal "with harsh economic reality: a grant of liberty . . . could spell privation if not accompanied by the pittance of a small annuity."[17] No wonder then that "for some poor people, the life of a slave appeared better than that of a free man" (Temin 2013: 132).

In fact, voluntary self-sale into slavery is well-attested in late classical antiquity and in the Middle Ages,[18] and for the Byzantine Empire (Rotman 2004: 238–241). In early modern Russia, there is some evidence that "scions of the important, genealogically ranked families . . . sold themselves into slavery" (Hellie 1982: 36). In North America, Galenson (1984: 1) reports that "between one-half and two-thirds of all white immigrants to the British colonies between the Puritan migration of the 1630s and the Revolution came under indenture"—in effect "as voluntary slaves" (Silver 2016[a]: 76).

For the classical period at Rome, likewise, much evidence confirms voluntary enslavement's juridical and economic significance—and illustrates how Roman jurisprudents struggled to reconcile free persons' right to choose servitude with the law's protection of minors who lacked juridical capacity to enslave themselves. In this context, the law was attentive both to the protection of good-faith purchasers of apparently enslaved persons as well as to the rights of free persons involuntarily forced into slavery. Some free persons may actually have been parties to fraud (*dolus malus*) and therefore deprived of their freedom as punishment (*capitis deminutio maxima*)—although Ulpian makes clear that *dolus malus* does not encompass mere failure to clarify one's free status at the time that one acquiesces to sale into slavery.[19] In any event, the fact that some initially free individuals may have been estopped (I actually mean estopped, a result different from merely "impeded") by their own

17. Frier 1993: 229. On these annuities, see Boyer 1965: 342–355; Champlin 1991: 133–134; Frier 1993, esp. 229–230.

18. Rio 2016: 42–45; 2012, passim.

19. *Dig.* 40.12.14: rectissime praetor calliditati eorum, qui, cum se liberos scirent, dolo malo passi sunt se pro seruis uenum dari, occurrit. . . . Dolo autem non eum fecisse accipimus, qui non ultro instruxit emptorem, sed qui decepit. Such fraud might encompass a multitude of scams ranging, for example, from a preconceived claim for damages for mistreatment of a free individual purposefully presented as a slave (akin to the action for *hybris* available in Classical Athens for [mis]treatment of a free person in the induced belief that he was a slave [below, pp. 15–17]) through a plot to place the putative slave into a position providing opportunity to appropriate the buyer's property), etc.

wrongful behavior from a return to free status (in Roman terms, denied the right to assert their freedom, *proclamare in libertatem*) does not justify modern scholars' denying the existence of, or minimizing the importance of, the Roman institution of self-enslavement.

Evidence for Self-Enslavement as a Roman Institution

Voluntary servitude is treated in juridical and literary sources as a fundamental Roman configuration. Writing in the Early Empire, Dio Chrysostomus notes the many free men who had voluntarily entered into servitude."[20] In his humorous second-century CE sketch *On Those Employed for Pay*, Lucian critiques voluntary slavery (in Greek, *ethelodouleia*), explaining that many highly educated and skilled individuals embrace it to avoid the poverty and hunger otherwise afflicting them: high pay and a pleasant life entice them to surrender their freedom, unwisely (in Lucian's opinion).[21] At the famous, although fictional, banquet hosted by Petronius's Trimalchio, a rich freedman attributes the origin of his wealth to his decision, as a free man, to opt for voluntary slavery.[22] During the reign of Domitian (95–98), Clement, bishop of Rome, providing examples of altruism among non-Christians, cites the many persons who have sold themselves into slavery in order that they might support their families through the proceeds generated by the sale.[23] Juvenal elliptically alludes to the "men who offer themselves for sale under the spear-sign of ownership" (3.33).[24] Labeo and Caecilius confirm the existence of a specific venue where people were accustomed to congregate in order to seek self-sale

---

20. *On Slavery and Freedom II* (15).23: μύριοι δήπου ἀποδίδονται ἑαυτοὺς ἐλεύθεροι ὄντες, ὥστε δουλεύειν κατὰ συγγραφὴν ἐνίοτε ἐπ' οὐδενὶ τῶν μετρίων, ἀλλ' ἐπὶ πᾶσι τοῖς χαλεπωτάτοις. Cf. ibid. §13.

21. ἐπὶ τὸν τοιοῦτον βίον ἀφικνοῦνταί τινες . . . οὕτο γὰρ ἂν αὐτοῖς ἡ ἀπολογία προαναιροῖτο καὶ ἡ πρώτη ὑπόθεσις τῆς ἐθελοδουλείας, οἱ μὲν δὴ πολλοὶ τὴν πενίαν καὶ τὴν τῶν ἀναγκαίων χρείαν προθέμενοι ἱκανὸν τοῦτο προκάλυμμα (36.5). On the need to read Lucian not for "basic historic information but (for) the second-century Zeitgeist," see Bozia 2015: 13 and passim.

22. *Satyr.* 57.4: 'quare ergo seruiuisti?' quia ipse me dedi in seruitutem . . . et nunc spero me *sic* uiuere ut nemini iocus sim. . . . glebulas emi, lamellulas paraui, uiginti uentres pasco et canem . . . mille denarios pro capite solui. Although Gamauf (2017) finds voluntary self-sale into slavery during the High Empire to be "plausible" (2017: 3. Themenstellung), he argues that there was no legal basis for such a phenomenon as early as the first century CE (the putative time of composition of the *Satiricon* attributed to Petronius).

23. First Letter to the Corinthians, §55: πολλοὶ ἑαυτοὺς παρέδωκαν εἰς δουλείαν, καὶ λαβόντες τὰς τιμὰς ἑτέρους ἐψώμισαν.

24. Translation: Braund 2004, s.v. (praebere caput domina uenale sub hasta).

into slavery.[25] Plautus identifies the Tuscan neighborhood as the area where men sell themselves.[26]

Voluntary self-enslavement is identified in Roman legal materials as a principal source of unfree status. The First Title of the *Digest* specifies "slavery by choice" as one of only three channels into servitude (the others being hostile capture and birth to a mother who is herself enslaved): under Roman law (*ius civile*) any free person over twenty years of age could allow himself to come into someone else's ownership by "sharing in the purchase price."[27] Justinian's *Institutes* offers the same tripartite source of enslavement—by capture, by birth, and whenever "a free man over twenty years of age has allowed himself to be sold in order to share in the purchase price."[28] In describing the Roman formulation of sale by "mancipation," a ceremonial and symbolic but efficacious process, Gaius's *Institutes* establishes that free persons (as well as already enslaved individuals) could be bought through this mechanism.[29] But freedmen's obligations to their former masters complicated their ability to sell themselves into fresh slavery: a patron without knowledge of the sale could ultimately seek to have it annulled.[30] Soldiers, however, were absolutely forbidden to enter into self-chosen servitude:[31] since free status was requisite for

25. *Dig.* 21.1.17.12: quaeritur, si quis in asylum confugerit aut eo se conferat, quo solent uenire qui se uenales postulant, an fugitiuus sit. . . . Cf. Silver 2009: 246–247; 2014: 577–578; Ramin and Veyne [1981] 2001: 269–270. On the physical parameters of Roman slave markets, see Fentress et al. 2005: 180–240; Trümper 2009.

26. *Curc.* 482: in Tusco uico, ibi sunt homines qui ipsi sese uenditant. This might, however, be a reference solely to men selling themselves in a prostitutional context (an interpretation argued against in Silver 2014). Cf. Strong 2016: 160 (who sees the Tuscan area as "a center of Roman male prostitution)."

27. 1.5.5.5 (Marcianus): serui autem in dominium nostrum rediguntur aut iure ciuili aut gentium: iure ciuili, si quis se maior uiginti annis ad pretium participandum uenire passus est: iure gentium serui nostri sunt, qui ab hostibus capiuntur aut qui ex ancillis nostris nascuntur. See Wieling 1999.

28. 1.3.4: Serui autem aut nascuntur aut fiunt. nascuntur ex ancillis nostris: fiunt aut iure gentium, id est ex captiuitate, aut iure ciuili, ueluti cum homo liber maior uiginti annis ad pretium participandum sese uenumdari passus est.

29. 1.119–120: est mancipatio . . . imaginaria quaedam uenditio . . . eaque res ita agitur . . . aes tenens ita dicit: HUNC EGO HOMINEM EX IURE QUIRITIUM MEUM ESSE AIO . . . eo modo et seruiles et liberae personae mancipantur.

30. *Dig.* 40.12.4 (Gaius): patrono conceditur pro libertate liberti litigare, si eo ignorante libertus uenire se passus est.

31. *Dig.* 48.19.14 (Macer): si miles . . . in seruitutem se uenire passus est, capite puniendum Menander scribit. Cf. Ramin and Veyne [1981] 2001: 250, n. 16.

service in the Roman army,[32] voluntary enslavement was incompatible with military obligations.

Protection of Minors

Legal recognition of compensated self-imposed servitude did present societal and juridical challenge. Free minors lacked the capacity lawfully to choose slavery, but (in the absence at Rome of systematic registration of births and dates of birth[33]) determination of age was often uncertain. According to Papinian, a self-enslaved free man younger than twenty at the time of opting for slavery was entitled to have his servitude set aside—in contravention of the general rule that the law would not nullify servitude once the volunteer had received a share of the purchase price:[34] when a free man (or woman[35]) had entered voluntarily into slavery and had received payment therefor, he (or she) lost the legal right to escape slavery through assertion of free status (in Latin, *proclamatio in libertatem*), a procedure otherwise available to free persons who had been improperly deprived of their liberty.[36] Nevertheless, under a ruling by Constantine in 323 CE (preserved in the Theodosian Code),

32. *Dig.* 49.16.11 (Marcian); Dig. 48.19.14 (Macer); *CTh.* 7.13.8; CPL 102; Plin. *Ep.* 10.29–30. Conversely, a free man's evasion of military service was punished by enslavement: see Cic. *Pro Caec.* 34.99. Cf. Buckland [1908] 1970: 401. (Silver 2016b: 205 argues that the Roman army did, in fact, utilize large numbers of slaves but only for functions not combat-related).

33. From the time of Augustus, a form of "birth certificate" was known and could be used by individuals, but no standardized cataloguing was ever achieved, nor were such filings legally requisite or determinative. See Schulz 1942–1943; Geraci 2001–2002: 675–696; Sanchez-Moreno Ellart 2002, 2004.

34. *Dig.* 4.4.9.4: Papinianus ait, si maior annis uiginti, minor uiginti quinque se in seruitutem uenire patiatur, id est si pretium participatus est, non solere restitui. . . . The reference in Papinian's rule to a "person under the age of 25" reflects the fact that "a person under the age of 25 has in most cases a right of *restitutio in integrum*, but not in this case" (Buckland [1908] 1970: 428). On the critical juridical importance of the volunteer slave's actual "participation in the price" paid for cession of his liberty, see below, pp. 97 ff.

35. *Dig.* 40.13.3 (Pomp.): eis, qui se passi sint uenire, ad libertatem proclamandi licentiam denigari. Quaero, an et ad eos, qui ex mulieribus, quae se passae sint uenire, nascuntutur, ita senatus consulta pertinent? See also *Cod.* 7.16.16 (Latin text below at n. 45).

36. *Dig.* 40.14.2 (Saturninus): qui se uenire passus esset maiorem, scilicet ut pretium ad ipsum perueniret, prohibendum de libertate contendere diuus Hadrianus constituit. Cf. *Dig.* 40.13.3 (text set forth in preceding note), 40.12.23.pr. (Paul.) (si usum fructum tibi uendidero liberi hominis pretium participantis). Even slaves were protected under the lex Fabia from being held or sold by someone other than their master: lege Fabia tenetur, qui ciuem Romanum ingenuum libertinumue seruumue alienum celauerit uendiderit uinxerit comparauerit (*Collatio legum Mosaicarum et Romanarum* 14.2.1, in Riccobono et al., eds. [1940–1943] 1964: II, 577).

a free person unlawfully sold into slavery as a minor by his father was not precluded from obtaining freedom on maturity even when he had as an adult undertaken a managerial role (*actum administravit*) for his putative master.[37] (Payment for voluntary entrance into bondage did not have to be received in cash: recompense might be provided through the volunteer's obtaining of a key position [*ad actum gerendum*] that might facilitate the accumulation of servile assets through a *peculium*.[38]) Similarly, under a further ruling by Constantine, recognition of a free individual's free status is not precluded, even in old age, even when as a minor he had been raised as a supposed slave and as an adult had accepted without protest his sale to a new master for whom he had undertaken an executive function (*actu administrato*): ignorance of his true situation vitiated his apparent acceptance of sale into slavery, and nullified his acceptance of a post that, under other circumstances, would have constituted sufficient payment for his surrender of liberty.[39] Freedmen (*libertini*) likewise were entitled to restoration of free status if their original manumission had occurred before they reached the age of fourteen, but they had remained in servitude, not fully cognizant of their liberation,[40] even in cases where, as adults, motivated by desire for profit (*quaestus*), they had accepted fresh sale into slavery. But even under these circumstances, voluntary assumption of servitude would be legally binding if the newly self-enslaved individual had actually possessed full knowledge of his free status prior to participating for personal financial advantage in a (re)sale into slavery.[41]

---

37. *CTh.* 4.8.6.pr.-1: libertati a maioribus tantum impensum est, ut patribus, quibus ius uitae in liberos necisque potestas permissa est, eripere libertatem non liceret. Si quisquam minor uenumdatus actum maior administrauit, quoniam minoris emptio scientiam non obligat, eum ad libertatem uenientem emptionis actusque a maiore administrati praescriptio non tenebit.

38. *Dig.* 28.3.6.5: irritum fit testamentum, quotiens ipsi testatori aliquid contigit, puta si . . . maior annis uiginti uenum se dari passus sit ad actum gerendum pretiumve participandum. For the importance and income-generating potential of posts available exclusively or largely to slaves such as *dispensator* or *procurator*, see Chapter 1, pp. 43–45; Chapter 2, pp. 69–70, 77–79, this chapter, n. 2.

39. *CTh.* 4.8.6.2: Nec uero ille, qui apud quempiam pro seruo educatur, ac maior effectus uendenti ueluti domino acquieuit actuque administrato iam paene extremam relegit libertatem, (quoniam neque maior effectus originem suam nouerat, neque eam, quam ignorauerat, uenditionem patiens deseruisse iudicandus est) minori similis, eadem emptionis atque actus administrati praescriptione non alligabitur, sed utrique dabitur assertio.

40. For the frequent absence of clear juridical and/or economic distinction between slaves and freedmen ("manumission as legal fiction"), see Chapter 2, section on "The Manumission of Skilled Slaves: Facilitating Commerce through Legal Fiction."

41. *CTh.* 4.8.6.3: Paria (*referencing 4.8.6.2*) etiam in libertinis erunt, qui quaestu quodam in eandem rursus seruitutem relabuntur. sed eorum hac exceptione causa distinguenda est, ut, qui

These rulings by Constantine neatly juxtapose two challenges that arise in virtually all sophisticated legal systems: (1) how to protect the interests of persons who lack juridical capacity to engage in acts entirely lawful for individuals of unimpaired capacity,[42] while (2) guarding against harm to third parties collaterally involved, in good faith, in substantive transactions involving these persons. Efforts to protect minors, for example, from the effects of self-enslavement—and to liberate free persons improperly held in servitude—might, of course, adversely affect persons who inadvertently might have purchased individuals whom they had believed to be properly and lawfully enslaved. As in Constantine's decision regarding *libertini*, Roman law tended to conclude that even victimized minors should be held to their self-enslavement as adults if they had known in maturity (and before subsequent self-enslavement) that they were actually free,[43] provided that they had received personal recompense for their election to enter into servitude. Thus the Emperor Gordian ruled in 239 CE that persons were lawfully entitled to assert their entitlement to liberty (*libertatis defensio*) even if they had permitted themselves to be sold into slavery without revealing their alleged true status (*dissimulata condicione sua*)—but only if they had not personally benefited from sharing in the purchase price.[44] The Emperors Diocletian and Maximian in 293 CE similarly held that a woman's free status could not be adversely affected by the fact that she (although a free person) had been performing work appropriate to a slave (*ministerium*). Despite her behavior—a potential source of confusion about her status—legal force would be denied to a document (of which she had been unaware) purporting to convey her as a slave in a dotal transfer: this was especially so since persons under twenty years of age could not under any condition alter their status and become

---

impuberes intra annum quartum decimum manumissi ac deinceps in seruitio retenti ignorata libertate non utantur, maioresque uenumdati actum gerant, ab assertione non arceantur: quum illi aetati tributae libertatis ignoratio aut obliuio concessa est. qui uero memoria firma uenditioni post factae non nescius innectitur, huius legis beneficio carebit.

42. For various aspects of ancient legal regulation of incapacity, see the essays in Yiftach, ed., 2017, especially articles on guardianship in ancient Egypt (Depauw), in Rome (Du Plessis), and in historical perspective (N. Cohen).

43. Because of Roman practices such as the abandonment of free infants, many persons serving as slaves might have been unaware that they were actually free. In fact, "le cas de *l'homo liber seruiens* était fréquent" (Ramin and Veyne [1981] 2001: 249). On the *liber homo bona fide seruiens*, see Heinemeyer 2013: 159–171; Reggi 1958, esp. 473.

44. *Cod.* 18.1.pr.: Dispar causa est eius, qui dissimulata condicione sua distrahi se passus est, et eius qui pretium participatus est. nam superiori quidem non denegatur libertatis defensio, posteriori autem, et si ciuis Romanus sit et participatus est pretia, libertas denegatur.

slaves rather than free persons (implying, of course, that free *adults* could legally sell themselves into servitude).[45]

Protection against Wrongful Sale of a Free Person

Permitting free persons' voluntary entry into servitude carried the inherent risk that these *liberi* might actually have been forced or tricked into slavery against their will, a wrongful deprivation of liberty absolutely forbidden by Roman law.[46] In the absence of the new slaves' uncompelled consent to, and obtaining of compensation for, loss of liberty, a sale was not valid where buyer and seller both knew, or even where the buyer alone knew, that the person being transferred was in fact free.[47] Improperly enslaved individuals might have been acquired, however, "in good faith" (*bona fide*), by original or subsequent purchasers without protest from victims intimidated into silently accepting their situation—or whose protests might have been disregarded as lacking verisimilitude in a society that did not provide clear external indicia for differentiating persons of slave and free status—a recurrent pattern in communities where slavery was pervasive.

In various "slave economies" over vast periods of human history,[48] coercive unlawful enslavement of free persons has been a recurrent but largely ineradicable outrage. In antebellum North America, slavery was entirely

45. *Cod.* 7.16.16: Si ministerium quasi libera exhibuisti ac te nesciente quasi ancilla in dotem data conscriptum instrumentum est, nihil haec libertati tuae nocere potuerunt, maxime cum te minorem aetate fuisse commemores et placuerit minores uiginti annis nulla ratione mutare statum ac pro liberis seruos fieri, ne ante libertatem inconsulte amittant, quam aliis propter aetatis rationem sine consilio praestare non possunt.

46. *Dig.* 21.2.8 (Julian); *Dig.* 40.12.18 (Ulp,); *Dig.* 40.12.20.4 (Ulp,); *Dig.* 40.15.1.4 (Ulp.).

47. *Dig.* 18.1.70 (Licinnius Rufinus): liberi hominis emptionem contrahi posse plerique existimauerunt, si modo inter ignorantes id fiat. Quod idem placet etiam, si uenditor sciat, emptor autem ignoret. Quod si emptor sciens liberum esse emerit, nulla emptio contrahitur. Cf. *Dig.* 18.1 (Paul.), 4 (Pomponius), 6.pr. (ibid.).

48. For the much disputed description of Rome as a "slave economy" (also termed a "slave society": an entity in which the contribution of a huge number of enslaved persons to the totality of wealth production was so substantial that its overall economy was largely dependent on slaves): see Harper and Scheidel 2018; MacGaw 2014; Joshel 2010: 7–12; Schiavone 2000: 112; Andreau and Descat 2006: 23–27; Verboven 2011: 88 (who argues that "the economy of Roman Italy may be characterized as a 'freedman economy'"). On the large number of freedmen in Italy, see Verboven 2011: 89–92 and Chapter 3 below, section on "Generally High Rates of Manumission?" Despite the ubiquitous presence of unfree individuals in virtually all human communities prior to the nineteenth century CE, few true "slave economies" have actually been attested: Lenski 2018; Hunt 2018: 50–52; Vlassopoulos 2016: 81–85, 95–97; Klees 1998: 1–18.

racially based: the physical appearance of White persons generally and easily protected them from enslavement, but free Blacks—in some slave states a major portion of the non-White population[49]—were not infrequently kidnapped and forced into unlawful servitude.[50] In pre-colonial Africa, sale of slaves to distant locations was utilized to reduce propinquity between a society's master class and the enslaved,[51] ipso facto reducing victims' access to persons who might aid those improperly subjected to servitude. In classical Athens, another slave society, the homogeneous appearance of the various residents of Attica made it difficult to distinguish, by dress or physical characteristic alone, free persons from slaves. Although some modern scholars have sought to find in sepulchral art and obtuse literary allusions markers of attire differentiating slaves from free persons,[52] the author of the satiric *Constitution of the Athenians* insists that at Athens no difference in dress or physical appearance distinguishes citizen, foreigner, or slave,[53] an egalitarianism confirmed—and decried—by Plato.[54] Court presentations routinely posit a similarity of appearance among local inhabitants. During a raid on a citizen's farm, for example, by persons seeking to enforce a judgment, the debtor's son was carried off: he was assumed to be a slave (Demosthenes 47.61). The maltreatment of a free woman, described at Demosthenes 47.58–59, demonstrates the difficulty of differentiating female slaves from other women. Greek sources even tell of a young man who was sent into a neighbor's garden to pluck flowers in the hope

49. This was especially true in Delaware and Maryland: see U.S. Bureau of the Census 1918: 57. On free Blacks in the United States prior to the Civil War, see Berlin 1974; Litwack 1961.

50. See Wilson 1994; Lubet 2010. Cf. von Daack 2012.

51. See Kopytoff and Miers 1977: 13–14.

52. Dalby 2002 finds in literary materials a suggestion that courtesans wore more elaborate clothing (and of finer quality) than other female residents of Attika. But he concedes that in general "their dress was like that of other women" (2002: 119). Bäbler claims that "female slaves on grave-stelai are usually depicted wearing a characteristic long-sleeved dress or '*kandys*,' which seems to have been a kind of 'slave garment'" (2001, n. 5 and related text). Cf. Bäbler 1998: 20–32. But other specialists disagree: "slave figures dress in the same way as the (free) women with whom they appear" (Lewis 2002: 140). Rihll (2011: 50, 54) finds slaves "generally indistinguishable" from citizens "in appearance and, apparently, in demeanour." Davies 1994 sees the iconography of grave stelai as suggestive of the "solidarity" of women and their slaves.

53. Xen. *Ath. Pol.* 1.10: εἰ νόμος ἦν τὸν δοῦλον ὑπό τοῦ ἐλευθέρου τύπτεσθαι . . . . πολλάκις ἂν οἰηθεὶς εἶναι τὸν Ἀθηναῖον δοῦλον ἐπάταξεν ἄν· ἐσθῆτά τε γὰρ οὐδὲν βελτίων ὁ δῆμος αὐτόθι ἢ οἱ δοῦλοι καὶ οἱ μέτοικοι, καὶ τὰ εἴδη οὐδὲν βελτίους εἰσίν. Similarly: Sommerstein 2009: 136.

54. *Rep.* 563b: . . . οἱ ἐωνημένοι καὶ αἱ ἐωνημέναι μηδὲν ἧττον ἐλεύθεροι ὦσι τῶν πριαμένων. ἐν γυναιξὶ δὲ πρὸς ἄνδρας καὶ ἀνδράσι πρὸς γυναῖκας ὅση ἡ ἰσονομία καὶ ἐλευθερία γίγνεται. . . .

that, mistaking the intruder for a slave, the neighbor might strike or bind him and thus become subject to damages for *hybris* (Demosthenes 53.16).

At Rome, likewise, slaves were difficult to differentiate from free persons.[55] There were no legal restrictions on slaves' appearance or demeanor,[56] and both enslaved and free inhabitants (male and female) wore the same everyday garb (tunic and cloak),[57] "creating a degree of homogeneity in external appearance."[58] Because both *liberi* and *servi* often lived at or near levels of bare subsistence—and even that often derived from burdensome toil[59]—their bodies uniformly would have tended to show the effects of inadequate nutrition and of arduous labor. Not surprisingly, then, artistic representations seldom picture individuals who can be identified as slaves on the basis of appearance alone.[60] In real life, for example, it might be difficult to distinguish mistress from female servant.[61] This uniformity generated numerous legal decisions and juridical issues relating to the actions and circumstances of slaves who had been mistakenly believed to be free, and of free people who had been improperly subjected to servitude. For spectacular example, a large

55. *Dig.* 18.1.5 (Paul.): difficile dinosci potest liber homo a seruo. Some modern scholars go further: at Rome "slaves and free were almost impossible to distinguish" (Gamauf 2016: 387). Others, however, claim that some Roman authors (especially Plautus) posit as an ideological trope that "some men and women were unmistakably free and noble by nature," and that accordingly "slaves were unmistakable as a group and . . . . the free were recognizable among themselves" (Stewart 2012: 74): cf. McCarthy 2000: 167–170. For a similar view in North American slave context, see Sypher 1942: 108–121.

56. Sen. *Clem.* 1.24.1: dicta est aliquando a senatu sententia, ut seruos a liberis cultus distingueret; deinde apparuit, quantum periculum immineret, si serui nostri numerare nos coepissent. Cf. Lampridius, *Alex. Seuerus* 27; Morley 2011: 280; Bradley 1994: 95–99; 2011(b): 366. Only in late antiquity did the Theodosian Code slightly reduce slaves' freedom of dress (*CTh.* 14.10.1, 14.10.4). By the fourth century CE, at least a few slaves were subjected to the wearing of collars—coercive necklaces resistant to removal, and naming on a permanently attached pendant tag of bronze the slave and (frequently) his/her owner, and sometimes offering a reward for the slave's return if he/she had left the locus of subjugation (*fugit*). Although relatively rare (and never mentioned in ancient textual sources), a number of these necklaces have survived from late antiquity, but none prior to the fourth century. See Trimble 2016: 449–452, 457–462; Hunt 2018: 203 (Fig. 12.2 and related text). Cf. Thurmond 1994; Binsfeld 2010; Heinen, ed., 2010.

57. See, for example, App. *Bell. Civ.* 2.122.

58. George 2011: 399. In agreement: Bradley 2011(a): 261.

59. See Chapter 1, section on "Financial Inequality: Wealthy Slaves, Impoverished Free Persons."

60. See Kolendo 1978; George 2002.

61. *Dig.* 47.10.15.15 (Ulp.): si quis uirgines appellasset, si tamen ancillari ueste uestitas, minus peccare uidetur: multo minus, si meretricia ueste feminae, non matrum familiarum uestitae fuissent. si igitur non matronali habitu femina fuerit et quis eam appellauit uel ei comitem abduxit, iniuriarum tenetur.

number of enslaved persons were liberated in 104 BCE pursuant to a senatorial decree after Nicomedes III of Bithynia, monarch of a state allied with Rome, complained that a number of his free subjects had been improperly subjected to Roman servitude after being seized by tax collectors (*publicani*).[62] Even without royal involvement, a runaway slave successfully passing as a free man came to occupy the highest judicial office in Rome, the praetorship—forcing legal experts to debate the continuing validity of decisions rendered before his unmasking (in the great Ulpian's view, the slave-praetor's decisions remained valid).[63] Similarly, parties to an arbitration were bound by the decision rendered by a slave dissembling as a free man,[64] even though (persons known to be) *servi* could not issue binding arbitral determinations.[65] Complex rules of law were developed to deal with the validity of documents witnessed by persons believed to be free but who were in fact enslaved,[66] to resolve the status of issue born from slaves who had been thought to be free,[67] and to evaluate arrangements (*institutiones*) intended to benefit persons erroneously assumed to be unenslaved.[68]

Roman jurisprudents likewise developed sophisticated legal guidance to distinguish between a free person's legally binding voluntary assumption of contractual enslavement and the coercive unlawful imposition of servitude.

---

62. Diod. Sic. 36.3.1–2: τοὺς πλείους τῶν Βιθυνῶν ὑπὸ τῶν Δημοσιῶν διαρπαγέντας δουλεύεον ἐν ταῖς ἐπαρχίαις. τῆς δὲ συγκλήτου ψηφισαμένης ὅπως μηδεὶς σύμμαχος ἐλεύθερος ἐν ἐπαρχίᾳ καὶ τῆς τούτων ἐλευθερώσεως. . . . Kerremens argues that this senatorial edict more likely occurred after 102 BCE (2016: 830–832).

63. *Dig.* 1.14.3: Barbarius Philippus cum seruus fugitiuus esset, Romae praeturam petiit et praetor designatus est. sed nihil ei seruitutem obstetisse ait Pomponius, quasi praetor non fuerit: atquin uerum est praetura eum functum. et tamen uideamus: . . . quae edixit, quae decreuit, nullius fore momenti? . . . et uerum puto nihil eorum reprobari.

64. *Cod.* 7.45.2: si arbiter datus a magistratibus, cum sententiam dixit, in libertate morabatur, quam is postea in seruitutem depulsus sit, sententia ab eo dicta habet rei iudicatae auctoritatem.

65. *Dig.* 4.8.9.pr. (Ulp.): sed si in seruum compromittatur et liber sententiam dixerit, puto, si liber factus fecerit consentientibus partibus, ualere.

66. Just. *Inst.* 2.10.7: sed cum aliquis ex testibus testamenti quidem faciendi tempore liber existimabatur, postea uero seruus apparuit, tam diuus Hadrianus Catonio Uero quam postea diui Seu nerus et Antoninus rescripserunt, subuenire se ex sua liberalitate testamento, ut *sic* habeatur atque si ut oportet factum esset, cum eo tempore quo testamentum signaretur omnium consensu hic testis liberorum loco fuerit, nec quisquam esset qui ei status quaestionem moveat.

67. For example, Gaius 1.85–86: si quis cum aliena ancilla, quam credebat liberam esse, coierit, siquidem masculi nascantur, liberi sint, si uero feminae, ad eum pertineant, cuius mater ancilla fuerit. . . . ex libera et seruo alieno, quem sciebat seruum esse, serui nascantur.

68. Just. *Inst.* 2.15.4; *Dig.* 28.5.41 (Iulianus); *Cod.* 6.24.3 (Seuerus).

Here the would-be slave's actual receipt of payment ("participation in the price," in Latin *participans pretium*) was the determinative differentiation.[69] Self-sale of a free man into slavery was not generally a fortuitous, ad hoc undertaking negotiated without assistance directly by the parties (future master and former freeman). To the contrary, "sharing" in the consideration paid to obtain ownership of a previously free individual reflected the reality that at Rome, voluntary entry into slavery by free persons was well-organized, indeed institutionalized: a market venue had been created,[70] a place in which slave dealers and previously free individuals mutually benefited from "participating in the purchase price" of the fresh volunteer-slave.[71]

Gordian's imperial edict of 239 demonstrates the decisive impact of actual receipt of payment in legitimatizing an individual's voluntary cession of liberty. "Participation in the price" cements the master/slave relationship: even a Roman citizen, so compensated, cannot thereafter assert an entitlement to freedom (*libertatis defensio*). But the absence of payment—in a fashion perhaps akin to the Common Law's vitiation of contractual obligations in the absence of "consideration"—allowed a volunteer slave later to assert his free status even if at the time of sale he had acquiesced in his enslavement without making known his allegedly free status.[72] Another imperial judgment of 225 further illustrates this general rule: a woman—even if she were a Roman citizen and even if she had been purchased from the imperial fisc—was not entitled to her freedom if she had consented to enter servitude "in order to share in (the) purchase price" (provided that at the time of sale she had not been a minor).[73] Ulpian similarly emphasizes the decisive importance of a free man's "participation" in the proceeds generated by his sale into slavery: free

---

69. See, for example, *Dig.* 1.5.5.5; *Dig* 4.4.9.4; *Dig.* 28.3.6.5; *Dig.* 40.12.7.pr.; *Dig.* 40.12.23.pr.; *Dig.* 40.13.1; *Dig.* 40.14.2; *Cod.* 7.16.5.1; *Cod.* 7.18.1; *Cod.*18.1.pr.; Just. *Inst.* 1.3.4. Several of these cases have been discussed above ("Protection of Minors").

70. *Dig.* 21.1.17.12: see above, n. 25 and related text.

71. Sen. *Ben.* 4. 13.3: Multa quae summam utilitatem aliis adferunt, pretio gratiam perdunt. Mercator urbibus prodest, medicus aegris, mango uenalibus; sed omnes isti, quia ad alienum commodum pro suo ueniunt, non obligant eos, quibus prosunt.

72. *Cod.* 7.18.1: Dispar causa est eius, qui dissimulata condicione sua distrahi se passus est, et eius, qui pretium participatus est. nam superiori quidem non denegatur libertatis defensio, posteriori autem, et si ciuis Romanus sit et participatus est pretia, libertas denegatur.

73. *Cod.* 7.16.5.pr.-1: non ideo minus in libertatem proclamare potest ea, quam ancillam tuam esse dicis, quia eam uendente fisco comparasti. Sed nec hoc ad praescriptionem operatur, quod uenditionis tempore maior uiginti annis fuit, cum aetatis adlegatio non alias possit praescriptionem adversus ciuem Romanum accomodare, quam si participandi pretii gratia consensum seruitati dedisse probetur.

men brought into slavery are entitled to their liberty unless they had allowed themselves to be sold in order to "participate in the price" paid for them (*ut participaverint pretium*). In the absence of such payment, the putative slave is entitled to his freedom even if he were an adult at the time of entering into slavery, and even if both the "slave" and the buyer knew that the person being sold was free.[74] In a case in which a would-be slave had not participated in the purchase price, and therefore would generally have been entitled to his liberty,[75] the praetor was specifically authorized to examine the motivation and behavior (*calliditas*) of a person who, although knowing himself to be free, had "permitted" his own sale into slavery. If that person had engaged in fraud (*dolus malus*[76]), he would not be allowed his freedom. But a mere failure to inform the buyer voluntarily of one's free status did not constitute *dolus malus*: a person who had passively allowed a buyer to assume that he was free was entitled subsequently to assert and obtain his freedom from the unknowledgeable purchaser[77]—so long as the putative slave had not participated in the purchase price.[78]

It is often assumed that legal rights seeming to protect those held in slavery were merely theoretical, of no real-world applicability, and that *domini* were not likely actually to be adversely affected by provisions purporting to protect

---

74. *Dig.* 40.12.7.pr.-2: liberis etiam hominibus, maxime si maiores uiginti annis uenum se dari passi sunt uel in seruitutem quaqua ratione deduci, nihil obest, quo minus possint in libertatem proclamare, nisi forte se uenum dari passi sunt, ut participauerint pretium. si quis sciens liberum emerit, non denegatur uendito in libertatem proclamatio aduersus eum qui comparauit, ciuiusque sit aetatis qui emptus est, idcirco quia non est uenia dignus qui emit, etiamsi scientem prudentemque se liberum emerit. Cf. *Dig.* 40.12.33 (Paul.): qui sciens liberum emit, quamuis et ille se pateretur uenire, tamen non potest contradicere ei qui ad libertatem proclamat: sed si alii eum ignoranti uendiderit, denegabitur ei proclamatio.

75. *Dig.* 40.12.14.1 (Ulp.): in ea causa is qui se uenire passus est, ut ei ad libertatem proclamatio denegetur. . . .

76. Labeo defines *dolus malus* as encompassing "every form of cunning, deception, or machination employed to dupe, swindle, or deceive another person" (omnem calliditatem fallaciam machinationem ad circumueniendum fallendum decipiendum alterum adhibitam" (*Dig.* 4.3.1.2). See Kaser 1962; Carcaterra 1970; Procchi 2007.

77. *Dig.* 40.12.14 (Ulp.): rectissime praetor calliditati eorum, qui, cum se liberos scirent, dolo malo passi sunt se pro seruis uenum dari, occurrit. Dedit enim in eos actionem, quae actio totiens locum habet, quotiens non est in ea causa is qui se uenire passus est, ut ei ad libertatem proclamatio denegetur. Dolo autem non eum fecisse accipimus, qui non ultro instruxit emptorem, sed qui decepit.

78. *Dig.* 40.13.1.pr. (Ulp.): maiores uiginti annis ita demum ad libertatem proclamare non possunt, si pretium ad ipsum qui ueniit peruenerit: ex ceteris autem causis, quamuis maior uiginti annis se uenum dari passus sit, ad libertatem ei proclamare licet.

victims of economic or social standing inferior to that of the master class.[79] To the contrary, however, in this context the *causa liberalis*—an action to free an individual held in servitude, an iconic process in Roman law, the subject of an entire title in the *Digest* (40.12)—seems to have been of considerable practical significance: the relative ease of transition at Rome between freedom and slavery, especially the seemingly remarkable frequency of manumission,[80] combined with the homogeneity of the free and slave populations to ensure that individuals in servitude were likely to command easy access, through personal and/or familial relations, to non-enslaved individuals able to vindicate their rights. Consanguineous support was so readily available to persons purportedly in illegal servitude that the praetor had developed detailed rules to determine priority among a multitude of persons who might be seeking to assert the rights of persons in bondage.[81] Relatives could seek to free even enslaved persons satisfied with their bondage (except for those who had "participated in the price" paid for their voluntary entry into slavery).[82] In the case of persons of impaired capacity, the praetor allowed not only close friends and relatives but even outsiders to intervene on their behalf if they had been improperly enslaved.[83] Even women and patrons were authorized to act on behalf of putative victims.[84]

79. de Ligt 2002b: 26–38; Kleijwegt 2011: 115–116. Cf. Lanni 2016: 53–54.

80. See below, this chapter, section on "Manumission Pursuant to Contract."

81. Si plures ex memoratis personis existant, qui uelint pro his litigare, praetoris partes interponendae sunt, ut eligat, quem potissimum in hoc esse existimat. quod et in pluribus patronis obseruari debet (*Dig.* 40.12.5.1 [Ulp.]). Cf. Buckland [1908] 1970: 659.

82. Si quando is, qui in possessione seruitutis constitutus est, litigare de condicione sua non patitur . . . in hoc casu aequum est quibusdam personis dari licentiam pro eo litigare: ut puta parenti . . . nam etiamsi nolit filius, pro eo litigabit . . . parenti dabitur hoc ius, quia semper parentis interest filium seruitutem non subire. . . . uisum est cognatis etiam hoc dari debere (*Dig.* 40.12.1.pr.-2 [Ulp.]). liberis etiam hominibus, maxime si maiores uiginti annis uenum se dari passi sunt uel in seruitutem quaqua ratione deduci, nihil obest, quo minus possint in libertatem proclamare, nisi forte se uenum dari passi sunt, ut participauerint pretium (*Dig.* 40.12.7.pr. [Ulp.]).

83. Si furiosus et infans est qui in seruitutem trahitur, non solum necessariis personis, sed etiam extraneis hoc permittatur (*Dig.* 40.12.6 [Gaius]). Cf. Buckland [1908] 1970: 659.

84. *Dig.* 40.12.3.2–3 [Ulp.]): cum uero talis nemo masculus est, qui pro eo litiget, tunc necessarium est dari facultatem etiam matri uel filiabus uel sororibus eius ceterisque mulieribus quae de cognatione sunt uel etiam uxori . . . et si libertum meum uel libertam dicam, idem erit dicendum.

Self-Purchase: Complement to Self-Sale

A slave claiming to have been "purchased with his own money" has the right to litigate against his master, on whose good faith he has relied, regarding the master's failure to free him, at Rome in the office of the urban prefect, and in the provinces with the governors.

—*Digest of Roman Law* 40.1.5 (Marcianus)[85]

For the Romans, slaves' "purchase of freedom with their own money" (*redemptio suis nummis*) constituted an economically coherent coda to the voluntary assumption of slavery by skilled free individuals—albeit a *redemptio* largely ignored by contemporary scholars, and in antiquity only reluctantly acknowledged by Roman jurisprudents. In modern times—despite Romanists' torrential output of specialized studies on virtually every aspect of *ius Romanum*—the first substantial legal investigation of manumission through a slave's own funds, appeared only in 2013.[86] In English, to my knowledge, no legally oriented study of *redemptio servi suis nummis* appeared between 1908 and 2020.[87] In antiquity, fundamental principles of Roman law precluded even the jurisprudential conceptualization, and certainly the juridical recognition, of slaves' "own money," a servile asset that was, as a formalistic legal matter, doctrinally impossible, but economically a reality that *ius Romanum* accommodated through its easy acceptance of "legal fictions."[88] Indeed, the Roman jurisprudents gingerly acknowledged that "one must close one's eyes" to the clear incompatibility between legal recognition of a slave's

---

85. Si quis dicat se suis nummis emptum, potest consistere cum domino suo, cuius in fidem confugit et queri, quod ab eo non manumittatur, Romae quidem apud praefectum urbis, in prouinciis uero apud praesides. See also *Dig.* 1.12.1.1 (Ulp.).

86. Heinemeyer's analysis of "der Freikauf des Sklaven mit eigenem Geld." Earlier, relatively cursory discussions include Finkenauer 2009: 345–357 and 2010: 42 ff.; Horsmann 1986: 308–321; Michel 1962 [1996]: 157–167; Seuffert 1907. Cf. also Zolnierczuk 1976 (in Polish; *non vidi*).

87. See Buckland's brief discussion in *The Roman Law of* Slavery, 1908: 636–640. Watson's Roman Slave Law (1987) makes no mention of the subject. Koops 2020 does treat "freedom purchase agreements" (48–57) but concludes that "a master was under no legally enforceable obligation and merely under a moral obligation to uphold agreements made with his slaves" (49). On the efficacy of agreements between slaves and masters, see below in this chapter, pp. 107–113.

88. See Chapter 2, pp. 59–63.

ownership of assets and legal insistence that slaves, qua slaves, had no capacity to own anything: in Ulpian's formulation, in using the expression "purchased with his own cash" we "close our eyes" to juridical doctrine and give legal effect to economic reality.[89]

* * *

Self-liberation took the form of a fictitious acquisition of a slave by a third party, who in fact was utilizing the slave's own money (literally "his own coins," *suis nummis*) to effectuate his manumission. Ulpian explains that a slave can be properly said to have been purchased into freedom through his own money whenever a nominal buyer pays for the liberating acquisition not through the buyer's own funds but with the slave's money[90]—"whether" the slave's funding is coming "from his *peculium*, or whether from a fortuitous gain, or whether even from the benevolence or generosity of a friend, or by the slave's delayed payment or by the slave's making a commitment or providing for a third-party payment (*se delegante*) or recognizing a personal obligation."[91] Despite the diverse means through which a slave might pay the purchase price from "his own funds"—an indication of the sophisticated nature of money at Rome, extending far beyond coined precious metals to encompass many forms of "credit currency" and "bank money"[92]—the complete absence of any expenditure of his own funds by the putative buyer is requisite.[93] As with other Roman "legal fictions,"[94] this pragmatic artifice would have preserved the juridical dogma of slaves' absolute legal nullity while actually sanctioning slaves' capacity to utilize their own funds

89. uerum coniuentibus oculis credendum est suis nummis eum redemptum, cum non nummis eius, qui eum redemit, comparatur. proinde siue ex peculio . . . redemptus sit, credendum est suis nummis eum redemptum (*Dig.* 40.1.4.1). Cf. *Dig.* 15.1.41 (Ulp.): cum eo uerbo abutimur, factum magis demonstramus quam ad ius ciuile referimus obligationem. The interrelationship between receipt of payment on entry into slavery, and the tendering of payment on departure, is discussed below, this chapter, section on "Manumission Pursuant to Contract."

90. Latin text, preceding n. 89.

91. siue ex peculio . . . siue ex aduenticio lucro, siue etiam amici beneficio uel liberalitate uel proregante eo uel repromittente uel se delegante uel in se recipiente debitum redemptus sit (40.1.4.1[Ulp.]). On this passage, see Heinemeyer 2013: 32–33.

92. See Harris 2006a, 2006b, 2008, and 2019(a); Jones 2006: 252; Howgego 1992: 13–15; Lo Cascio 2003a: 13; 2003b: 148–149, all rejecting an earlier orthodoxy "that all Roman money consisted of coins" (Harris 2008: 174).

93. *Dig.* 40.1.4 (Ulp.): satis est enim, quod is, qui emptioni suum nomen accommodauerit, nihil de suo inpendit.

94. See Chapter 2, pp. 50, 59–63, 70–71, 79 ff.)

and payment mechanisms to negotiate, and to enter into, bilateral arrangements with their owners and others.

The jurisprudent Marcellus confirms that in cases of self-purchased manumission the money paid to the master might come entirely from his own slave's resources,[95] implicitly confirming the reality of actual ownership of a *peculium* by the slave generating the fund.[96] Marcellus posits a case in which an owner, intending to sell a *servus*, instead had freed him in return for money received directly from the slave. If the servant's funds had actually belonged to the master, in reality and not in legal dogma alone, then the master in accepting this payment would have been receiving only money that already belonged to him, thus forgoing (to the owner's disadvantage) the fresh additional funds he would have received from a third-party purchaser.[97] In a more complex case, a slave had entered into an agreement with his master to fund his own manumission, and had actually paid the price negotiated, but before effectuation of the agreed-upon manumission, his master had died, bequeathing to the slave both his freedom and his *peculium*. On these facts, the preclassical jurisprudent Alfenus Varus[98] concludes that the heirs were obligated to return the slave's money (*peculium suum*)—provided that prior to his death the master had not accounted for these funds as his own.[99]

Although this form of manumission through a slave's own money had long been attested in the Roman world,[100] its legal efficacy was explicitly confirmed sometime between 161 and 169 CE through an imperial letter (*constitutio*) of Marcus Aurelius and Verus.[101] More than three hundred years prior, the Roman comic playwright Plautus had already made a number of allusions to

95. On slaves' multiple sources for generating personal property and funds, see Chapter 2, section on "Generating the *Peculium*."

96. On slaves' "ownership" of their *peculia*, see Chapter 2, section on "Owning Assets through the Peculium."

97. *Dig.* 37.15.3: Titius puerum emit, quem post multos annos uenire iussit: postea exorartus accepto ab eo pretio eum manumisit . . . a suo seruo. . . .

98. Consul 39 BCE.

99. Seruus pecuniam ob libertatem pactus erat et eam domino dederat: dominus prius quam eum manumitteret, mortuus erat testamentoque liberum esse iusserat et ei peculium suum legauerat . . . si eam pecuniam dominus, posteaquam accepisset, in suae pecuniae rationem habuisset, statim desisse eius peculii esse: sed si interea, dum eum manumitteret, acceptum seruo rettulisset, uideri peculii fuisse et debere heredes eam pecuniam manumisso reddere (*Dig.* 40.1.6).

100. See Brinkhof 1978: 133 ff.; Ankum 1974: 6; Jacota 1966: 219 ff.

101. *Epistula diuorum fratrum ad Urbium Maximum*: *Dig.* 40.1.4.pr.

manumission through one's own monies. In *Stichus*, for example, a *servus* about to waste his *peculium* on carnal pleasure is mocked for being about to consume the monies needed for his freedom.[102] In *Poenulus*, freedmen insist that they had purchased their liberty with their own money, an accomplishment that protagonists in *Aulularia* aspire to.[103] Pliny the Elder, who lived during the first century CE, marvels at the substantial sums certain actors have been able to pay for their manumission.[104] In a declamation attributed to Quintilian, another author of the first century CE, the speaker notes that slaves generally purchase their liberty at considerable expense.[105] Suetonius, writing in the late first and early second centuries CE, reports that the well-known educator Staberius Eros gained his freedom through a transaction funded by "his own money."[106]

In surviving Roman legal materials, numerous allusions to self-purchase "suggest that the practice was common."[107] Especially in Book 40 of the *Digest* (dealing with manumission), jurisprudents analyze a vertiginous variety of legal implications and permutations relating to a slave's purchase of his freedom with "his own money."[108] For example, even where a slave undertakes the process of gaining manumission through self-purchase but fails initially to pay from "his own money" the sum requisite for his manumission, Ulpian believes that he is still entitled to freedom if he should subsequently satisfy the required payment through services (*operae*) or from any other asset that he might later acquire through his own merit.[109] Papinian insists that an agreement to free a slave is legally enforceable—"freedom can be extracted even from an unwilling owner!"—when a master has accepted

102. Line 751: (*Stich.*) Uapulat peculium, actum est. (*Sang.*) Fugit hoc libertas caput.

103. Plaut. *Poen.* ll. 518–519: quom argentum pro capite dedimus, nostrum | dedimus, non tuom. Plaut. *Aul.* 309–310: censen uero adeo talentum magnum exorari pote | ab istoc sene ut det, qui fiamus liberi? Cf. Plaut. *Asin.* 650–652, 673; *Most.* 300; *Pers.* 34–38; *Rud.* 1408–1410.

104. *N.H.* 7.58: pretium hominis in seruitio geniti maximum ad hanc diem . . . hoc in nostro aeuo ne modice histiones, sed hi libertatem suam mercati etc.

105. *Decl. Min.* 388.23: uindictam magno redimere solent.

106. *Gramm.* 13: suomet aere emptus.

107. Hopkins 1978: 129. Gardner 1993: 36: "legal evidence indicates that it was not uncommon for slaves to secure manumission by paying a sum of money to their owners."

108. Koops has found almost 200 references in the *Digest* "deal(ing) with the complications arising from (slaves') purchase of freedom" (2020: 54).

109. *Dig.* 40.1.4.10: suis autem nummis redemptus etsi totum pretium non numerauit, ex operis tamen ipsius accesserit aliquid, ut repleri pretium possit, uel si quid suo merito adquisierit, dicendum est libertatem competere.

money from a third party in return for a commitment to free a slave. In fact, Papinian sees this situation as analogous to that of the slave "redeemed with his own money" and notes that "often" the money received for manumission from a third party is actually the slave's own funds.[110] Similarly, in cases of contingent testamentary manumission, a slave's payment of money was the most common condition imposed for obtaining freedom.[111]

Slaves controlling *peculia* (see Chapter 2) were obviously in a position to purchase their freedom with "their own funds," if they were able to persuade their owners to accept such an exchange. But in some cases—those in which Self-Purchase was a contractual complement to Self-Sale—the owner had no right to reject slaves' tender of funds. In these cases, the *servus*, originally a free man (or woman), was bound by his voluntary contractual entry into servitude; his (or her) master was bound by agreement to free the slave on tender of an agreed purchase price which the slave might generate in his new employment. Anticipated mutual benefit underlay such agreements. And here for both future owner and future slave, there were substantial potential benefits in facilitating the cycle that led free persons to enter voluntarily into slavery, with the expectation of regaining their freedom through "self-purchase." Roman business had only limited use for free persons and considerable need for skilled slaves; the Roman economy's fostering of "slave enterprise" deprived free persons of economic opportunity. Both might benefit from the cycle that led free persons to enter voluntarily into slavery, and returned them to freedom through "self-purchase." We proceed to examine the functioning of this cycle, and its importance to the Roman economy and to the Roman commonwealth.

Manumission Pursuant to Contract

Large numbers of free men sell themselves into slavery pursuant to written agreements, sometimes on immoderate, even extremely harsh terms.

—Dio Chrysostomus[112]

---

110. *Dig.* 40.1.19: si quis ab alio nummos acceperit, ut seruum suum manumittat, etiam ab inuito libertas extorqueri potest, licet plerumque pecunia eius numerata sit, maxime si frater uel pater naturalis pecuniam dedit: uidebitur enim similis ei qui suis nummis redemptus est.

111. Buckland [1908] 1970: 496–497. Cf. Amelotti 1966; Champlin 1991: 139.

112. 15.23: Greek text, this chapter, n. 20. For *syngraphai* as "written contracts," see Cohen 2015(a): 102, n. 31; Harris 2015: 14; Mirhady 2004: 57–58; Scafuro 2003/2004: 11, n. 37.

Despite decades of intensive study of virtually every aspect of Roman slavery,[113] to my knowledge no attention has ever been given to the relationship—in my opinion structurally important to Roman economy and society—between slaves' receipt of payment for entry into slavery and slaves' expenditure of payment for departure from slavery.[114] Inattention to this interconnection has left scholars confused, and even mystified, as to the motives for, the mechanics of, and the significance of manumission through slaves' own money. Koops, in an otherwise insightful study of "The Practice of Manumission through Negotiated Conditions in Imperial Rome," constructs a detailed framework for "the practice of manumission" but concedes that "the one modality that escapes this framework is the *emptio suis nummis*" (2020: 70). Mouritsen finds the process of manumission through one's own money "anomalous."[115] Gardner dismisses self-purchase with one's own funds as "an unattractive proposition that was to be avoided in favor of other modalities."[116] Andreau suggests that a would-be "purchaser with his own money" could through this mechanism compel his original owner to agree to free him, but offers no evidentiary support for this assertion.[117] Brunt claims that purchase *suis nummis* was merely a means, through transfer to a third party, of avoiding impediments to an owner's manumission of slaves by the advantageous manumission

113. See, among many others, the multitudinous publications of the Forschungen zur antiken Sklaverei and of the Groupe international de recherches sur l'esclavage dans l'antiquité. Cf. Cohen 2014(b): 194–195 (Guide to Further Reading).

114. Although a few scholars have given some consideration to the phenomenon of self-sale into slavery (see above nn. 6 and 11, this chapter), and a few others have studied the phenomenon of self-purchase (see this Chapter, section on "Self-Purchase: Complement to Self-Sale," especially nn. 86, 87), only Morris Silver has explored the economic significance of self-sale: "forcibly taken slaves (including born-slaves) would be insufficiently incentivised by *peculia*. . . . the *peculium* economy is nevertheless able to stand as a dominant Roman socio-economic reality because the slaves forming its base are slaves by contract/self-sellers" (Silver 2016: 69–70).

115. Mouritsen 2011: 174.

116. Koops 2020: 71, correctly characterizing Gardner 1993: 36–39. Cf. Behrends 1980: 60–62; Jacota 1966.

117. Andreau 2004b: 117. The imperial edict of Marcus Aurelius and Verus (discussed below, this chapter, pp. 125–126) did authorize an action to compel not the original owner but a third-party "accommodation purchaser" to manumit a slave whose payment for his freedom "with his own money" had actually been accepted by the original owner (see *Dig.* 40.1.4.1–7 [Ulp.]).

vindicta ("by the rod"):[118] such avoidance, however, could presumably have been accomplished merely through transfer of a slave to a master who had the legal capacity to manumit "by the rod"—without any need for "slaves' own money," with its concomitant complexity of juridical fiction. *Faute de meilleur*, Weiler finally explains such purchase as merely a "special type" of termination of servitude.[119]

To better explain the financial purpose and commercial significance of this form of liberation from slavery, I proceed to examine the importance and nature of the Roman cycle of initial self-sale into slavery through contractual arrangements providing for the ultimate self-purchase of liberty by originally free individuals who had voluntarily entered into slavery pursuant to agreements governing the terms of their enslavement. For the individual free person of entrepreneurial inclination and/or business talent, voluntary entry into slavery would have been far more enticing—and presumably much more frequent—if the volunteers were able, simultaneously with entry into slavery, to negotiate with their owners-to-be a binding right of redemption through future payment from "their own monies." As we have seen in Chapter 2, Roman law and practice did acknowledge a slave's right to utilize his *peculium* partly or entirely for his own benefit. But by Roman legal shibboleth, of course, slaves could not enter into agreements with their masters. Yet in the Greco-Roman world, *servi* seem often to have done so—and these agreements were not treated as informal arrangements of convenience, giving rise to no legal obligation. To the contrary, such covenants could be enforced or confirmed by legal procedures, or through other effective mechanisms. Moreover, in the late Republic and Early Empire these arrangements might have helped to satisfy Rome's pressing need for skilled slaves and perhaps to elucidate Rome's otherwise inexplicably high rates of manumission—although we have no numerical evidentiary basis for determining how frequently voluntary sale into slavery was in fact coupled with the simultaneous arrangement of self-purchase. The very possibility of this coupling, however, provides considerable insight into the Roman economy and Roman society.

---

118. Brunt 1983(a): 146. On manumission *uindicta*, which in contrast to informal forms of manumission bestowed citizenship instead of mere Latin status, see Robleda 1976: 110–114; Treggiari 1969: 20–25; Berger 1953: 577, s.v. Cf. Tondo 1967. On "informal" manumission and "Latin status," see below, n. 186. On forms of manumission, see below, n. 193.

119. "Sonderformen einer Beendigung des Sklavenstatus" (Weiler 2003: 243–250).

Agreements between Slave and Master

Roman sources confirm the existence of agreements between slaves and masters, including written arrangements governing the terms of voluntary entry into slavery. Writing in Greek during the early imperial period, Dio Chrysostomus reports that "large numbers of free men sell themselves into slavery pursuant to written agreements (*syngraphai*), sometimes on immoderate, even extremely harsh terms."[120] Dio's reference to "sometimes harsh terms" implies that some would-be slaves and future masters did enter into mutual agreements that were relatively favorable to the volunteer. As with all compacts, however, the actual terms of an agreement governing entry into slavery and providing for the possible purchase of manumission were likely to vary on the basis of such factors as the parties' relative negotiating strength and/or skill, anticipated future benefits, individual access to reliable and useful information, and so forth. Cicero, however, seems to be referring to agreements unduly unfavorable to volunteer slaves when he asks whether there can be any question concerning the servitude of those men who, influenced by their desire to obtain a *peculium*, reject no servile term as excessively harsh.[121] Alfenus Varus alludes to a form of bilateral agreement that provided for manumission through the slave's own funds.[122] Marcianus confirms a *servus*'s right to sue his master pursuant to these arrangements: "a slave claiming to have been 'purchased with his own money,' has the right to litigate against his master, on whose good faith he has relied, regarding the master's failure to free him, at Rome in the office of the Urban Prefect, and in the provinces with the governors."[123] Discussing a spectacular cause célèbre of the first century CE,[124] Tacitus alludes to a slave's agreement with his master for manumission through payment by the slave. When this undertaking was violated by the master, Pedanius Secundus, a wealthy Roman of senatorial

120. Dio Chrysostomus 15.23: Greek text, this chapter, n. 20. Cf. Dio Chrysostomus 15.23 §13.

121. *Paradoxa stoicorum* (5) 39: an eorum seruitus dubia est, qui cupiditate peculii nullam condicionem recusant durissimae seruitutis? See B. Cohen 1951: 138; Silver 2016(a): 77.

122. *Dig.* 40.1.6: seruus pecuniam ob libertatem pactus erat et eam domino dederat.

123. *Dig.* 40.1.5 (Marcianus): Latin text, this chapter, n. 85. Cf. *Dig.* 1.12.1.1 (Ulp.).

124. Some 400 slaves were executed under Roman traditional law (*lex maiorum*) that required the killing of all enslaved members of a household whose *dominus* had been murdered by a household slave. Regarding this savage retribution, which generated enormous civil unrest and violent protest at Rome, see Tac. *Ann.* 14.42–45, *Ann.* 13.32; Miceli 2020: 381; Cohen 2014(b): 193; Harries 2013: 51 ff.; Schiavone 2000: 108 ff.; Wolf 1988; Saller 1987: 65–66. Cf. my discussion above, Chapter 2, n. 161 and related text.

standing then serving as urban prefect of Rome, he was murdered by his slave (who presumably saw little chance for justice in filing a complaint with the office of his owner, the urban prefect).[125] In connection with self-purchase, Ulpian makes reference to the "full faith of contract" (*fidem contractus*) between slave and master.[126] These agreements between slave and putative master (the buyer under the "fictitious purchase" *suis nummis*) might even explicitly acknowledge the actual true nature of the transaction—that the slave has a contractual entitlement to his freedom.[127] In another apparent example of an agreement for manumission between servant and master, a certain Ericthonius is described on a still unpublished funerary inscription as entitled to be manumitted when he has attained thirty years of age (unfortunately, he died at twenty-eight).[128] A slave could even obtain a right to manumission (*ut manumittatur*) as a third-party beneficiary of an agreement entered into between or among free persons, an arrangement binding on his owner even if this master was not originally a party to the agreement (which might require, for example, that a slave be freed if a particular covenant were violated.

Agreements between masters and slaves were not limited to issues relating directly to enslavement and/or to manumission. Cicero, for example, mentions that a slave functionary (*vilicus*)[129] of his brother Quintus had decided not to proceed with a commitment to Quintus personally to serve as contractor on some new residential construction at a price of 16,000 *sesterces*, because Quintus had increased the scope of the work, but not the amount to be paid to his slave employee![130] Much earlier, slaves of the elder Cato reportedly entered into recurring business arrangements with their master pursuant

125. *Ann.* 14.42.1: praefectum urbis Pedanium Secundum seruus ipsius interfecit, seu negata libertate cui pretium pepigerat sive amore exoleti incensus et dominum aemulum non tolerans.

126. *Dig.* 40.1.4.2 (Ulp.): ab initio enim hoc agi debet, ut imaginaria fieret emptio et per fidem contractus inter emptorem et seruum agatur.

127. *Dig.* 40.1.4.6 (Ulp.): exprimetur in contractu (uelut in emptione) hoc "ut manumittatur."

128. RMO Leiden EDCS-58700011: Dis manibus / Ericthonio animae / sanctissimae–hic / cum deberet ann(is) XXX / manumitti ann(os). / XXIIX / decessut / C(aius) Cilnius–Philetus / filio carissimo /fec(it) (set forth in Koops 2020: 49, n. 57). Cf. CIL 10. 4917. See Silver 2016a: 85.

129. On Roman *uilici* ("stewards/bailiffs") as always (or virtually always) enslaved, see Chapter 1, n. 126.

130. Epist. *Ad Quint. Frat.* 3.1.5–6: Nicephorum, uilicum tuum, sane probaui quaesiuique ex eo ecquid ei de illa aedificatiuncula Lateri de qua mecum locutus es mandauisses; tum is mihi respondit se ipsum eius operis HS xvi conductorem fuisse, sed te postea multa addidisse ad opus, nihil ad pretium; itaque id se omisisse.

to which they borrowed money from their owner to purchase *servi* whom they trained and then resold at a profit.[131]

At Athens, despite slaves' supposedly total deprivation of legal rights,[132] unfree persons still made arrangements with their owners providing for a sharing of revenues generated by slaves' autonomous business activities (*apophora*), and in some cases even for their manumission as part of these agreements. In the fourth century BCE, a group of slaves—Xenôn, Euphraios, Euphrôn, and Kallistratos --entered into a written agreement to lease the most significant bank at Athens, that of Pasiôn, from their own masters, the bank's owners. The lease set forth the terms pursuant to which for ten years they paid rent of a full talent per year,[133] operating this major banking business and retaining all profits beyond the rental obligation. At the end of this period they received their freedom.[134] Similarly, a group of "nine or ten" slave leather-workers are reported (Aeschines 1.97) to have operated a workshop: the slave in charge (*hêgemôn tou ergastêriou*) paid their master a fixed sum of three obols per day, while the other slaves paid two. Unfree craftsmen employed in the construction trades are known to have received monetary compensation; when living outside the master's quarters, these artisans paid a portion of their compensation to their owners and kept the remainder.[135] *Apophora* agreements also were entered into by *douloi* skilled in the production of pottery.[136] Even individual slaves exploiting mineral resources are known to have shared their revenue with their masters (Andocides 1.38). In Menander's *Epitrepontes*, a charcoal-maker,[137]

131. Plut. *Cato Mai.* 21.7: Greek text at Chapter 1, n. 87.

132. Slaves' legal nullity at Athens: Harrison 1968: 163–172; Ferrucci 2012: 99; Rihll 2011: 51–52; Klees 1998: 176–217. Slaves' only entitlement was perhaps the right not to be murdered: Antiph. 5.47, 6.4. Cf. Isok. 18.52, Dem. 59.9.

133. Perhaps US$600,000, calculating on the basis of Purchase Power Equivalency. For ancient societies, in my opinion, it is entirely nugatory (and largely irrelevant) to relate the value of their coinages to the unstable modern values of equivalent physical amounts of precious metals. On determination of Purchasing Power Equivalency at Athens, see Cohen 1992: xiv.

134. Dem. 36.13–14 (Greek text at Chapter 1, n. 137), 37. See Cohen 1992: 76, 80–82.

135. See Randell 1953; Burford 1972.

136. See Webster 1973. On *apophora* agreements in Greece, Rome, and the United States, see Chapter 1, pp. 45–46.

137. Charcoal was of enormous importance in the Greco-Roman world: in addition to its use for heating and other purposes, virtually all warm food was cooked by charcoal. See Veal 2012: 26–27; Faas 2003: 130; Forbes 1966: 61; Renfrew 2004: 83.

living outside the city with his wife, pays to his owner only a portion of his income.[138]

Similarly, Roman slaves appear autonomously to have operated workshops in a variety of commercial areas, including leather-crafting, wool-working, baking, and the production of bricks, lamps, and terra sigillata[139]—paying a portion of their income to their owners and retaining the rest. A construction craft worker, for example, is said to have been paying an annual fee (*annuam mercedem*) to his master.[140] Roman slaves such as Callistus operated banks on their own: these enslaved bankers were sometimes entitled not merely to a portion, but to all of the business's ongoing profits—with the owner benefiting from compensation at the time of the slaves' manumission or from prior periodic payments similar to those otherwise due a lender.[141] Writing during the High Empire, Artemidôros, in his treatise on interpreting dreams, explains that the appearance of a creditor in a slave's dream signifies a "master seeking an *apophora*."[142]

These agreements were not chimerical.[143] Because slaves at Athens and at Rome were generally unable to initiate lawsuits,[144] scholars have deemed meaningless a master's commitment to free a slave upon mutually agreed terms.[145] In both classical Athens and classical Rome, however, special exceptions allowed some agreements between master and slave to be enforced through the courts, explicitly including at Rome agreements for manumission through a slave's own monies (this chapter, pp. 112–113). Moreover,

138. σὺ δὲ ταυτί, γύναι, | λαβοῦσα πρὸς τὸν τρόφιμον ἐνθάδ' εἴσφερε | Χαιρέστρατον. νῦν γὰρ μενοῦμεν ἐνθάδε, | εἰς αὔριον δ' ἐπ' ἔργον ἐξορμήσομεν | τὴν ἀποφορὰν ἀποδόντες (ll. 376–380).

139. See Wiedemann [1987] 1997: 33; Prachner 1980; Harris 1980a; Tapio 1975.

140. Source (in Latin) at Chapter 1, n. 141.

141. *Dig.* 2.13.4.2. Autonomous slave bankers at Rome are discussed more fully in Chapter 1, pp. 47–48.

142. 3.41: Δανειστὴς οἰκέτην δεσπότην σημαίνει ἀποφορὰν ἀπαιτοῦντα.

143. On the legal implications of agreements between master and slave, see Jacota 1966 and Knütel 1993.

144. Athens: Plato, *Gorg.* 483b; Dem. 53.20. Roman slave unable to enter into a contract or be a party to a civil lawsuit: Metzger 2014; Bürge 2010; Burdese 1981; Biscardi 1975.

145. Koops's formulation is typical: "(A) master was under no legal enforceable obligation and merely under a moral obligation to uphold agreements made with his slaves" (2020: 49). Cf. Mouritsen 2011: 171: "a slave could enter an agreement, *pactio*, with his owner concerning his manumission, but it was not binding for the master"; Hopkins 1978: 126 ("not a legal contract . . . could not be enforced by individual slaves").

slaves involved in mercantile matters could rely upon so-called soft law,[146] the informal sanctions of commercial exclusion and ostracism that discouraged violation of the moral expectations of the universe of parties engaged in business[147]—deterrence reinforced where relevant by social (and sometimes religious) pressures. In fact, legal science increasingly has been recognizing that access to the court system is not the sole factor reifying a business commitment.[148] At Athens, and in early Republican Rome, an interplay of commercial and communal values provided strong impetus to compliance with obligations, "whatever (the parties') respective social, economic and legal status."[149] Moreover, Athenian arbitration often provided a channel for resolution of disagreements for those unable or unwilling to use formal juridical procedures.[150] In the modern world, many parties purposefully opt *ab initio* for mandatory arbitration, abjuring recourse to state tribunals.[151]

At Athens the courts had come to accommodate commercial needs arising from the creation in the fourth century BCE of businesses (*ergasiai*) operated by slaves with little if any involvement by their masters.[152] Thus, fourth-century tribunals did accept slaves and free non-citizens as parties and witnesses in commercial litigation—in contravention of the general rules allowing access to *polis* courts only to citizens of that *polis* and allowing servile testimony only when obtained through torture.[153] Athenian courts also recognized slaves' responsibility for their own business debts[154] and accepted mercantile "agency" as a mechanism to overcome slaves' remaining business incapacities.[155]

---

146. Alonso 2013 discusses the pervasive presence throughout Roman Egypt of what he terms "soft law" (2013: 404). On the importance of "soft law" in ancient Greece, see Vélissaropoulos-Karakostas 2018; Barta 2011, *passim*.

147. For the application of such sanctions among Roman artisans, see Hawkins 2012, 2016: 51–52.

148. Vélissaropoulos-Karakostas 2002: 131, 136, 138, n. 16; Karablias 1997: 148; Scafuro 1997: 31–42, 129–131 (*pace* E. Harris 2018b).

149. Aubert 2013: 192, alluding to archaic Roman experience and discussing Athenian agreements between masters and slaves.

150. Scafuro 1997: 117–141, 34–42; Lanni 2016: 44–46.

151. See Born 2014: Chs. 1 and 2; Hensler 2003.

152. Cohen 1992: 90–101.

153. See Thür 2005: 150–162, esp. 151, and 1977; Humphreys 1985.

154. See Cohen 2012; Dimopoulou 2012; Maffi 2008; Talamanca 2008.

155. See Cohen 2017: 132–133 (*pace* E. Harris 2013).

At Rome, several studies have demonstrated how the law made similar adaptations to business reality, progressively extending in the second and third centuries CE slaves' rights independently to access the law courts in commercial situations.[156] Although the "letter of the law" continued into the High Empire to treat as unenforceable agreements between slave and owner,[157] at about the same time Hermogenianus alludes to a number of situations in which slaves exceptionally have the right to sue masters, explicitly citing those cases where individuals redeemed through their own monies have not been manumitted "contrary to their reliance on an agreement" with the master providing for liberation *suis nummis*.[158] Marcianus even earlier had confirmed the Roman courts' availability for suits in which a slave was seeking to enforce an agreement for manumission against a master on whose "good faith" the slave had relied in arranging a purchase "with his own monies."[159] Ulpian, citing Julianus, even extends this right of suit retroactively to permit litigation against his former master seeking return of the monies advanced by a former slave who had self-funded his manumission: these funds must be repaid by the master if it could be established that the putative slave had actually been a free man "serving in good faith," for example as a result of a misunderstanding of his true status.[160] But if a slave had sued his master, and had failed to prove that he had been "redeemed through his own monies," he

156. See, for example, Jacota 1966; Guarino 1967: 295; Morabito 1981:109–111.

157. See, for example, *Cod.* 7.16.36: post certi temporis ministerium ancillae liberam eam esse cum ea paciscendo conuentionis obtemperandi legi domina nullam habet necessitatem utque hoc uerum est, ita e contrario si filios suos constituta cum his libera in ministerium tibi tradere promisisse probetur, parere placitis non compellitur (294 CE). See also *Cod.* 7.14.8, 7.16.10, 7.16.20, 4.6.9. Cf. Koops 2020: 49–50.

158. uix certis ex causis aduersus dominos seruis consistere permissum est: id est . . . si qui suis nummis redemptos se et non manumissos contra placiti fidem adseuerent . . . sed et si quis fidem alicuis elegerit, ut nummis eius redimatur atque his solutis manumittatur, nec ille oblatam pecuniam suscipere uelle dicat, contractus fidem detegendi seruo potestasa tributa est (*Dig.* 5.1.53). Similarly, Ulpian: qui se dicit suis nummis redemptum, si hoc probauerit . . . compellendus erit manumittere eum qui se suis nummis redemit (*Dig.* 5.1.67).

159. *Dig.* 40.1.5 (Marcianus): Latin text, this chapter, n. 85. On this passage, see Kleijwegt 2011: 113–115.

160. *Dig.* 12.4.3.5: si liber homo, qui bona fide seruiebat, mihi pecuniam dederit, ut eum manumittam, et fecero: postea liber probatus an mihi condicere possit, quaeritur, et Iulianus scribit competere manumisso repetitionem. Cf. the similar case of the female dancer Paris, ibid.

not only lost the case, but could be sent to the mines in servitude if his master preferred not to have him returned in chains.[161]

Legal opinions carefully protected both a slave's right to sue his master in the event that he had received the slave's own money and nonetheless refused to manumit—but also protected the slave's money if it had been improperly alienated. In an opinion that Ulpian endorses as "elegant," Julianus opines that a slave who had deposited monies with a ficuciary to be paid out to his master for his freedom could recover the funds from that depositary if the fiduciary had disbursed the monies as though they belonged to the fiduciary itself. But if the depositary had indicated the source and purpose of the money in paying it out, and had so notified the slave, the depositary was not liable.[162] (The slave, if not liberated, could still sue the master in a *causa liberalis* or other appropriate action, but the jurisprudents' structuring of the legal question implies that such a suit was not a plausible remedy [in this particular case] for some factual reason, such as perhaps the slave's sale by an insolvent owner to a purchaser who had no knowledge of the anticipated *redemptio suis nummis*.)

Although even former masters, as "patrons" of former slaves, could not normally be sued by ex-*servi*, in the case of slaves manumitted through their own funds, this prohibition did not apply: here, if a former owner "broke faith," he could be sued by the person freed *suis nummis*.[163] In Paulus's words, "liberty can be wrung even from an owner" if that freedom has been purchased with the slave's own money.[164]

---

161. *Dig.* 48.19.38.4 (Paul.): qui se suis nummis redemptum non probauerit, libertatem petere non potest: amplius eidem domino sub poena uinculorum redditur uel, si ipse dominus malit, in metallum damnatur.

162. *Dig.* 16.3.1.33 (Ulp.): eleganter apud Iulianum quaeritur, si pecuniam seruus apud me deposuit ita, ut domino pro libertate eius dem, egoque dedero, an tenear depositi. Et scribit, si quidem *sic* dedero quasi ad hoc penes me depositam teque certiorauero, non competere tibi depositi actionem, quia sciens recepisti, careo igitur dolo: si uero quasi meam pro libertate eius numerauero, tenebor. Quae sententia uera mihi uidetur: hic enim non tantum sine dolo malo non reddidit, sed nec reddidit: aliud est enim reddere, aliud quasi de suo dare.

163. *Dig.* 2.4.10.pr. (Ulp.): sed si hac lege emi ut manumittam, et ex constitutione diui Marci uenit ad libertatem: cum sim patronus, in ius uocari non potero. Sed si suis nummis emi et fidem fregi, pro patrono non habebor.

164. *Dig.* 40.1.19 (Pap.): si quis ab alio nummos acceperit, ut seruum suum manumittat, etiam ab inuito libertas extorqueri potest, licet plerumque pecunia eius numerata sit . . . qui suis nummis redemptus est.

Economic Significance of Self-Funded Emancipation

Rome needed highly skilled slaves; impoverished free persons needed the economic opportunities largely available only to slaves. Free people accordingly were able to negotiate agreements governing their entry into slavery and providing for their eventual liberation through payment to their master of at least a portion of the funds accumulated in the servile *peculium*. This cycle of liberty/slavery/liberty accordingly proffers an explanation for a phenomenon that has baffled modern scholarship: why did Roman masters free slaves on terms seemingly so favorable to the unfree? However, this circular pattern affected only a self-selected group of adept individuals—a cycle that, although quite significant for the Roman economy, does not establish, or even necessarily suggest, an unusually widespread process of emancipation permeating all levels of servitude.

Needed: Skilled Volunteers for Enslavement

By early imperial times, the Roman economy was producing significant wealth from extensive networks of complex businesses almost entirely operated by slaves.[165] These concerns—working within a legal and commercial system that valorized "slave enterprise" and deterred competition from non-enslaved persons—often reserved important roles for skilled unfree businessmen and had only limited use for non-enslaved persons.[166] Free individuals—even if talented and ambitious—were accordingly largely relegated to dispiriting poverty (a dystopia that is the subject of Chapter 1).

But there was no superfluity of skilled slaves. In fact, in the late Republic and Early Empire, slaves overall are estimated to have been a clear minority, even in Italy, where they constituted probably only about 20 percent of the peninsula's inhabitants.[167] (At Rome itself, in the time of Augustus, the percentage of enslaved inhabitants has recently been estimated at less than

165. See Chapter 1, pp. 41–48.

166. For slaves' quasi-monopoly on lucrative senior positions in Roman enterprises, see Chapter 1, pp. 27, 41–48; Chapter 2, section on "The Manumission of Skilled Slaves: Facilitating Commerce through Legal Fiction."

167. Kay 2014: 178–183; Temin 2013: 136; Scheidel 2011: 289; 2012b: 92; Launaro 2011: Table 1.1 at 16. A few scholars argue for a higher ratio, up to 35 percent: Morley 2011: 265; Hopkins 1978: 101 (Table II.1) (cf. Beloch 1886: 418, 435–436). All such estimates are speculative: see Introduction, pp. 6–8; Scheidel 2005: 64–66; Koops 2020: 41.

10 percent.[168]) In other areas of the Roman world, *servi* are believed to have been proportionately even a smaller percentage of inhabitants than in Italy.[169]

Increasing the supply of slaves was, at best, challenging. In addition to voluntary entry into slavery by free persons, Roman law recognized only two sources of lawful servitude—hostile capture and birth to a slave mother.[170] Yet by imperial times, the Roman Empire had attained a stability and had expanded to a point where only rarely did military victories generate significant numbers of additional unfree persons: the total number of slaves resulting from hostile capture has been estimated as far fewer under the Empire than it had been in the Republican period.[171] Data from Italy and Alexandria suggest a low proportion of females among the slave population, inhibiting increase, or even replacement, of the servile population through births in captivity.[172] Reproduction was also adversely affected by low life expectancy (especially in cities, mines, and malarial areas of the countryside) and by servile family dissolutions imposed by slave owners. As a result, even Scheidel, who questions the adequacy of data arguing for low proportions of females among the enslaved population of the Roman Empire, nevertheless concludes that natural reproduction among the slave population even in late Republican Italy would have been approximately 50 percent less than requisite replacement levels.[173] Moreover, the vast majority of *servi* worked outdoors in agricultural pursuits and within households as domestic servants[174]—and

168. Morley 2013: 42 (50,000 slaves in a total population of perhaps 650,000). Hermann-Otto estimates that slaves might have constituted only 5 percent of the Roman population (2013: 63).

169. Hopkins 1978: 99, n. 99. Scheidel identifies slaves as constituting perhaps 10 percent of the overall population of the Roman Empire (2011: 289).

170. See above, this chapter, nn. 27 and 28 with related text.

171. Boese, who has made the most detailed calculations (1973: 51–142), estimates that in the period between 200 and 31 BCE about 1.8 million slaves were produced by hostile capture, and that in the years between 31 BCE and 180 CE, the total fell to only approximately 400,000 (1973: 87, 109). Such figures, however, represent only a "credible guess" (Scheidel 2011: 293). Nevertheless, some commentators have construed the increase in prices for manumitted slaves recorded on the Delphic manumission inscriptions, dating from the third to the first centuries BCE, as likely confirmation of a reduced supply of war captives during that period, contributing to a rise in the value of such slaves as might be available. See Hunt 2018: 1; Hopkins and Roscoe 1978: 134–171.

172. Treggiari 1975a, 1975b, *P. Oxy.* 3197 (Alexandria). Bagnall and Frier (1994: 342–343), however, found greater balance in Egyptian male/female servile sex ratios prior to manumission.

173. Scheidel 1997: 166. Cf. Harris 1999: 64–72; Scheidel 2005; Straus 2004.

174. Slaves in Egypt, where census texts are relatively well-preserved, appear to have worked primarily as domestics (Bagnall and Frier 1994: 181–312; Bagnall, Frier, and Rutherford

thus never had the opportunity to develop the skills useful or requisite for business functions. Although slaves by natality (in Latin *vernae* [m. and f.]), and presumably some captives, often received significant vocational education,[175] thus potentially augmenting the supply of skilled workers, many free persons are reported to have entered voluntarily into servitude,[176] again suggesting that *vernae* and captives were insufficient to meet the ongoing needs of Roman commerce. Yet in apparent counterpoint to the needs of a city and empire struggling to generate and maintain skilled slaves in numbers adequate to commercial requirements, modern scholars have posited an unprecedently elevated and exceptionally generous rate of manumission, especially for skilled *servi*.

Generally High Rates of Manumission?

Extrapolating from the multitudinous evidence for self-purchase of freedom by skilled slaves,[177] commentators have, erroneously in my opinion, assumed a high rate of manumission of dependent persons throughout Roman society. It is often asserted that Rome freed its private slaves "more often and in greater numbers than any other slave-based society in history."[178] Scheidel (1997: 160) has estimated that in the early Roman Empire, every five years 10 percent of slaves over twenty-five years of age were freed, a proportion that would far exceed rates of manumission statistically attested in other societies.[179] Liberation of slaves purportedly was so pervasive that some historians believe that virtually all urban slaves expected to be manumitted[180]—and on average

1997: 57–88). In most of the Empire, rural slaves outnumbered urban, although proportions were about equal for Italy alone (Scheidel 2011: 292, Table 14.1 [Hypothetical Distribution of the Free and Slave Population of the Roman Empire]).

175. See above Chapter 1, n. 112 and related text.

176. Dio 15.23. Cf. n. 20 above, this chapter.

177. See above, this chapter, especially n. 107 and related text.

178. Mouritsen 2016: 402. Cf. Mouritsen 2011: 120–131.

179. Except possibly in Brazil in the waning years of slavery in the nineteenth century: Luna and Klein 2003: 162–163; Nishida 1993: 365, 376. In Louisiana, for example, in the early nineteenth century, manumission required court action, a provision that has permitted statistical confirmation of a rate of liberation far below that postulated for the early Roman Empire (see Cole 2005; Hall 2000; Whitman 1995).

180. Alföldy 1986: 296, 319. See Nicolet 1994: 605; Patterson 1991: 320; Brunt 1971: 121; Weaver 1972: 1. Cf. Horsmann 1986: 319 and Vittinghoff 1990: 188.

after only six years of service.[181] In short, "the ancient sources clearly suggest," according to Perry, "that manumission was routine and commonplace."[182]

Moreover, this alleged extremely high frequency of emancipation was supposedly accompanied by extraordinary generosity in the conditions of manumission: in sharp contrast to other ancient societies where freed slaves were absolutely excluded from citizenship,[183] Roman slaves who had been "formally" manumitted generally received the full civil and other rights of natural-born citizens,[184] limited only by minor political disabilities imposed on all Roman citizens possessing middling economic resources.[185] The result,

181. This problematic assertion is based solely on a rhetorical flourish by Cicero, who in his Eighth Philippic (43 BCE) dramatically called on the Roman elite to make all possible sacrifice to free the Roman people who were already in the sixth year of hoping for freedom (from Caesar's domination), a period longer, he claims, than obedient and conscientious war captives (*captivi*) usually spent in servitude. (Cic. *Phil.* 8.32: cum in spem libertatis sexennio post sumus ingressi diutiusque seruitutem perpessi quam captiui frugi et diligentes solent, quas uigilias, quas sollicitudines, quos labores liberandi populi Romani causa recusare debemus?). But Cassius Dio (53.25.4) more soberly suggests twenty years as an appropriate period of service for *captiui* before possible manumission. See Harris 1980b: 133–134; Rink 1993: 46–47; Cohen 2000: 144.

182. Perry 2014: 5.

183. Athens, for example, denied citizenship not only to "freed slaves" but even "free men who migrated from other Greek states, or from the 'barbarian' world, or even their children born and raised in [an Athens] that labelled them aliens" (Finley 1982: 26). (In actual practice, however, some persons of servile origin did successfully penetrate citizens' ranks: see Forsdyke 2018; Cohen 2018a, 2018b). Although citizenship at Athens was limited to persons born from two parents both of whom had been citizens, some Greek jurisdictions insisted on two, three, or even more generations of citizen-progenitors as antecedents (Aristot. *Pol.* 1275b23–24). In rare cases, persons of slave origin might gain Athenian citizenship by naturalization, but this was no routine procedure: naturalization required on an individual basis a specific resolution of the male citizen body in Assembly. In principle, such grants were reserved for persons who had been extraordinary benefactors of the state. See Osborne 1981–1983: 4, 204–206; Cohen 1992: 88–89, 102–106.

184. Formal manumission was a liberation involving governmental participation or confirmation. (Gaius, *Inst.* 1.16 specifies as *legitima manumissio* (1) manumission *testamento* [by will], (2) manumission *censu* [by enrollment], and (3) manumission *uindicta*—a patterned ceremony requiring the presence of a Roman magistrate.) Before Augustan legislation, only formal manumission was recognized, and all persons thus obtaining freedom became Roman citizens. The Lex Junia (317 BCE?) recognized "informal" manumission resulting in so-called Junian Latin status, rather than citizenship for persons so liberated. Informal manumission could be effectuated, for example, merely through the presence of witnesses (*inter amicos*), by written communication from master to slave (*per epistulam*), etc. On forms of manumission, see Treggiari 1969: 20–31; Buckland [1908] 1970: 437–572; Hawkins 2016: 133. On Junian Latinity, see Weaver 1997; Rawson 2010; Roth 2010. By Gaius's time, "libertinorum tria sunt genera: aut ciues Romani aut Latini aut dediticiorum numero sunt (*Inst.* 1.12): see Lewis 2015: 171–172.

185. The offspring of freedmen, however, were eligible to hold, and did hold, local magistracies throughout the Empire. See Chapter 2, n. 162.

according to Frank, was that as much as 90 percent of the residents of Rome were of slave origin (carrying, in Frank's racist phrase, "Oriental blood in their veins"); Gordon asserted that 20 percent of municipal officeholders in Italy during the second century CE, were of slave origin.[186] Even Tacitus reported the assertion that by Nero's time most *equites* and many senators were actually descendants of men who had been enslaved.[187]

But this model of rampant liberation is not mandated by historical sources. No ancient quantitative or archival material or other evidence establishes, or even suggests, the frequency of manumission at Rome, absolutely or relatively, or the overall ratio of manumission to enslavement.[188] Similarly, the actual number of voluntary slaves, or even their quantity relative to those forced into, or born into, servitude, cannot today be determined, nor the number of manumissions effectuated through self-purchase, nor the proportion of such redemptions to total liberations.[189] There is also uncertainty as to the number of slaves involved in commerce, and the ratio of such slaves to the totality of unfree persons: some scholars believe that even skilled slaves were employed primarily in satisfying the owner's domestic household requirements.[190]

Moreover, because of the unique nature of commercial slavery at Rome—with its *peculia*, *praescriptiones*, *institores*, and other sophisticated mechanisms—comparative evidence from other places and other eras, even Mediterranean venues, provides slight if any insight. But clearly, even if manumission were the norm for skilled slaves active in business pursuits,[191] the vast majority of unfree persons—those employed in agriculture and mining, or in routine service functions—would still have had virtually no access to

---

186. See Frank 1916: 690; Gordon 1931: 70. Similarly: Barrow 1928; Duff 1928. These authors, propounding the "orthodoxy" of their time, condemned the "racial impurity" that allegedly arose from such supposedly widespread introduction of slaves into the citizen body. As fascism and bigotry lost favor in the academy in the 1950s, scholars condemned racist assertions, but often continued to accept the epigraphic material supposedly underlying the belief in widespread manumission (see McKeown 2007: 11–29; cf., for example, Weiss 2004; Prachner 1980).

187. *Ann.* 13.27: et plurimis equitum, plerisque senatoribus non aliunde originem trahi. Cf. Juvenal 8.45.

188. See Introduction, pp. 6–8.

189. Silver 2011: 75.

190. In Hawkins's opinion, funerary inscriptions (including material from *columbaria*) "suggest that slave or freed artisans who were attached to large households were more likely to have been employed by their owners to meet the internal needs of those households than to have worked in commercial enterprises" (2016: 127). Cf. Joshel 1992: 93–95.

191. "les artisans et les commerçants": Dumont 1987: 65.

emancipation;[192] freedom "was ordinarily available only to those who were judged to be especially meritorious—which excluded the average farmhand, porter, and quarry-worker,"[193] for whom manumission never was more than "a fragile prospect."[194] In Bradley's words, "most of the servile population probably never achieved freedom at all" (1987: 83).

There is furthermore no academic consensus even concerning the frequency of manumission through slaves' self-purchase. Some savants insist that *redemptio suis nummis* was relatively rare.[195] Others assert that it was omnipresent: every skilled slave could expect freedom immediately upon his generation of funds sufficient to purchase manumission, which supposedly meant that "for skilled slaves, chattel slavery was effectively transformed into a medium-term labour 'contract.' "[196] But Hopkins, the foremost proponent of the ubiquity of self-redemption, was unable to point to any law entitling slaves to obtain freedom upon tender of payment, or to any mechanism for determining the price to be paid for such freedom, or even to any "Roman evidence for frequent self-purchase of manumission." Hopkins candidly concedes that in arguing for virtually universal manumission of skilled slaves at Rome, his "arguments are plausible, but they do not constitute proof."[197]

In contrast, Mouritsen, perhaps the leading exponent of the rarity of self-purchase, insists that "payment was considered the exception rather than the norm": he argues tautologically that because self-purchase (in his opinion) necessarily involved the rupture of all further relationship with the former owner while freedmen's continuing dependence on their former master was an elemental and essential aspect of Roman manumission, self-redemption

192. Watson 1987: 23; Hermann-Otto 1994: 369–398; Schumacher 2001: 292–293.

193. Harris 2008: 527. Similarly Wiedemann 1985; Harris 1980b.

194. Bradley 1987: 111.

195. Mouritsen 2016: 412, 2011: 159–185; Badian 1982: 168.

196. Hopkins 1978: 126, 128–129; Alföldy 1986: 286–331 ("Sklaverei"); 1972: 97–129. Roth terms Hopkins's and Alföldy's assertions of pervasive self-purchase a "view (that) did not catch on" (2010: 92). Nonetheless, many scholars recognize the Roman "ideal of regular manumission" (Wiedemann 1985: 164). Cf. Klees 2002: 117; Bang 2008: 278; Kleijwegt 2002; Horsley 1998: 50; Dumont 1987: 66–67; Fabre 1981: 272–277 (frequent self-purchase in the Republican period). Although Zelnick-Abramovitz believes that at Rome "usually manumitted slaves paid their manumittors for freedom," she notes that funding could come from sources other than the slave's "own money" (2013: 2, 67 [online version]).

197. Hopkins 1978: 128.

must have been infrequent.[198] But he offers no justification or evidence for his insistence that self-purchase involved a total separation of slave from master, merely citing Garnsey (1981), who first asserted that all future relation with a former master was terminated by slaves' formalistic purchase of freedom "with their own money," phraseology that for Garnsey referred not to an actual transfer of funds but rather to a legal fiction convenient for ending a relationship.[199] But Garnsey offers no evidentiary support for this hypothesis—only supposition from "logic." Self-purchase with a slave's own funds—he asserts—"created a freedman who was to all intents and purposes independent of any patron . . . . how surprising and illogical it would have been, if a slave who had purchase(d) his freedom should have found himself in his new status subject to more rather than less constraint."[200]

Yet consistency and logic have seldom been achieved in discussions of Roman manumission. Although Garnsey insists that a slave would not "illogically" have paid for freedom from constraint, substantial evidence establishes that manumission often left the freedman, in many respects, in a position unchanged from his prior situation (see Chapter 2, on "The Manumission of Skilled Slaves: Facilitating Commerce through Legal Fiction").

Advocates of the rarity of self-purchase still insist that overall, Rome experienced an extremely high level of manumission of its slave population.[201] Under all present theories, the key "question—'Why did the Romans free so many slaves?'—is still unanswered."[202] Proffered explanations are uniformly unpersuasive.

According to a major strand of scholarly opinion, in acquiring and retaining slaves, Roman households did not act with financial rationality.

---

198. Mouritsen 2011: 172–174. *Idem.* 2016: 412: "*seruus suis nummis emptus*. . . . the key to understanding it probably lies in the outcome, which was a freedman who had no relationship whatsoever with his former master, familial, moral or legal. . . . rather than a diminished patronal authority it seems that a clear break between the parties was preferred, which further suggests that payment was considered the exception rather than the norm."

199. In agreement: Verboven 2011: 96–97.

200. Garnsey (1981) 1998: 33–34. Evidence does survive, however, for one modest reduction in ties between original *dominus* and *libertus*: freedman's request for continuing sustenance can be rejected, where redemption has been effectuated through payment from the former slave's "own money": *Dig.* 25.3.5.22 (Ulp.): si quis liberti liberto ali se desideret uel ab eo, quem ex causa fideicommissi manumisit quemque suis nummis redemit, non debet audiri, ut et Marcellus scribit, exaequatque eum, qui mercedes exigendo ius libertorum amisit.

201. See, for example, Mouritsen 2016: 402; 2011: 120–131.

202. Dari-Mattiacci 2011: 3. Similarly: Bradley 2011a: 256, 259; Patterson 2009: 23; Engerman 2008. This interrogatory was first formulated by Hopkins (1978: 115–131).

Maucourant asserts that Roman decision-making, "embedded" in legal and social institutions, was unresponsive to "market" considerations.[203] "Economic motives" supposedly "played only a small role in Roman manumission."[204] Thus the Roman aristocratic model is said to have called for a plethora of servants, each handling minutely delineated functions requiring far less than a slave's full-time effort, resulting in the ownership and maintenance of excessive numbers of often unneeded *servi*, ostentatiously accoutered in extravagantly costly dress, practicing an extreme, and uneconomic, specialization of servile functions. For example, in an elite home, food would not be prepared by a single servant fully occupied by a variety of tasks, but by teams of slaves—supervisory cooks, sous-chefs, a variety of bakers and other culinary specialists—as set forth in the *Satyricon*'s description of the operations of Trimalchio's home.[205] When Piso allegedly assigns a multitude of functions to a single servant, Cicero attributes to him a meanness of household operation, reflecting a contemptible persona, not an economically rational striving for economy and efficiency.[206]

Similarly, manumission of slaves was not an effort at loss minimization, but supposedly "a moral and political act with significant honor consequences."[207] "The notion of 'profitable' manumission would have been out of tune with the ideology of the Roman elite, for whom the ability to make generous gestures with little concern for the economic consequences was a reflection of wealth and status."[208] Indeed, according to some scholars, "the most

---

203. Maucourant 2004. But investigation of such institutions "should complement, rather than replace, investigation of the market forces that influenced . . . the Roman economy" (Kehoe 2006a: 181).

204. López Barja de Quiroga 1998: 160. Even Scheidel, a strong advocate of economic rationality with regard to Roman slavery, insists that "the importance of status value of slaveownership . . . should not be underrated" (2012(b): 97). Hopkins, who believes that "in the final analysis, the liberation of so many slaves was acceptable to masters only because it was profitable," nevertheless concedes that some masters "freed slaves as an ostentatious token of their wealth and power" (1978: 128).

205. See Puglisi 1987. However, although the dinner at Trimalchio's home features a pageant of precisely delineated servants, Trimalchio, a former slave, has long been seen not as an avatar of aristocratic values, but as the incarnation of *nouveau riche* distortion of elite aspirations: see, for example, Hales 2013, esp. 161–164; Veyne 1961, esp. 213; Gagé 1974: 139; D'Arms 1981: 97–120.

206. *Piso* 67: serui sordidati ministrant . . . idem coquus, idem atriensis; pistor domi nullus, nulla cella; panis et uinum a propola atque de cupa.

207. Meyer 2012/2013: 45.

208. Mouritsen 2011: 196, who does acknowledge that while a small number of enormously wealthy individuals may have been able to indulge in such blatant disregard of their economic

important factor" motivating an owner's decision to manumit was "the personal relation between a master and slave."[209] On this premise, slaves working in close proximity with the master—especially females in domestic service who could come to develop a sexual and/or affectionate connection with the *dominus*—were most likely to acquire freedom;[210] by such reasoning, skilled *servi* would have been least likely to be manumitted, because Roman legal principles and business institutions discouraged interaction between owners and their slaves operating businesses, facilitating hierarchical organization in which slaves worked with and answered to other slaves. Because skilled *servi* seldom worked closely with their masters,[211] they would seldom have been manumitted.

Although some (possibly many) slaves might have been freed because of a master's affection for and/or generosity to an individual slave with whom he had close personal relations—Cicero's Tiro, for example—both Roman evidence and comparative material argue persuasively against attributing Roman freeing of slaves primarily to generosity and relational bonhomie. Even strong advocates of the connection between manumission and intimacy have acknowledged that in reality "most of those performing more responsible roles"—in which slaves normally worked without direct contact with their *dominus*—"eventually would be freed" (Mouritsen 2011: 196). Surveys of New World slavery—where, in contrast to Rome, statistical material is often available—consistently show that "only a small fraction of the instances of manumission can be explained by sexual or progeny relationships with the manumittor."[212] As for supposed Roman benevolence toward those in inferior positions, no one has yet explained why kindness would have been so much greater in the Roman Republic or Empire than in all other human slaveholding societies: both the Republic and the Empire for centuries

---

interest, "less affluent owners would probably not have been able to afford such disregard for their future slave supply" (ibid.).

209. Perry 2014: 54. See also Strack 1914: 8; Mouritsen 2011: 198.

210. See Perry 2014: 59; Weiler 2001: 127–131; Smadja 1999: 356, 361; Madden 1996; López Barja de Quiroga 1998.

211. See Chapter 1, section on "Legal Inequality: The Privileging of Servile Enterprise."

212. Dari-Mattiacci 2013: 3–4. Cf. Whitman 1997: 95 (U.S.); Johnson 1979: 264 (Argentina); Schwartz 1974: 616 (Brazil); Brana-Shute 1989: 190 (Suriname); Handler and Pohlmann 1984: 400, 406 (Barbados).

were engaged almost constantly in the murder and looting of vast swaths of humanity.[213]

Moreover, minimization of the economic rationality of wealthy Romans disregards the enormous amount of evidence and analysis to the contrary collated over more than three decades—effectively commencing with D'Arms's iconic *Commerce and Social Standing in Ancient Rome*[214]—demonstrating that while the Roman elite affected to disregard and disdain "rational" financial behavior, in reality they sought intensively and diligently to maximize their income and assets, while minimizing the transparency of their profit-seeking behavior. Roman business and social organization "permit(ted) a man of *dignitas* to exploit fresh opportunities for gain" by utilizing others (D'Arms 1981: 46). Thus, already in the late Republic, upper-class Romans were pursuing personal enrichment through joint ventures lightly camouflaged as "loans" to businessmen or through businesses conducted by their slaves.[215] Nominal adherence by wealthy Romans to the social primacy of non-economic considerations (*patria instituta ac mores*) did not mean that wealthy Romans really disdained material advantage, seeking to reduce their financial well-being through gratuitous divesting of assets. "Aristocratic codes of behavior have generally proved feeble defenses against the temptations of really big money" (Stone 1965: 335). *A fortiori,* "Roman society was not marked by altruism" (Hopkins 1978: 117).

The other leading academic explanation of manumission, entirely contradictory to the economically "irrational" thesis, asserts that "freedom in exchange for cash was a commercial transaction, governed on the owner's side not by morality or benevolence but by considerations of financial gain and loss" (Bradley 1994: 159). "The liberation of so many slaves was acceptable to masters only because it was profitable" (Hopkins 1978: 128). But neither Hopkins, the foremost advocate of "profitable" manumission, nor anyone else

---

213. Even the Romanophile historian Polybius, in describing the slaughter that followed the capture of New Carthage (Cartagena) in 209 BCE, clinically ascribes to the Romans a terroristic tradition of murdering all the inhabitants (including animals) of cities that dared to resist Roman power: ποιεῖν δέ μοι δοκοῦσι τοῦτο καταπλήξεως χάριν (10.5.4). See Harris 2016: Chap. 2.

214. See D'Arms 1981: 20–96, 149–171; Tchernia 2011: 19–55. Similarly: Pleket 1983: 137, 1984: 14; Schleich 1984: 39–42; Giardina 2002: 333; Nonnis 2003: 272; Cébeillac-Gervasoni 1998: 174; Giardina and Gurevič 1994: 28; Rathbone 2003: 203–204. In part, D'Arms was anticipated by Robert (1968: 598–599).

215. Verboven 2004. In Veyne's words, "les revenus épongés par les détenteurs du sol étaient prêtés aux négotiants, ou encore, les détenteurs transformaient en négotiants leurs esclaves" (2001: 162 = 1979: 280).

has been able definitively to delineate the profitability that accrued to masters from freeing slaves.

For example, some scholars argue that without the incentive of a slave's personal benefit from his efforts slave labor is inherently inefficient, especially as to functions requiring skill and initiative,[216] and that Rome therefore used the hope of manumission—arising from the frequency and speed of servile liberation—as a spur, as a "carrot," to eliminate "laziness and shoddy work" and thus to produce profitability from slave labor.[217] Yet this explanation assumes a far-sighted and coordinated policy pursued by large numbers of slaveholders—of which there is no indication in our sources. In contrast to this possibly illusionary, and at best unassured, hope of an evanescent future freedom, there is overwhelming evidence for slaves' widespread possession of *peculia*, of which those held by skilled and diligent slaves would likely have been substantial (as discussed throughout this work). But by legal dogma these monies belonged to the master. By the letter of the law, a slave owner would have been receiving only his own money in accepting payment from the *peculium* of a slave being manumitted. In taking even the entire *peculium* as a charge for a slave's freedom, the master would have been forfeiting the additional funds he would have received from a third-party purchaser if on sale of the slave the *dominus* had actually been entitled both to receive the purchase price from the outside buyer and to retain the assets constituting the slave's *peculium*.[218]

But the master would have needed the slave's cooperation to liquidate a *peculium*: monetization and liquidation of a significant *peculium* would have been a difficult and complex process, not easily or always attainable. The difficulties of terminating a functioning commercial *peculium* were in fact often insurmountable:[219] transactional costs were likely to be unreasonably high, and the ultimate amount of proceeds available to the master, unpredictable. And Hopkins notes that the supposed impetus might have the opposite effect ("the slave might also cheat his master to speed his chances of buying freedom").[220]

---

216. See Fenoaltea 1984; Findlay 1975; Scheidel 2008.

217. Hopkins 1978: 126. Cf. Koops 2020: 65; Dari-Mattiacci 2013; Temin 2013: 127; Garnsey 1996: 87; Bagnall and Frier 1994: 71, 342–343.

218. *Dig.* 37.15.3: accepto ab eo pretio eum manumisit . . . a suo seruo . . . acceptis nummis dederit libertatem.

219. See Chapter 2, section on "Retaining *Peculium* Assets after Manumission," especially pp. 66–69.

220. Hopkins 1978: 126.

But options would not have been available to a slave owner bound by a contractual commitment to free a person who had entered servitude pursuant to a written agreement in order to pursue commercial opportunities unavailable to the unenslaved—and who, originally dissatisfied with his economic position as a free man, was now (after garnering economic success as a slave) in a position to regain his freedom through "self-purchase," ready to emerge economically and socially enhanced. The cycle is complete: from impoverished freedom to slavery—from slavery to a prosperous freedom. Ulpian seems to recognize this circular progression explicitly, when he characterizes the Constitution of Marcus Aurelius and Verus as "restoring" freedom to the slave who has purchased his liberty with "his own monies."[221]

Here economic considerations once again modify legal dogma. The imperial rescript of Marcus Aurelius and Verus significantly does not provide for the mandatory immediate freeing of the slave who has bought his liberty with his own funds. Rather it provides that such a slave is brought into a condition (*in eam condicionem redigitur*) from which, at his option, he may obtain freedom (*ut libertatem adipiscatur*).[222] As rendered by the standard English translation of the *Digest*, "a man who is purchased with his own cash obtains a status whereby he may secure freedom."[223] A volunteer slave thus might opt for immediate freedom—albeit a liberty that might be constricted by some continuing obligations to his former master, now his *patronus*.[224] Alternatively, economic considerations might motivate the volunteer slave to choose to continue, at least temporarily, in his enslavement: many lucrative positions were available only to the unfree.[225] Yet, at a later time[226] he could,

---

221. *Dig.* 5.1.67: qui se dicit suis nummis redemptum, si hoc probauerit, exinde liber erit ex quo redemptus est, quia constitutio non liberum pronuntiari praecipit, sed restitui ei libertatem iubet.

222. *Dig.* 40.1.4.pr. (Ulp.): is qui suis nummis emitur, in eam condicionem redigitur, ut libertatem adipiscatur.

223. Translation Watson, ed., 1999. Cf. Gaius I.175, where the indicative mood shows the immediacy of acquisition of guardianship: patroni autem liberi eandem tutelam adipiscuntur, quam et pater eorum habuit.

224. Because of the responsibilities and dependence inherent in the continuing relationship between former *dominus* and erstwhile *seruus*, in the absence of an original agreement to the contrary, a freedman's situation was in important respects not entirely free. See Chapter 2, section on "The Manumission of Skilled Slaves: Facilitating Commerce through Legal Fiction."

225. See Chapter 1, section on "Legal Inequality: The Privileging of Servile Enterprise."

226. See *Dig.* 40.1.6 (dealing with the consequences of late manumission of a slave who had entered into an agreement for his freedom upon provision of required payment: seruus pecuniam ob libertatem pactus erat et eam domino dederat: dominus prius quam eum

on tendering the price of manumission, obtain his freedom—but a liberty now not "far worse than his prior servitude."[227] In short, Roman masters in relevant situations freed skilled Roman slaves not by choice, but because of lack of choice: they were contractually bound to proffer freedom to slaves who had so negotiated their entry into servitude.

---

manumitteret, etc. [Alfenus Uarus]). Cf. *Dig.* 40.1.5 (si quis dicat se suis nummis emptum, potest consistere cum domino suo [Marcianus]).

227. For manumitted freedom as a condition far worse than prior servitude, see Epict., *Diss.* 35–36 (ἐμπέπτωκεν εἰς δουλείαν πολὺ τῆς προτέρας χαλεπωτέραν). For modern scholars' facile assumption that no free person would willingly choose servitude, see above, this chapter, pp. 84–86.

4

Businesswomen

IN SERVITUDE AND IN FREEDOM

MODERN SCHOLARSHIP HAS tended to assume the absence of women—both free and slave—from significant business activities at Rome.[1] Free females supposedly were limited to routine domestic pursuits:[2] even "women in artisanal and entrepreneurial families preferred to allocate their time to household tasks."[3] Female slaves are often portrayed as performing only lowly and/or erotically degrading domestic tasks. An unfree woman's situation supposedly "was principally defined by her sexual availability . . . gendered assumptions about the relationship between sexual conduct and social status shaped Roman authors' and lawmakers' interpretation of female slaves' standing and worth."[4] For enslaved women there was allegedly only a single route to an improved personal situation and to expeditious manumission—the

1. Jakab 2013: 134: "The traditional view gives the impression that women were almost totally excluded from business." The typical study "elides the many female owners in Roman society" (Saller 1999: 187, faulting, for example Kirschenbaum 1987: ix, who only "very occasionally acknowledges the reality of women owners"). Andreau even asserts that at Rome "there are no women to be found in active financial life" (1999: 66), "les femmes n'avaient pas le droit d'exercer le métier d'*argentarius* (1997: 497, n. 44).

2. Purportedly, women's economic activity "doveva sempre avvenire all'interno di un quadro rassicurante di valori femminili 'tradizionali'" (D'Aloja 2016: 661–662). "The nature of (women's) active involvement (in business), especially in the case of married women, is unclear. Some are slaves, many freed, few certainly freeborn" (Gardner 1986: 232–233).

3. Hawkins 2016: 255.

4. Perry 2016: 1, 4–5. Cf. Petron. *Satyr.* 75.11 (nec turpe est quod dominus iubet). See Saller 1999: 193–196 (esp. 195: "the sexual honor [of free women] distinguished them from slaves, who did not have such honor, a distinction at the heart of the aetiology of the festival of *ancillae*"). Tout court, "les riches Romains traitaient leur *familia* servile comme un véritable harem" (Veyne 1991: 255). In explaining the concept of "corruption" of slave(s) (*corruptio serui*), Ulpian offers numerous examples of how this might occur in the context of enslaved men; for

Roman Inequality. Edward E. Cohen, Oxford University Press. © Oxford University Press 2023.
DOI: 10.1093/oso/9780197687345.003.0005

possibility of winning their owners' tolerance, affection, or love through sexual submission.[5]

In fact, however, many unfree females *were* involved in commerce, where their position and prospects corresponded largely to the same factors of entrepreneurial accomplishment and contractual arrangement that facilitated the progress of similarly situated male slaves.[6] Business managers (*institores*), most of whom were slaves, might be male or female.[7] "Apprenticeship" positions, leading to increased responsibility, were frequently filled by female slaves.[8] For both unfree servile businessmen and unfree servile businessswomen, the *peculium* was the mechanism for wealth creation and possible manumission.[9] It has even been asserted that "the institution of slavery [at Rome] allowed fuller exploitation of female human capital as compared with [the situation in] later Europe."[10]

In this chapter, we will explore the widespread involvement of women in Roman business, and the legal and economic significance, implications, and complications of this phenomenon.

Women in Commerce

At Rome "adult women handle their business matters for themselves."[11]

—Gaius, *Institutes*, 1.190–191

---

women, the only form cited is sexual (*Dig.* 11.3.1). On sexual "honor" as the essence of the free *mater familias*, see *Dig.* 50.16.46.1 (Ulp.). Cf. Saller 1998: 88; Gardner 1995; Strong 2016: 18 ff. (on *pudicitia* as the essence of the *femina bona*).

5. Gardner 1986: 225: "statistics are lacking, (but) there will quite often have been a man, either the patron himself wishing to marry her, or another wishing to buy her freedom. . . ." On female slaves manumitted in order to marry their owners: Weiler 2001, 2003; Weber 2008; Mouritsen 2011: 192; Weaver 1972: 18.

6. "In business life, women who were slaves had in effect the same legal standing as men" (Gardner 1986: 233).

7. *Dig.* 14.3.7.1 (Ulp.), text below at n. 37. Cf. Aubert 1994: 14 ("in most cases cited by the jurists the manager is a person-in-power [*alieni iuris*]"), 53.

8. Bradley 1991: 103–124; Jerrard 2000: 2–3, 6. Cf. Smuts and Stromback 2001: 5.

9. See Halbwachs 2016: 448: "At this lowest rung of the social hierarchy, a differentiation by gender is not discernible, and female slaves acted more or less as independently as male slaves within the context of their *peculia*." Cf. Kaser and Knütel 2014: 292–295. For the interaction between Roman commerce and the realia of enslavement and manumission, see Chapters 2 and 3.

10. Saller 2012: 79–80.

11. Mulieres enim quae perfectae aetatis sunt, ipsae sibi negotia tractant.

Even in the absence of statistical information concerning the relative and absolute number of businesswomen at Rome and in its empire—an arithmetical dearth encountered, of course, in the analysis of every aspect of the ancient classical world[12]—numerous examples do survive of both free and enslaved women who were engaged in an enormous variety of elevated mercantile undertakings, including widespread participation as principals in financial transactions, as buyers and sellers of substantial real estate, and in the ownership and operation of maritime vessels. Women also are encountered in less exalted pursuits. Not only female slaves, but also manumitted females and even a few free-born women worked as hairdressers, personal attendants, masseuses, and such,[13] but even in these prosaic jobs some female slaves appear to have functioned as independent contractors, rather than as servants of a single household.[14] Women worked as doctors (*medicae*),[15] midwives (*obstetrices*), and in various other health-related positions;[16] wet-nurses (*nutrices*) in Roman Egypt entered into detailed agreements governing their terms of service.[17] Females functioned as secretaries and scribes,[18] and in retail business, especially in textiles and perfume.[19] They are attested as vendors of a multitude of common and specialized products (fish, seeds, beans, barley, preserved foods, honey, etc.[20]). Free women (and slaves male and female) appear also as functionaries in productive industries, frequently, for example,

---

12. On the pervasive lack of statistics for the ancient Mediterranean world, see Introduction, pp. 6–8.

13. Joshel 1992: Table 5.2; Groen-Vallinga 2013: 304, n. 50.

14. Joshel 1992: 98.

15. On the high prestige of female medical experts, see, for example, Ausonius, *Parentalia* 6.6; *Codex Just*. 7.7.1.5a; IGGR UV.507 (Greek inscription from Roman Pergamum). See further Masci 2001: 139–141, #47 (cf. Cristifori 2011: 159–160); CILX.3980; CIL VI.9477. Cf. Berg 2003: M. Alonso 2011; Lamberti 2014: 69.

16. See Galen, *On Prognosis* 8.8. Cf. Treggiari 1976: 86–89; Milnor 2011: 610; Kampen 1981: 116; Parker 1997: 137; Pleket 1969: ##12, 20, 26.

17. Eichenauer 1988: 270. Some *nutrices* were born free: see Günther 1987: 79–80; Cristofori 2004: 543.

18. *Ann. Epig.* 1982: 46; Treggiari 1976: 78; Kampen 1981: 118, nn. 49–50.

19. Textiles: Juv. *Sat.* 8.42–43. See Dixon 2000/2001, 2004: 65–68; Jerrard 2000. Perfumes: Treggiari 1979: 70.

20. See, for example, CIL I.3021; III.6672; VI.9684; VI.9801; XIV.2850. Cf. Holleran 2012: 57 (n. 206), 201; 2013, 321–322; Treggiari 1979: 72, 78; Kampen 1981: 118, 157 (n. 53, fig. 45); Dixon 2001: 128–129.

as bottlers of olive oil (*diffusores olearii*),[21] and as producers (*officinatores*) of bricks from clay-yards in the environs of Rome.[22] (Some 43 women were among the 150 attested owners [*domini, -ae*] of such clay beds,[23] and more than 20 females are recorded as lessees thereof.)

Women active in commerce are mentioned frequently in papyri and in the so-called Archive of the Sulpicii from Puteoli, a unique collection of financial documents on wooden tablets discovered in the nineteenth and twentieth centuries in areas near Mount Vesuvius. In fact, twenty-three tablets (about a quarter of the total number of items preserved in the Archive) record business transactions involving women.[24] Roman funeral inscriptions (despite their brevity and their tendency to memorialize females through family relations rather than by business activity) likewise confirm women's general business importance. More than 200 women are identified by occupation on surviving epitaphs at Rome covering a period ranging from the first century BCE to the third century CE.[25] Some 62 individual fields of female remunerative activity are recorded—even though women's business involvement tends to be described on these epitaphs with less specificity than men's.[26]

Women undertook complex real-estate transactions, even buying on a privately negotiated basis enormously expensive properties from prominent Romans such as Pliny the Younger.[27] (Pliny sold his interest—possibly worth 900,000 *sesterces*—for 700,000 *sesterces* to Corellia, who negotiated the price on an exclusive basis [*non expectata auctione*]). The late Republic recorded a number of similar transactions—such as Servilia's acquisition of

---

21. See Chic García 1988: nos. 4, 9, 11, 16, 22, 33, 34, 41.

22. In fact, the majority of known *officinatores* were slaves or former slaves: see Steinby 1978: cols. 1516–1519; Helen 1975: 23; D'Aloja 2016: 652–653; Gourevitch and Rapsaet-Charlier 2001: 161–163; Aubert 1994: 224.

23. Helen 1975: 22–23, 94, 112–113, 123.

24. Jakab 2013: 130.

25. Becker 2016: 915–916; Joshel 1992: 69, Table 3.1. Far more men are identified by métier on such stones.

26. Groen-Vallinga 2017: 131. Cf. Becker 2016: 915 ("the Roman epigraphic habit . . . favors the story of its male inhabitants"); Hawkins 2016: 164 ("female slaves and freedwomen are both attested in far fewer trades than men").

27. Pliny, *Ep*. 7.11.

valuable farms, again allegedly at a substantial discount through an auction process involving Julius Caesar,[28] and Crassus's purchase of real estate in the suburbs from Licinnia, one of the Vestal Virgins—also supposedly at a favorable price.[29] As a group, Roman women of high standing had acquired so much property that during the Civil Wars the Second Triumvirate considered confiscating these assets to meet its pressing needs for revenue, but was supposedly dissuaded through an elegant presentation by a female speaking on behalf of the women who would have been affected.[30] Offering insight into women's business activities under the High Empire, a *responsum* of the Emperor Caracalla concerns an elaborate real-property deal in which both buyer and seller were female: the seller provided financing for the transaction and was entitled to impose harsh penalties in the event of the other woman's default.[31]

Women were importantly engaged in maritime commerce, the principal channel of wholesale trade in classical antiquity.[32] Amphoras carried on ships were often stamped with women's names, attesting to their managerial and/or ownership involvement in viniculture and in the related transportation by ship of wine in bulk, both businesses important to overall maritime import and export.[33] Preserved inscriptions record women as owners of ships.[34] These female proprietors sometimes appointed men to

---

28. Caesar: Suet. *Jul.* 50.2: Seruiliam, cui . . . super alias donationes amplissima praedia ex auctionibus hastae minimo addixit.

29. Crassus: Plut. *Crass.* 1.2: Λικιννίᾳ . . . ἦν δὲ προάστειον αὐτᾷ καλόν, ὅ βουλόμενος λαβεῖν ὀλίγης τιμῆς ὁ Κράσσος καὶ διὰ τοῦτο προσκείμενος ἀεὶ τῇ γυναικὶ καὶ θεραπεύων . . . τὴν δὲ Λικιννίαν οὐκ ἀνῆκε πρότερον ἢ τοῦ κτήματος κρατῆσαι.

30. Quint. *Inst.* 1.1.6; App. *Bell.Ciu.* 4.32.

31. *Cod.* 4.54.1 (Antoninus to Claudia Diotima: 216): si ea lege praedium uendidisti, ut, nisi intra certum tempus pretium fuisset exsolutum, emptrix arras perderet et dominium ad te pertineret, fides contractus seruanda est.

32. "Le vrai commerce a toujours été, dans l'Antiquité grecque et romaine . . . le commerce en gros par voie de mer" (Biscardi 1982: 28). See Schiavone 2020: 12; Ste. Croix 1974: 42; Bleicken 1985: 73; Garland 1987: 85; Cohen 2015b: 395–396.

33. See, for example, ILS 8574(a), (b); CIL III.12020; CIL III.14371 (all recording Calvia Crispinilla). For other attestations of women's names on amphoras, see ILS 8573; CIL XI.6695; CIL XI.6623; CIL X.6252. On the capital-intensive requirements of vineries, see Pliny, *Nat. Hist.* 14.5–6; Cato, *de re rust.* 1.7.

34. CIL XV.3691, XV.3729, XV.3845–3847. Women are attested as shipowners even into late antiquity: a female shipowner reportedly paid for the mosaics of a sixth-century CE church on Kos (Mentzou-Meimare 1982: #97; cf. Nikolaou 1994: 142–143). In the ninth century,

captain vessels—and were then legally responsible for any contracts that the male subordinate might have entered into.[35] Indeed, Ulpian insists that for purposes of liability "it matters little" (*parvi refert*) whether a vessel is commanded by a man or a woman,[36] or even by an enslaved woman.[37] In a long-sustained imperial effort to ensure an adequate supply of grain imports at Rome, the Emperor Claudius even initiated the award of special privilege (the *ius quattuor liberorum*) to businesswomen originally enslaved but later manumitted, commendation for their entrepreneurial involvement in the building of merchant vessels—an incentive continued by his successors at least until well into the second century.[38] Because so many female moneylenders mentioned in the *Codex* (of Justinian) were freedwomen, "it seems quite likely that (they) had learned the business of maritime trade as slaves."[39] A further indication of women's prominence in maritime lending: female financiers are recipients of two of the *Codex*'s four surviving *rescripta* dealing with nautical loans (*nauticum foenus*).[40] (Women's prominence here is not anomalous: of some 2,500 rescripts on private legal matters dating from 117 to 305 CE and preserved in the *Codex*, approximately a quarter [about 650] are addressed to female

---

many women appear to have ownerd vessels, including Theodora, wife of Emperor Theophilos and regent for Emperor Michael (*Theophanes Continuatus* 88–89). Cf. Chrestou 2016: 246; Nikolaou 2005: 295; Thurn, ed. 1973: 51).

35. Et si a muliere magister nauis praepositus fuerit, ex contractibus eius ea exercitoria actione ad similitudinem institoriae tenetur (*Cod.* 4.25.4: Diocletianus et Maximianus Antigonae 293). On this rescript, see Sirks 2018: 89; Connolly 2010: 106–107. Cf. *Dig.* 14.3.7.1 (n. 37 below): nam et si mulier praeposuit, competet institoria.

36. Parui autem refert, qui exercet masculus sit an mulier (*Dig.* 14.1.1.16).

37. *Dig.* 14.3.7.1: parui autem refert, quis sit institor, masculus an femina, liber an seruus proprius uel alienus; item quisquis praeposuit: nam et si mulier praeposuit, competet institoria exemplo exercitoriae actionis, et si mulier sit praeposita, tenebitur etiam ipsa. Sed et si . . . ancilla praeposita, competit institoria actio.

38. Suet. *Claud.* 18–19: Urbis annonaeque curam sollicitissime semper egit . . . et naues mercaturae causa fabricantibus magna commoda constitutuit pro condicione cuiusque, ciui uacationem legis Papiae Poppaeae, Latino ius Quiritium, feminis ius quattuor liberorum, quae constituta hodieque seruantur.

39. Benke 2012: 227.

40. *Rescripta* were "authoritative legal answers relating to individual legal disputes or attendant legal processes, issued in response to petitions submitted to the Imperial chancellery" (Halbwachs 2016: 444). Cf. Connolly 2010; Peachin 1996; Honoré 1992; Nörr 1981.

petitioners.[41]) One of these *rescripta*, in 286 CE, denies the claim of a certain Aurelia Cosmiana for an enhanced yield on a maritime loan, ruling that she had not assumed the usual obligation of maritime risk (*periculum ex navigatione maris*):[42] lenders were entitled to an augmented return (beyond the maximum 12 percent per annum otherwise permitted[43]) only if they had agreed to forfeit repayment if exigencies of the sea had resulted in destruction of the collateral supporting the loan. Invoking public interest (*ratio publici iuris*), the second rescript (also from Emperors Diocletian and Maximianus) held that another female lender, Aurelia Iuliana, *was* entitled to repayment on a loan on which she had undertaken "maritime risk" even though the underlying collateral had not arrived at the agreed-upon destination: assumption of "maritime risk" eliminated an obligation of repayment only if cargo were lost because of a calamity such as a sea storm, not because the imperial government had seized goods in another port in response to the borrower's taking on unlawful merchandise.[44]

Surviving evidence illustrates the multitude of roles played by women in Roman finance and provides a virtual "catalog of legal texts showing women as creditors or debtors"[45]—reflecting the reality that at Rome "adult women handle their business matters for themselves."[46] Cicero, for example, is known

---

41. On imperial responses to female petitioners, see Reduzzi Merola 2012; Osaba 2000; Volterra [1973] 1993; Huchthausen 1992; Anagnostou-Cañas 1984. Cf. Huchthausen 1974, 1976; Sternberg 1985; Connolly 2010.

42. *Cod.* 4.33.3 (Diocletianus et Maximianus Aureliae Cosmianae, 286 CE): cum dicas pecuniam te ea lege dedisse, ut in sacra urbe tibi restitueretur, nec incertum periculum, quod ex nauigatione maris metui solet, ad te pertinuisse profitearis, non dubium est pecuniae creditae ultra licitum te usuras exigere non posse. On the context of this ruling, see Halbwachs 1999: 359–362. Cf. Halbwachs 2016; Jakab 2009: 157–186 ("Lieferungskauf bei den römischen Juristen)."

43. For the 12 percent limit often prevailing, see Cic. *Att.* 5.21.13; *Frag. Vaticana* (Pap. 3 resp.) 11; Andreau 2020: 81–82; Soricelloi 2016: 350. On limitations and fluctuations in Roman interest rates, see Andreau 2015: 94–97; Camodeca 1992: 165–198; Cardilli 1997; Petrucci 1997; Foraboschi and Gara 1981, 1982. On the legal structuring of Roman interest, see Petrucci 2002: 67–102; Salazar Revuelta 1999: 153 ff.

44. *Cod.* 4.33.4: cum proponas te nauticum foenus ea condicione dedisse, ut post nauigium, quod in Africam dirigi debitor adseuerabat, in Salonitanorum portum naue delata fenebris pecunia tibi redderetur, ita ut nauigii dumtaxat quod in Africam destinabatur periculum susceperis, perque uitium debitoris, nec loco quidem nauigii seruato, illicitis comparatis mercibus quae nauis continebat fiscum occupasse: amissarum mercium detrimentum, quod non ex marinae tempestatis discrimine, sed ex praecipiti auaritia et inciuili debitoris audacia accidisse adseueratur, adscribi tibi iuris publici ratio non permittit.

45. Benke 2012: 219. Cf. Halbwachs 1997.

46. Gaius 1.190: Latin text at n. 11 (above).

to have been indebted to two unrelated women, and to have been the creditor of a third.[47] About the same time (in or about 66 BCE) Gaius Visellius Varro reportedly became indebted to a woman (Otacilia Laterensis) in the stupendous amount of 300,000 *sesterces* (according to her books of account).[48] Varro, however, claimed that the "loan" was actually a sham transaction whose "repayment" was intended discreetly to transfer funds to his then-lover Otacilia. Without regard to the actual veracity of Varro's denial, the claim of a purported loan would have blatantly lacked credibility if it were inconceivable that a woman at Rome might, as a principal, lawfully have advanced monies in such a large amount. To the contrary, Roman law generally held that money lent by women—even in the absence of any male authorization of the advance—created for the recipient a binding obligation of repayment.[49] At Puteoli, a number of loans involving women are preserved in the Archive of the Sulpicii,[50] including financial transactions with women who had originally been enslaved.[51] (The Archive also references loans to and from men still enslaved, acting either for the slaves' own account through their *peculia* or on behalf of their owners.[52]) Freeborn females also were active at Puteoli: Caesia Priscilla, for example, appears as a principal in a variety of financial dealings

47. See Shatzman 1975: 416–420; Cic. *Att.* 12.51.3 (borrowing from Caerellia in 45 BCE).

48. Val. Max. 8.2.2: C. Uisellius Uarro gravi morbo correptus trecenta milia nummum ab Otacilia Laterensi, cum qua commercium libidinis habuerat, expensa ferri sibi passus est eo consilio, ut, si defessisset, ab heredibus eam summam peteret, quam legati genus esse uoluit, libidinosam liberalitatem debiti nomine colorando, euasit deinde ex illa tempestate aduersus uota Otaciliae, quae offensa quod spem praedae sua morte non maturasset, ex amica obsequenti subito destrictam feneratricem agere coepit, nummos petendo, quos ut fronte inuerecunda, ita inani stipulatione captauerat. De qua re C. Aquilius uir magnae auctoritratis et scientia iuris civilis excellens iudex adductus adhibitis in consilium principibus ciuitatis prudentia et religione sua mulierem repulit. For juridical analysis of this passage, and in particular of the form of contract (*litteris*?), see von Lübtow 1952; Watson 1965: 32–36. Cf. Liebs 2007: 65–78; Soricelli 2016: 368.

49. Gaius 2.81: Ideoque si quando mulier mutuam pecuniam alicui sine tutoris auctoritate dederit, quia facit eam accipientis, cum scilicet et pecunia res nec mancipi sit, contrahit obligationem. For female freedom from male *tutores* in making such advances, see below, pp. 47–59.

50. On surviving Roman business documentation from the Pompeii area, see above, n. 15 and related text.

51. TPSulp. 99 (Marcia Fausta borrowing 2,000 *sesterces*); TPSulp. 82 (Patulcia Erotis, auction transaction).

52. TPSulp. 58, Pyramus Caesiae Priscillae ser(uus); TPSulp. 56 (March 7, 52 CE), Niceros colonorum coloniae | Puteolanae seruus arcarius | (see Gröschler 1997: 261–262).

(loans, deposits, remittances) amounting to a total of 24,000 *sesterces*;[53] Lollia Saturnina, a woman of high birth, provided two advances, one for 2,000 *sesterces* and another in an amount not now ascertainable.[54] Another financing involved the elevated amount of 30,000 *sesterces* provided by a woman, Magia Pulchra, to a male borrower.[55] We even know of a transaction (albeit involving only the relatively small sum of 1,600 *sesterces*) in which both the lender and the borrower were women.[56] In Roman Egypt, a database of 349 loans made between 30 BCE and 284 CE reveals women as borrowers in about 22 percent of the financings, and as lenders in about the same percentage.[57] Approximately 42 percent of the loans by women were to female borrowers.[58]

Military personnel also obtained funds from women. For example, in the High Empire, Antoninus in 212 ruled that a soldier seeking return of property pledged against a loan was not obligated to pay further interest to a female creditor (*creditrix*) once he had tendered to her full payment of his obligation together with any interest due to the time of tender, and might seek redress from the governor (*praeses*) in her absence.[59] Even the walls of Pompeii attest to female finance: a number of graffiti refer to a certain Faustilla as a woman who had advanced several loans secured by property of limited value.[60]

Females monitored and recorded monetary transactions, and served as accountants[61]—and even participated in the provision of revenues to the government through tax-farming.[62] Although Roman customs (*mores*) tended

---

53. TPSulp. 58, 71.

54. TPSulp. 54, 73. See Gardner 1999: 14; Andreau 1999: 26.

55. TPSulp. 63. See Camodeca 1999: 158.

56. TPSulp. 60 (March 20, 43 CE). For variant exegeses of this financing, see Jakab 2013: 145–147; Gardner 1999: 17–18; Gröschler 1997: 67–96; Bove 1984: 150; Rowe 2001: 230; Wolf 2010b: 85.

57. Lerouxel 2006.

58. Lerouxel 2006: Résultats généraux #13.

59. *Cod.* 4.32.6 (Antoninus A. Antigono). Si creditrici, quae ex causa pignoris obligatam sibi rem tenet, pecuniam debitam cum usuris testibus praesentibus obtulisti eaque non accipiente obsignatam eam deposuisti, usuras ex eo tempore quo obtulisti praestare non cogeris. Absente uero creditrice praesidem super hoc interpellare debueras.

60. CIL IV.4528; IV.8203; IV.8204. These loans seem to have carried high interest rates: Lázaros Guillamón 2010: 260; Soricelli 2016: 369.

61. *Dig.* 15.1.27.pr. (Gaius); *Dig.* 15.1.1.2–3 (Ulp.). See García Garrido 1958: 13 ff. and 22 ff.; Aubert 1994: 66.

62. See below, this chapter, p. 140, n. 88 .

to restrict elite women's overt involvement in the routine operations of a business entity, free women, in my opinion, did engage in various financial businesses, including banking,[63] but in a manner compatible with traditional Roman values—through the physical intermediation of their slaves and other dependents.[64]

Gender Equality and Inequality

Legal authorities ancient and modern have observed that "in many aspects of Roman Law the situation of women is inferior to that of men."[65] Females were barred from governmental positions. The male head of the family (*pater familias*) held dictatorial dominance (*patria potestas*) over all members of his household. Roman law even imposed a "male guardianship over women." It limited women's rights of inheritance and circumscribed females' capacity to provide potentially lucrative guarantees and sureties. Conservative social values and juridical precepts ("law in the books") tenaciously upheld "the appearance of male authority over property."[66] And yet, in actual practice ("law in action"[67]) juridical reality accommodated the needs of women working in commerce, facilitating the significant female involvement in business chronicled in the preceding section. Roman commercial law even purported to be gender-blind: any right available to a male was in general automatically extended to a female, and on issues and procedures relating to "commercial law"[68] women seem largely to have enjoyed juridical equality. Efforts to "protect" women by excluding them from competition with men for profitable

63. See below, section on "Female Bankers?"

64. Cf. Jakab 2013: 148: "A woman of some property, owning slaves or having freeedmen, could take part in all business without any restriction——through her dependants, acting for her as intermediaries."

65. Papinian, *Digest* 1.5.9 "In multis iuris nostri articulis deterior est condicio feminarum quam masculorum." See Pavón 2019: 196–197; Mercogliano 2011: 4–8: (http://www.teoriaestoriadeldirittoprivato.com/index.php?com=statics&option=index&cID=248#_ftmref32): Perry 2016: 436–437; Herrmann-Otto 2002; Gardner 1995.

66. Culham 2004: 151–152.

67. For the frequently inconsistent interaction of dogma and practice in Roman law and society, see Chapter 1, n. 8 and related text.

68. Because Roman law never developed a unitary system of rules governing commerce, modern studies of so-called Roman commercial law generally focus on various individual topics relating to business activity, principally *res* and *obligationes*. See Chapter 2, pp. 63–65.

financial opportunities were largely nullified in reality, albeit often not in legal theory.

Gender Neutrality in Roman Commercial Law

Avoiding direct contradiction of traditional legal doctrines espousing male supremacy, Roman law enunciated principles that obliquely imposed gender neutrality in business undertakings and disputes. Jurisprudents, for important example, insist that in legal context "the phrase 'if someone' encompasses men as well as women."[69] Thus, Roman jurisprudents felt that it was of no moment whether assets were managed by slave businesswomen or enslaved males: actions *de peculio* were authorized in either case.[70] Ulpian clarifies: "when an action under the Edict is granted 'to him,' and not explicitly also 'to her,' nevertheless the action is available to a person of the female sex."[71] In Gaius's words, "there can be no doubt that the term 'man' encompasses the feminine as well as the masculine."[72] However, as Ulpian observes, this is a normal, not an absolute and universal rule: "a statement employing the masculine gender generally (*plerumque*) extends to either gender."[73] Moreover, despite the presumed inclusion of females in any rule applicable to males, statements pertaining to females as a class do not necessarily encompass males.[74] Nonetheless, it is clear that through the law's commitment to gender

69. *Dig.* 50.16.1 (Ulp.): uerbum hoc "si quis" tam masculos quam feminas complectitur. In legal context, the masculine form of other words likewise encompasses both male and female: *seruus* (*Dig.* 50.16.40.1 [Ulp.]); *parens* (*Dig.* 50.16.51 [Gaius]); *patronus* (*Dig.* 50.16.52 [Ulp.]; *filius* (*Dig.* 50.16.84 (Paul.]). See Saller 1999: 185, n. 12; Benke 2000: 43–45.

70. *Dig.* 15.1.27.pr. (Gaius): ancillarum nomine et filiarum familias in peculio actio datur. See also *Dig.* 15.1.3.2 (Ulp.): parui autem refert, seruus quis masculi an mulieris fuerit: nam de peculio et mulier conuenietur. Cf. *Dig.* 15.1.3.12 (Ulp.): et circa rerum amotarum actionem filiae familias nomine in id quod ad patrem peruenit competit actio de peculio.

71. *Dig.* 15.1.1.3: de eo loquitur, non de ea; sed tamen et ob eam quae est feminini sexus dabitur ex hoc edicto actio.

72. *Dig.* 50.16.152: "hominis" appellatione tam feminam quam masculum contineri non dubitatur.

73. *Dig.* 50.16.195.pr. (Ulp.): pronuntiatio sermonis in sexu masculino ad utrumque sexum plerumque porrigitur.

74. *Dig.* 31.45.pr. (Pomponius): si ita sit scriptum: "filiabus meis centum aureos do," an et masculi generis et feminini liberis legatum uideatur? Nam si ita scriptum esset: "filiis meis hosce tutores do," responsum est etiam filiabus tutores datos esse. Quod non est ex contrario accipiendum, ut filiarum nomine etiam masculi contineantur: exemplo enim pessimum est feminino uocabulo etiam masculos contineri. Cf. *Dig.* 2.4.10.5 (Ulp.); *Dig.* 43.29.3.1 (Ulp.); *Dig.* 50.16.56.1 (Ulp.)

neutrality, Roman women came to enjoy many of the same legal rights as men in dealing with commercial property and commercial obligations. "An adult Roman woman is able to hold property, to negotiate, to enter contracts, to dispose of her property, and to become liable for her tortuous conduct."[75] For the law, it made virtually no difference, Ulpian insists, whether a business person engaging in maritime commerce, for example, was male, female, or even an enslaved woman.[76]

In contrast, the Roman law of succession did discriminate against women, possibly "to ensure that at least a sizeable portion of large patrimonies would always pass directly into male hands."[77] In fact, prior to the time of Hadrian, women could not even make testamentary arrangements without satisfying a number of obstructive and time-consuming formalities to which men were not subject.[78] The inheritance rights of females were inferior to those of males: women might more easily be disinherited by will[79] and were at least theoretically precluded under the Lex Voconia from inheriting more than 100,000 *sesterces*[80] (although this limitation might be easily evaded through a *fideicommissum* which effectively allowed women to receive inheritances of unlimited amounts[81]). In the event of intestacy, however, shares in father's estates were allocated on equal terms to sons and daughters (who during the lifetime of the *pater familias* had both been equally subject to patriarchal authority).[82]

---

75. Benke 2012: 220–221, assuming that an adult woman has not married *in manum* and so is not under her husband's control (for these caveats, see below, p. 43. For women's juridical equality in commercial context, see also Gardner 1995: 378, 1986: 163–203; Benke 2005. In agreement: Manzilas 2016: 169–171; Setälä 1998; Peppe 1984; Van Bremen 1983.

76. See above, nn. 36–37 with related text.

77. Gardner 1986: 176.

78. Gaius, *Inst.* 1.115a, 2.112, 2.118.

79. Gaius, *Inst.* 2.127–128.

80. See Cic. *De Rep.* 3.10.17: Uocania lege lata: quae quidem ipsa lex utilitatis uirorum gratia rogata in mulieres plena est iniuriae. Cur enim pecuniam non habeat mulier? . . . Cf. Cic. *Uerr.* 2.1.104, 112. See Paul. *Sent.* 4.8.20; Gaius *Inst.* 1.115a, 2.112, 2.118, 2.127–128 (disinheritance); Cato, *ORF*³ Fr. 158; Gell. *N.A.* 17.6.8; Quint. *Decl. Min.* 264.12–13. For discussion of the alleged inferior position of women under this legislation (enacted in 169 BCE), see Benke 2002; Weishaupt 1999, *passim*; Gardner 1986: 171–77); Hallett 1984: 92 ff.; Vigneron 1983, esp. 144, nn. 20–23.

81. Gaius *Inst.* 2.274: item mulier, quae ab eo, qui centum milia aeris census est, per legem Uoconiam heres institui non potest, tamen fideicommisso relictam sibi hereditatem capere potest.

82. Dixon 2016: 466–467; McDonnell 2006: 174; Saller 1999.

But the juridical category of greatest female inferiority appears to have been the Law of Persons—with its "male guardianship over women," its limitations on females' right to provide guarantees and sureties, and its provisions for dictatorial dominance over the family by the *pater familias* and his *patria potestas*. But here, too, reality and dogma differed greatly—to the considerable advantage of female entrepreneurs.

"Positions Suitable Only for Men"

Women were barred from positions in governmental operations—precluded by legal dogma from holding military posts and excluded by custom from filling state and political offices (*officia civilia*). According to Ulpian, "women have been banned from all civil and public offices and accordingly are not able to be judges, nor hold magistracies, nor bring legal claims, nor represent or intervene on behalf of another nor serve as procurators."[83] Yet Paulus points out that the ban on women's holding public positions is not based on any alleged incapacity but merely reflects custom: "not everyone is able to be appointed as a judge . . . for some people are prevented by law (*lex*[84]) from being judges . . . some by custom (*mores*) . . . someone who has been expelled from the Senate is prevented by law (*lex*), women and slaves by custom (*mores*), not because they lack judgment (*iudicium*), but because it has become accepted, that they do not fill public offices."[85] Similarly, the praetor denied other public *officia* ("duties," "business services," or "offices") to women since these *officia* were appropriate only for men (*virilia*). Thus women could not make judicial applications on behalf of others (*postulare*)—because "involving themselves in the cases of others" involved "performing services appropriate only for men (*virilia officia*)" and was thus "contrary to the restraint appropriate to their sex."[86] According to Lactantius, Roman (male) public opinion

---

83. *Dig.* 50.17.2.pr.-1: feminae ab omnibus officiis ciuilibus uel publicis remotae sunt et ideo nec iudices esse possunt nec magistratum gerere nec postulare nec pro alio interuenire nec procuratores existere.

84. "The primary meaning of *lex* is that of a statute, law, passed in the way legally prescribed by the competent legislative organs" (Berger 1953, s.v.).

85. *Dig.* 5.1.12.2: non autem omnes iudices dari possunt . . . quidam enim lege impediuntur ne iudices sint . . . quidam moribus. . . . lege impeditur, qui senatu motus est. moribus feminae et serui, non quia non habent iudicium, sed quia receptum est, ut ciuilibus officiis non fungantur. See Gaius 1.190, discussed below, pp. 156–158.

86. *Dig.* 3.1.1.5 (Ulp.): edictum proponitur in eos, qui pro aliis ne postulent: in quo edicto excepit praetor sexum et casum . . . sexum: dum feminas prohibet pro aliis postulare, et ratio

shuddered at the nightmare of women in the Senate House, in the military and in magistracies, and in high command.[87]

But even in governmental matters, female exclusion from official duties or opportunities was never total. Women were openly associated with tax collection, for example, through tax-farming partnerships (*societates publicanorum*) that consistently provided a large portion of total public revenues: in a case preserved in the *Digest*, a female tax-partner, Moschis, is memorialized as in debt to the imperial treasury (*fiscus*) as a result of her involvement in such a governmental revenue-providing enterprise.[88] Women also sometimes appeared as advocates in the law courts.[89] Even when represented by others, women litigants were expected to participate actively in court proceedings. In a *responsum* of 294 CE, Diocletian refuses to reverse a judgment in a case in which a female litigant failed to protest in court against a verdict and thereafter did not take an appeal after judgment had been rendered.[90] But when women did assert themselves in public matters, they might be faulted for being overly aggressive: Ulpian claims that the praetor had imposed the ban on applications (*postulationes*) by females only in the second quarter of the first century BCE[91] after Carfania, "an extremely shameless woman," had

quidem prohibendi, ne contra pudicitiam sexui congruentem alienis causis se immisceat, ne uirilibus officiis fungantur mulieres.

87. Quin etiam feminis curiam reseruauit, militiam et magistratus et imperia permisit. Quanta erit infelicitas urbis illius, in qua uirorum officia mulieres occupabunt! Lact. *Epit.* 38.4–5, criticizing Cicero's admiration for Plato, who in the *Republic* proposed allowing women to serve in the institutions enumerated.

88. *Dig.* 49.14.47.pr. (Paul.): Moschis quaedam, fisci debitrix ex conductione uectigalis, heredes habuerat. . . . On women's involvement in governmental fiscal activity, see Klingenberg 1983. On tax-farming at Rome, see Chapter 5, nn. 30–31 and related text.

89. See, for example, *Dig.* 48.2.1 (Pomponius): non est permissum mulieri publico iudicio quemquam reum facere, nisi scilicet parentium liberorumque et patroni et patronae et eorum filii filiae nepotis neptis mortem exequatur; *Dig.* 48.2.2 (Papinianus): certis ex causis concessa est mulieribus publica accusatio, ueluti etc.; *Dig.* 49.14.16 (Ulp.): feminis quoque, quamuis delationibus prohibentur, tamen ex beneficio Traiani deferre se permissum est. Cf. Lamberti 2012; Milnor 2011: 615.

90. *Just. Cod.* 2.9 [10]: Impp. Diocletianus et Maximianus Ulpiae . . . quae constituta sunt, ut aduocatorum error litigatoribus non noceat, tibi etiam opitulari possunt, cum te praesentem neque causae palam ex continenti, id est triduo proximo, contradixisse neque post sententiam appellationis remedio, si tibi haec displicebat, usam proponas. See Crook 1995: 142.

91. Carfania died in 48 BCE: Val. Max. 8.3.2. See Bauman 1992: 231, n. 29.

annoyed a magistrate by brazen behavior in pursuing an application—an affront to Roman customs (*mores*).[92]

Roman *mores* did underlie social practices that scholars have sometimes erroneously attributed to formal legal prohibitions rather than to voluntary compliance with societal values. Serving as a guardian (*tutor*) over children was another "manly undertaking" (*virile munus*) from which, in the opinion of some scholars, women were uniformly banned by law.[93] In fact, Roman women did sometimes act as guardian of children (*tutela impuberis*).[94] Nonetheless, by the letter of the law, adult women themselves supposedly always required guardians.[95] This allegedly universal "guardianship over women" (*tutela mulierum*) provides yet a further example of the use of a Roman "legal fiction" to formalistically preserve legal dogma, while the law "in action" facilitates a very different reality (see below in this chapter, section on "Male Guardianship over Women"). Similarly, as we shall now proceed to discuss, the relative invisibility of women in banking has been ascribed to an imagined legal ban promulgated by modern scholars—rather than to the tendency of females active as principals in banking to operate through male dependents, avoiding the censure of Roman social customs that denigrated elite women's excessive public exposure to everyday commercial duties performed in interaction with men.

Female Bankers?

Female involvement in banking has deep roots in the ancient Mediterranean world. At Athens in the fourth century BCE, for example, women (including females of slave origin) were markedly present in the banking ("trapezitic"[96]) business. Archippê, wife of Pasiôn, the owner of the most significant Athenian

92. *Dig.* 3.1.1.5 (Ulp.): origo uero introducta est a Carfania improbissima femina, quae inuerecunde postulans et magistratum inquietans causam dedit edicto. On Carfania, see Chiusi 2013; Höbenreich and Rizzelli 2003: 61–72; Berrino 2002; Benke 1995: 203–212, 244–250; Cantarella 1995: 527–530; Cenerini 2009: 76–77.

93. See, for example, D'Aloja 2016: 656–657; Cantarella 1989: 596–600.

94. Gaius concedes in his book *On the Provincial Edict* (preserved only in excerpts) that the ban on female guardians was only "generally" (*plerumque*) true (*Dig.* 26.1.16.pr.: tutela plerumque uirile officium est)——thereby confirming by implication that women qua women were not absolutely banned from service as guardians.

95. See Gagliardi 2012; Giunti 2012: 366–379; Chiusi 1994. For women's management of their children's property, see below, p. 44.

96. For Greek and Latin terminology, see n. 111 below.

bank, was thoroughly conversant with trapezitic activities: she had access to the bank's records, and had detailed knowledge of its complex operations.[97] Indeed, after her husband's death, Archippê (herself possibly of slave origin[98]) had such control over the bank's records that she was even accused of having destroyed them, allegedly to prevent the development of legal claims against Pasiôn's successor, her second husband Phormiôn.[99] Women at Athens sometimes participated in bank-related matters even independent of a familial role. In one of the few instances in which information has survived regarding the circumstances that generated a specific bank deposit, it is a woman, Antigona, who induces a would-be business purchaser to marshal the substantial funds, forty *mnai*, to be deposited in a *trapeza* as an apparent "good-faith deposit." Even her adversary in the litigation arising from a notorious Athenian business scandal concedes her leading role in this complex financial transaction.[100] Although Athenian forensic protocol mandated that women who were not adversarial to the speaker should not be publicly identified by name, even in connection with their business activities,[101] a (presumably fictitious) woman Korinthia *is* identified as a banker in a comedic work that has been attributed to Menander,[102] suggesting that unfree women were, on occasion at least, openly involved in Athenian *trapezai*. In fact, Athenian banking was so dominated by wives and slaves that a *trapezitês* often would appoint a highly regarded slave as his successor and would direct his widow, on the principal's death, to marry the slave-successor. Thus a speaker in an Athenian litigation appeals to the jurors' personal knowledge ("anyone could cite many examples" of slaves who had been freed by their owners, entrusted with the master's bank, and married at the owner's direction to his widow[103])—and then proceeds to

97. Dem. 36.14: ἡ πάντ᾽ ἀκριβῶς ταῦτ᾽ εἰδυῖα.

98. See Cohen 1992: 76–77, n. 73.

99. Dem. 36.18: τὰ γράμμαθ᾽ ἡ μήτηρ ἠφάνικε πεισθεῖσ᾽ ὑπὸ τούτου, καὶ τούτων ἀπολωλότων οὐκ ἔχει τίνα χρὴ τρόπον ταῦτ᾽ ἐξελέγχειν ἀκριβῶς.

100. Hyp. *Ath.* §§4–5. On this episode, see Lanni 2004: 163–164; Zelnick-Abramovitz 2005: 217–218, 220; Scafuro 1997: 61–64; Cohen 2016: 720.

101. Institutions situated in the male world of the community sought to avoid all contact with, and even mention of, respectable living women. This effort reflected an ethical norm so deeply held that in Athenian litigation, speakers consistently employed complex circumlocution even to avoid mentioning their own female relatives by name. See Schaps 1971. Cf. Gould 1980: 45; Bremmer 1981.

102. K-A 8.1152: see Thür 2001: 147–152.

103. Dem. 36.29: καὶ πολλοὺς ἂν ἔχοι τις εἰπεῖν τοιούτους.

offer a number of prominent Athenian examples.[104] This trapezitic practice was not limited to Athens. In Aigina, for example, Strymodôros had married his wife to Hermaios, "his own slave."[105] At Assos, the banker Hermias (himself originally a slave) is said to have arranged the marriage of his niece and adopted daughter, Pythias, to his former teacher, the eminent philosopher Aristotle—who then proceeded to reside at Assos between 348/7 and 345/4.[106] (While there is no affirmative evidence that Aristotle, like others married to bankers' wives or daughters, engaged personally in trapezitic activities during this period, we do know that in the *Politics* he famously observed that although philosophers actually did possess an unusual capacity to amass riches, they eschewed this opportunity because of their deprecation of such nugatory activity.[107]) In any event, Aristotle after his sojourn in Asia Minor returned to Athens and his teaching, thinking, and research.

Roman bankers (*argentarii, nummularii, coactores argentarii, mensarii*[108]) operated businesses that accepted deposits and made loans from those deposits, thus qualifying (in modern parlance) as "true banks" rather than mere coin-changers or pawnbrokers.[109] These banks are generally recognized

---

104. Οὐδ᾽ αὐτὸν λέληθεν, οὐδ᾽ ὑμῶν πολλούς, ὅτι Σωκράτης ὁ τραπεζίτης ἐκεῖνος, παρὰ τῶν κυρίων ἀπαλλαγεὶς ὥσπερ ὁ τούτου πατήρ, ἔδωκε Σατύρῳ τὴν ἑαυτοῦ γυναῖκα, ἑαυτοῦ ποτὲ γενομένῳ. ἕτερος Σωκλῆς . . . . καὶ πολλοὺς ἂν ἔχοι τις εἰπεῖν τοιούτους (Dem. 36.28–29).

105. καὶ οὐ μόνον ἐνθάδε ταῦτα ποιοῦσιν οἱ περὶ τὰς ἐργασίας ὄντες ταύτας . . . ἀλλ᾽ ἐν Αἰγίνῃ ἔδωκεν Στρυμόδωρος Ἑρμαίῳ τῷ ἑαυτοῦ οἰκέτῃ τὴν γυναῖκα, καὶ τελευτησάσης ἐκείνης ἔδωκε πάλιν τὴν θυγατέρα τὴν ἑαυτοῦ (Dem. 36.29).

106. See Diogenes Laertios 5.1.3. Cf. Green 2003; Chroust 1972.

107. Aristot. *Politics* 1259a17–18: ῥᾴδιόν ἐστι πλουτεῖν τοῖς φιλοσόφοις, ἂν βούλωνται, ἀλλ᾽ οὐ τοῦτ᾽ ἐστὶ περὶ ὃ σπουδάζουσιν.

108. Based on the presence or absence of these descriptive terms, scholars have differentiated "bankers" (businesspersons receiving deposits and making loans from these deposits) from other Roman "notable financiers" (see Andreau 2015: 85; 2010: 145–147; Ioannatou 2006; Verboven 2008[b]). On the distinctions underlying the differing denominations of financial businesses, see Soricelli 2016: 351–369.

109. See Kay 2014: 107–128; 2018: 133–135; Harris 2019a: 172–173, 2011b: 236–238; von Reden 2012: 281; Andreau 1999: 40. Johnston 1999: 87 skillfully summarizes the mechanisms (*mutuum* [see *Dig.* 16.3.28 (Scaeuola)], "deposita irregularia") through which Roman bankers were able to lend out deposits despite Roman law's *stricto sensu* prohibition of depositee's use of objects on deposit (Andreau 2020: 95–96). For definition of a "true bank," in Roman context, see Andreau 1987: 3–20; in the context of Athenian and modern finance, see Cohen 1992: 8–11, 22–25. Cf. Levine 1997. I know of no one who accepts Bürge's opinion that "there were no banks in Rome; the Roman bank is a modern fiction" (1987: 508).

as cumulatively a significant factor in Roman finance.[110] Although there was no legal barrier to a free person's operation of a bank (in Latin, *mensa*[111]) for his or her own account,[112] the majority of cases discussed in Roman law sources involve slaves operating banks directly through their *peculia*,[113] or concern slaves or former slaves (or both together) working as *institores* (managers) in a bank owned by someone else.[114] Yet, according to prevailing scholarly belief, at Rome "the profession of *argentarius* (banker) was officially banned to women" (Andreau 1999: 31); "women were not allowed to be bankers" (Gardner 1986: 235).[115]

---

110. Rathbone and Temin 2008: 384; Andreau 2015: 85–86; Kaye 2014: 236 ("banks appear to have been ubiquitous in the Roman world of the second and early first centuries BC"); Harris 2019a: 172 ("the banks' potential contribution to the money supply was considerable").

111. Paralleling *trapeza* ("table"), the ancient and modern Greek word for "bank." The Greek and Latin terms both reflect the origin of deposit-accepting financial businesses from "tables" set up in markets as work surfaces for the exchange of the multiple currencies of Aegean and Mediterranean polities. Greeks working at the tables were *trapezitai*; Romans, *mensularii* or *mensarii*. For Hellenic terminology, see Thompson 1988: 829; Bogaert 1966: 169–170; Cohen 1992: 67–68. For Roman, Petrucci 1991: 1–62; Fadda 1903: 17 ff.; De Ruggiero 1961: 658 ff., s.v. *argentarii*.

112. *Dig.* 16.3.28 (Scaeuola); *Dig.* 2.14.47.1 (Scaeuola); *Dig.* 5.3.18.pr. (Ulp.); *Dig.* 34.3.23 (Pap.). Cf. *Dig.* 14.3.7.1 (Ulp.). See Petrucci 2002: 104–105. For Roman law's general indifference to gender distinctions, and Roman society's frequent countervailing inclination to sexism, see below, pp. 33–37.

113. A bank operated by a slave for his own account is termed (*mensa*) *peculiaris argentaria*. See *Dig.* 2.13.4.2–3 (Ulp.); si seruus argentariam faciat (potest enim), si quidem uoluntate domini fecerit. . . . sed si inscio domino fecit . . . . si seruus peculiarem faciat argentariam, dominus de peculio uel de in rem uerso tenetur. Cf. *Dig.* 31.77.16 (Pap.): mensae negotium ex causa fideicommissi cum indemnitate heredum per cautionem susceptum emptioni simile uidetur. As Petrucci (2002: 124) observes, "si deve considerare implicita l'esistenza di uno schiavo che esercita la *mensa peculiaris* che forma oggetto del fedecommesso." Cf. also *Dig.* 2.13.9.1 (Paul.): nihil interest, si successores aut pater aut dominus argentarii eiusdem fuerunt professionis; *Dig.* 34.3.28.9 (Scaeuola): rationes actus rei meae quae per mensam eius uidetur extra mensam in diem mortis meae gesta est, exigatis eoque nomine eum liberetis. See Burdese 1982: 756 ff.; Petrucci 1999: 218 ff. On books of account (*rationes*), and their wide utilization, see Chapter 2, pp. 56–57.

114. Slaves: *Dig.* 14.3.5.3 (Ulp.); *Dig.* 14.3.19.1 (Pap.); *Dig.* 40.7.40.8 (Scaeuola); *Cod.* 4.25.3 (Rescript of Alex. Seu., 230 CE); *Dig.* 14.5.8 (Paul.) (financial business not explicitly identified as bank); *Dig.* 14.3.13 pr. (Ulp.) habebat quis seruum . . . praepositum . . . mutuis pecuniis accipiendis) (lending business not necessarily operating as bank). Freedmen: *Dig.* 14.3.19.1 (Pap.): si dominus, qui seruum institorem apud mensam pecuniis accipiendis habuit; *Dig.*14.3.20 (Scaeuola): Lucius Titius mensae nummulariae quam exercebat habuit libertum praepositum. Cf. Petrucci 2002: 103–137; 1991: 199, 207, 322; Cerami and Petrucci [2002] 2010: 61 ff.; Chapter 1 above, pp. 47–48.

115. In agreement: Pavón 2019: 201; Benke 2012: 225–226.

Epigraphic evidence, however, shows that women were the owners of virtually all the slaves known through inscriptions to have been active in Roman banking[116]—a phenomenon reifying women's important financial interest, but probably not quotidian presence, in Roman banking operations. Such indirect participation in banking by slaveowners would be consonant with Roman law's strong discouragement of personal involvement in business by male or female slave-owners: limitations on masters' financial liability were effective only when a *dominus* was not directly engaged in, or even knowledgeable of, mercantile operations.[117] Such limited activity in mundane banking matters appears to parallel female trapezitic involvement at Athens, where women are not attested as participating in the everyday activities of a métier that was corporally demanding (receiving and protecting often-bulky collateral goods, physically safeguarding valuables, etc.) and socially interactive (dealing with male customers and male competitors), but where females, often of slave origin, took on a critically important, but largely opaque role within banking businesses.

The sole evidentiary basis for a purported prohibition of women bankers at Rome is a single statement, preserved without context, attributed to the jurisprudent Callistratus,[118] usually translated to the effect that "women are held to be excluded from the office of banker since this is a masculine type of work" (*feminae remotae videntur ab officio argentarii, cum ea opera virilis sit*).[119] In my opinion, this is an incorrect translation of the Latin text, based on a misunderstanding of the way in which women generally functioned in Roman business. Eva Jakab offers insight into such dealings through her 2013

---

116. See CIL VI.4422; VI.4423; VI.4424; VI.7600 ("sans doute": Andreau 1987: 95); VI.8727; VI.9155; VI.37381. Owners' gender is not, however, preserved in all surviving inscriptions that mention banking slaves. In at least one case, an attribution to female ownership is likely but not absolutely certain: the banker L. Rubrius Dossenus appears to have been related to Rubria, owner of a slave (Philodamus) who was engaged in banking (see Herzog 1919: #5 [= I.L.L.R.P 990], Herzog *R.E.*, "Nummularius," coll. 1440 ff.; Barlow 1982: 249, 259, n. 3)—but Andreau is skeptical that "le maître de Philodamus soit une femme"(1987: 497, n. 44).

117. For this and other reasons for slave-owners' absence from ongoing business operations, see Chapter 1, pp. 42–43.

118. Unlike many other legal statements excerpted in the *Digest*, this observation appears alone, without context and "lacks substantial reasoning" (Benke 2012: 226).

119. 2.13.12. Translation: MacCormack in Watson, ed., [1985] 1999 (still the sole English-language translation of the entire *Digest*) s.v. Similarly, Frier and McGinn 2004: 461: "Women are held to be excluded from the position of banker, since this is a male job." Cf. Petrucci's Italian paraphrase: "Donne, cui era interdetto, secondo la nota affermazione di Callistrato, l'*officium* di *argentarius*" (1991: 323). Pavón's French paraphrase: "les femmes ne pouvaient pas être non plus *argentariae* ou banquières, parce q'il s'agissait d'un *officium uirile*" (2019: 201).

study of the many substantial "financial transactions by women" recorded in the well-known and extensive Archive of the Sulpicii.[120] Jakab has perceptively observed a "surprising fact" that "until now nobody has taken notice of,"[121] that in most cases women "had their business transactions carried out by slaves and freed persons to a particularly large extent,"[122] "phenomena (that) can be reasonably explained by the desire of women for discretion. Female participants in business tried to avoid personal appearances at public places."[123] Women were expected to pursue commerce in such a way "that they did not involve themselves personally (*se immesceant*) in outside activities (*alienis causis*), contrary to the restraint appropriate to their sex."[124] Accordingly, women's utilization of subordinates at Puteoli explains why females were the owners of virtually all the slaves known through inscriptions to have been active in Roman banking (see above note 116 and related text). The Callistratus passage accordingly should be understood in its literal Latin meaning (and not in the "technical"—and misleading—translations presently prevailing): at Rome women "seem absent" or "separated" (*remotae videntur*),[125] from the practice of banking, "since this is a business suitable to men (*virilis*)." Roman legal authors knew how to write "women are excluded" from certain positions: *feminae remotae sunt ab etc.*, not *feminae remotae videntur ab etc.*[126]

Other Roman texts do confirm that women actually did work as bankers at Rome. Moreover, a governmental ban on female bankers would have been (1) in conflict with Roman law's general insistence in commercial matters

---

120. The name of the Archive "relates to the family [familia] of the Sulpicii, businessmen from Puteoli" (Jakab 2013: 128). See above, this chapter, pp. 130, 134–135.

121. Jakab 2013: 148.

122. Halbwachs 2016: 449, n. 27.

123. Jakab 2013: 148.

124. *Dig.* 3.1.1.5 (Ulp.): "ne contra pudicitiam sexui congruentem alienis causis se immisceant" (in the context of restrictions on women making judicial applications on behalf of others: see above, this chapter, n. 86 and related text).

125. Even in legal literature, *uideri* often (but not always) carries its basis meaning of "seem": cf., for example, *Dig.* 16.3.1.33 (Ulp.).

126. *Dig.* 50.17.2.pr. (Ulp.): feminae ab omnibus officiis ciuilibus uel publicis remotae sunt et ideo nec iudices esse possunt etc. Cf. *Dig.* 5.1.12.2 (Paul.): quidam enim lege impediuntur ne iudices sint, quidam natura, quidam moribus. In legal Latin, *remotus* (fem. plur. *remotae*) often means "discharged" (in the sense of "removed," rather than "banned"): see, for example, Gaius, *Inst.* 1.182, senatus censuit ut si tutor pupilli pupillaeue suspectus a tutela remotus sit; *Dig.* 5.2.8.15 (Ulp.): hunc puto remouendum a querella.

on legal equality between men and women, the *sine qua non* for the well-documented phenomenon of women's recurring prominence in Roman financial matters;[127] (2) in conflict with the Roman tendency to depend on *mores* ("customs") rather than juridical exclusions to disadvantage women (no other private profession is known to have excluded females through an absolute legal ban); and (3) in conflict with Roman banking's freedom from direct governmental regulation. For banks (and virtually every other business) the Roman world eschewed governmental regulations establishing rules for business operation or organization.[128] "Roman banking law" did not even impose governmental regulations common in modern systems such as capital requirements, guidance on permissible loans, and loan-to-value ratios.[129]

Women Possibly Involved in Banking at Rome

A female banker is the subject of a rescript issued in 155 by Antoninus concerning funds that had allegedly been deposited with her: the petitioner seeks confirmation from his female adversary's records that the monies claimed to be on deposit are actually owed to him. But the Emperor answers that access to her account books (*rationes*) is subject to the trial judge's discretion.[130] Since the acceptance of monetary deposits is an essential characteristic of a

---

127. See above, this chapter, pp. 137–138.

128. Because banking was a significant factor in the Roman economy (and a commonplace phenomenon in everyday Roman life), some juridical rules did come into existence relating to banks and bankers, a congeries of specialized directions that cumulatively are sometimes characterized by modern scholars as elements of Roman "banking law" ("diritto bancario": Petrucci 2002: 22; cf. Andreau 2020: 103–106 ["professional law"]). The Praetor's Edict, for example, contained evidentiary requirements mandating the availability in litigation of certain banking records (see below, this chapter, nn. 133–135 and related text). But these and other rules related to the operations of the judicial system, and only peripherally and coincidentally to the conduct of financial businesses.

129. Scholars, however, sometimes assume that such regulation did exist at Rome. Thus Andreau (1999: vii) in his volume on *Banking and Business in the Roman World* promises to "examine the way in which Rome and the various cities of the Empire controlled and regulated banking and private business." Andreau does recognize, however, that "the vast majority of businessmen, whether or not they were bankers, were private entrepreneurs, and the State and the cities did not intervene in their affairs" (5). Not until the third century CE does he find two "unfortunately indirect and fleeting references to exceptional measures applicable solely to the banking business" (CIL VI.1035 and CIL VI.1101), allusions so arcane that many scholars deny their applicability to "banking" (see, for example, re CIL VI.1 101, Gordon and Gordon 1965: 91–92 ("money-lenders? money-changers or silversmiths? . . . shorthand writers? scribes?").

130. *Cod.* 2.1.1. Imperator Antoninus. Ipse dispice, quemadmodum pecuniam, quam deposuisse te dicis, deberi tibi probes. Nam quod desideras, ut rationes suas aduersaria tua exhibeat, id ex causa ad iudicis officium pertinere solet. On *rationes,* see Chapter 2, pp. 56–57.

mensa (or "true bank"[131]), a dispute concerning funds on deposit would seem to identify the underlying business as a bank.[132] Gardner, however, believing from the Callistratus passage that women were absolutely precluded from becoming bankers, argues that "the praetor's edict obliged bankers to put their account books into evidence in any litigation concerning clients" (1987: 235–236) and that therefore the woman must have been not a banker but some other type of deposit-holder. In fact, although litigants' own banking records in principle were available to them as a legal right,[133] accessibility to such material in practice was subject to highly nuanced juridical determinations,[134] and so the rescript advises the petitioner, "as is usual" in such cases, to seek a court ruling allowing access to his accounts.[135]

Another example of a woman involved in banking: during the Early Empire a female slave, Helena, is identified on a surviving inscription as an *argent(aria)*, a female banker.[136] Although the feminine ending *-aria* is not preserved on the inscription, the female name "Helena" *is* fully preserved, and the natural restoration for the surviving "argent" ("bank-"[137]) on the stone is *argent(aria)* ("'female banker")—as the editors of Volume 6 of the Corpus Inscriptionum Latinarum (CIL) had made clear already in the nineteenth century.[138]

Some scholars have identified a further female banker in a passage from the *Digest* dealing with a *negotiatrix*'s bequest of silver to her daughter.[139] (The

131. See above, nn. 108–111 and related text.

132. As Crifo pointed out long ago: 1964: 151 ff.

133. *Dig.* 2.13.4.1 (Ulp.).

134. *Dig.* 2.13.4.2–3 (Ulp.) offers examples of the kinds of complex issues that might preclude provision of these materials to a litigant. Cf. *Dig.* 2.13.6 (Ulp.), 8 (Ulp.), 9 (Paul.), 10 (Gaius). See Petrucci 2002: 118–123; Andreau 2001: 129–131; Juglar 1894: 15.

135. "id ex causa ad iudicis officium pertinere solet" (full Latin text at n. 130 above).

136. CIL VI.5184: Helena Artemae | Augustae l(iberti) argent(aria) | cui is dedit ollam I mort.

137. As Andreau has noted, in Roman inscriptions "les mots *argentarius* etc. désignaient ou concernaient des manieurs d'argent de métier . . . le mot *argentarius* est fréquemment abrégé . . . l'absence de la fin du mot n'est pas gênante, car il n'y a guère de confusion possible avec d'autres noms de métiers." (1987: 676, 679). Nonetheless, because Andreau accepts the prevailing view that women could not be bankers, he proffers the restoration "Helena Artemae | Augustae l(iberti) argent(arii)," insisting that "il est de beaucoup préférable d'attribuer la fonction à l'homme, et non à la femme" (1987: 97). In agreement: Gummerus 1915: 160.

138. CIL VI at 6.8727–28 ("item *argentaria* n. 5184").

139. *Dig.* 34.2.32.4: cum (Q. Ceruidius Scaeuola) quaereretur de tali legato: "hoc amplius filia mea dulcissima e medio sumito tibique habeto ornamentum omne meum muliebre cum auro

word *negotiatrix* is, in Latin, the female form of *negotiator*, a term defined in some dictionaries as a "banker."[140] In the relevant extract, Scaevola rules that the inheritance at issue encompassed only the silver she owned for her own personal use, not necessarily the stock of silver employed in her business. Although *negotiator* is often used in contrast to *mercator* (a "trader" or "dealer"),[141] surviving references seldom provide information sufficient to permit identification of the business pursuits undertaken by one identified as a *negotiator* or *negotiatrix*: the *Oxford Latin Dictionary* accordingly proffers for this term the nondescriptive translation "one who engages in commerce." This businesswoman may well have been involved in banking activities, but reference to her as a *negotiatrix* dealing in silver does not, ipso facto, rule out the possibility that she may have been only a merchant dealing in silver or silver products. The word *argentaria*, albeit the basic and clearest term in Latin for a "female banker,"[142] literally means a person "concerned with silver."[143] Gardner has even suggested that the *negotiatrix* here "might have described herself as an *argentaria*," thereby avoiding ambiguity.[144] This, of course, *is* the term recorded for and applied to Helena, the female banking slave who appeared in our preceding example. Even in Helena's case, however,

---

et si qua alia muliebria apparuerint," cum testatrix negotiatrix fuerit, an non solum argentum, quod in domo uel intra horreum usibus eius fuit, legato cedit, sed etiam quod in basilica fuit muliebre: respondit, si testatrix habuit proprium argentum ad usum suum paratum, non uideri id legatum, quod negotiandi causa uenale proponi soleret, nisi de eo quoque sensisse is qui petat probet. Translation (Watson, ed., [1985] 1999): "(Scaeuola) was also asked about a legacy of the following kind: 'Further, let my dearest daughter take from the residue and have for herself all my women's jewelry, together with the gold and other female accoutrements.' Since the testatrix was a businesswoman (*negotiatrix*), do not merely the silver that was kept at home or in store for her own use but also the women's silver articles kept at her commercial premises pass under the legacy? (Scaeuola) has given it as his opinion that if the testatrix had silver of her own acquired for her own use, the silver which she used to put up for sale in the course of business is not regarded as part of the legacy, unless the claimant proves that her intention had embraced this too."

140. *Lewis and Charles Latin Dictionary*, s.v. *negotiator*: "one who does business by wholesale, a wholesale dealer, a banker."

141. See, for example, Cic. *Uerr.* 2.2.77 (postulo ut mihi respondeat qui sit is Uerrucius, mercator an negotiator. . . .), *Planc.* 26 [64] (negotiatoribus comis, mercatoribus iustus).

142. Andreau 1987: 676.

143. *Oxford Latin Dictionary*, s.v.

144. 1986: 235. In *Digest* 34.2.32.4 (above, n. 96), the *negotiatrix* does not describe herself: there survives only an excerpt from a legal discussion by Scaeuola cited in abbreviated form by Paulus in Book 2 of his *Uitellius* (which in turn is excerpted in the *Digest*, shorn of context and content).

scholars who accept the Callistratus passage as banning women from banking have felt constrained to deny even an *argentaria*'s (female banker's) involvement in banking.

Fathers' (and Sometimes Mothers') Power over Family Members

A seminal characteristic of Roman society and law is the enormous power (*patria potestas*) granted to the household's male progenitor (*pater familias*), a masculine authority unique (*proprium*) to *ius Romanum*, or so the Romans thought.[145] Under *patria potestas* only the head of a Roman household is *sui iuris* ("under his [her] own legal authority"): all other family members—principally slaves and children—are subject to his power, and possess no legal capacity, or even persona, of their own.[146] If *patria potestas* had encompassed the spouses of *patres familiarum*, formal legal doctrine would then have precluded (and even law "in action" might have impeded) wives' functioning as independent businesswomen.

Wives, however, did not fall under marital control. Although husbands acquired authority equivalent to *patria potestas*[147] over spouses who had entered into so-called marriages *in manu*,[148] by the imperial period this form of union was long extinct.[149] Under its replacement, "free marriage" (*matrimonium sine manu*) which by the late Republic had already become the dominant mode of matrimony,[150] wives remained members of their natal families, free of their husband's authority, but subject still to their own father's control. On her

---

145. Gaius, *Inst.* 1.55: item in potestate nostra sunt liberi nostri . . . quod ius proprium ciuium Romanorum est. fere enim nulli alii sunt homines qui talem in filios suos habent potestatem, qualem nos habemus. Fathers were said once to have the power even of life and death (uitae necisque potestas) over subordinate family members (Gaius 1.52; Pap. [*libro singulari de adulteris*] *Collatio* 4.8.1). By the classical period, however, this right had long vanished (Frier and McGinn 2004: 191).

146. See Gaius, *Inst.* 1.48, 52, 55. Cf. Pahud 2013: 119–147; Kehoe 2011: 144–147; Frier and McGinn 2004: 18–22; Johnston 1999: 30–31. For the substantial economic impact of *patria potestas*, see Chapter 1, pp. 40–47.

147. A wife in *manum* "was legally in the position of a daughter" (Jakab 2016: 505). See Astolfi 2004; Treggiari 1991; Volterra 1991.

148. Gaius *Inst.* 1.110, 112, 1.137–137a. (In Latin, "manus" was literally the "hand" of the husband.). For the situation of Roman wives as portrayed in non-legal ("literary") sources, see Höbenreich and Rizzelli 2003: 112–166.

149. Tac. *Ann.* 4.16; Gaius *Inst.* 1.123, 136. See Gardner 1986: 11–15; Frier and McGinn 2004: 54–55.

150. Lewis 2015: 165; Cantarella 2016: 425.

father's death, a married woman legally became *sui iuris* ("under her own legal authority"), head of her own household as a *mater familias* ("mother of the family" or "mother of the household"),[151] a designation linguistically parallel to *pater familias* ("father of the family" or "father of the household"). Since life expectancies were low,[152] *matres familiarum* would not have been rare.

In fact, for the words *mater familias* there survive "an abundance of literary evidence"[153] and a multitude of ancient juridical discussions.[154] Modern philological studies have shown that the phrase had in varied contexts a broad range of meanings, but that in legal context it frequently, and explicitly, denoted a woman who was fully independent and juridically responsible (*sui iuris*).[155] Although it is sometimes suggested that the appellation *mater familias* is merely a synonym for *matrona* ("married woman," "respectable lady"), with which it is "interchangeable,"[156] "not a technical term (unlike *pater familias*),"[157] Ulpian describes the status of *matres familiarum* as directly equivalent to that of *patres familiarum*: "of Roman citizens, some are male heads of households (*patres familiarum*) . . . some are female heads of households (*matres familiarum*). . . . Male heads of households are those who are in their own power (*potestas*) . . . female heads of households are in like case."[158] The Romans recognized that households could be constituted in a variety of formulations.[159] According to a fragment attributed to Ulpian, where male and female were both *sui iuris*, Roman law recognized both as "heads

---

151. Fiori 1993–1994; Kunkel 1930.

152. Saller 2007: 90–91; Bagnall and Frier 1994.

153. McGinn 1998: 151. See, for example, Liv. 8.22.3; Quint. *Inst. Orat.* 5.10,.62; Gell. *Att. Noct.* 18.6.8–9; Val. Max. 6.1.8 and 8 *absol.* 12; Sen. *Ep.* 97.5; TLL, s.v. *mater familias* 440; Cic. *Cael.* 32, 57; Nepos, praef. 6; Serv. *Verg. Aen.* 11.476; Tert. *Virg. Vel.* 11.6.

154. Sampling of juridical allusions: *Dig.* 1.7.25.pr. (Ulp.); *Dig.* 11.7.20.1–2 (Ulp.); *Dig.* 23.2.41.1 (Marcel.); *Dig.* 48.20.5.1 (Ulp.); *Dig.* 50.16.46.1 (Ulp.); *Cod.* 9.9.28(29) (Constant.) (326CE).

155. See Wolodkiewicz 1983; Kunkel 1930. Cf. Treggiari 1991: 34–35.

156. McGinn 1998: 149.

157. Frier and McGinn 2004: 298. In agreement: Gardner 1986: 6; Perozzi 1947: 327; Bonfante 1925: 9: "materfamilias è titolo meramente onorifico che in epoca storica non ha valore giuridico."

158. "Ciuium Romanorum quidam sunt patres familiarum . . . quaedam matres familiarum . . . patres familiarum sunt, qui sunt suae potestatis . . . simili modo matres familiarum (*Dig.* 1.6.4). Translation from Watson, ed., 1985, 1999 (slightly adapted).

159. *Dig.* 50.16.195.1 (Ulp.): "familiae appellatio . . . uarie accepta est: nam et in res et in personas deducitur."

of households," in this context explicitly equating the *pater familias* and the *mater familias.*[160] A *mater familias* might thus be both the head (*caput*) of her own household—and (if she had no slaves of her own) its sole member, the totality (*finis*) of her own family[161]—thus attaining a legal autonomy sufficient for all commercial purposes. In short, a woman without children but independent of anyone else's control (*sui iuris*) was still denominated a *mater familias.*[162]

Where a woman *did* have children, recognition as *mater familias* seems to have carried the inherent right to manage the affairs of one's minor offspring after the death of the juveniles' father.[163] Even grandmothers are known to have managed the affairs of grandchildren.[164] With imperial consent, women might openly and lawfully serve as tutors over their own children.[165] Throughout the Roman East, influenced by Greek legal traditions, mothers routinely acted as formal guardians of their offspring.[166] In the second century CE, for example, Babatha, a Jewish woman from Roman Arabia, brought a legal action to assume management of her children's assets[167]---and as proof of her right to control this property proffered documents that had been drafted with provisions satisfying Roman requirements for a legal case installing herself as guardian (*actio tutelae*), suggesting the regularity of such

160. Sui iuris sunt familiarum suarum principes, id est pater familiae itemque mater familiae (Tit. Ulp. 4.1). (Neither son nor daughter was *sui iuris* if that person's father were alive even if s[he] had begotten his own offspring.)

161. *Dig.* 50.16.195.5 (Ulp.): mulier autem familiae suae et caput et finis est. *Dig.* 50.16.196 (Gaius): familiae appellatione et ipse princeps familiae continetur. feminarum liberos in familia earum non esse palam est, quia qui nascuntur, patris familiam sequuntur.

162. Fiori 1993–1994: 474: "l'espressione *materfamilias* non postula necessariamente un rapporto di maternità fisica, ma di maternità (in atto o anche solo in potenza) sociale."

163. *Dig.* 3.5.(30) 31.6 (Ulp.): quamquam mater filii negotia secundum patris uoluntatem pietatis fiducia gerat, tamen ius actoris periculo suo litium causa constituendi non habebit, quia nec ipsa filii nomine recte agit aut res bonorum eius alienat uel debitorem impuberis accipiendo pecuniam liberat.

164. *Dig.* 3.5.33(34) (Paul.): auia nepotis sui negotia gessit: defunctis utrisque auiae heredes conveniebantur a nepotis heredibus negotiorum gestorum actione. See Halbwachs 2014; Schmidt-Ott 1993: 197 ff.

165. *Dig.* 26.1.18.pr. (Neratius): feminae tutores dari non possunt, quia id munus masculorum est, nisi a principe filiorum tutelam specialiter postulent. For mothers so serving, see Gagliardi 2017: 223–227.

166. Gagliardi 2017: 231–236; Hübner 2009: 68; Vuolanto 2002.

167. P Yadin 28–30. For the Babatha archives, see Chiusi 2020; Czajkowski 2017; Meyer 2007: 53–56; Cotton 2002: 18.

female administration in the Eastern Empire. This assumption of a guardianship role brings the *mater familias* in the eastern part of the Empire transparently into direct commensurability, indeed parity, with the *pater familias*, for there (especially after promulgation of the *Constitutio Antoniniana*) *patria potestas* itself had been "reduced to a sort of guardianship over minor children, with the father in fact frequently labelled as guardian."[168]

Prohibition of Credit Enhancement by Women: *Senatus consultum* Velleianum

The shibboleth "functions suitable only for men!" (*virilia officia*) was also trotted out in an effort to deny women a place in "intercession" (*intercessio*: literally "stepping in"). In essence, intercession was a form of credit enhancement that involved the assumption of another person's debt,[169] either directly by replacing that person as obligor,[170] or indirectly through guaranteeing payment of the debt and/or providing security for its requital,[171] or through obligating oneself alongside the original borrower. Because of the ruinous consequences of defaulting on Roman debt,[172] as consideration for intercession substantial fees might be obtained from a debtor unable to meet his or her obligations. Since *intercessio* did not require an actual advance of funds (*mutui datio*),[173] "Internal Rates of Return" here might be enormously high. Because of women's prominence in Roman finance,[174] females might be

---

168. Alonso 2020: 48. Cf. Taubenschlag 1916, passim.

169. *Dig.* 16.1.2.5 (Ulp.): intercedit: suscipit enim in se alienam obligationem . . . Berger 1953, s.v.: "to assume on oneself another's debt or a liability for another."

170. A creditor clearly would accept only a replacement who enhanced collectability of the underlying obligation: see *Dig.* 16.1.15 (Iulianus) discussed below, n. 173.

171. See *Dig.* 16.1.8.pr. (Ulp.); *Dig.* 46.1.48.pr. (Pap.); *Cod.* 4.29.6.pr. (Alexander Severus) (228).

172. See Chapter 1, p. 43.

173. For example, at *Dig.* 16.1.15 (Iulianus), a woman is posited to have invoked the *s.c.* Uelleianum as a defense (*exceptio*) in a case where she had promised to have a third party accept a payment to her as settlement of a debt owed to the third party by the person for whom she is "stepping in." The payment was made to her, but the third party did not release the debt. Iulianus is of the opinion that her *exceptio* must be rejected: otherwise the woman could retain her profit (*lucrum*) while avoiding the related obligation. She did not, according to the jurisprudent, actually involve herself in someone else's debt (*aliena obligatio*) and therefore should not be allowed to retain her gain (non enim uideri potest alienam obligationem recusare, cum maneam debito obligatus, et ipsa de lucro agat ac potius reddere cogatur quod non debitum acceperat, quam pro alio soluere).

174. See above, this chapter, pp. 128–136.

expected to be highly visible in this process, and richly rewarded therefor. Yet, a series of laws and imperial decisions (most notoriously the *senatus consultum* Velleianum adopted in the mid-first century CE[175]) provided that a woman might avoid responsibility for her involvement in *intercessio*: on objection (*exceptio*) the Velleianum legislation prohibited enforcement of an action against a female who had "stepped in."[176] Such exculpation seemingly would have prevented women from engaging in this potentially highly profitable line of business: no creditor would have accepted women as credit enhancers, no debtor would have paid for such "enhancement," if a woman "stepping in" could avoid her obligations merely by asserting her gender (as the jurisprudent Paulus observed).[177]

Yet, in principle the *senatus consultum* Velleianum became an integral part of Roman law—and ultimately was even received into various modern European codes, surviving in the South African Roman-Dutch law until 1969.[178] Roman legal experts justified the provision by asserting that it would not be "right" (*aequum*) for females to function as guarantors and serve as sureties because these were "functions suitable only for men" (*virilia officia*).[179] Indeed, female exclusion was allegedly for the benefit of the women themselves, since otherwise because of the intellectual incapacity of their sex (*sexus inbecillitas*) they would be seduced and deceived in many instances.[180] Paulus, however, more candidly admits that the ban on female *intercessio* was intended not only to deprive women of "work and employment" (*opera*

175. *Dig.* 16.1.2 (Ulp,): et primo quidem temporibus diui Augusti, mox deinde Claudii edictis eorum erat interdictum, ne feminae pro uiris suis interfecerent. postea factum est senatus consultum, quo plenissime feminis omnibus subuentum est. On the *s.c.* Velleianum, see Finkenauer 2013; Benke 2001, 2012: 227–30; Dixon 1984: 362–69.

176. *Dig.* 16.1.2.1 (Ulp.): factum est senatus consultum quo . . . de obligationibus feminarum, quae pro aliis reae fierent . . . quod ad fideiiussiones et mutui dationes pro aliis, quibus intercesserint feminae, pertinet, tametsi ante uidetur ita ius dictum esse ne eo nomine ab his petitio neue in eas actio detur. For the mechanism of *exceptio*, see, e.g., *Dig.* 16.1.6 (Ulp.).

177. *Dig.* 16.1.11: si mulier tamquam in usus suos pecuniam acceperit alii creditura, non est locus senatus consulto: alioquin nemo cum feminis contrahet, quia ignorari potest, quid acturae sint.

178. See Thomas 1976: 243, n. 7.

179. *Dig.* 16.1.2.1 (Ulp.): Cum eas uirilibus officiis fungi et eius generis obligationibus obstringi non sit aequum. . . .

180. *Dig.* 16.1.2.2–3 (Ulp.): quia opem tulit mulieribus propter sexus inbecillitatem multis huiuscemodi casibus suppositis atque obiectis . . . nam deceptis, non decipientibus opitulatur.

nudumque ministerium), but also to ensure that familial wealth remained safely under male control in accord with Roman tradition (*moribus*).[181]

In reality, however, the Velleianum law seems to have been largely or entirely ineffective: the statute did not actually invalidate women's assumption or guarantee of others' debts, but merely permitted objection to efforts to enforce the guarantee or assumption. But that *exceptio* would be upheld only if the woman truly was an innocent party[182]—raising the factual issue of fault: "female mental weakness, not female capacity merited protection," "there was no aid for women who acted with cunning."[183] Moreover, to avoid the Velleianum provisions, women could structure transactions so that technically they did not fall within the parameters of *intercessio*: direct loans to an individual (albeit with the same purpose and effect as "stepping in"),[184] assistance to another provided through *mandatum* rather than *intercessio*,[185] and innumerable other possibilities for sophisticated structuring that would allow women to continue operating in this area of finance.[186] In fact, 150 years or more after the adoption of the Velleianum legislation, female "stepping in" remained so important that Paulus devoted an entire monograph to *Intercessions by Women*.[187] Moreover, a full title of the *Digest* (16.1) is devoted to multitudinous issues related to the Velleianum provisions—discussions that in number and detail are themselves testimony to the wide range and

181. *Dig*. 16.1.1 (Paul.): Uelleiano senatus consulto plenissime comprehensum est, ne pro ullo feminae intercederent. Nam sicut moribus civilia officia adempta sunt feminis et pleraque ipso iure non ualent, ita multo magis adimendum eis fuit id officium, in quo non sola opera nudumque ministerium earum uersaretur, sed etiam periculum rei familiaris.

182. *Dig*. 16.1.6 (Ulp.): exceptionem senatus consulti replicatione doli repellendam.

183. *Dig*. 16.1.2.3 (Ulp.): eis subuenit, si non callide sint uersatae: hoc enim diuus Pius et Seuerus rescripserunt. nam deceptis, non decipientibus opitulatur et est et Graecum: ταῖς ἀπατώσαις γυναιξὶν τὸ δόγμα τῆς συγκλήτου βουλῆς οὐ βοηθεῖ (id est: decipientibus mulieribus senatus consultum non opitulatur). infirmitas enim feminarum, non calliditas auxilium demeruit.

184. *Dig*. 16.1.11 (Paul.): si mulier tamquam in usus suos pecuniam acceperit alii creditura, non est locus senatus consulto.

185. Paulus (quoting Pomponius) shows how a woman can avoid the Velleianum provisions by structuring an "intercessio" as an undertaking by *mandatum*. *Dig*. 16.1.22: si mulieri dederim pecuniam, ut eam creditori meo soluat uel expromittat, si ea expromisserit, locum non esse senatus consulto Pomponius scribit, quia mandati actione obligata in rem suam uidetur obligari.

186. *Dig*. 16.1.4.1 (Ulp.): dum uult Titio donatum, accepit a me mutuam pecuniam et eam Titio donauit, cessabit senatus consultum. Sed et si tibi donatura creditori tuo nummos numerauerit, non intercedit. . . .

187. Paulus libro singulari de intercessionibus feminarum (*Dig*. 16.1.24).

high importance of women's financial undertakings even after adoption of the legislation,[188] suggesting that a legal provision meant to deprive women of opportunity actually had enhanced the strategic position of female financiers. If *intercession*-like activities went well for the businesswoman, she might graciously accept the profits. If they went poorly, she might invoke the Velleianum legislation in an effort to void her obligations. But considerations of reputational damage and business necessity would have precluded female financiers from frivolously invoking the provision.

Male Guardianship over Women

> *Women require the authorization of a tutor in these situations: if they bring suit by statute or in a statutory trial; if they obligate themselves; if they conduct a transaction in the ius civile; if they allow their freedwomen to remain in cohabitation with another person's slave; if they dispose of certain assets (res mancipi).*[189]

As Gaius makes clear in his second-century CE *Institutes* (the sole treatment of Roman law principles preserved directly from the classical period), guardianship over adult women was a fundamental doctrine of Roman law[190]—but a dogma that in logic had no reasonable basis: there was no persuasive justification (*nulla pretiosa ratio*) for placing adult Roman women into tutelage.[191] Gaius insists that the common belief advanced to justify this guardianship over women—that females are often hoodwinked because of their

---

188. "The multiplicity of records which have come down to us and the broad casuistry on this topic provide evidence (of) the highly complex tripartite legal relationships in which women were involved" (Halbwachs 2016: 450, n. 33).

189. *Tituli ex Corpore Ulpiani* 11.27: tutoris auctoritas necessaria est mulieribus quidem in his rebus: si lege aut legitimo iudicio agant, si se obligent, si ciuile negotium gerant, si libertae suae permittant in contubernio alieni serui morari, si rem mancipii alienent (translation: Frier and McGinn 2004: 453 [adapted]).

190. *Tutela mulierum* was seen by jurisprudents as unique to Roman law (*ius ciuile*), although the Romans believed it compatible with similar institutions that generally prevailed among foreigners (*ius gentium*). See Gaius 1.193: apud peregrinos non similiter, ut apud nos, in tutela sunt feminae; sed tamen plerumque quasi in tutela sunt: ut ecce lex Bithynorum, si quid mulier contrahat, maritum auctorem esse iubet aut filium eius puberem. Modern scholars agree: "subjection of women's legal acts to some male authority was virtually universal in antiquity" (Crook 1967: 114). Cf. Faraguna 2017: 273.

191. Gaius 1.190: Latin text at n. 11 (above).

flightiness of mind (*levitas animi*)—is "specious rather than true."[192] (Ulpian even suggests that men in business context needed protection from the superior cunning or craftiness [*calliditas*] of Roman women![193]) Accordingly, although conservative social values and juridical precepts ("law in the books") could not abandon "the appearance at least of men's control over the disposal of property,"[194] in practice ("law in action"[195]) guardianship over women was largely of theoretical and historical—not practical—significance.[196]

In reality, according to Gaius, Roman adult women handled their affairs for themselves,[197] an assertion confirmed by The Rules (*Regulae*) attributed to Ulpian: the guardians of male and female children do manage the business dealings (*negotia*) of their wards; the "guardians" of women do not.[198] Accordingly, tutors of male and female children had to account in court for their handling of their wards' interests once the minors had attained adulthood (*pubertas*); in contrast, a woman (or someone on her behalf) could not bring suit against a tutor for maladministration in the management of her affairs.[199] There could be no "maladministration," since "unlike the tutors of minors, they did not administer."[200] In some cases, for appearance's sake a tutor might be allowed formalistically to interpose his "authority" (*auctoritas*) to "permit" a woman to take a limited number of actions formally requiring a guardian's consent (instituting legal actions, disposing of certain substantial

192. Gaius 1.190: Nam quae uulgo creditur, quia leuitate animi plerumque decipiuntur et aequum erat eas tutorum auctoritate regi, magis speciosa uidetur quam uera. Cf. Val. Max. 9.1.3: de feminis . . . quas et imbecillitas mentis. . . . Although Cicero repeats this canard (mulieres omnis propter infirmitatem consili maiores in tutorum potestate esse uoluerunt [*Pro Mur.* 27]), nowhere in his multitudinous writings does he actually indicate a belief in women's need for guidance. To the contrary, he is awed by his wife Terentia's capability (albeit not her probity): see Dixon 1984 [2003]: 343.

193. See above n. 181 and related text.

194. Gardner 1986: 21.

195. For the interaction of dogma and practice see Chapter 1, n. 8 and related text.

196. By the High Empire, guardianship over women was "une institution qui à Rome n'est pas à cette epoque qu'un vestige du passé" (Méléze [Modrzejewski] 1974: 292).

197. Gaius 1.190: Latin text at n. 11, above.

198. *Tituli ex Corpore Ulpiani* 11.25: Pupillorum pupillarumque tutores et negotia gerunt et auctoritatem interponunt; mulierum autem tutores auctoritatem dumtaxat interponunt.

199. Gaius 1.191: unde cum tutore nullum ex tutela iudicium mulieri datur. At ubi pupillorum pupillarumue negotia tutores tractant, eis post pubertatem tutelae iudicio rationem reddunt.

200. Gardner 1986: 21.

assets [*res mancipi*[201]], entering into important transactions, permitting a freedwoman of hers to cohabit with a slave owned by someone else).[202] But if a guardian actually attempted to negate a woman's wishes, according to Gaius he was often compelled by the praetor, even involuntarily, to yield to the woman's supervening direction.[203] The availability of recourse to the praetor was probably sufficient to ensure that tutors generally followed women's directions: "that a tutor's consent *could* be compelled does not entail that it usually *had* to be."[204] Cicero even alludes to the existence of "guardians who are controlled by the power of their adult female wards."[205]

Considerable evidence shows that in reality this guardianship had been of limited importance from an early period.[206] Even at its inception, the guardian's power had extended only to action on matters relating to *res mancipi* (essentially slaves held anywhere and real property located in Italy[207]), "the main elements of wealth when the form was devised."[208] These assets as a class, however, increasingly became less significant as the enormous expansion of Roman power during the Late Republic resulted in the diversification of Romans' tangible and intangible assets far beyond *res mancipi*. This new range of dominance and wealth was accompanied by an unprecedented development of businesses of significant commercial complexity.[209] But no sizable or

201. On *res mancipi*, see below n. 207 and related text.

202. Gaius 1.190: in quibusdam causis dicis gratia tutor interponit auctoritatem suam. Matters requiring tutors' authorization: tutoris auctoritas necessaria est mulieribus quidem in his rebus: si lege aut legitimo iudicio agent, si se obligent, si ciuile negotium gerant, si libertae suae permittant in contubernio alieni serui morari, si rem mancipi alienent (*Tituli ex Corpore Ulpiani* 11.25).

203. Gaius 1.190: saepe etiam inuitus auctor fieri a praetore cogitur.

204. Gardner 1995: 21.

205. *Pro Mur.* 27: genera tutorum quae potestate mulierum continerentur.

206. Guardianship is already present in outline in the Twelve Tables (Tab. V.3 [UTI LEGASSIT SUPER PECUNIA TUTELAUE SUAE REI, ITA IUS ESTO], Tab. V.6 [QUIBUS TESTAMENTO TUTOR DATUS NON SIT, IIS EX LEGE XII TABULARUM AGNATI SUNT TUTORES]: see Crook 1967: 119). Beyond that, Romans seem to have had no clear tradition concerning the origin and development of *tutela maiorum* other than that it was "ancient": see Cicero, *Pro Mur.* 27 (n. 175 above). For modern speculation on the history of the guardianship over women, see Schultz 1951: 180–191; Thomas 1975: 44–45; Solazzi 1973, s.v.

207. Gaius 2.14a–17. See Capogrossi Colognesi 2016: 524–525; Vacca 1988: 54–74; Arangio-Ruiz 1956: 178.

208. Buckland [1931] 2011: 116. Cf. DuPlessis 2017: 168.

209. On this transmutation, see Chapter 1, pp. 41–42.

multifaceted company could function through exclusive dependence on a sole proprietor. Roman businesses accordingly came to operate largely through managers acting for principals, with many dependents sometimes serving a single master.[210] Yet women (prominent in the new economy, as we have seen above) were free to appoint as managers whomever they wished: their tutors' "authority" was irrelevant since the making of such appointments was not an item of *res mancipi*.[211] Tutors' authority was also irrelevant to women's making of loans—again not a *res mancipi*. Without assent from a guardian, therefore, women could buy and sell and deal in virtually all assets.

Even before the imperial period, businesswomen did enter into significant transactions, usually without any reference in our sources to tutors, occasionally with mention of tutors whose consent appears perfunctory. Cicero's multitudinous forensic and epistolary writings are illustrative. He alludes to the commercial and political activities of Sassia,[212] who placed one of her freedmen into a well-equipped apothecary shop in Larinum and made lavish expenditures to procure juridical influence,[213] but Cicero makes no mention of a guardian or guardians who might be monitoring her activities.[214] Cicero's own wife, Terentia, was able to pursue investment opportunities, to offer substantial real estate for sale, and to manumit slaves,[215] managing her wealth, in Cicero's words, "with a spirit stronger than that of any man"[216]—but no male is mentioned who might have "authorized" her activities.[217] The wealthy Caesennia (known from Cicero's speech *Pro Caecina*) purchased substantial

210. Pesaresi 2008: 9–11; di Porto 1984: 31 ff.; Serrao 1989: 17 ff. For Roman law's adaptation to commerce that functioned through agent-like managers, see Chapter 1, pp. 40–41.

211. *Frag. Uat.* 325 (Diui Diocletianus et Constantius Aureliae Pantheae: mulier quidem facere procuratorem sine tutoris auctoritate non prohibetur [293 CE]). *Frag. Uat.* 327 (libro XV responsorum): mulierem quoque et sine tutoris auctoritate procuratorem facere posse).

212. On Sassia, see Ige 2003: 47–50; Dixon 1984 [2003]: 347, n. 19.

213. *Pro Roscio Amer.* IX.27.

214. *Pro Cluentio* passim, esp. 63 (178): quae (Stratoni) . . . ornatam Larini medicinae exercendae causa tabernam dedit.

215. Investments: Cic. *Ep. Att.* 2.4.5, 2.15.4. Sale of real estate: Cic. *Ep. Fam.* 14.1.5 (scribis te uicum uenditurам). Manumission of slaves: Cic. *Ep. Fam.* 14.4.4 (de familia liberata . . . primum tuis ita promissum est, te facturam esse ut quisque esset meritus). Cf. Plut. *Cic.*, esp. 41.

216. Cic. *Ep. Fam.* 14.7.2: cohorterer uos quo animo fortiores essetis nisi uos fortiores cognossem quam quemquam uirum. Et tamen eius modi spero negotia esse ut et uos istic commodissime sperem esse et me aliquando cum similibus nostri rem publicam defensuros.

217. Crook 1967: 115: "(W)e hear a good deal about the business transactions of Cicero's wife Terentia, but never who her guardian was."

real property, and thereafter entered into a medium-term leasing arrangement for the property.[218] Although she is known to have had a tutor from her own family, there is no indication of his involvement in the real-estate purchase. She did, however, confer with friends and other relatives prior to the acquisition, and ultimately makes use of a certain Aebutius (who is not her guardian) to negotiate the actual transaction.[219] Clodia (according to Cicero's lurid account) was a principal in significant undertakings—advances of money on a flagrantly liberal basis, manumission of slaves, and sales of property.[220] Cicero does refer to her brothers, who were officially her tutors, but indicates that they had no real knowledge or understanding of her dealings[221]—and allegedly were never consulted by her regarding such matters.[222]

Of course, in forensic narratives, the manner of allusion to a guardian's authorization (or the absence of any reference) may merely reflect the speaker's rhetorical or juridical crafting of his argument.[223] Roman forensic addresses as rhetorical contrivances would virtually always present evidence tendentiously—or even with outright falsity. Nonetheless, it would be in the advocate's interest not to undermine his argument by making assertions whose premises are contrary to generally known factual reality. Since persuasion was a speaker's dominant motive, the presence of a general phenomenon may be confirmed by a claim that presupposes such a phenomenon, even if we cannot establish (or strongly doubt) the truth of the speaker's specific factual assertion. An assertion dependent on premises blatantly inconceivable or transparently untrue would be inherently unpersuasive. Thus when Cicero asserts the absence of Clodia's agnatic relatives from any supervision, or even knowledge, of her affairs, this may be an untrue statement. But if male

---

218. Cic. *Pro Caecina* 17, 94.

219. Cic. *Pro Caecina*, esp. 11–18. See Frier 1985: 3–20; Damon 1997: 222–224; Gardner 1986: 21–22; Rantz 1982.

220. Loan: auro opus fuit; sumpsit a Clodia; sumpsit sine teste, habuit quamdiu uoluit (*Pro Caelio* 13 [31]). Manumission of slaves: *Pro Caelio* 29 [68]) (n. 222 below); Sale of property: *Ep. Att.* 12.44.2, 12.32.2.

221. *Pro Caelio* 29 (68): "at propinquis" inquit "placuit." Cur non placeret, cum rem tute ad eos non ab aliis tibi adlatam sed a te ipsa compertam deferre diceres?

222. *Pro Caelio* 29 (68): sunt serui illi de cognatorum sententia . . . manu missi. Tandem aliquid inuenimus quod ista mulier de suorum propinquorum sententia atque auctoritate fecisse dicatur.

223. Gardner 1998: 246: "(W)e have to be wary of omissions and simplifications in our (literary) sources." On Cicero's artifice in advocacy, see Crook 1995: 141–144; Clarke 1953: 63 ff.; Frier 1985: xiv ("the 'Ciceronian court' (was) dominated by rhetorical advocacy").

guardians of women in Republican Rome had in general actually controlled their wards' activities, Cicero would have had to craft a different explanation for the guardians' failure to intervene in Clodia's improprieties.

But when one looks not to rhetorical presentations but to documentary evidence, the same evanescence of guardians is found, for example in the Archives of the Sulpicii.[224] Jakab's detailed study of the many financial transactions involving women from Puteoli (dating from 29 to 61 CE)[225] concludes that "all (these) businesswomen acted without a guardian," a phenomenon contrary to legal dogma ("as taught and learned in [modern] textbooks") and surprising even to the author of the study ("How was this possible?").[226] Outside Italy, the pattern is similar. In Roman Egypt, for example, papyri provide information on 110 women acting without a tutor.[227] Prefects in Egypt also are attested as appointing guardians who had been nominated by the future adult female wardsthemselves.[228]

In fact, women's right to select and to replace their own guardians provided women with a mechanism for effective control over their putative controllers.[229] Guardianship over an adult female traditionally arose through a deceased husband's appointment by will of a guardian for a widow who had been married *in manu*, a traditional mode of marriage at Rome that subjected a female to the control (*manus*) of her husband.[230] Such wills might name a number of men as possible appointees: the widow was given the power to select one as guardian (sometimes for a number of transactions, sometimes only for a single transaction)—and thereafter, if she so wished, to discharge him at her discretion and to appoint a successor from the original testamentary

224. On this material from Puteoli, see above, this chapter, p. 130.

225. These financial transactions are discussed above, this chapter pp. 134–135.

226. Jakab 2013: 125–126, 145, 148. Jakab suggests that "the widely accepted practice of contracting through slaves and freedmen released women (in fact) from a guardian's authorization" (2013: 148).

227. Sijpesteijn 1982: 158–71.

228. See *P. Oxy.* 12.1467 (FIRA III no. 27); Taubenschlag 1955: 177.

229. Gaius 1.150–53; in persona tamen uxoris quae in manu est recepta est etiam tutoris optio, id est, ut liceat ei permittere quem uelit ipsa tutorem sibi optare . . . quo casu licet uxori tutorem optare uel in omnes res uel in unam forte aut duas (151) ceterum aut plena optio datur aut angusta . . . (153) qua optiones plurimum inter se differunt. Nam quae plenam optionem habet potest semel et bis et ter et saepius tutorem optare; quae uero angustam habet optionem, si dumtaxat semel data est optio, amplius quam semel optare non potest. . . .

230. On marriage *in manu*, see above, this chapter, nn. 148–149 and related text.

list of nominees.[231] If a woman wanted to enter into a transaction for which a guardian's approval was needed, and the tutor demurred, he might avoid conflict by "absenting" himself (without regard to how nearby he actually remained)—in which case the female ward could move to replace him (because of his "unavailability") with a successor "guardian" of her choice (possibly only for the issue in dispute).[232] Despite the virtual extinction of *in manu* marriage during the Late Republic,[233] for centuries thereafter juridical discussions continued to give prominence to *in manu* matrimony (despite its constantly diminishing importance in real life).[234] By the time of Gaius, *in manu* marriage was defunct, but Gaius, in setting forth "law in the books," continues to discuss and analyze its juridical characteristics and implications.

Limited as it had become under the Republic, guardianship over women was progressively curtailed during the Empire. Under Augustan legislation, even the formality of guardianship was abrogated for any woman with three children (four in the case of a freedwoman). Another early Emperor, Claudius, abolished the one form of guardianship that women had previously been unable to avoid—the so-called *tutela legitima* of male relatives over "adult" females who at age twelve were deemed to have attained maturity and were therefore moved from being the wards of a male relative ("agnate") guardian over minors to becoming the wards of a male relative serving as guardian over female adults. Once this *tutor legitimus* had been eliminated, all guardians became powerless—all equally subject to a female ward's ability to replace them, subject to a female ward's power to compel them to confirm her wishes, subject to the female ward's ability to ignore them.

Factually, women continued to be of importance in Roman commerce, but *tutela mulierum* was now totally neutered. Yet in Roman legal dogma

---

231. Even agnatic guardians could be changed through a pro-forma surrender of rights, via *cessio (hereditatis)* and *coemptio fiduciae causa*. Gaius I.115: si qua uelit quos habet tutores deponere et alium nancisci, illis tutoribus auctoribus coemptionem facit. Cf. Buckland [1931] 2011: 60–61, 119, and 257.

232. Gaius I.173: senatusconsulto mulieribus permissum est in absentis tutoris locum alium petere; quo petito prior desinit; nec interest quam longe abrit is tutor. See, for example, Riccobono et al. FIRA III #69, vv. 18–24 and FIRA III #25, in which a woman Maeuia Dionysarion requests from the Prefect of Egypt the appointment of Iulius Alexander as her "guardian." Cf. Crook 1967: 115: "she could get a temporary guardian of her choice"; Watson 1967: 25 and 121–122.

233. See above, this chapter, pp. 150–151.

234. See Gardner 1986: 11–15; Benke 2012: 222 ("manus seems not to have been a regular implication of marriage from the end of the Republic onward").

it continued to be treated as an essential institution. As late as 293–294 CE, formal law (in conservative Egypt) continued to present guardianship over women as operational.[235] But finally, in the Theodosian Code of 438 CE, there is no mention of *tutela mulierum*. Legal fiction had become legal fact.

235. *Frag. Uat.* 325. See Dixon 1984 [2003]: 348.

5

Servile Imperialism

IN POWER, IN SERVITUDE

Many emperors—although they were the masters of the citizens—were themselves the slaves of their own former slaves: they were ruled by the counsels and by the whims of their freedmen.

—Pliny the Younger, *Panegyricus*[1]

Although much attention has been lavished on individual "freedmen" (*liberti*) who, especially in the first century CE, attained leading, even dominant roles in the Empire, as a group the Emperor's Slaves (in Latin, *Caesaris servi*) until relatively recently have been almost invisible in the massive modern academic literature devoted to ancient servitude,[2] a scholarly oblivion that belies their astounding importance, richly documented, in Roman life and history. *Tout court*, the Roman Empire was run to a considerable extent by an imperial administration consisting almost entirely of slaves and former slaves, thousands of whom even today (despite the relatively small number of individuals

1. §88: plerique principes cum essent ciuium domini, libertorum erant serui; horum consiliis, horum nutu regebantur. Cf. Tac. *Hist.* 2.92.2: seruilia ingenia . . . (serui libertique) in domum Caesaris transgressi atque ipsis dominis potentiores.

2. Weaver, author of the only monograph in English on imperial slaves and ex-slaves, notes "the grievous neglect," "the patent neglect of this subject" prior to his own study (1972: 2, 12). D'Arms finds it difficult to explain this "scholarly neglect" (1975: 335 ff.). Clarke asserts that Weaver had "virtually created on his own . . . a whole new world of beavering slave and freedmen bureaucrats working behind the Roman Emperors" (2005: 67). In truth, however, shortly before Weaver's 1972 volume, monographs on this subject had appeared in German and French (Chantraine 1967; Boulvert 1970: see also Wolf's unpublished 1965 Münster dissertation). Since 1972, despite the general flood of work on classical slavery, relatively little has been published on servile power and influence within the imperial administration (see Osgood 2011a: 271, n. 28). (Eck's editing in 2005 of the epigraphic evidence for imperial slaves and ex-slaves is almost entirely a reproduction of the materials earlier gathered by Weaver.) But this evanescence may be ending: see, for example, MacLean 2018: 104–130.

Roman Inequality. Edward E. Cohen, Oxford University Press. © Oxford University Press 2023.
DOI: 10.1093/oso/9780197687345.003.0006

involved in managing the empire) remain known by name, by significant relationships, and by employment history.[3]

This imperial staff is referred to in Roman sources by such appellations as "the emperor's household" (*domus principis*) or as "the emperor's 'service' (*paratus*) of slaves and freedmen."[4] In modern scholarly literature it has become fashionable to speak of the *familia Caesaris* ("Caesar's family"),[5] a recent formulation not attested in antiquity,[6] but accurately descriptive because the emperor's civil service was in fact organized and functioned analogously to the Roman *familia*, the basic constituent element of much of Roman life. Like the imperial administration, the Roman aristocratic private "family" was based on, and encompassed, long-term, quasi-permanent symbiotic relationships among masters and dependents—free, slave, and formerly slave.[7] Just as the structure of private Roman life and law mandated the conduct of commerce through the master's allocation of critical functions to his slaves and former slaves, and the exclusion of free persons from mercantile roles,[8] considerations of reliance, loyalty, continuity, and control motivated the *princeps* to administer his *imperium* essentially through his slaves and former slaves, epigraphically attested as *Caesaris servi* and *Augusti liberti*,

3. This information survives in more than four thousand sepulchral, dedicatory and other inscriptions found largely in Rome (and to a lesser extent in Italy and in virtually all regions of the Empire). See Chantraine 1967; Weaver 1972; Boulvert 1970, 1974. "(M)ost of the inscriptions are brief, but nearly all give some information, however exiguous, about wives, family relationships, ages, etc. and nearly half of them mention occupations and official posts held and membership of *collegia*, benefactions and municipal honours received, if any" (Weaver 1972: 9). Cf. Cooley 2012: 53–54; MacLean 2018: 3–4.

4. *Domus principis*: Tac. *Ann.* 11.28.1. *Serui liberti paratus principis*: Tac. *Ann.* 11.12.3. Cf. Plin. *Epist.* 8.16.2 (seruis res publica quaedam et quasi ciuitas domus est); Tac. *Ann.* 2.40.3 (multi e domo principis), 4.6.4 ([Caesaris] modesta seruitia, intra paucos libertos domus), 12.1.1 (principis domus), 13.47.1 (Graptus domum principum edoctus), *Hist.* 2.92.2 ([serui libertique] in domum Caesaris transgressi). For the expansive inclusiveness of the Roman family (*familia*), however, see Chapter 1, n. 97.

5. See, for example, Hunt 2018: 76–78, 80, 82, 119; MacLean 2018: passim, esp. Ch. 4; Taylor 2016: 354; Bruun 2014b: 617; Morley 2011: 283; Mouritsen 2011: 93–94, 179, 298; Eck, ed., 2005: Introduction; Schumacher 2001b, 2011: 598, 602–603; Millar 1992: 69–83; Barrow 1928: 139. Winterling notes that, *stricto sensu*, the term is historically inaccurate (1999: 115–116).

6. Weaver 1972: 299–300.

7. Only the head of a Roman household is *sui iuris* ("under his [or her] own legal power"): all other household members—principally slaves and offspring—are subject to his power (see Chapter 4, pp. 150–153; Chapter 1, pp. 39–41 and n. 97. Cf. Bryenb 2016: 322–323, 326–328; Mouritsen 2016: 404–405; Dixon 2016: 4; Hesberg 2005; Rilinger 1997: 73 ("Aus dem aristokratischen Haus entwickelte sich der Kaiserhof").

8. See Chapter 1, section on "Legal Inequality: The Privileging of Servile Enterprise."

respectively.[9] And just as within the private Roman household, where for slaves of economic talent and accomplishment even after "manumission" the boundary between freedom and slavery was often somewhat imperceptible, analogously for important *Caesaris servi* gaining "freedom" was a chimera, a virtual oxymoron.[10] Imperial slaves of skill and accomplishment tended, as they progressed in their careers, to take on a formally "free" status as *liberti* (and on occasion even to be named as quasi-aristocratic members of the praetorian or equestrian groupings)—but in reality they remained members of Caesar's family, still dependents of their master, evoking the same envy and fear from free persons that they often aroused when still formalistically enslaved. In present-day academic discourse, however, these individuals are almost always treated not as slaves, but as free persons whose servile origins deprived them of the respect and prestige to which they would otherwise have been entitled. Yet markedly successful slaves serving in the emperor's administration did enjoy significant rewards while still enslaved; thereafter they often became markedly successful "freedmen," likely enjoying even more of these rewards, but still deprived of many of the prerogatives otherwise available to free persons: in either capacity, free or slave, they were still in reality *Caesaris servi*.[11]

And just as the valorization of "slave enterprise" over free enterprise in the private sector resulted in a class of privately owned slaves and ex-slaves decried for their conspicuous wealth,[12] the Principate was so dominated by present and former imperial slaves that a litany of literary voices repetitiously charges that although Emperors often treated citizens like slaves, these autocrats were themselves frequently the slaves of their own slaves[13] and former slaves,[14]

---

9. MacLean 2018: 105; Bruun 2014(b): 617; Osgood 2011(a): 203–205; Oost 1958: 113.

10. See below in this chapter, pp. 175 ff.

11. Formalistically after manumission they are epigraphically denominated as *Augusti liberti* (for whom relatively prolific information survives) rather than as *Caesaris serui* (for whom only sparse data are preserved). For the reality, however, reifying the nomenclature, see below, pp. 19 ff.

12. See Chapter 1; Chapter 2, pp. 49–50 and section on "Owning Assets through the *Peculium*."

13. Dio charges that Claudius "more conspicuously than any of his peers was ruled by slaves" (περιφανέστατα . . . ἐδουλοκρατήθη [60.2.4]). Indeed, according to Dio, Claudius was enslaved even though he himself ruled over all the Romans and their subjects (καὶ τῶν Ῥωμαίων ἁπάντων καὶ τῶν ὑπηκόων αὐτῶν κρατῶν ἐδεδούλωτο) (60.2.5).

14. Plin., *Panegyr*. 88 (Latin text above, n. 1); Martial 9.79.1: oderat ante ducum famulos turbamque priorem et Palatinum Roma supercilium; Tac. *Hist*. 1.49: (Galba) amicorum libertorumque, ubi in bonos incidisset, sine reprehensione patiens, si mali forent, usque

inferior individuals whose arrogant dominance in governmental administration, belying their slave status and servile origins, was strongly resented by the free, but cowed, Roman populace.[15] (Such criticism, however, was invariably directed against rulers and imperial slaves no longer in power—for the critics a salutary protocol.[16])

Still, the phenomenon of Servile Imperialism—the dominance of even the highest ranks of the imperial service by slaves and ex-slaves—should not be exaggerated, either in its scope or its longevity. This ascendancy arose, and reached its acme, in the first century CE, and thereafter "freed slaves' sway . . . decline(d) gradually,"[17] although persons not born free are attested as continuing to hold important administrative positions well into the third century.[18] Moreover, the Roman Empire functioned through a large number of domestic groupings operating by imperial consent and practical necessity almost entirely autonomously of the central government at Rome.[19] From these centers of authority, slaves (entirely) and even *liberti* (largely) were excluded: free persons, usually men of property, here exercised authority and discretion.

Unfree Masters of Empire

The imperial government did not need, and did not encompass, a huge bureaucracy. The cooperation of the emperor's subjects was ensured by the coercive reality of the emperor's powerful military force—legions posted

---

ad culpam ignarus. See also Tac. *Ann.* 11.38, 12.2, 13.6.3 (Claudius . . . seruilibus iussis obtemperaturus); Suet. *Claud.* 28–29.

15. Tac. *Ann.* 12.53: Pallanti, quem repertorem eius relationis (*sc. s.c. Claudianum*) ediderat Caesar, praetoria insignia et centies quinquagies sestertium censuit consul designatus . . . adseuerauit Claudius contentum honore Pallantem intra priorem paupertatem subsistere. et fixum est aere publico senatus consultum quo libertinus sestertii ter milies possessor antiquae parsimoniae laudibus cumulabatur. Cf. Plin. *Epist.* 8.6.3–4: quis adeo demens . . . ut primus in senatu laudare Pallantem posset. Mitto quod Pallanti seruo praetoria ornamenta offeruntur - quippe offeruntur a seruis. . . .

16. Tiberii Gaique et Claudii ac Neronis res florentibus ipsis ob metum falsae, postquam occiderant recentibus odiis compositae sunt: Tac. *Ann.* 1.1.

17. Schumacher 2011: 598.

18. See Hunt 2018: 80–82; Bruun 2014a: 284; Mouritsen 2011: 95–98; Harper 2011: 437; Schlinkert 1996: 237–284. In the fourth century, however, there was a substantial resurgence of servile power, especially by palace eunuchs.

19. See Introduction, p. 4. For an overview of Roman Society in historical context, see Alföldy 1988; Peachin, ed., 2011.

strategically in provinces throughout the Empire,[20] a presence perceptible to the general population through interaction between citizens and soldiers, contacts often unavoidable despite the general segregation of the armed forces from the resident inhabitants.[21] In many provinces, a deeply engrained inclination, even before Roman conquest, to accede to monarchical control, obviated the need for large numbers of administrators working directly for imperial overlords and allowed instead a significant delegation of administrative functions to local units[22] that actually performed many governmental tasks entirely without direct supervision,[23] but always subject to the emperor's absolute right to ultimate decision-making.[24] Acceptance of imperial authority manifested itself in obedience to the serious commands (or even occasional whims) of provincial governors—often senators and former high officials[25]—who were sent out periodically from Rome, possessing dominant authority (*imperium*) over their assigned territories. These personages exercised a power derived from the emperor, who directly appointed certain provincial governors (*legati Augusti*) and indirectly entitled others (*proconsules*, who were technically assigned their provinces by the Senate in cooperation with the emperor). In addition, the emperor sometimes appointed members of the *equestrian* order as *procuratores* charged with special assignments such as managing imperial properties, collecting non-recurring taxes, or auditing the accounts of municipal officials.[26] These appointees, however, were few in

---

20. For the deployment of legions at various periods, see Tac. *Ann.* 4.5 (23 CE); Dio 55.23–24 (early third century CE); ILS 2288 (Antonine and late Severan period). Cf. the tabular presentation at Pollard 2006: 210, Table 11.1. Despite legalistic ornamentation, the imperial regime's authority ultimately depended on its armed forces: see Eck 2016; Birley 2007a.

21. On the "separation of soldiers from civilians" and "the social exclusivity of the army as a whole" (Pollard 2006: 224), see Shaw 1983; MacMullen [1984] 1990; Pollard 1996; various papers in Goldsworthy and Haynes, eds., 1999. For civilian interaction with local military units and (especially) veterans, see Isaac 1992: 115–118; Alston 1999, 1995: 81–96; Pollard 2000: 85–104. For military officers acting as de facto judges in outlying provinces, see Palme 2014: 492; Birley 2007b: 318–324.

22. For local governmental structures, see Roselaar 2016: 124–131.

23. See, for example, Fournier 2010 (local administration in Greek-speaking provinces); González 1986 and Caballos 1996 (municipal regulations in Spain). Cf. Giménez-Candela 1981 and Weiss 2001.

24. Richardson 2016: 119; Osgood 2011a: 129–130.

25. Millar 2002: 271–320; Ando 2000: 152–174.

26. See Gleason 2006: 240–241; Eck 2000: 280.

number, with small staffs:[27] it has been plausibly estimated that in the initial two centuries CE, "the central government dispatched in any given year around 160 elite officials to govern its 55 million subjects."[28] These few "elite officials," however, were augmented by larger numbers of imperial slaves.[29]

In the Republican period, the collection of taxes and other financial functions had been intermeshed within the general governance of Rome and its domains. This control of monetary matters by provincial praetorian and consular officials had fostered corruption and had facilitated unjust extraction of revenues by "tax-farming companies" (*societates vectigalium*) and others working in concert with governors not directly supervised by the central government.[30] In the High Empire, by contrast, monetary functions, systematically separated from provincial governance, were concentrated within the imperial administration at Rome, thereby—at least in principle[31]—reducing the opportunity for malfeasance by individual governors and their associates, but increasing opportunities for self-aggrandizement by persons of slave origin working as imperial staff—some of whom gained enormous wealth and overwhelming power. The sway of Claudius's "freedmen," for example, was notorious: according to Suetonius, the future Emperor Vespasian gained his command in Britain only through Narcissus;[32] Callistus supposedly humiliated his former owner by making him wait outside his door while others were freely admitted.[33]

Most imperial slaves, however, were far removed from administrative power. Some were not even involved in the provision of governmental services, working instead on the maintenance of the emperor's vast personal property—his many residential villas and gardens in and near Rome, and in

---

27. Cic. *Q. fratrem* 1.1.10–14. Cf. Nelis-Clément 2000; Brunt 1990: 271.

28. Ando 2006: 179.

29. Quantification of the slave component of the imperial administration has proven elusive, but the number of "slaves and seconded soldiers performing administrative duties throughout the empire" in the first and second centuries has been estimated at perhaps 10,000 (Kelly 2004: 111) and perhaps twice that number (Harris 2016: 168, n. 62).

30. On Roman "tax-farming,"' see Tan 2017: 40–67. Cf. Kiser and Kane 2007; Fleckner 2020: 247–248; Shaw 2022: 78–127.

31. In practice, "tax farming did not disappear altogether under the emperors, (but it was) progressively pruned way back" (Tan 2017: 65–66). Similarly: Lo Cascio 2007: 632. Cf. Lo Cascio 2000: 183–184; Sirks 2018: 106–108.

32. *Uesp.* 4.1: "Narcissi gratia."

33. Sen. *Epist.* 47.9.

other parts of Italy and throughout the Empire.[34] Of those slaves who *were* involved with the provision of public services, many had slight, if any, discretion in the implementation of imperial functions, and therefore virtually no opportunity for personal advancement or advantage, as they toiled, anonymously, in mining and quarrying, and in building and maintaining roads, mail service, and public works.[35] Like the private *servi* engaged in domestic service and agriculture, little is known individually of these low-skilled, low-profile, interchangeable imperial slaves.

Far different was the situation of the imperial slaves with direct access to the emperor—his doctors, his food-tasters, his valets, his guards and stewards, the persons responsible for official functions like written communications or aesthetic activities. Many of these functionaries were able to rise to levels at which they had the resources to pay for the sepulchral inscriptions that attest to their successful careers, and sometimes allude to their humbler initial assignments—employment, for example, as lower-level managers (*vicarii*), financial assistants (*arcarii*), or record-keepers (*tabellarii*).[36] Those who gained high positions, however, often ignore in their epitaphs earlier lowly jobs and make reference only to relatively exalted posts in the imperial bureaucracy: assignments as overseers (*praepositi*), personal assistants to officers of importance (*proximi*), placements as senior managers (*procuratores*).[37] While imperial slaves and "freedmen" could attain great power and high emoluments in a variety of administrative divisions (Narcissus, for example, dealing with imperial correspondence [*ab epistulis*]; Polybius working on cultural matters [*a studiis*]),[38] the likeliest path to wealth and power appears to have involved governmental financial functions, especially those which offered employees considerable authority and concomitant opportunity to generate, for themselves, substantial personal income through contact with monetary assets.

---

34. See Millar 1992: 175–201; Brunt 1990: 134–162; Hunt 2018: 76. On the Emperor's agricultural property outside Italy, see Kehoe 2006b: 298–99, 306–309.

35. On the role, for example, of the imperial *serui* in the building and maintenance of aqueducts during the Principate, see Frontinus, *de acquis* passim; Barrow 1928: 137–141. Cf. Hodge [1992] 2002; Evans 1994.

36. Relevant examples: CIL VI.64; CIL VI.8719; CIL VI.9052. For context: Osgood 2011a: 38–39; Schumacher 2011: 599.

37. Weaver 1972: 200–258.

38. Suet. *Claud.* 28; Sen. *Dial.* 11.6.5. See Seitz 1969.

Like privately owned slaves,[39] *Caesaris servi* possessed *peculia* in which they had a proprietary interest. The highly fragmentary work *De Iure Fisci* ("Legal Regulations for the Treasury"), preserved in a fifth-century CE manuscript discovered in 1816,[40] contains language that seems to confirm other evidence suggesting that each slave working on governmental fiscal matters had a 50 percent interest in his own *peculium*.[41] As long as they did not work in derogation of imperial interest (*in fraudem portionis Caesaris*), they were free to enter into contracts, to buy and to deal, and to manage their own property.[42] Accordingly, some imperial slaves, while formally still in servitude, did accumulate considerable wealth.

The father of Claudius Etruscus, for prominent example, was a slave from Smyrna (on the west coast of Asia Minor) who in servitude entered the imperial administration under Tiberius and ultimately became, under the Flavians, the highest fiscal official in the Empire, the secretary *a rationibus* ("master of accounts").[43] An encomium for him written by the first-century poet Statius provides detail of his career.[44] Admitted by Vespasian to the elite equestrian order after decades as an imperial slave,[45] according to the poet he had advanced at unusual speed through the various ranks of governmental service, always at the emperor's side, privy to secrets, eventually allegedly controlling all imperial revenues and expenditures, himself attaining extraordinary personal

39. See Chapter 2, especially section on "Owning Assets through the *Peculium*."

40. Only two incomplete pages of an apparently much longer work survive. The fragments were identified at Verona about the same time as the sole surviving manuscript of Gaius's *Institutes*. Cf. n. 63 below.

41. See Ulp. 20.16: seruus publicus populi Romani partis dimidiae testamenti faciendi habet ius. *Fr. de iure fisco* (12.1–3) provides explicitly that *Caesaris libertae* have the right to bequeath 50 percent of their property as they wish, with the remainder going to the imperial treasury: libertae Caesaris tam manumissione quam beneficio coniunctionis effectae si testatae decedant dimidium, si interstatae, <to>tum fisco uindicatur. Cf. CIL.VI.2354.

42. *Fr. de iure fisci*: 6.10–14: Caesaris ab ad<minist>ratione reru<m su>arum itemque comm<un>ium rerum comme<r>cio non prohibentur: ideo et stipulari ab his et <e>mere donatum<u>e accipere possumus, nisi cum in fr<a>udem portionis Caesaris fiat. Buckland thought that this right applied indiscriminately to imperial slaves and freedmen, although "as the whole passage is dealing with slaves, it seems probable that this (passage) refers to the *peculium* of *serui* Caesaris" ([1908] 1970: 325).

43. On the father of Claudius Etruscus, whose own name has not survived, see Stat. *Silvae* 1.5.65, 3.3; Mart. 6.83, 7.40; PIR^2 c 763. Cf. Weaver 1965, 1972: 284–294. On the *officium a rationibus*, see most recently Klodzinski 2017.

44. See Newlands 2002, passim. Cf. Hulls 2011.

45. Stat. *Silvae* 3.3.143: atque idem in cuneos populo seduxit equestres.

fortune.[46] Over many decades he served emperors in succession, from Tiberius to Domitian, entrusted with the "wealth of the world and of all its peoples."[47] While still enslaved,[48] he had married well: Etrusca, the aristocratic scion of a wealthy family, sister of a former consul, had added the prestige of high free pedigree to the talent and wealth of an enslaved administrator.[49]

Like the father of Etruscus, Pallas achieved high position and considerable wealth, apparently while still enslaved. He too ultimately became the imperial "master of accounts" (*a rationibus*), a position that allowed him personally to garner such vast financial benefits while serving Emperor Claudius that, supposedly, upon the emperor's inquiry as to why imperial revenues were inadequate, Claudius was informed (presumably apocryphally) that the shortfall would disappear if the *princeps* were to become a "partner" of his favorite "freedmen" Pallas and Narcissus.[50] Together with Callistus, Pallas and Narcissus were believed to be virtually in control of the entire Empire during Claudius's regime.[51] He became proverbially identified as enormously wealthy.[52] His own assets were so great, and his longevity so extended, that an impatient Nero reportedly plotted to poison him in order to obtain, perhaps justifiably as an imperial freedman's heir under Roman law principles, access to his fortune.[53] Yet Pallas first appears in surviving sources as himself the property of Antonia Minor, daughter of Octavia (sister of the first Roman

46. quam diues in usus | natorum totoque uolens excedere censu | testis adhuc largi nitor inde adsuetus Etrusci, | cui tua non humiles dedit indulgentia mores (Stat. *Silvae* 3.3.147–50).

47. Stat. *Silvae* 3.3.86–88: iam creditur uni | sanctarum digestus opum partaeque per omnes | diuitiae populos magnique impendia mundi. . . .

48. iura tamen geniali cordi | . . . iungere festa | conubia et fidos domino genuisse clientes (Stat. *Silvae* 3.3.108–110).

49. quis sublime genus formamque insignis Etruscae | nesciat? . . . . |nec uulgare genus; fasces summamque curulem frater et Ausonios enses mandataque fidus | signa tulit. . . . | (119) *sic* quicquid patrio cessatum a sanguine, mater | reddidit (Stat. *Silvae* 3.3.111–20).

50. Suet. *Claud.* 28: (Claudius) libertorum praecipue suspexit . . . ante omnis Narcissum *ab epistulis* et Pallantem *a rationibus*. . . ut querente eo quondam de fisci exiguitate non absurde dictum sit, abundaturum, si a duobus libertis in consortium reciperetur.

51. Pliny, *N. H.* 33.134–135: liberatos . . . tres Claudii principatu Callistum, Pallantem, Narcissum . . . adhuc rerum potiantur. Tacitus refers to Claudius' freedmen as "quos penes potentia" (*Ann.* 11.28). For the close association of high power with freedmen, see Cic. *Uerr.* II 2.13; Plin. *N.H.* 36.60; Suet. *Cal.* 56.1.

52. On Pallas's enormous fortune, see, for example, Juv. *Sat.* 1: 108–109.

53. Tac. *Ann.* 14.65.1: libertorum potissimos ueneno interfecisse creditus est, Doryphorum . . . Pallantem, quod immensam pecuniam longa senecta detineret. Cf. Dio 62.14.3; Suet. *Nero* 35.5.

emperor), and mother of the future Emperor Claudius, Nero's adoptive father.[54] Although little is known of his origins and early life, he appears still to have been in servitude in 31 CE, by which time he had already obtained "a position of great trust and confidence in the household of Antonia Minor."[55] (His relationship with Antonia was so close that she entrusted him with the delicate and dangerous task of delivering to Emperor Tiberius her letter warning of a purported plot against the emperor by his trusted and powerful Praetorian Prefect, Sejanus.[56]) Although nothing is known of his prior governmental career, Pallas appears in the year 48 in Tacitus's *Annals* (11.29.1) as one of three senior imperial officials seeking to deal with the alleged effort of Messalina, Claudius's wife, to depose Claudius and replace him with her lover Silius. Ultimately Claudius yielded to Pallas so much authority that he was, reportedly, virtually the "ultimate authority" (*arbitrium*) of imperial power.[57] Although Tacitus characterizes Pallas as already extraordinarily high in the emperor's regard in 48,[58] the historian offers no indication as to whether Pallas was a "slave" ' or a "freedman" at this time. When Nero finally deprived him of the authority he had obtained under Claudius, Nero (according to Tacitus) found that Pallas—as if himself an imperial figure not subject to normal juristic strictures—had already arranged that he should not have to answer for his prior actions and that his accounts, as controller of state resources (*a rationibus*), should be accepted without question as "balanced."

Imperial "Freedmen"?

The Roman Empire itself rested on a fundamental fiction. In reality a military dictatorship,[59] for hundreds of years it persisted in self-presentation as an evolved continuation of the Roman Republic, directed by a leading citizen (*princeps*) to whom power had been constitutionally delivered pursuant

54. On Antonia, whose enormous importance in the Julian Principate tends to be overshadowed by the mesmerizing persona of Augustus's wife Livia, see Kokkinos 2002, esp. 6–33.

55. Oost 1958: 115.

56. Jos. *Ant. J.* 18.182. Cf. Dio 66.14.1–2.

57. Tac. *Ann.* 13.14: Nero demouet Pallantem cura rerum quis a Claudio impositus uelut arbitrium regni agebat.

58. *Ann.* 11.29.1: flagrantissimaque eo in tempore gratia Pallas.

59. Tac. *Ann.* 1.1.1, 1.2 ([Augustus] insurgere paulatim, munia senatus magistratuum legum in se trahere); App. *Praef.* 14.60, *Civ.* 1.24; Dio 53.17.1–2, 53.18.2. See Eck 2016a, 2016b; Birley 2007a; Béranger 1953: 31–40, 55–61.

to age-old and ageless protocols and traditions.[60] This imperial *imaginaire*—the Empire's "'self-image,' how it sees itself in fantasy, with a large element of idealization and wish fulfillment"[61]—still functioned through consuls, praetors, *quaestors*, senators, equestrians, and numerous other officials and groupings of the defunct Republic.[62] Rome was supposedly governed by "laws" (*leges*) "which the people orders and enacts," by plebeian statutes adopted by majorities, by resolutions of the Senate, and by judgments of its *princeps*[63]—all in reality actually fashioned by and administered by a government functioning largely through the slaves (*servi*) and ex-slaves (*liberti*) of the *princeps*.

Within this complex fantasy intermixing elements of *l'imaginaire* and *Realpolitik*, a clear and consistent perception of actual governmental structure and of actual personal status is largely absent—and apparently undesirable. Although (for example) the Romans professed to understand the propriety, and juridical necessity,[64] of segregating the emperor's personal wealth from state resources that were under the emperor's control,[65] in practice there seems to have been no clear boundary (but no absence of ambiguity) between public assets and the property owned by an individual *princeps*.[66] If

60. "(T)he change from republic to principate appears chimerical, at once . . . a momentous shift in sovereignty from the people to a monarchy, and yet also a return to an idealized constitutionalism" (Ando 2011: 38).

61. Loraux [1984] 1993: 3 (Translator's Note), with reference to *l'imaginaire* of classical Athens.

62. Tac. *Ann.* 3.7: eadem magistratuum uocabula.

63. Constant iura populi Romani ex legibus, plebiscitis, senatus consultis, constitutionibus principum . . . lex est, quod populus iubet atque constituit. Plebiscitus est, quod plebs iubet atque constituit (Gaius 1.2–3). Roman private law was also governed by praetorial and curule edicts and by *responsa* of jurisprudents (edictis eorum, qui ius edicendi habent, responsis prudentium: Gaius 1.2–3). Cf. *Dig.* 1.1.7 (Papinian). For an incisive survey of the sources of Roman law as perceived and enunciated in the High Empire, see Ibbetson 2015: 25–26, 28–40. Cf. de Zulueta's brief but nuanced discussion (1953: 13–23). For a more extensive analysis, see Kunkel 1973: 81–131.

64. We know the titles of ancient works that appear to focus on legalistic considerations governing the interrelationship between the *Fiscus* (the imperial treasury) and the *Aerarium* (the Treasury "of the people"): Callistratus, *de iure fisci et populi*; Paulus, *de iure fisci*. A few fragments likely attributable to such a work have survived (Fragmentum [fragmenta] *de iure fisci*). See above, n. 38 and related text. Cf. Liebs 1989; Baviera 1940.

65. Even Nero promised the Senate that he would keep the two separate: discretam domum et rem publicam (Tac. *Ann.* 13.4.2). On the original governmental *Aerarium* and the new *Fiscus* introduced under the Principate, see Bolla 1938: 19–20; Garzetti 1944, esp. 327; Millar 1963.

66. On the "severe technical problem" (Harris 2016: 187) of distinguishing state assets from the Emperor's personal holdings (*priuata res Caesaris*), see Brunt 1990: Chapters 7 and 16; Maiuro

an emperor's slaves truly were the personal property of the *princeps* himself, then pursuant to the requirements of Roman law, manumission of an imperial slave during the emperor's lifetime would have resulted in his continued connection with his former owner (and now imperial patron). Instead of the burdens of servitude, after liberation the freedman would owe to the emperor *obsequium*, *operae*, and *bona*, just as any private slave upon manumission remained under obligation to, and in relationship with, his "former owner."[67] On the emperor's death an imperial slave would have passed to the *princeps*'s heirs pursuant to private-law juridical principles of succession. A new emperor would have employed his own slaves to manage his new domains.

But actual practice was quite different. The assassinated emperor Caligula was succeeded by Claudius, who—although a member of the Julian family as a grandson of Octavia—was not a descendant of his predecessor. Caligula's slaves therefore should have passed to his heirs (presumably his sisters since his daughter and wife had been murdered shortly before he was killed), but hundreds of funereal inscriptions, set up by persons serving under both *principes*, attest to an unbroken continuity of imperial service under Claudius.[68] As we have seen earlier in this chapter, the father of Claudius Etruscus, even after gaining his freedom, continued to serve successor emperors without apparent change in duties; Pallas, although a "freedman," similarly passes seamlessly from high service under Claudius to similar executive heights under the new Emperor Nero. Epaphroditus was manumitted under Nero, but continued to serve through many successions: he is recorded years later serving Domitian, successor to Vespasian and Titus.[69]

In fact, Pallas's power and success enormously annoyed an aristocratic intimate of Emperor Trajan, Pliny the Younger, who decades after Claudius's death was still fulminating with irony, sarcasm, understatement, overstatement, and outrage against the accomplishments, pretensions, and arrogance of this imperial servant. In a letter to Montanus,[70] Pliny describes how he had

---

2012; Sitek 2017: 49–60; Jones 1950; Sutherland 1945: 159; Buckland [1908] 1970: 318–319. On ambiguity in Roman concepts of "ownership," see Chapter 2, n. 64 and related text.

67. See Chapter 2, section on "The Manumission of Skilled Slaves: Facilitating Commerce through Legal Fiction," especially nn. 140–142 with related text.

68. Osgood 2011a: 38. See Bellen 1974; Chantraine 1967; Boulvert 1970, 1974.

69. ILS 9505. See Eck 1976.

70. Plin. *Ep*. 8.6. Syme (1968: 150) has suggested that Montanus, otherwise unattested outside Pliny's letters, can be identified as Lucius Uenuleius Montanus Apronianus, a Roman senator who was consul during part of the year 92.

come upon a monument bearing an inscription recording the Senate's award to Pallas of the accoutrements of praetorian status and of 15 million *sesterces* for his fidelity and faithfulness to his masters (*patroni*): Pallas had accepted the praetorian status, but had rejected the money.[71] For Pliny, bestowing such public honors and offers of cash on "Pallas the slave" (*Pallanti servo*) is an outrageous indecency (*publicum dedecus*), even if Pallas were to have been the least self-aggrandizing and most faithful guardian of the imperial assets (*abstinentissimus fidelissimusque custos principalium opum*).[72] While modern scholars are unable to determine in what year Pallas obtained his freedom,[73] by Pliny's judgment an imperial slave could never be free of his servile origins. Even if (like the father of Etruscus), he had controlled all the resources of the Roman Empire, even if (like Pallas) he had enslaved the Senate itself, as a servile individual he could never be accepted as the equal of a freeborn soul (*ingenuus animus*: §17). He was "dirt" (*caenum*) and "filth" (*sordes*).[74] Even though Pliny knows that ultimately Pallas, at least formalistically, was denominated a freedman (*libertus*, 8.6.12, 8.6.16), he recurringly refers to Pallas as a slave—*servus* (8.6.4, 8.6.16), *mancipium* (8.6.14). Pliny even insists sarcastically that the "praetorian" slave should have been wearing not the golden ornaments of exalted status awarded by the Senate but the iron (ring) of a slave.[75] Tacitus agrees: Nero's negativity toward Pallas was engendered by Pallas's being a slave.[76]

Nero's condescending dismissal of Pallas as "servile" reflected Roman imperial "reality." Legally, a reigning emperor appears to have had unlimited power in determining the status and situation of members of his household. While other Romans, even holders of traditional offices, were bound by specific rules closely guiding the mechanisms and effects of purported manumissions, in situations relating to the freedom of a member of his household, the emperor's mere will was sufficient: according to Paulus (interpreting a "law"

71. Plin. *Ep.* 8.6.1: huic senatus ob fidem pietatemque erga patronos ornamenta praetoria decreuit et sestertium centies quinquagies, cuius honore contentus fuit. Cf. Plin. *Ep.* 7.29.2.

72. Plin. *Ep.* 8.6.4 (*Pallanti seruo*), 8.6.3 (*publicum dedecus*), 8.6.7 (abstinentissimus fidelissimusque custos principalium opum).

73. Oost 1958; PIR^2 A 858; MacLean 2018: 107.

74. *Ep.* 7.29.3. See Roller 2001: 270–271.

75. Plin. *Ep.* 8.6.4: compellendum ad usum aureorum anulorum; erat enim contra maiestatem senatus, si ferreis praetorius uteretur.

76. *Ann.* 13.2: neque Neroni infra seruos ingenium. Cf. below n. 84 and related text.

of Augustus), the *princeps* need not comply with any prevailing procedures. When he has merely "willed it" (*voluit*), the object of his would-be liberation is deemed manumitted.[77] But the manumission did not terminate the emperor's superordinate interest. According to Ulpian, it was more than clear that the property (*bona*) of his own freedman is not free of a *princeps*'s continuing rights.[78] Pallas, albeit the manumitted slave of Nero's predecessor, had remained in the imperial household as Nero's "freedman." But Emperor Nero saw him not as "free," but as "servile."

Characterizations of imperial freedmen as "slaves" would mirror the Roman practice of treating manumission of private slaves as a mere transfiguration of prior servitude into a fresh vassalage: the newly liberated "freedmen" (*liberti*) are routinely termed "slaves" (*servi*).[79] Similarly, Roman authors recurrently identify sometimes as freedmen, sometimes as slaves, persons who had originally served as imperial *servi* and had now been "freed." This conflation is encountered sometimes within a single sentence, in which the same individuals are indiscriminately referred to as "slaves" and as "freedmen"—sometimes even in narratives in which the author has in the same work explicitly reported the imperial administrator's transition from original enslavement to subsequent "freedom." For example, the Emperor Claudius, prior to the invasion of Britain, had dispatched to Gaul his powerful "freedman" Narcissus,[80] but the Roman soldiers there mocked their new leader with cries of "Io Saturnalia," imputing servility to the "freedman" Narcissus through reference (according to Dio) to the Cronian festivities where slaves comported themselves as masters,[81] thus expressing their view that this "slave" had no right to command free men. Likewise, according to Tacitus, rebellious natives in Britain were contemptuous of the slave Polyclitus, earlier identified by the historian as an imperial freedman (*libertus*) sent by the Emperor Nero to take command of Roman forces, to impose a peace on rebellious natives, and to resolve conflicts among high-ranking Roman officials. The enemy, however, not cognizant of

---

77. *Dig.* 40.1.14.1: imperator cum seruum manumittit, non uindictam imponit, sed cum uoluit, fit liber is qui manumittitur ex lege Augusti.

78. *Dig.* 38.16.3.8: principem ad bona libertorum suorum admitti plus quam manifestum est.

79. See Chapter 2, pp. 75–79.

80. Narcissus was one of a triumvirate of freedmen reportedly "in control" of Roman affairs under Claudius: see above, nn. 48 and 49 with relevant text.

81. Dio 60.19.3: οὔτε τι ἐκείνῳ εἰπεῖν ἐπέτρεψαν, συμβοήσαντες ἐξαίφνης τοῦτο δὴ τὸ θρυλούμενον 'ἰὼ σατουρνάλια,' ἐπειδήπερ ἐν τοῖς Κρονίοις οἱ δοῦλοι τὸ τῶν δεσποτῶν σχῆμα μεταλαμβάνοντες ἑορτάζουσι.

"the power of freedmen" (*libertinorum potentia*) at Rome, marvels at how the commander and the legionnaires of powerful Roman forces could obey "slaves."[82] Again, in seeking to identify that select group of free persons entitled to admission into the "equestrian order," the elder Pliny characterizes the mass of freed men (*servitute liberati*) as slaves (*servitia*) with no valid claim to equestrian pretensions.[83] In explaining Pallas's relationship with Nero, Tacitus advances the same presupposition of interchangeable equivalence—at least verbally—between "slaves" and freedmen: the emperor felt an existential superiority to "slaves," but Pallas's doleful arrogance, extending far beyond the limits appropriate to a "freedman," had brought disgust upon himself.[84] Similarly, Pallas's brother Felix, ruling over Judea, wielded regal power "with all the instincts of a slave."[85] For Florus, Sextus Pompeius's powerful freedmen were "filthy slaves" (*foeda servitia*).[86] "Filthy slave" (here *foedum mancipium*) is also Tacitus's term for Vitellius's freedman, Asiaticus, an important military commander, who for Tacitus was "a freedman" but one ultimately punished on Vitellius's defeat with "the death of a slave."[87] Foreign adversaries in the first century CE saw Roman commanders as "regal freedmen" (*libertos regios*) and "slaves in command" (*servilia imperia*)—and preferred war to subservience to such spurious "masters."[88]

The ambiguous perception—and ambiguous actual situation—of both important private and imperial *liberti* corresponded to the requirements

82. *Ann.* 14.39: missus est e libertis Polyclitus, magna Neronis spe posse auctoritate eius non modo inter legatum procuratoremque concordiam gigni, sed et rebellis barbarum animos pace componi . . . sed hostibus inrisui fuit apud quos . . . nondum cognita libertinorum potentia erat; mirabanturque quod dux et exercitus tanti belli confector seruitiis oboedirent. Church and Brodribb translation of *seruitiis oboedirent*: "cringing to slaves."

83. *H.N.* 33.9: Tiberii principatu nono anno in unitatem uenit equester ordo . . . passimque ad ornamenta ea etiam seruitude liberati transiliant . . . ita dum separatur ordo ab ingenuis, communicatus est cum seruitiis.

84. Neque Neroni infra seruos ingenium, et Pallas tristi adrogantia modum liberti egressus taedium sui mouerat (*Ann.* 13.2.3–4).

85. Claudius . . . Iudaeam prouinciam equitibus Romanis aut libertis permisit, e quibus Antonius Felix per omnem saeuitiam ac libidinem ius regium seruili ingenio exercuit (*Hist.* 5.9). On Felix, see Tac. *Ann.* 12.54; Suet. *Claud.* 28; *PIR*² I.695.

86. *Epit.* 2.18.2: so characterizing Menas and Menecrates.

87. Postulante exercitu ut libertum suum Asiaticum equestri dignitate donaret. . . (Uitellius) honorauit Asiaticum anulis, foedum mancipium (*Hist.* 2.57). Asiaticus (is enim libertus) malam potentiam seruili supplicio expiauit (*Hist.* 4.11).

88. Tac. *Ann.* 4.23: Maurorum auxiliis . . . qui . . . libertos regios et seruilia imperia bello mutauerant.

of Roman economy, society, and imperial government. Just as business would often have been crippled if slaves performing commercially important functions in family businesses—the foundational bases of the Roman economy[89]—had actually left the *familia* upon manumission,[90] the imperial administration would likewise have been hobbled by the loss of key administrators and managers. Because these key slaves stayed on in similar role and similar situation even after manumission by emperor or private owner, popular conflation of their situation before and after liberation was natural. In both private and governmental context, the clear distinction between slavery and freedom was seen not immediately in the case of so-called *liberti*, but in the next generation, with the children of *liberti*, who were known as *ingenui* and who, by explicit legal dogma, were granted the juridical entitlements of other men born free. A generation late, legal fact and legal fiction finally coalesce.

89. See Chapter 1, pp. 41–45.

90. For commercial dependence on skilled slave managers and operators, see Chapter 1, section on "Legal Inequality: The Privileging of Servile Enterprise."

Works Cited

Abatino, B., and G. Dari-Mattiacci. 2011. *Agency Problems and Organizational Costs in Slave-Run Businesses*. Amsterdam Center for Law and Economics. Working Paper No. 2011: 13. Amsterdam.

Abatino, B., and G. Dari-Mattiacci. 2020. "Agency Problems and Organizational Costs in Slave-Run Businesses." In Dari-Mattiacci and Kehoe, eds., Vol. 1, pp. 273–306.

Abatino, B., G. Dari-Mattiacci, and E. Perotti. 2011. "Depersonalization of Business in Ancient Rome." *Oxford Journal of Legal Studies* 31.2: 365–89.

Abel, R. 1982. "Law as Lag: Inertia as a Social Theory of Law." *University of Michigan Law Review* 80: 785–809.

Albanese, B. 1979. *Le persone nel diritto privato romano*. Palermo.

Alfani, G. 2010. "Wealth Inequalities and Population Dynamics in Northern Italy during the Early Modern Period." *Journal of Interdisciplinary History* 40: 513–549.

Alfani, G. 2015. "Economic Inequality in Northwestern Italy: A Long-Term View (Fourteenth to Eighteenth Centuries)." *The Journal of Economic History* 75: 1058–1096.

Alfani, G., and R. Frigeni. 2016. "Inequality (Un)perceived: The Emergence of a Discourse on Economic Inequality from the Middle Ages to the Age of Revolution." *Journal of European Economic History* 1: 22–66.

Alfani, G., and M. Di Tullio. 2019. *The Lion's Share: Inequality and the Rise of the Fiscal State in Preindustrial Europe*. Cambridge.

Alföldy, G. 1972. "Die Freilassung von Sklaven und die Struktur der Sklaverei in der römischen Kaiserheit." *Rivista storica dell'antichità* 2: 97–129.

Alföldy, G. 1986. "Die Freilassung von Sklaven und die Struktur der Sklaverei in der römischen Kaiserzeit." In *Die römischen Gesellschaft. Ausgewählte Beiträge*, pp. 286–331. Stuttgart.

Alföldy, G. 1987. *Die römische Gesellschaft. Ausgewählte Beiträge*. Wiesbaden.

Alföldy, G. 1988. *The Social History of Rome*. Baltimore, MD.

Alföldy, G. 2011. *Römische Sozialgeschichte*. 4th ed. Stuttgart.

Allen, R. 2009. "How Prosperous Were the Romans? Evidence from Diocletian's Price Edict (AD 302)." In Bowman and Wilson, eds., 327–345.

Alonso, J. 2013. "The Status of Peregrine Law in Egypt: 'Customary Law' and Legal Pluralism in the Roman Empire." *Journal of Juristic Papyrology* 43: 351–404.

Alonso, J. 2020. "The *Constitutio Antoniniana* and Private Legal Practice in the Eastern Empire." In Czajkowski, Eckhardt, and Strothmann, eds., pp. 43–64.

Alonso, M. 2011. "Medicae y obstetrices en la epigrafía latina del imperio romano. Apuntes en torno a un análisi comparativo." *Classica et Cristiana* 6: 267 ff.

Alston, R. 1995. *Soldier and Society in Roman Egypt: A Social History*. London.

Alston, R. 1999. "The Ties that Bind: Soldiers and Societies." In Goldsworthy and Haynes, eds., pp. 175–195.

Amelotti, M. 1966. *Il testamento romano attraverso la prassi documentale*. Florence.

Amirante L. 1983. "Lavoro di giuristi sul peculio. Le definizioni da Q. Mucio a Ulpiano." In *Studi in onore di Cesare Sanfilippo* III, pp. 1–15. Milan.

Anagnostou-Cañas, B. 1984. "La femme devant la justice provinciale dans l'Egypte romaine." *Revue historique de droit français et étranger* 62.3: 337–360.

Anagnostou-Canas, B. 1991. *Juge et sentence dans l'Egypte romaine*. Paris.

Andermahr, A. 1998. *Totus in Praediis: Senatorischer Grundbesitz in Italien in der Frühen und Hohen Kaiserzeit*. Bonn.

Ando, C. 2000. *Imperial Ideology and Provincial Loyalty in the Roman Empire*. Berkeley, CA.

Ando, C. 2006. "The Administration of the Provinces." In Potter, ed., pp. 177–192.

Ando, C. 2010. "Imperial Identities." In *Local Knowledge and Microidentities in the Imperial Greek World*, edited by T. Whitmarsh, pp. 17–45. Cambridge.

Ando, C. 2011a. "Law and the Landscape of Empire." In *Figures d'empire, fragments de mémoire: Pouvoirs (pratiques et discours, images et representations), et identités (sociales et religeuses) dans le monde romain imperial (Ier s. av. J.-C.–Ve s. ap. J.C.)*, edited by S. Benoist, A. Daguey-Gagey, and C. Hoët-van Cauwenberge, pp. 25–47. Villeneuve d'Ascq.

Ando, C. 2011b. *Law, Language and Empire in the Roman Tradition*. Philadelphia.

Ando, C. 2012. *Imperial Rome AD 193 to 284: The Critical Century*. Edinburgh.

Ando, C. 2013. "Pluralisme juridique et l'intégration de l'empire." In *Les voies de l'intégration à Rome et dans le monde romain*, edited by S. Benoist, S. Demougin, and G. de Kleijn, pp. 5–19. Leiden.

Ando, C. 2014a. "Postscript: Cities, Citizenship, and the Work of Empire." In *The City in the Classical and Post-Classical World: Changing Contexts of Power and Identity*, edited by C. Rapp and H. Drake, pp. 240–256. Cambridge.

Ando, C. 2014b. "Pluralism and Empire, from Rome to Robert Cover." *Critical Analysis of Law: An International and Interdisciplinary Law Review* 1: 1–22.

Ando, C. 2015a. *Roman Social Imaginaries: Language and Thought in Contexts of Empire*. Toronto.

Ando, C. 2015b. "Fact, Fiction, and Social Reality in Roman Law." In *Legal Fictions in Theory and Practice*, edited by M. Del Mar and W. Twining, pp. 295–324. Heidelberg.

Ando, C. 2015c. "Exemplum, Analogy and Precedent in Roman Law." In *Exemplarity and Singularity: Thinking through Particulars in Philosophy, Literature, and Law*, edited by M. Lowrie and S. Lüdemann, pp. 111–122. New York.

Ando, C. 2016a. "Making Romans: Citizens, Subjects and Subjectivity in Republican Empire." In *Cosmopolitanism and Empire: Universal Rulers, Local Elites and Cultural Integration in the Ancient Near East and Mediterranean*, edited by M. Lavan, R. Payne, and J. Weisweiler, pp. 169–185. Oxford.

Ando, C. 2016b. "Legal Pluralism in Practice." In du Plessis, Ando, and Tuori, eds., pp. 283–293.

Ando, C. 2017. "Afterword." In Kehoe and McGinn, eds., pp. 183–191.

Ando, C. 2019. "Self, Society, Individual, and Person in Roman Law." In *Self, Self-Fashioning, and Individuality in Late Antiquity: New Perspectives*, edited by M. Niehoff and J. Levinson, pp. 375–392. Tübingen.

Ando, C., ed. 2016. *Citizenship and Empire in Europe 200–1900: The Antonine Constitution after 1800 Years*. Stuttgart.

Andreau, J. 1974. *Les Affaires de Monsieur Jucundus*. Rome.

Andreau, J. 1987. *La vie financière dans le monde Romain: les métiers de manieurs d'argent (IVe siècle av. J.-C.–IIIe siècle ap. J.-C.)*. Rome.

Andreau, J. 1992. "L'Affranchi." In Giardina, ed., pp. 219–246.

Andreau, J. 1999. *Banking and Business in the Roman World*. Cambridge.

Andreau, J. 2001. *Banques et affaires dans le monde romain: IVe siècle av. J.-C.–IIIe siècle ap. J.-C.* Paris.

Andreau, J. 2004a. "Sur les choix économiques des notables Romains." In Andreau, Frances, and Pittia, eds., pp. 71–85.

Andreau, J. 2004b. "Les esclaves 'hommes d'affaires' et la gestion des ateliers et commerces." In Andreau, Frances, and Pittia, eds., pp. 111–126.

Andreau, J. 2010. *L'économie du monde romain*. Paris.

Andreau, J. 2013. "Freedmen in the *Satyrica*." In Prag and Repath, eds., pp. 114–124.

Andreau, J. 2015. *The Economy of the Roman World*. Ann Arbor, MI (English-language version of *L'économie du monde romain*, 2010).

Andreau, J. 2020. "Banking, Money-Lending, and Elite Financial Life in Rome." In Dari-Mattiacci and Kehoe, eds., Vol. 2, pp. 81–111.

Andreau, J., and R. Descat. 2006. *Esclave en Grèce et à Rome*. Paris.

Andreau, J., and R. Descat. 2009. *Gli schiavi nel mondo greco e romano*. Bologna.

Andreau, J., P. Briant, and R. Descat, eds. 1997. *Économie antique: Prix et formation des prix dans les économies antiques*. Saint-Bertrand-de-Comminges.

Andreau, J., J. Frances, and S. Pittia, eds. 2004. *Mentalités et choix économiques des Romains*. Bordeaux.

Angelini, P. 1971. *Il "Procurator."* Milan.

Ankum, H. 1974. "Towards a Rehabilitation of Pomponius." In *Daube Noster: Essays in Legal History for David Daube*, edited by A. Watson, pp. 1–13. Edinburgh.

Apathy, P. 1979. Review of J. Brinkhof, *Peculium in het klassieke Romeinse recht. Zeitschrift der Savigny-Stiftung für Rechtsgeschichte* (Romanist. Abt.) 96: 398–407.

Apicella, M., L. Haack, and F. Lerouixel, eds. 2014. *Les affaires de Monsieur Andreau: Économie et société du monde romain (Scripta antiqua, 61)*. Bordeaux.

Arrangio-Ruiz, V. 1950. "Sul problema della doppia cittadinanza nella Repubblica e nell'Impero Romano." In *Scritti giuridici in onore di F. Carnellutti*, Vol. 4, pp. 53–77. Padova.

Arrangio-Ruiz, V. 1956. *La compravendita in diritto romano*, Vol. 1. Naples.

Astolfi, R. 2004. *Il matrimonio nel diritto romano classico*. Padua.

Atkins, M., and R. Osborne, eds. 2006. *Poverty in the Roman World*. Cambridge.

Aubert, J.-J. 1994. *Business Managers in Ancient Rome: A Social and Economic Study of Institores 200 BC–AD 250*. Leiden.

Aubert, J.-J. 2002. "A Historian's Point of View." In Aubert and Sirks, eds., pp. 182–192.

Aubert, J.-J. 2013. "*Dumtaxat de peculio*: What's in a Peculium, or Establishing the Extent of the Principal's Liability." In du Plessis, ed., pp. 192–206. Edinburgh.

Aubert, J.-J. 2015. "Commerce." In Johnston, ed., pp. 213–245.

Aubert, J.-J., and M. Sirks. 1990. "Slave-Owning Slaves and the Structure of Slavery in the Early Roman Empire." *Kodai* 1: 24–35.

Aubert, J.-J., and M. Sirks. 2002. "Preface." In Aubert and Sirks, eds., pp. v–vii.

Aubert, J.-J., and M. Sirks, eds. 2002. *Speculum Iuris: Roman Law as a Reflection of Social and Economic Life in Antiquity*. Ann Arbor, MI.

Baba, M. 1990. "Slave-Owning Slaves and the Structure of Slavery in the Early Roman Empire." *Kodai* 1: 24–35.

Bäbler, B. 1998. *Fleissige Thrakerinnen und wehrhafte Skythen. Nichtgriechen im klassischen Athen und ihre Archäologische Hinterlassenschaft*. Stuttgart.

Bäbler, B. 2001. "Review of E. Cohen 2000." *Bryn Mawr Classical Review* 2001.05.19.

Badian, E. 1982. "Figuring Out Roman Slavery." *Journal of Roman Studies* 72: 164–169.

Badian, E. 1983. *Publicans and Sinners: Private Enterprise in the Service of the Roman Republic*. Ithaca, NY.

Bagnall, R. 1992. "Landholding in Late Roman Egypt: The Distribution of Wealth." *Journal of Roman Studies* 82: 128–149.

Bagnall, R., and B. Frier. 1994. *The Demography of Roman Egypt*. Cambridge.

Bagnall, R., B. Frier, and I. Rutherford. 1997. *The Census Register P. Oxy. 984: The Reverse of Pindar's Paeans*. Brussels.

Bagnall, R., J. Keenan, and L. MacCoull. 2011. *A Sixth-Century Tax Register from the Hermopolite Nom*e (Vol. 51: American Studies in Papyrology). Cincinnati, OH.

Baldus, C. 2016. "Possession in Roman Law." In du Plessis, Ando, and Tuori, eds., pp. 537–552.

Bang, P. 2002. "Romans and Mughals: Integration in a Tributary Empire." In *The Transformation of Economic Life under the Roman Empire*, edited by L. de Blois and J. Rich, pp. 1–27. Amsterdam.

Bang, P. 2008. *The Roman Bazaar: A Comparative Study of Trade and Markets in a Tributary Empire*. Cambridge.

Barja de Quiroga, P. 1998. "Junian Latins: Status and Number." *Athenaeum* 86: 133–163.

Barja de Quiroga, P. 2007. *Historia de la manumisión en Roma: De los orígines a los Severos*. Madrid.

Barlow, C. 1982. *Bankers, Moneylenders and Interest Rates in the Roman Republic*. London.

Barrow, R. 1928. *Slavery in the Roman Empire*. London.

Barta, H. 2011. *"Graeca non leguntur?" Zu den Ursprüngen des europäischen Rechts im antiken Griechenland*, Vol. 1. Wiesbaden.

Bassignano, M. 1986. "Review of H.-G. Pflaum, Les carrières procuratoriennes équestres sous le haut-empire romain." (Supplément). *Epigraphica* 48: 258–268.

Bauman, R. 1992. *Women and Politics in Ancient Rome*. London.

Baviera, G. 1940. "Fragmenta de iure fisci." In *Fontes Iuris Romani Anteiustiniani*, edited by S. Riccobono, G. Baviera, C. Ferrini, G. Furlani, and V. Arangio-Ruiz. Vol. 2: *Auctores*: 627–630. 2nd edition. Florence.

Beard, M. 2014. "Foreword." In *The Roman Guide to Slave Management*, edited by J. Toner, pp. vi–ix. New York.

Beard, M. 2015. *SPQR: A History of Ancient Rome*. New York.

Beard, M., J. North, and S. Price. 1998. *Religions of Rome, 1: A History*. Cambridge.

Beare, R. 1978. "Were Bailiffs Ever Free Born?" *Classical Quarterly* 28: 398–401.

Becker, H. 2016. "Roman Women in the Urban Economy: Occupations, Social Connections, and Gendered Exclusions." In *Women in Antiquity: Real Women across the Ancient World*, edited by S. Budin and J. Turfa, pp. 714–725. Oxford.

Behrends, O. 1971. "Die Prokuratur des klassischen römischen Zivilrechts." *Zeitschrift der Savigny-Stiftung für Rechtsgeschichte* (Romanist. Abt.) 88: 215–299.

Behrends, O. 1980. "Prinzipat und Sklavenrecht. Zu den geistigen Grundlagen der augusteischen Verfassungsschöpfung." In *Rechtswissenschaft und Rechtsentwicklung*, edited by U. Immenga, pp. 53–88. Göttingen.

Bellen, H. 1974. "Die 'Verstaatlichung' des Privatvermögens der römischen Kaiser im 1. Jahrhundert n. Chr." In *Aufsteig und Neidergan der römischen Welt*, I, edited by W. Haase and H. Temporini, pp. 91–112. Berlin.

Bellen, H., and H. Heinen. 2001. *Fünfzig Jahre Forschungen zur Antiken Sklaverei an der Mainzer Akademie 1950–2000*. Stuttgart.

Beloch, J. 1902. "Zur griechischen Wirtschaftsgeschichte." *Zeitschrift für Sozialwissenschaft* 5: 1–97.

Bengtsson, E., A. Missiaia, M. Olsson, and P. Svensson. 2018. "Wealth Inequality in Sweden, 1750–1900." *Economic History Review* 71.3: 772–794.

Benke, N. 1988. "Zu Papinians *actio ad exemplum institoriae actionis.*" *Zeitschrift der Savigny-Stiftung für Rechtsgeschichte* (Romanist. Abt.) 105: 592–633.

Benke, N. 1995. "Women in the Courts: An Old Thorn in Men's Sides."*Michigan Journal of Gender and Law* 3.1: 195–256.

Benke, N. 2000. "In Sola Prudentium Interpretatione: Zur Methodik und Methodologie römischer Juristen." In *Norm und Entscheidung: Prolegomena zur Theorie des Falls*, edited by B. Feldner and N. Forgó, pp. 1–85. Vienna.

Benke, N. 2001. "Why Should the Law Protect Roman Women? Some Remarks on the *Senatus Consultum Velleianum* (ca. 50 A.D.)." In *Gender and Religion in Europe: European Studies*, edited by K. Børresen, S. Cabbibo, and E. Specht, pp. 41–56. Rome.

Benke, N. 2002. "Review of Weishaupt 1999." *Zeitschrift der Savigny-Stiftung für Rechtsgeschichte* (Romanist. Abt.) 119: 488–510.

Benke, N. 2005. "Aemilia Pudentilla: A Landowning Lady." In *Ex iusta causa traditum: Essays in Honour of Eric H. Pool*, edited by R. van den Bergh, pp. 19–31. Pretoria.

Benke, N. 2012. "Gender and the Roman Law of Obligations." In *Obligations in Roman Law: Past, Present, and Future*, edited by T. McGinn, pp. 215–246. Ann Arbor, MI.

Benton, L. 2002. *Law and Colonial Cultures: Legal Regimes in World History 1400–1900*. Cambridge.

Benton, L. 2007. "Empires of Exception: History, Law, and the Problem of Imperial Sovereignty." *Quaderni di Relazioni Internazionali* 8: 54–67.

Benz, L., E. Stärk, and G. Vogt-Spira, eds. 1995. *Plautus und die Tradition des Stegreifspiels: Festgabe für E. Lefèvre zum 60. Gebgurtstag*. Tübingen.

Béranger, J. 1953. *Recherches sur l'aspect idéologique du principat*. Basel.

Berg, R. 2003. "Donne medico a Pompei?" In Buonopane and Cenerini, eds., pp. 131–154.

Berg, R., ed. 2016. *The Material Sides of Marriage: Women and Domestic Economies in Antiquity*. Rome.

Berger, A. 1953. *Encyclopedic Dictionary of Roman Law*. Philadelphia.

Bernard, S. 2017. "Workers in the Roman Imperial Building Industry." In Verboven and Laes, eds., pp. 62–86.

Berrino, N. 2002. "'Femina improbissima' e 'inquietans': Il divieto di 'postulare pro aliis.'" *Quaderni di Invigilata Lucernis* 24: 15 ff.

Besnier, R. 1976. "L'état économique de Rome de 264 à 133 av. J.C." *Revue historique de droit français et étranger* 54: 5–33.

Bianchi, E. 1997. *Fictio juris: Ricerche sulla fizione in diritto romano dal periodo arcaico all' epoca augustea*. Padua.

Bianchi, E. 2007. "Attività commeriale fra privato e pubblico in età imperiale." In *Fides Humanitas Ius: Studii in onore di Luigi Labruna*, edited by C. Cascione and C. Masi Doria, pp. 423–438. Naples.

Biezunska-Malowist, I. 1977. *L'Esclavage dans l'Egypte gréco-romaine Seconde Partie: Période romaine*. Wroclaw.

Binsfeld, A. 2010. "Collaria." In *Handwörterbuch der antiken Sklaverei*, edited by H. Heinen. s.v. Stuttgart.

Birks, P. 1986. "Fictions Ancient and Modern." In *The Legal Mind: Essays for Tony Honoré*, edited by N. MacCormick and P. Birks, pp. 83–101. Oxford.

Birley, A. 2007a. "Making Emperors: Imperial Instrument or Independent Force?" In *A Companion to the Roman Army*, edited by P. Erdkamp, pp. 379–394. Malden, MA.

Birley, A. 2007b. "Two Types of Administration Attested by the Vindolanda Tablets." In *Herrschen und Verwalten: der Alltag der römischen Administration in der hohen Kaiserzeit*, edited by R. Haensch and J. Heinrichs, pp. 306–324. Cologne.

Bisazza, G. 2003. *Lo iussum domini e la sostituzione negoziale nell'esperienza romana*. Milan.

Biscardi, A. 1975. "La capacità processuale dello schiavo." *Labeo* 21: 143–171.

Biscardi, A. 1982. "Introduction à l'étude des pratiques commeriales dans l'histoire des droits de l'Antiquité." *Revue internationale des droits de l'antiquité*, 3d ser., 29: 21–44.

Biscotti, B. 2004. "Ancora sulle proprietà in diritto romano." *Index* 32: 1–25.

Black, A., and G. Bell, eds. 2011. *Law and Legal Institutions of Asia: Traditions, Adaptations and Innovations*. Cambridge.

Bleicken, J. 1985. *Die athenische Demokratie*. Paderborn.

Blois, L. de, ed. 2001. *Administration, Prosopography and Appointment Policies in the Roman Empire: Proceedings of the First Workshop of the International Network (Impact of Empire. Roman Empire 27 BC–AD 406)*. Amsterdam.

Blois, L. de, and J. Rich, eds. 2002. *The Transformation of Economic Life under the Roman Empire*. Amsterdam.

Blouin, K. 2014. *Triangular Landscapes: Environment, Society, and the State in the Nile Delta under Roman Rule*. Oxford.

Blume, L., and S. Durlauf. 2015. "Review Essay: *Capital in the Twenty-First Century*." *Journal of Political Economy* 123: 749–777.

Boatwright, M. 2000. *Hadrian and the Cities of the Roman Empire*. Princeton, NJ.

Bodel, J. 1999. "The Cena Trimalchionius." In *Latin Fiction: The Latin Novel in Context*, edited by H. Hofmann, pp. 38–51. London.

Bodel, J. 2005. "*Caveat Emptor*: Towards a Study of Roman Slave-Traders." *Journal of Roman Archaeology* 18: 181–915.

Bodel, J. 2008. "From *Columbarium* to Catacombs: Communities of the Dead in Pagan and Christian Rome." In *Commemorating the Dead: Texts and Artifacts in Context*, edited by L. Brink and D. Green, pp. 177–242. Berlin.

Bodel, J. 2011. "Slave Labour and Roman Society." In Bradley and Cartledge, eds., pp. 311–336.

Boese, W. 1973. *A Study of the Slave Trade and the Sources of Slaves in the Roman Republic and the Early Roman Empire*. Dissertation, University of Washington.

Bogaert, R. 1966. *Les Origines antiques de la banque de dépôt: Une mise au point accompagnée d'une esquisse des opérations de banque en Mésopotamie*. Leyden.

Bogaert, R. 1973. "Changeurs et banquiers chez les Pères de l'Église." *Ancient Society* 4: 239–270.

Boldizzoni, F. 2011. *The Poverty of Clio: Resurrecting Economic History*. Princeton, NJ.

Bolkestein, H. 1939. *Wohltätigkeit und Armenpflege im vorchristlichen Altertum*. Utrecht.

Bolla, S. 1938. *Die Entwicklung der Fiskus zum Privatrechtssubjekt mit Beiträgen zur Lehre vom Aerarium*. Prague.

Bond, S. 2016. *Trade and Taboo: Disreputable Professions in the Roman Mediterranean*. Ann Arbor, MI.

Bonfante, P. 1925. *Corso di diritto romano. I. Diritto di famiglia*. Rome.

Booth, A. 1979. "The Schooling of Slaves in First-Century Rome." *Transactions of the American Philological Association* 109: 11–19.

Born, G. 2014. *International Commercial Arbitration*. Alphen aan den Rijn, Netherlands.

Boulvert, G. 1970. *Esclaves et affranchis impériaux sous le Haut-Empire romain: Rôle politique et administratif*. Naples.

Boulvert, G. 1974. *Domestique et fonctionnaire sous le Haut-Empire romain*. Paris.

Bove, L. 1984. *Documenti di operazioni finanziarie dall'archivio dei Sulpicii: Tabulae Pompeianae di Murécine*. Naples.

Bowes, K. 2021a. "When Kuznets Went to Rome: Roman Economic Well-Being and the Reframing of Roman History." *Capitalism: A Journal of History and Economics* 2.1: 7–40.

Bowes, K., ed. 2021b. *The Roman Peasant Project 2009–2014: Excavating the Roman Rural Pool*. Philadelphia.

Bowes, K., et al. 2017. "Peasant Agricultural Studies in Southern Tuscany: Convertible Agriculture and the Importance of Pasture." In *The Economic Integration of Roman Italy: Rural Communities in a Globalising World*, edited by T. de Haas and G. Tol, pp. 170–199. Leiden.

Bowman, A. 1985. "Landholding in the Hermopolite Nome in the Fourth Century AD." *Journal of Roman Studies* 75: 137–163.

Bowman, A. 2009. "Quantifying Egyptian Agriculture." In Bowman and Wilson, eds., pp. 177–204.

Bowman, A., and A. Wilson. 2009. "Preface." In Bowman and Wilson, eds., pp. v–vii.

Bowman, A., and A. Wilson, eds. 2009. *Quantifying the Roman Economy: Methods and Problems*. Oxford.

Boyer, L. 1965. "La fonction sociale des legs d'après la jurisprudence classique." *Revue historique de droit français et étranger* (4. sér.) 43: 333–408.

Bozia, E. 2015. *Lucian and His Roman Voices: Cultural Exchanges and Conflicts in the Late Roman Empire*. New York.

Bradley, K. 1987. *Slaves and Masters in the Roman Empire: A Study in Social Control*. Oxford.

Bradley, K. 1990. "*Servus Onerosus*: Roman Law and the Troublesome Slave." *Slavery and Abolition* 11: 135–157.

Bradley, K. 1991. *Discovering the Roman Family*. Oxford.

Bradley, K. 1994. *Slavery and Society at Rome*. Cambridge.

Bradley, K. 2011a. "Slavery in the Roman Republic." In Bradley and Cartledge, eds., pp. 241–264.

Bradley, K. 2011b. "Resisting Slavery at Rome." In Bradley and Cartledge, eds., pp. 362–384.

Bradley, K., and P. Cartledge, eds. 2011. *The Cambridge World History of Slavery*, Vol. 1: *The Ancient Mediterranean World*. Cambridge.

Brana-Shute, R. 1989. "Approaching Freedom: The Manumission of Slaves in Suriname, 1760–1828." *Slavery and Abolition* 10.3: 40–60.

Bransbourg, G. 2022a. "The Roman Coinage under the Antonines Revisited: An Economy of Silver, Not Gold." In *The Uncertain Past*, edited by M. Ivan, D. Jew, and B. Danon, pp. 135–194. Cambridge.

Bransbourg, G. 2022b. "Gold or Silver Standard: Choice or Necessity? The Middle Class and the Fifth Century Collapse of Roman Silver Coinage." *Revue Belge de Numismatique et de Sigillographie* 168: 73–106.

Braund, S. 2004. *Juvenal and Persius*. Loeb Classical Library. Cambridge, MA.

Braudel, F. 1981. *The Structures of Everyday Life*. New York (published originally in French as *Les structures du quotidien*, Paris, 1967).

Bremmer, J. 1981. "Plutarch and the Naming of Greek Women." *American Journal of Philology* 102: 425–426.

Bresson, A. 2016. *The Making of the Ancient Greek Economy: Institutions, Markets, and Growth in the City-States*. Princeton, NJ.

Bresson, A., and J.-J. Aubert. (forthcoming). "Accounting." In Lo Cascio, Bresson, and Velde, eds., pp. XX–XX.

Bretone, M. 2011. "Finzioni e formule nel diritto romano." *Materiali per una storia della cultura giuridica* 31.2: 295–313.

Bricault, L. 2005. *Recueil des inscriptions concernant les cultes isiaques*, I–III. Paris.

Brinkhof, J. 1978. *Een Studie over het Peculium in het klassieke Romeinse recht* (abstract in German). Meppel.

Brousseau, E., and J.-M. Glachant. 2008. *New Institutional Economics: A Guidebook*. Cambridge.

Bruhns, H. 2014. "Cambridge, Bordeaux ou Heidelberg: À quoi servent les 'classiques'?" In Apicella, Haack, and Lerouixel, eds., pp. 29–42.

Brunt, P. 1971. *Italian Manpower (225 BC–AD 14)*. Oxford.

Brunt, P. 1983a. "Marcus Aurelius and Slavery." In *Modus Operandi: Essays in Honour of Geoffrey Rickman*, edited by M. Austin, J. Harries, and C. Smith, pp. 139–150. London.

Brunt, P. 1983b. "Review of D'Arms 1981." *Journal of Economic History* 43: 314–315.

Brunt, P. 1987. *Italian Manpower 225 B.C.*–A.D. 14. 2nd ed. Oxford.

Brunt, P. 1988. "The Army and the Land in the Roman Revolution." In *The Fall of the Roman Republic and Related Essays*, pp. 240–275. Oxford.

Brunt, P. 1990. *Roman Imperial Themes*. Oxford.

Bruun, C. 1989. "The Name and Possessions of Nero's Freedman Phaon." *Arctos* 23: 41–53.

Bruun, C. 1990. "Some Comments on the Status of Imperial Freedmen (The Case of Ti. Claudius Aug. lib. Classicus." *Zeitschrift für Papyrologie und Epigraphik* 82: 271–285.

Bruun, C. 2008. "La *familia publica* di Ostia antica." In *Epigrafia 2006: Attti della XIVe Rencontre sur l'épigraphie in onore di Silvio Panciera*, edited by M. Caldelli, G. Gregori, and S. Orlandi, pp. 537–556. Rome.

Bruun, C. 2014a. "Roman Government and Administration." In Bruun and Edmonson, eds., pp. 274–298.

Bruun, C. 2014b. "Slaves and Freed Slaves." In Bruun and Edmonson, eds., pp. 605–626.

Bruun, C., and J. Edmonson, eds. 2014. *Oxford Handbook of Roman Epigraphy*. Oxford.

Bryen, A. 2008. "Visibility and Violence in Petitions from Roman Egypt." *Greek, Roman, and Byzantine Studies* 48: 181–200.

Bryen, A. 2016a. "Reading the Citizenship Papyrus (P.Giss. I 40)." In Ando, ed., pp. 29–44. Stuttgart.

Bryen, A. 2016b. "Crimes against the Individual: Violence and Social Crimes." In du Plessis, Ando, and Tuori, eds., pp. 322–332.

Bücher, K. 1893. *Die Entstehung der Volkswirtschaft*. Tübingen.

Buchwitz, W. 2010. "Fremde Sklaven als Erben: Sozialer Aufstieg durch Dritte." In *Homo, caput persona: La costruzione giuridica dell'identità nell'esperienza romana*, edited by A. Corbino, M. Humbert, and G. Negri, pp. 393–425. Pavia.

Buchwitz, W. 2012. *Servus alienus heres: die Erbeinsetzung fremder Sklaven im klassischen römischen Recht*. Vienna.

Buckland, W. [1908] 1970. *The Roman Law of Slavery*. 2nd ed. Cambridge.

Buckland, W. [1931] 2011. *The Main Institutions of Roman Private Law*. Cambridge.

Buckland, W., and A. McNair. [1952] 1965. *Roman Law and Common Law: A Comparison in Outline.* 2nd ed., revised by F. Lawson. Cambridge.

Buecheler, F. 1862. *Petronii Arbitri Satirarum Reliquiae*. Berlin.

Buongiorno, P. 2013. "Arcaismo continuismo desuetudine nelle deliberazioni senatorie di età giulio-claudia." *Iura* 61: 218–258.

Buongiorno, P. 2015. "Norme di derivazione non romana nelle fonti del diritto di età imperiale: Il senatus consultum 'de iustis nuptiis inter patruos fratrumque filias' (49 d.C.)." In *Il diritto romano e le culture straniere. Influenze e dipendenze interculturali nell'antichità*, edited by F. Lamberti, P. Gröschler, and F. Milazzo, pp. 5–32. Lecce.

Buonocore, M. 1984. *Schiavi e liberti dei Volusii Saturnini: Le iscrizioni del colombario sulla via Appia antica*. Rome.

Buonopane, A. 2003. "*Medicae* nell'Occidente romano: Un'indagine preliminare." In A. Buonopane and F. Cenerini, eds., pp. 113–130.

Buonopane, A. and F. Cenerini, eds. 2003. *Donna e lavoro nella documentazione epigrafica, Atti del II Seminario sulla condizione femminile nella documentazione epigrafica*. Faenza.

Buraselis, K. 2007. *ΘΕΙΑ ΔΩΡΕΑ: Das göttlich-kaiserliche Geschenk. Studien zur Politik der Severer und zur* Constitutio Antoniana. Vienna.

Burdese, A. 1971. "'Actio ad exemplum institoriae' e categorie sociali." *Bullettino del Istituto di diritto romano* 74: 61–82.

Burdese, A. 1981. "Controversie giurisprudenziali in teme di capacità degli schiavi." In *Studi in onore di A. Biscardi*, I, pp. 147–180. Milan.

Burdese, A. 1982. "Considerazioni in tema di peculio c. d. profettizio." In *Studi in onore di C Sanfilippo*, I, pp. 69–111. Milan.

Burdese, A. 1993. *Manuale di diritto privato romano*. Turin.

Burford, A. 1972. *Craftsmen in Greek and Roman Society*. London.

Bürge, A. 1987. "Fiktion und Wirklichkeit: soziale und rechtliche Strukturen des römischen Bankwesens." *Zeitschrift der Savigny-Stiftung für Rechtsgeschichte* (Romanist. Abt.) 104: 465–558.

Bürge, A. 1993. "*Cibaria*: Indiz für die sociale Stellung des römischen Arbeitnehmer?" In *Ars boni et aequi: Festschrift für W. Waldstein zum 65. Geburtstag*, edited by M. Schermaier and Z. Vegh, pp. 63–78. Stuttgart.

Bürge, A. 2010. "Lo schiavo (in)dipendente e il suo patrimonio." In *La costruzione giuridica dell' identità nell'esperienza romana: Dall' epoca di Plauto a Ulpiano*, edited by A. Corbino, M. Humbert, and G. Negri, pp. 369–391. Pavia.

Burton, G. 2001. "The Imperial State and Its Impact on the Role and Status of Local Magistrates and Councillors in the Provinces of the Empire." In *Administration, Prosopography and Appointment Policies in the Roman Empire*, edited by L. De Blois, pp. 202–214. Amsterdam.

Butcher, K., and M. Ponting. 2015. *The Metallurgy of Roman Silver Coinage from the Reform of Nero to the Reform of Trajan*. Cambridge.

Buti, I. 1976. *Studi sulla capacità patrimoniale dei "servi."* Naples.

Caballos, A. 1996. "Testimonios recientes con referencía a municipios." In *Teoría y práctica del ordenamiento municipal en Hispania*, edited by E. Ortiz de Urbina and J. Santos, pp. 175–210. Vitoria.

Caballos, A. 2001. "Der Aufstieg localer Eliten Spaniens in die Reichselite." In de Blois, ed., pp. 255–271.

Cairns, J., and P. du Plessis. 2007. "Introduction: Themes and Literature." In Cairns and du Plessis, eds., pp. 3–8.

Cairns, J., and P. du Plessis, eds. 2007. *Beyond Dogmatics: Law and Society in the Roman World (Edinburgh Studies in Law)*. Edinburgh.

Caldelli, M., and C. Ricci. 1999. *Monumentum familiae Statiliorum: Un riesame*. Rome.

Calpino, T. 2014. *Women, Work and Leadership in Acts*. Tübingen.

Camodeca, G. 1992. *L'Archivio puteolano dei Sulpicii*. I. Naples.

Camodeca, G. 1994. "Riedizione del trittico ercolanense TH 77+78+80+53+92 del 26 gennaio 69." *Cronache Ercolanensi* 24: 137–146.

Camodeca, G. 1999. *Tabulae Pompeianae Sulpiciorum: Edizione critica dell'archivio puteolano dei Sulpicii*. 2 Vols. Rome.

Camodeca, G. 2006. "Cura secunda della Tabula cerata londinese con la compravendita della puella Fortunata." *Zeitschrift für Papyrologie und Epigraphik* 157: 225–230.

Camodeca, G. 2017. *Tabulae Herculanenses: Edizione e commento*. Rome.

Canbakal, J. 2013. "Wealth and Inequality in Ottoman Bursa, 1500–1840." Paper presented at the Economic History Society Annual Conference, York.

Cancrini, F., C. Delplace, and S. Marengo, eds. 2001. *L'evergetismo nella Regio V (Picenum)*. Tivoli.

Cantarella, E. 1987. *Pandora's Daughters: The Role and Status of Women in Greek and Roman Antiquity*. Translation, with revisions, by M. Fant. Baltimore, MD (originally published as *L'ambiguo malanno*, 1981).

Cantarella, E. 1989. "La vita delle donne." In *Storia di Roma: Caratteri e morfologie*, Vol. 4, edited by A. Gabba and E. Schiavone, pp. 596–600. Turin.

Cantarella, E. 1995. "Afrania e il divieto dell'avvocatura per le donne." In *Vicende e figure femminili in Grecia e a Roma: Atti del convegno, Pesaro 28–30 aprile 1994*, edited by R. Raffaelli, pp. 527 ff. Ancona.

Cantarella, E. 2016. "Women and Patriarchy in Roman Law." In du Plessis, Ando, and Tuori, eds., pp. 419–431.

Capogrossi Colognesi, L. 2016. "Ownership and Power in Roman Law." In du Plessis, Ando, and Tuori, eds., pp. 524–536.

Carcaterra, A. 1970. *"Dolus Bonus"/ "Dolus Malus": Esegesi di D. 4.3.1.2–3*. Naples.

Cardilli, R. 1997. "Il periculum e le usurae nei giudizi di vuona fede." In Tafaro, ed., pp. 13–60.

Carlsen, J. 1995. *Vilici and Roman Estate Managers until AD 284*. Rome.

Carlsen, J. 2010. "Recruitment and Training of Roman Estate Managers in a Comparative Perspective." In Roth, ed., pp. 75–90.

Carrié, J.-M. 2005. "Developments in Provincial and Local Administration." In *The Cambridge Ancient History*, 2nd ed., Vol. XII: *The Crisis of Empire A.D. 193–337*, edited by A. Bowman, A. Cameron, and P. Garnsey, pp. 269–312. Cambridge.

Cartledge, P. 1998. "The Economy (Economies) of Ancient Greece." *Dialogos* 5: 4–24.

Cartwright, E. 2014. *Behavioral Economics* (Routledge Advanced Texts in Economics and Finance), 2nd ed. New York.

Casavola, F. 1960. *Lex Cincia: Contributo alla storia delle origini della donazione romana*. Naples.

Cébeillac-Gervasoni, M. 1998. *Les magistrats des cités italiennes de la seconde guerre punique à Auguste: Le Latium et la Campanie*. Rome.

Cecconi, G. 2006. "Romanizzazione, diversità culturale, politicamente corretto." *Mélanges de l'École française de Rome. Antiquité* 118: 81–94.

Cenerini, F. 2009. *La donna romana*. Bologna.

Cerami, P., A. Di Porto, and A. Petrucci. 2004. *Diritto commerciale romano*. 2nd ed. Turin.

Cerami, P., and A. Petrucci. [2002] 2010 (3rd edition). *Lezioni di diritto commerciale romano*. Turin.

Champlin, E. 1991. *Final Judgments: Duty and Emotion in Roman Wills, 200 B.C.–A.D. 250*. Berkeley, CA.

Champlin, E. 2005. "Phaedrus the Fabulous." *Journal of Roman Studies* 95: 97–123.

Chantraine, H. 1967. *Freigelassene und Sklaven im Dienst der römischen Kaiser: Studien zu ihrer Nomenklatur*. Wiesbaden.

Chantraine, H. 1980. "Freigelassene und Sklaven Kaiserlicher Frauen." In *Studien zur antiken Sozialgeschichte: Feschrift Friedrich Vittinghoff*, edited by W. Eck, H. Galsterer, and H. Wolff, pp. 389–416. Cologne.

Cherry, D. 1996. "Intestacy and the Roman Poor." *Tijdschrift voor Rechtsgeschiedenis* 64: 155–172.

Chic Garcia, G. 1988. *Epigrafia anfórica de la Bética*. II. Seville.

Chioffi, L. 2003. *Capuanae*. In A. Buonopane and F. Cenerini, eds., pp. 163–192.

Chiusi, T. 1993. *Contributo allo studio dell'editto de tributoria actione*. Accademia Nazionale dei Lincei, 19. Rome.

Chiusi, T. 1994. "Zur Vormundschaft der Mutter." *Zeitschrift der Savigny-Stiftung für Rechtsgeschichte* (Romanist. Abt.) 111: 155–196.

Chiusi, T. 2001. *Die actio de in rem verso im römischen Recht*. Munich.

Chiusi, T. 2007a. "Zum Zusammenspiel von Haftung und Organisation im römischen Handelsverkehr. Scientia, voluntas und peculium in D. 14.1.19–20." *Zeitschrift der Savigny-Stiftung für Rechtsgeschichte* (Romanist. Abt.) 124: 94–112.

Chiusi, T. 2007b. "Diritto commerciale romano? Alcune osservazioni critiche." In *Fides Humanitas Ius. Studii in onore di L. Labruna*, edited by C. Cascione and C. Doria, Vol. 2, pp. 1025–1041. Naples.

Chiusi, T. 2013. "*Fama* and *Infamia* in the Roman Legal System: The Cases of Afrania and Lucrretia." In *Judge and Jurist: Essays in Memory of Lord Rodger of Earlsferry*, edited by A. Burrows, D. Johnston, and R. Zimmermann, pp. 143–165. Oxford.

Chiusi, T. 2020. "Legal Interactions in the Archive of Babatha: P. Yadin 21 and 22." In Czajkowski, Eckhardt, and Strothmann, eds., pp. 100–114.

Chrestou, I. 2016. "Innkeepers, Ship-owners, Prostitutes: Three 'Female' Business Activities." In Berg, ed., pp. 243–247.

Christes, J. 1979. *Sklaven und Freigelassene als Grammatiker und Philologen im antiken Rom*. Wiesbaden.

Christophilopoulos, A. 1973. "Νομικοὶ νομῳδοὶ νομοδῖκται εἰς τὴν ἑλληνικὴν Ἀνατολήν." In *Δίκαιον καὶ ἱστορία. Μικρὰ μελετήματα*, pp. 310–321. Athens.

Chroust, A.-H. 1972. "Aristotle's Sojourn in Assos." *Historia* 21.2: 170–176.

Cienfuegos, S. 2007. *Banca, navegación y otras empresas en el derecho romano*. Mexico City.

Cimarosti, E. 2005. "Schiave e liberte pubbliche nella documentazione epigrafica: note a CILA, 541." In *Donna e vita cittadina nella documentazione epigrafica (Atti del II Seminario sulla condizione femminile nella documentazione epigrafica)*, edited by A. Buonopane and F. Cenerini, pp. 447–456. Verona.

Clarke, G. 2005. "Paul Richard Carey Weaver." *Australian Academy of the Humanities, Proceedings* 30: 66–71.

Clarke, M. 1953. *Rhetoric at Rome: A Historical Survey*. London.

Cloud, D. 2002. "The Pompeian Tablets and Some Literary Texts." In McKechnie, ed., pp. 231–246.

Coffee, N. 2017. *Gift and Gain: How Money Transformed Ancient Rome*. Oxford.

Cohen, B. 1951. "Peculium in Jewish and Roman law." *Proceedings of the American Academy for Jewish Research* 20: 135–234.

Cohen, D. 1995. *Law, Violence and Community in Classical Athens*. Cambridge.

Cohen, E. 1973. *Ancient Athenian Maritime Courts*. Princeton, NJ.

Cohen, E. 1992. *Athenian Economy and Society: A Banking Perspective*. Princeton, NJ.

Cohen, E. 2000. *The Athenian Nation*. Princeton, NJ.

Cohen, E. 2002. "Introduction" to *Money, Labour and Land in Ancient Greece*, edited by P. Cartledge, L. Foxhall and E. Cohen, pp. 1–7. London.

Cohen, E. 2005. "Commercial Law." In *A Companion to Ancient Greek Law*, edited by M. Gagarin and D. Cohen, pp. 290–302. Cambridge.

Cohen, E. 2012. "Juridical Implications of Athenian Slaves' Commercial Activity." In *Symposion 2011 (Akten der Gesellschaft für Griechische und Hellenistische Rechtsgeschichte)*, edited by B. Legras and G. Thür, pp. 213–223. Vienna.

Cohen, E. 2014a. "Private Agreements Purporting to Override Polis Law." In *Symposion 2013 (Akten der Gesellschaft für Griechische und Hellenistische Rechtsgeschichte)*, edited by M. Gagarin and A. Lanni, pp. 277–286. Vienna.

Cohen, E. 2014b. "Sexual Abuse and Sexual Rights: Slaves' Erotic Experience at Athens and Rome." In *A Companion to Greek and Roman Sexualities*, edited by T. Hubbard, pp. 184–198. Oxford.

Cohen, E. 2015a. *Athenian Prostitution: The Business of Sex*. Oxford.

Cohen, E. 2015b. "Maritime Profiteering in Fourth-Century Athens." In Ἄξων: *Studies in Honor of Ronald S. Stroud*, edited by A. Matthaiou and N. Papazarkadas, pp. 393–409. Athens.

Cohen, E. 2016. "The Athenian Businesswoman." In *Women in Antiquity: Real Women across the Ancient World*, edited by S. Budin and J. Turfa, pp. 714–725. Oxford.

Cohen, E. 2017. "Overcoming Legal Incapacity at Athens: Juridical Adaptations Facilitating the Business Activity of Slaves." In Yiftach and Faraguna, eds., pp. 127–143.

Cohen, E. 2018a. "Slaves Operating Businesses: Legal Ramifications for Ancient Athens—and for Modern Scholarship." In *Ancient Greek Law in the Twenty-First Century*, edited by P. Perlman, pp. 54–69. Austin, TX.

Cohen, E. 2018b. "Slaves Telling Tales at Athens: A Response to Sara Forsdyke." In Thür, Yiftach, and Zelnick-Abramovitz, eds., pp. 367–376.

Cohen, E. 2018c. "Legal Status at Athens: The Fallacy of Modern 'Corrective Interpretations' of Ancient Evidence." In *Scritti di diritto greco in onore di Alberto Maffi*, edited by B. Biscotti, pp. 15–33. Milan.

Cohen, N. 2017. "Modern Guardianship in Historical Perspective." In Yiftach and Faraguna, eds., pp. 11–27.

Cole, S. 2005. "Capitalism and Freedom: Slavery and Manumission in Louisiana, 1770–1820." *Journal of Economic History* 65: 1008–1027.

Connolly, S. 2010. *Lives behind the Laws: The World of the Codex Hermogenianus*. Bloomington, IN.

Cooley, A. 2012. *The Cambridge Manual of Latin Epigraphy*. Cambridge.

Cosgel, M., and A. Bowğaç. 2012. "Inequality of Wealth in the Ottoman Empire: War, Weather and Long-Term Trends in Eighteenth Century Kastamonul." *Journal of Economic History* 72: 308–331.

Cotton, H. 2002. "Jewish Jurisdiction under Roman Rule: Prolegomena." In *Zwischen den Reichen: Neues Testament und Römische Herrschaft*, edited by M. Labahn and J. Zangenberg, pp. 5–20. Tübingen.

Cotton, H. 2009. "Continuity of Nabatean law in the Petra Papyri: AMethodological Exercise." In *From Hellenism to Islam. Cultural and Linguistic Change in the Roman Near East*, edited by H. Cotton, R. Hoyland, J. Price, and D. Wasserstein, pp. 154–174. Cambridge.

Crawford, M. 1996. *Roman Statutes*. BICS Supplement 64. London.

Crifo, G. 1964. "Sul problema della donna tutrice." *Bullettino dell' Istituto di Diritto Romano* 67: 87–166.

Cristofori, A. 2004. *Non arma virumque: Le occcupazioni nell' epigrafia del Piceno*, 2nd ed. Bologna.

Cristofori, A. 2011. "Le occupazioni nell'epifgrafia dell'Epiro e dell'Illiria meridionale di età romano." In *Sulla rotta per la Sicilia: l'Epiro, Corciera e l'Occidente*, edited by G. De Sensi Sestito and M. Intrieri, pp. 141–177. Pisa.

Cristofori, A. 2016. "Lavoro e identità sociale." In A. Marcone, ed., pp. 149–74. Rome.

Crook, J. 1967. *Law and Life of Rome, 90 B.C–A.D. 212*. Ithaca, NY.

Crook, J. 1973. "Intestacy in Roman Society." *Proceedings of the Cambridge Philological Society* 19: 38–44.

Crook, J. 1995. *Legal Advocacy in the Roman World*. Ithaca, NY.

Culham, P. 2004. "Women in the Roman Republic." In *The Cambridge Companion to the Roman Republic*, edited by H. Flower, pp. 139–159. Cambridge.

Czajkowski, K. 2017. *Localized Law: The Babatha and Salome Komaise Archives*. Oxford.

Czajkowski, K. 2020. "Law and Romanization in Judaea." In Czajkowski, Eckhardt, and Strothmann, eds., pp. 83–100.

Czajkowski, K., and B. Eckhardt. 2020. "Introduction." In Czajkowski, Eckhardt, and Strothmann, eds., pp. 1–16.

Czajkowski, K., B. Eckhardt, and M. Strothmann, eds. 2020. *Law in the Roman Provinces*. Oxford.

D'Aloja, C. 2016. "Il lavoro femminile." In A. Marcone ed., pp. 639–662.

D'Arms, J. 1975. "Review of Weaver 1972." *American Journal of Philology* 96: 335–339.

D'Arms, J. 1976. "Notes on Municipal Notables of Imperial Ostia." *American Journal of Philology* 97: 387–411.

D'Arms, J. 1981. *Commerce and Social Standing in Ancient Rome*. Cambridge, MA.

Daack, K. von. 2012. *Freedom Has a Face: Race, Identity, and Community in Jefferson's Virginia*. Charlottesville, VA.

Dalby, A. 2002. "Levels of Concealment: The Dress of '*Hetairai*' and '*Pornai*' in Greek Texts." In *Women's Dress in the Ancient Greek World*, edited by L. Llewellyn-Jones, pp. 111–124. Swansea.

Damon, C. 1997. *The Mask of the Parasite: A Pathology of Roman Patronage*. Ann Arbor, MI.

Dari-Mattiacci, G. 2013. *Slavery and Information*. Amsterdam Law School Legal Studies Research Paper No. 2011–33. Amsterdam.

Dari-Mattiacci, G., and D. Kehoe, eds. 2020. *Roman Law and Economics*, Vol. 1: *Institutions and Organizations*; Vol. 2: *Exchange, Ownership and Disputes*. Oxford.

Darmezin, L. 1999. *Les Affranchissements par consécration en Béotie et dans le monde grec hellénistique*. Nancy.

Daube, D. 1965. "The Preponderance of Intestacy at Rome." *Tulane Law Review* 39: 253–62.

Daube, D. 1969. *Roman Law: Linguistic, Social and Philosophical Aspects*. Edinburgh.

David, J.-M. 1992. *Le patronat judiciaire au dernier siècle de la république romaine*. Rome.

Davies, G. 1994. "The Language of Gesture in Greek Art: Gender and Status on Grave Stelai." *Apollo* 140.389: 6–11.

Davies, J. 1998. "Ancient Economies: Models and Muddles." In Parkins and Smith, eds., pp. 225–256.

Davies, J. 2007. "Linear and Nonlinear Flow Models for Ancient Economies." In *The Ancient Economy: Evidence and Models*, edited by J. Manning and I. Morris, pp. 127–56. Stanford, CA.

De Callataÿ, F., ed. 2014. *Quantifying the Greco-Roman Economy and Beyond*. Bari.

De Certeau, M. 2011. *The Practice of Everyday Life* (translation of *Arts de faire*, 1980). Berkeley, CA.

Dekkers, R. 1935. *La fiction juridique: Étude de droit romain et de droit comparé*. Paris.

Dell'Agli, A., and T. Vigorita, eds. 1981. *Diritto e società nell' antica Roma: Scritti di diritto romano II (Francesco de Martino)*. Rome.

Del Lago, E., and C. Katsari, eds. 2008. *Slave Systems: Ancient and Modern*. Cambridge.

Del Mar, M. 2015. "Introducing Fictions: Examples, Functions, Definitions and Evaluations." In *Legal Fictions in Theory and Practice*, edited by M. Del Mar and W. Twining, pp. ix–xxix. Heidelberg.

De Martino, F. [1941] 1981. "Studi sull' 'actio exercitoria.'" *Rivista del diritto della navigazione* 7.1: 7–31 (reprinted in dell'Agli and Vigorita, eds., 1981, pp. 148–170).

De Martino, F. [1958] 1981. "Ancora sull' 'actio exercitoria.'" *Labeo* 4: 274–300 (reprinted in dell'Agli and Vigorita, eds., 1981, pp. 171–199).

Demougin, S. 1988. *L'ordre équestre sous les Julio-Claudiens*. Rome.

Dench, E. 2005. *Romulus' Asylum: Roman Identities from the Age of Alexander to the Age of Hadrian*. Oxford.

Depauw, M. 2017. "Legal Incapacity in Ancient Egypt." In Yiftach and Faraguna, eds., pp. 45–56.

Dhami, S. 2017. *The Foundations of Behavioral Economic Analysis*. Oxford.

Dimopoulou, A. 1999. *La rémunération de l'assistance en Justice: Étude sur la relation avocat-plaideur à Rome*. Athens.

Dimopoulou, A. 2012. "Le rôle des esclaves dans l'économie athénienne: réponse à Edward Cohen." In *Symposion 2011 (Akten der Gesellschaft für Griechische und Hellenistische Rechtsgeschichte)*, edited by B. Legras and G. Thür, pp. 225–236. Vienna.

Dimopoulou, A. 2014. "Ἄκυρον ἔστω: Legal Invalidity in Greek Inscriptions." In *Symposion 2013 (Akten der Gesellschaft für Griechische und Hellenistische Rechtsgeschichte)*, edited by M. Gagarin and A. Lanni, pp. 249–275. Vienna.

Diosdi, G. 1971. "'In bonis esse' und 'nudum ius Quiritium.'" In *Studi Volterra* II, pp. 130 ff. Milan.

Dixon, S. [1984] 2003. "Infirmitas Sexus: Womanly Weakness in Roman Law." *Tijdschrift voor Rechtsgeschiedenis* 52: 343–371 (= *Reading Roman Women : Sources, Genres and Real Life*, pp. 73–88 [revised], London, 2003).

Dixon, S. 2000–2001. "How Do You Count Them If They're Not There? New Perspectives on Roman Cloth Production." *Opuscula Romana* 25–26: 7–17.

Dixon, S. 2004. "Exemplary Housewife or Luxurious Slut? Cultural Representations of Women in the Roman Economy." In *Women's Influence on Classical Civilization*, edited by F. McHardy and E. Marshall, pp. 56–74. London.

Dixon, S. 2016. "Family." In du Plessis, Ando, and Tuori, eds., pp. 461–472.

Doria, C. 2012. "Status and Contract in Ancient Rome." In *Obligations in Roman Law: Past, Present, and Future*, edited by T. McGinn, pp. 102–130. Ann Arbor, MI.

Drinkwater, J. 2019. *Nero: Emperor and Court*. Cambridge.

Duff, M. [1928] 1958. *Freedmen in the Early Roman Empire*. Cambridge.

Dumont, J. 1987. *Servus: Rome et l'esclavage sous la république*. Rome.

Duncan-Jones, R. 1982. *The Economy of the Roman Empire: Quantitative Studies*, 2nd ed. Cambridge.

Duncan-Jones, R. 1990. *Structure and Scale in the Roman Economy*. Cambridge.

Du Plessis, P. 2012. "Theory and Practice in the Roman Law of Contracts." In *Obligations in Roman Law: Past, Present, and Future*, edited by T. McGinn, pp. 131–157. Ann Arbor, MI.

Du Plessis, P. 2017. "Once More on the Perpetual Guardianship of Women." In Yiftach and Faraguna, eds., pp. 165–172.

Du Plessis, P. 2020. "'Provincial Law' in Britannia." In Czajkowski, Eckhardt, and Strothmann, eds., pp. 435–461.

Du Plessis, P., ed. 2013. *New Frontiers: Law and Society in the Roman World*. Edinburgh.

Du Plessis, P., C. Ando, and K. Tuori, eds. 2016. *The Oxford Handbook of Roman Law and Society*. Oxford.

Eberle, L., and E. le Quéré. 2017. "Landed Traders, Trading Agriculturalists? Land in the Economy of the Italian Diaspora in the Greek East." *Journal of Roman Studies* 107: 27–59.

Eck, W. 1972. "Die Familie der Volusii Saturnini in neuen Inschriften aus Lucus Feroniae." *Hermes* 100: 461–484.

Eck, W. 1973. "Sozialstruktur des römischen Senatorenstandes in der hohen Kaiserzeit und statistische Methode." *Chiron* 3: 375–394.

Eck, W. 1976. "Neros Freigelassener Epaphroditus und die Aufdeckung der Pisonischen Verschwörung." *Historia* 25: 381–384.

Eck, W. 2000. "Provincial Administration and Finance." *Cambridge Ancient History* 2 II. 266–292. Cambridge.

Eck, W. 2013. "La loi municipale de Troesmis: données juridiques et politiques d'une inscription récemment découverte." *Revue historique de droit français et étranger* 91: 199–213.

Eck, W. 2016a. "Herrschafftssicherung und römische Heer unter Augustus." In *Studi su Augusto in occasione del XX centenario della sua morte*, edited by G. Negri and A. Valvo, pp. 78–93. Torino.

Eck, W. 2016b. "The Emperor, the Law and Imperial Administration." In du Plessis, Ando, and Tuori, eds., pp. 98–110.

Eck. W. 2020. "The *leges municipales* as a Means of Legal and Social Romanization of the Provinces of the Roman Empire." In Czajkowski, Eckhardt, and Strothmann, eds., pp. 314–331.

Eck, W., ed. 2005. *Repertorium Familiae Caesarum et Libertorum Augustorum (Paul Weaver)*, http;//altegeschichte.phil-fak.uni-koeln.de/500.html.

Eckhardt, B. 2020. "Law, Empire, and Identity between West and East: The Danubian Provinces." In Czajkowski, Eckhardt, and Strothmann, eds., pp. 416–435.

Eder, W. 1980. *Servitus Publica: Untersuchungen zur Entstehung, Entwicklung und Funktion der öffentlichen Sklaverei in Rom*.Forschungen zur antiken Sklaverei no. 13. Wiesbaden.

Edmonson, J. 2011. "Slavery and the Roman Family." In Bradley and Cartledge, eds., pp. 337–361.

Ehrlich, E. 2002. *Fundamental Principles of the Sociology of Law*. New Brunswick, NJ.

Eichenauer, M. 1988. *Untersuchungen zur Arbeitswelt der Frau in der römischen Antike*. Frankfurt.

Ellickson, R. 2020. "Ancient Rome: Legal Foundations of the Growth of an Indispensable City." In Dari-Mattiacci and Kehoe, eds., Vol. 2, pp. 159–210.

Elliott, C. 2020. *Economic Theory and the Roman Monetary Economy*. Cambridge.

Engerman, S. 1973. "Some Considerations Relating to Property Rights in Man." *Journal of Economic History* 32: 43–65.

Engerman, S. 2008. "Emancipation Schemes: Different Ways of Ending Slavery." In E. Del Lago and C. Katsari, eds., pp. 265–282. Cambridge.

Erdkamp, P. 2014. "How Modern Was the Market Economy of the Roman World?" *Œconomia* 4: 225–235.

Erdkamp, P. 2015. "Agriculture, Division of Labour, and the Paths to Economic Growth." In Erdkamp, Verboven, and Zuiderhoek, eds., pp. 18–39. Oxford.

Erdkamp, P., ed. 2013. *The Cambridge Companion to Ancient Rome*. Cambridge.

Erdkamp, P., K. Verboven, and A. Zuiderhoek, eds. 2015. *Ownership and Exploitation of Land and Natural Resources in the Roman World*. Oxford.

Eriksen, T. 2001. *Small Places, Large Issues: An Introduction to Social and Cultural Anthropology*, 2nd ed. London.

Erman, H. 1896. "*Servus Vicarius*, l'esclave de l'esclave romain." *Receuil publié par la Faculté de droit de l'Université de Lausanne*, pp. 391–532. Geneva.

Errington, R. 1988. "Aspects of Roman Acculturation in the East under the Republic." *Alte Geschichte und Wissenschaftsgeschichte. Festschrift für K. Christ*, edited by P. Kneissl and V. Losemann, pp. 140–157. Darmstadt.

Euzenmat, M., and J. Marion, eds. 1982. *Inscriptions antiques du Maroc*, Vol. II: *Inscriptions latines*. Paris.

Evans, H. 1994. *Water Distribution in Ancient Rome: The Evidence of Frontinus*. Ann Arbor, MI.

Ewald, W. 1995. "Comparative Jurisprudence (II): The Logic of Legal Transplants." *The American Journal of Comparative Law* 43: 489–510.

Faas, P. 2003. *Around the Roman Table*. London.

Fabiani, F. 2002. "L'augustalità nell'Etruria nord-occidentale: i casi di Luni, Lucca e Pisa." *Ostraka* 11: 99–112.

Fabre, G. 1981. *Libertus: Recherches sur les rapports patron-affranchi à la fin de la république romaine*. Rome.

Fadda, C. [1903] 1987. *Istituti commerciali del diritto romano: Gli argentarii ed il commercio bancario*. Napoli.

Faraguna, M. 2017. "Guardianship in Ancient Societies: Concluding Remarks." In Yiftach and Faraguna, eds., pp. 273–281.

Fenoaltea, S. 1984. "Slavery and Supervision in Comparative Perspective: A Model." *Journal of Economic History* 44: 635–689.

Fentress, E., J. Bodel, F. Coarelli, P. Braconi, and G. Pucci. 2005. "Selling People: Five Papers on Roman Slave Traders and the Buildings They Used." *Journal of Roman Archaeology* 18: 180–240.

Fercia, R. 2008. *La responsabilità per fatto di ausiliari nel diritto romano*. Padova.

Ferguson, J. 1917/18. "Aere conlato." *Classical Journal* 13: 515–520.

Ferrucci, S. 2012. "Schiavi banchieri: Identità e status nell'Atene democratica." In *Nuove e antiche schiavitù* , edited by A. Di Nardo and G. Lucchetta, pp. 98–109. Pescara.

Fiches, J.-L. 2013. "La romanisation, pourquoi pas? In *Contacts de cultures, constructions identitaires et stéréotypes dans l'espace méditerranéen antique*, edited by H. Ménard and R. Plana-Mallart, pp. 111–116. Monpellier.

Findlay, R. 1975. "Slavery, Incentives and Manumission: A Rhetorical Model." *Journal of Political Economy* 83: 923–934.

Finkenauer, T. 2008. "Direkte Stellvertretung bei Stipulationen?" *Zeitschrift der Savigny-Stiftung für Rechtsgeschichte* (Romanist. Abt.) 125: 440–497.

Finkenauer, T. 2009. "Anmerkungen zur *redemptio servi suis nummis*." In *Festschrift für Rolf Knütel*, edited by H. Altmeppen et al., pp. 345–357. Heidelberg.

Finkenauer, T. 2010. *Die Rechtsetzung Mark Aurels zur Sklaverei*. Mainz.

Finkenauer, T. 2013. "Der Verzicht auf die *exceptio SCti Velleiani* im klassischen Recht." *Tijdschrift voor Rechtsgeschiedenis* 81: 17–49.

Finley, M. 1964. "Between Slavery and Freedom." *Comparative Studies in Society and History* 6: 233–249.

Finley, M. 1965. "La servitude pour dettes." *Revue historique de droit français et étranger* 43: 159–184.

Finley, M. 1982. *Economy and Society in Ancient Greece*, edited by B. Shaw and R. Saller. New York.

Finley, M. 1986. *Ancient History: Evidence and Models*. New York.

Finley, M. [1973] 1999. *The Ancient Economy*, 3rd ed. Updated with a new foreword by I. Morris. Berkeley, CA.

Finley, M. [1980] 1998. *Ancient Slavery and Modern Ideology*. Princeton, NJ.

Fiori, R. 1993–94. "*Materfamilias*." *Bullettino dell'Istituto di Diritto Romano "Vittorio Scialoja*: 96–97: 455–498.

Flannery, K., and J. Marcus. 2012. *The Creation of Inequality: How Our Prehistoric Ancestors Set the Stage for Monarchy, Slavery and Empire*. Cambridge, MA.

Fleckner, A. 2010. *Antike Kapitalvereinigungen: Ein Betrag zu den konzepionellen und historischen Grundlagen der Aktiengesellschaft*. Cologne.

Fleckner, A. 2014. "The *Peculium*: A Legal Device for Donations to *personae alieno iuri subiectae*?" In *Gift Giving and the Embedded Economy in the Ancient World*, edited by F. Carlà and M. Gori, pp. 213–239. Heidelberg.

Fleckner, A. 2020. "Roman Business Associations." In Dari-Mattiacci and Kehoe, eds., Vol. 1, pp. 233–272.

Flohr, M. 2016. "Quantifying Pompeii: Population, Inequality, and the Urban Economy." In *The Economy of Pompeii*, edited by M. Flohr and A. Wilson, pp. 53–84. Oxford.

Fochesato, M., A. Bogaard, and S. Bowles. 2019. "Comparing Ancient Inequalities: The Challenges of Comparability, Bias and Precision." *Antiquity* 93.370: 853–869.

Földi, A. 1996. "Remarks on the Legal Structure of Enterprises in Roman Law." *Revue internationale des droits de l'antiquité* 43: 179–211.

Foraboschi, D., and A. Gara. 1981. "Sulla diffrerenza tra tassi di interesse in natura e in moneta nell'Egitto greo-romano." In *Proceedings of the XVIth International Congress of Papyrology*, edited by R. Bagnall, G. Browne, and E. Hanson, pp. 335–343. Chico.

Foraboschi, D., and A. Gara. 1982. "L'economia di crediti in natura (Egitto)." *Athenaeum* 60: 69–83.

Forbes, C. 1955. "The Education and Training of Slaves in Antiquity." *Transactions of the American Philological Association* 86: 321–360.

Forbes, R. 1966. *Studies in Ancient Technology*. Leiden.

Forsdyke, S. 2012. *Slaves Tell Tales and Other Episodes in the Politics of Popular Culture in Ancient Greece*. Princeton, NJ.

Forsdyke, S. 2018. "Slave Agency, Citizenship and the Law." In Thür, Yiftach, and Zelnick-Abramovitz, eds., pp. 345–366.

Forsdyke, S. (forthcoming). "How to Find a New Master: Slave Agency in Ancient Greece." In *Voiceless, Invisible and Countless: Subordinate Experience in Ancient Greece, 800–300 BCE.*, edited by S. Gartland and D. Tandy, pp. XX–XX.

Foucault, M. [1976] 1998. *The History of Sexuality*, Vol. 1. New York (originally published as *L'Histoire de la sexualité.* I. *La volenté de savoir*, Paris).

Fournier, J. 2010. *Entre tutelle romaine et autonomie civique. L'administration judicaire dans les provinces hellénophones del'Empire romain (129 av. J.-C.–235 apr. J.-C.* Athens.

Fowler, W. Warde. 1926. *Social Life at Rome in the Age of Cicero*. New York.

Foy, D. 2018. "An Overview of the Circulation of Glass in Antiquity." In Wilson and Bowman, eds., pp. 265–300.

Frank, T. 1916. "Race Mixture in the Roman Empire." *American Historical Review* 21.4: 689–708.

Frank, T. 1933. *Rome and Italy of the Republic. An Economic Survey of Ancient Rome*, Vol. 1. Baltimore, MD.

Friedländer, L. 1891. *Petronii Cena Trimalchionis*. Leipzig.

Friedländer, L. 1922. *Darststellungen aus der Sittengeschichte Roms in der Zeit von Augustus bis zum Ausgang der Antonine*. 10th ed. Leipzig.

Friedman, L. [1985] 2005. *A History of American Law*. New York.

Frier, B. 1980. *Landlords and Tenants in Imperial Rome*. Princeton, NJ.

Frier, B. 1985. *The Rise of the Roman Jurists: Studies in Cicero's pro Caecina*. Princeton, NJ.

Frier, B. 1989. *A Casebook on the Roman Law of Delict*. Atlanta, GA.

Frier, B. 1993. "Subsistence Annuities and Per Capita Income in the Early Roman Empire." *Classical Philology* 88: 222–230.

Frier, B., and D. Kehoe. 2007. "Law and Economic Institutions." In W. Scheidel, I. Morris, and R. Saller, eds., pp. 113–143. Cambridge.

Frier, B., and T. McGinn. 2004. *A Casebook on Roman Family Law*. Oxford.

Friggeri, R., G. Gregori, and M. Ceceri, eds. 2012. *Terme di Diocleziano. La collezione epigrafica*. Milan.

Fülle, G. 1997. "The International Organization of the Arretine *Terra Sigillata* Industry: Problems of Evidence and Interpretation." *Journal of Roman Studies* 87: 111–155.

Furubotn, E., and R. Richter, eds. 2005. *Institutions and Economic Theory: The Contribution Of The New Institutional Economics*. 2nd ed. Ann Arbor, MI.

Gagé, J. 1974. *Les classes sociales dans l'empire romain*. Paris.

Gagliardi, L. 2006. *Mobilità e integrazione delle persone nei centri cittadini romani*: aspetti giuridici. Milan.

Gagliardi, L. 2012. "La madre tutrice e la madre ἐπακολουθήτρια: osservazioni sul rapporto tra diritto romano e diritti delle province orientali." *Index. Quaderni Camerti di studi romanistici* 40: 423–446.

Gagliardi, L. 2017. "The Mother as Guardian of Her Children in Rome and in the Oriental Provinces of the Empire." In Yiftach and Faraguna, eds., pp. 221–242.

Galanter, M. 1989. *Law and Society in Modern India*. New Delhi.

Galsterer, H. 1986. "Roman Law in the Provinces." In *L'impero romano e le strutture economiche e sociali delle province*, edited by M. Crawford, pp. 13–27. Como.

Gamauf, R. 2009. "Slaves Doing Business: The Role of Roman Law in the Economy of a Roman Household." *European Review of History* 16.3: 331–346.

Gamauf, R. 2016. "Slavery: Social Position and Legal Capacity." In du Plessis, Ando, and Tuori, eds., pp. 386–401.

Gamauf, R. 2017. "Überlegungen zu Petron. 57,4 und zum Selbstverkauf als 'freiwilliger Sklave' im frühen Prinzipat." Oral presentation at la Société d'Histoire des Droits de l'Antiquité (SIHDA) 2017 (Bologna).

Gara, A. 1991. "La mobilità sociale nell'Impero." *Athenaeum* 79: 335–358.

García Garrido, M. 1957–1958. "Sobre los verdaderos límites de la ficción en derecho romano." *Anuario de Historia del Derecho Español* 27–28: 305–342.

García Garrido, M. 1958. *Ius uxorium: El régimen patrimonial de la mujer casada en derecho romano*. Rome.

García Garrido, M. 2001. *El Commercio, los negocios y las finanzas en el mundo romano*. Madrid.

Gardner, A., E. Herring, and K. Lomas, eds. 2013. *Creating Ethnicities and Identities in the Roman World*. London.

Gardner, J. 1986. *Women in Roman Law and Society*. Bloomington, IN.

Gardner, J. 1993. *Being a Roman Citizen*. London.

Gardner, J. 1995. "Gender-Role Assumptions in Roman Law." *Echos du Monde Classique/Classical Views* 39: 377–400.

Gardner, J. 1996. "Hadrian and the Social Legacy of Augustus." *Labeo* 83–100.

Gardner, J. 1998. *Family and* Familia *in Roman Law and Life*. Oxford.

Gardner, J. 1999. "Women in Business Life: Some Evidence from Puteoli." In *Female Networks and the Public Sphere in Roman Society, Acta Instituti Romani Finlandiae 22*, edited by P. Setälä and L. Savunen, pp. 11–27. Rome.

Gardner, J. 2001. "Making Citizens: The Operation of the Lex Irnitana." In de Blois, ed., pp. 215–229.

Gardner, J. 2011. "Slavery and Roman Law." In Bradley and Cartledge, eds., pp. 414–437. Cambridge.

Garland, R. 1987. *The Piraeus*. Ithaca, NY.

Garnsey, P. 1970. *Social Status and Legal Privilege in the Roman Empire*. Oxford.

Garnsey, P. 1975. "Descendants of Freedmen in Local Politics: Some Criteria." In *The Ancient Historian and His Materials: Essays in Honour of C. E. Stevens*, edited by B. Levick, pp. 167–180. Farnborough.

Garnsey, P. [1981] 1998. "Independent Freedmen and the Economy of Roman Italy under the Principate." *Klio* 63: 359–371 (reprinted in Garnsey 1998, pp. 28–44).

Garnsey, P. 1996. *Ideas of Slavery from Aristotle to Augustine*. Cambridge.

Garnsey, P. 1998. *Cities, Peasants and Food in Classical Antiquity: Essays in Social and Economic History*. Cambridge.

Garnsey, P. 1999. *Food and Society in Classical Antiquity*. Cambridge.

Garnsey, P. 2004. "Roman Citizenship and Roman Law in the Late Empire." In *Approaching Late Antiquity: The Transformation from Early to Late Empire*, edited by S. Swain and M. Edwards, pp. 133–155. Oxford.

Garnsey, P. 2014. "L'èconomie du Bas-Empire." In *Les affaires de Monsieur Andreau: Économie et société du monde romain*, edited by C. Apicella, M.-L. Haack, and F. Lerouxel, pp. 43–53. Bordeaux.

Garnsey, P., and R. Saller. 2009. *The Roman Empire: Economy, Society and Culture*, 2nd ed. London.

Garzetti, A. 1944. "*Aerarium* e *Fiscus* sotto Augusto; storia di una questione in parte di nomi." *Athenaeum* 21: 298 ff.

Geens, K. 2008. "Financial Archives of Graeco-Roman Egypt." In Verboven, Vandorpe, and Chankowski, eds., pp. 133–151. Leuven.

George, M. 2002. "Slave Disguise at Ancient Rome." *Slavery and Abolition* 23.2: 41–54.

George, M. 2011. "Slavery and Roman Material Culture." In Bradley and Cartledge, eds., pp. 385–413.

George, M., ed. 2013. *Roman Slavery and Roman Material Culture*. Phoenix Supp. 52. Toronto.

Geraci, G. 2001–2. "Le dichiarazioni di nascita e di morte a Roma e nelle province." *Mélanges de l'École française de Rome–Antiquité* 113: 675–711.

Gianfrotta, P., and A. Hesnard. 1989. "Les bouchons d'Amphore en pouzzolane." In *Amphores romaines et histoire économique: Dix ans de recherche. Actes du colloque (Sienne. 22–24 mai 1986)*. Collection de l'École française de Rome 114, pp. 393–414. Rome.

Giardina, A. 1994. "L'identità incompiuta dell'Italia romana." In *L'Italie d'Auguste à Dioclétien: Actes du colloque international, Rome, 25–28 mars 1992*, pp. 1–89. Rome.
Giardina, A. 2002. "Le Marchand." In Giardina, ed., pp. 315–347.
Giardina, A. ed. 2002. *L'Homme romain*. Paris.
Giardina, A., and A. Gurevič. 1994. *Il mercante dall'Antichità al Medioevo*. Rome.
Giliberti, G. 1984. *Legatum kalendarii: mutuo feneratizio e struttura contabile del patrimonio nell'età del principato*. Naples.
Giménez-Candela, T. 1981. "Una contribución al estudio de la ley Irnitana: la manumisión de esclavos municipals." *Iura* 32: 37–56.
Giunti, P. 2012. "Il ruolo sociale della donna romana di età imperiale: tra discriminazione e riconoscimento." *Index* 40: 342–379.
Glancy, J. 2002. *Slavery in Early Christianity*. Cambridge.
Gleason, M. 2006. "Greek Cities under Roman Rule." In Potter, ed., pp. 228–249.
Gofas, D. 1973. *Εἰσηγήσεις τοῦ Ρωμαϊκοῦ Δικαίου*. Athens.
Goldin, C. 1976. *Urban Slavery in the American South 1820–60*. Chicago.
Goldschmidt, L. 1891. *Universalgeschichte des Handelsrechts*. Stuttgart.
Goldsmith, R. 1987. *Premodern Financial Systems: A Historical Comparative Study*. Cambridge.
Goldsworthy, A., and I. Haynes, eds. 1999. *The Roman Army as a Community*. Portsmouth, RI.
Goldthwaite, R. 1980. *The Building of Renaissance Florence: An Economic and Social History*. Baltimore, MD.
González, J. 1986. "The *lex Irnitana*: A New Copy of the Flavian Municipal Law." *Journal of Roman Studies* 76: 147–243.
González, J., and M. Crawford. 1986. "The *Lex Irnitana*: A New Copy of the Flavian Municipal Law." *Journal of Roman Studies* 76: 147–241.
Goodman, M. "Babatha's Story." *Journal of Roman Studies* 81: 169–175.
Gordon, A., and J. Gordon. 1965. *Album of Dated Latin Inscriptions*, Vol. III. Berkeley.
Gordon, M. 1931. "The Freedman's Son in Municipal Life." *Journal of Roman Studies* 21: 65–77.
Gordon, W. 2007. *Roman Law, Scots Law and Legal History*. Edinburgh.
Gould, J. 1980. "Law, Custom and Myth: Aspects of the Social Position of Women in Classical Athens." *Journal of Hellenic Studies* 100: 38–59.
Gourevitch, D., and M.-T. Rapsaet-Charlier. 2001. *La femme dans la Rome antique*. Paris.
Green, P. 2003. "Politics, Philosophy and Propaganda: Hermias of Atarneus and his Friendship with Aristotle." In *Crossroads of History*, edited by W. Heckel and L. Tritle, pp. 29–46. Claremont, CA.
Greenridge, A. 1894. *Infamia: Its Place in Roman Public and Private Law*. Oxford.
Greif, A. 206. *Institutions and the Path to the Modern Economy: Lessons from Medieval Trade*. Cambridge.
Griffin, M. 1976. *Seneca: A Philosopher in Politics*. Oxford.

Grillo, R., et al., eds. 2009. *Legal Practice and Cultural Diversity*. Farnham, UK.

Groen-Vallinga, M. 2013. "Desperate Housewives?: The Adaptive Family Economy and Female Participation in the Roman Urban Labour Market." In *Women and the Roman City in the Latin West*, edited by E. Hemelrijk and G. Woolf, pp. 295–312. Leiden.

Groen-Vallinga, M. 2017. *The Roman World of Work: Social Structures and the Urban Labour Market of Roman Italy in the First Three Centuries AD*. Dissertation, Leiden.

Groen-Vallinga, M., and L. Tacoma. 2017. "The Value of Labour: Diocletian's Prices Edict." In Verboven and Laes, eds., pp. 104–132.

Gröschler, P. 1997. *Die tabellae-Urkunden aus den pompeianischen und herkulanensischen Urkundenfunden*. Berlin.

Grubbs, J. 2002. *Women and the Law in the Roman Empire: A Sourcebook on Marriage, Divorce and Widowhood*. London.

Gsell, S. 1932. "Esclaves ruraux dans l'Afrique romaine." In *Mélanges Gustave Glotz* 1: 397–415. Paris.

Guarino, A. 1963. *Storia del diritto romano*. Milan.

Guarino, A. 1967. "Tagliacarte." *Labeo* 13: 294–295.

Guarino, A. 1997. *Diritto privato romano*. Naples.

Gummerus, H. 1915. "Die römische Industrie. Das Goldschmied- und Juweliergewerbe." *Klio* 14: 129–189.

Gummerus, H. 1916. "Industrie und Handel." In *Pauly-Wissowa Realencyclopädie der classischen Altertumswissenschaft* 99: 1381–1535.

Günther, R. 1987. *Frauenarbeit-Frauenbindung. Untersuchungen zu unfreien und freigelassenen Frauen in der stadtrömischen Inschriften*. Munich.

Günther, S. 2018. "Roman Law: Opening the System." *Journal of Ancient Civilizations* 33.2: 267–282.

Habicht, C. 1975. "New Evidence on the Province of Asia." *Journal of Roman Studies* 65: 64–91.

Haensch, R. 1994. "Die Bearbeitungsweisen von Petitionen in der Provinz Aegyptus." *Zeitschrift für Papyrologie und Epigraphik* 100: 487–546.

Haensch, R. 1997. "Zur Konventsordnung in Aegyptus und den übrigen Provinzen des römischen Reiches." In *Akten des 21: Internationalen Papyrologenkongresses, Archiv für Papyrusforschung*, Vol. 3, edited by B. Kramer, W. Luppe, and H. Maehler, pp. 320–391. Leipzig.

Haferkamp, H., and T. Repgen, eds. 2017. *Wie pandektistich war die Pandektistik? Symposion aus Anlass des 80. Geburtstags von K. Luig am 11. September 2015*. Tubingen.

Halbwachs, V. 1997. *"Ipsae sibi negotia tractant": Frauen als Geschäftspartnerinnen im Spiegel römischrchtlicher Quellen*. Dissertation, Wien.

Halbwachs, V. 1999. "Ipsae sibi negotia tractant: Zur Frau als Geschäftspartnerin im Spiegel römischrechtlicher Quellen." In *Atti della 51a Sessione della SIHDA,*

Crotone-Messina 16–20 settembre 1997, edited by I. Piro, pp. 349–363. Sovertia Mannelli.

Halbwachs, V. 2014. "*Haec disceptatio in factum constitit*": Bemerkungen zur *pietas* im römischen Unterhaltsrecht." In *Meditationes de iure et historia: Essays in Honour of Laurens Winkel*, edited by R. van den Bergh and L. Wildenboer, pp. 371–82. Praetoria.

Halbwachs, V. 2016. "Women as Legal Actors." In du Plessis, Ando, and Tuori, eds., pp. 443–460.

Hales, S. 2013. "Freedmen's Cribs: Domestic Vulgarity on the Bay of Naples." In Prag and Redpath, eds., pp. 161–180.

Halkin, L. [1897] 1979. *Les esclaves publics chez les romains*. Brussels (reprint, New York, 1979).

Hall, G. 2000. *Databases for the Study of Afro-Louisiana History and Genealogy, 1699–1860*. New Orleans.

Hallett, J. 1984. *Fathers and Daughters in Roman Society*. Princeton, NJ.

Hamel, G. 1989. *Poverty and Charity in Roman Palestine, First Three Centuries C.E.* Berkeley, CA.

Hamza, G. 1980. "Aspetti della rappresentanza negoziale in diritto romano." *Index* 9: 193–229.

Handler, J., and J. Pohlmann. 1984. "Slave Manumissions and Freedmen in Seventeenth-Century Barbados." *William and Mary Quarterly* 41.3: 390–408.

Hansmann, H., R. Kraakman, and R. Squire. 2006. "Law and the Rise of the Firm." *Harvard Law Review* 119: 1335–1403.

Hansmann, H., R. Kraakman, and R. Squire. 2020. "Incomplete Organizations: Legal Entities and Asset Partitioning in Roman Commerce." In Dari-Mattiacci and Kehoe, eds., Vol. 1, pp. 199–232.

Harper, K. 2010. "The *SC Claudianum* in the Codex Theodosianus: Social History and Legal Texts." *Classical Quarterly* 60: 610–638.

Harper, K. 2011. *Slavery in the Late Roman World AD 275–425*. Cambridge.

Harper, K. 2012. Review of Mouritsen 2011. *American Historical Review* 117: 909–910.

Harper, K., and W. Scheidel. 2018. "Roman Slavery and the Idea of 'Slave Society.'" In Lenski and Cameron, eds., pp. 86–105.

Harries, J. 2013. "The *Senatus Consultum Silanianum*: Court Decisions and Judicial Severity in the Early Roman Empire." In du Plessis, ed., pp. 51–72.

Harris, E. 2013a. *The Rule of Law in Action in Democratic Athens*. New York.

Harris, E. 2013b. "Were There Business Agents in Classical Greece? The Evidence of Some Lead Letters." *The Letter: Law, State, Society and the Epistolary Format in the Ancient World*, edited by U. Yiftach-Firanko, pp. 105–124. Wiesbaden.

Harris, E. 2015. "The Meaning of the Legal Term *Symbolaion*, the Law about *Dikai Emporikai* and the Role of the *Paragraphe* Procedure." *Dike* 18: 7–36.

Harris, E. 2018a. "Some Recent Developments in the Study of Ancient Greek Law." *Journal of Ancient Civilizations* 33.2: 187–266.

Harris, E. 2018b. "Trials, Private Arbitration, and Public Arbitration in Classical Athens or the Background to [Arist.] *Ath. Pol.* 53, 1–7." In *Athenaion Politeiai tra storia, politica e sociologia: Aristotele e Pseudo-Senofonte*, edited by C. Bearzot, M. Canevaro, T. Gargiulo, and E. Poddighe, pp. 213–230. Milan.

Harris, W. 1980a. "Roman Terracotta Lamps: The Organization of an Industry." *Journal of Roman Studies* 70: 126–145.

Harris, W. 1980b. "Towards a Study of the Roman Slave Trade." In *Seaborne Commerce of Ancient Rome: Studies in Archaeology and History (American Academy in Rome: Memoirs* 36), edited by J. D'Arms and E. Kopoff, pp. 117–140. Rome.

Harris, W. 1991. "Demography, Geography and the Sources of Roman Slaves." *Journal of Roman Studies* 89: 62–75.

Harris, W. 1999. "Demography, Geography and the Sources of Roman Slaves." *Journal of Roman Studies* 89: 62–75.

Harris, W. 2006a. "A Revisionist View of Roman Money." *Journal of Roman Studies* 96: 1–24 (= Harris 2011b).

Harris, W. 2006b. "Una prospettiva revisionista sulla moneta romana." *Rivista di storia economica* 3: 287–306.

Harris, W. 2007. "The Late Republic." In Scheidel, Morris, and Saller, eds., pp. 511–539.

Harris, W. 2008. "The Nature of Roman Money." In Harris, ed., pp. 174–207.

Harris, W. 2011a. "Poverty and Destitution in the Roman Empire." In *Rome's Imperial Economy: Twelve Essays*, pp. 27–54. Oxford.

Harris, W. 2011b. "A Revisionist View of Roman Money." In *Rome's Imperial Economy: Twelve Essays*, pp. 223–256. Oxford.

Harris, W. 2016. *Roman Power: A Thousand Years of Empire*. Cambridge.

Harris, W. 2018. "The Indispensable Commodity: Notes on the Economy of Wood in the Roman Mediterranean." In Wilson and Bowman, eds., pp. 211–236.

Harris, W. 2019a. "Credit-Money in the Roman Economy." *Klio* 2019 101.1: 158–189.

Harris, W. 2019b. "A Strange Fact about Shipboard Coin Hoards Throws Light on the Roman Empire's Financial System." *Athenaeum* 107.I: 150–155.

Harris, W., ed. 2008. *The Monetary Systems of the Greeks and Romans*. Oxford.

Harrison, A. 1968. *The Law of Athens*, Vol. 1. Oxford.

Hartman, S. 1997. *Scenes of Subjection: Terror, Slavery, and Self-Making in Nineteenth-Century America*. New York.

Hasegawa, K. 2005. *The* Familia Urbana *during the Early Empire: A Study of Columbaria Inscriptions*. British Archaeological Reports International Series 1440. Oxford.

Hatzfeld, J. 1919. *Les trafiquants italiens dans l'Orient hellénique*. Paris.

Hausmaninger, H., and R. Gamauf. 2012. *A Casebook on Roman Property Law*. Translation by G. Sheets of *Casebook zum römischen Sachenrecht* (Vienna 2003). Oxford.

Hawkins, C. 2012. "Manufacturing." In Scheidel, ed., pp. 175–194.

Hawkins, C. 2013. "Labour and Employment." In Erdkamp, ed., pp. 336–351. Cambridge.

Hawkins, C. 2016. *Roman Artisans and the Urban Economy*. Cambridge.

Hawkins, C. 2017. "Contracts, Coercion, and the Boundaries of the Roman Artisanal Firm." In Verboven and Laes, eds., pp. 36–61.

Hawkins, C. (forthcoming) "Manumission and the Organization of Labour." In Lo Cascio, Bresson, and Velde, eds., pp. XX–XX. Oxford.

Haynes, I., and W. Hanson. 2004. "An Introduction to Roman Dacia." In *Roman Dacia: The Making of a Provincial Society*. Journal of Roman Archaeology Supplementary Series 56, edited by W. Hanson and I. Haynes, pp. 11–31. Portsmouth, RI.

Heinemeyer, S. 2013. *Der Freikauf des Sklaven mit eigenem Geld --- Redemptio suis nummis*. Berlin.

Heinen, H., ed. 2010. *Antike Sklaverie: Rückblick und Ausblick. Neue Beiträge zur Forschungsgeschichte und zur Erschliessung der archäologischen Zeugnisse*. Stuttgart.

Helen, T. 1975. *Organization of Roman Brick Production in the First and Second Centuries A.D.* Helsinki.

Hellie, R. 1982. *Slavery in Russia, 1450–1725*. Chicago.

Henderson, J. 2002. "The Law Is Not Mocked: Straightening out a Crooked Will (Phaedrus 4.5)." In McKechnie, ed., pp. 213–230.

Hensler, D. 2003. "Our Courts, Ourselves: How the Alternative Dispute Resolution Movement Is Re-Shaping Our Legal System." *Penn State Law Review* 108: 165–197.

Hermann-Otto, E. 1994. *Ex ancilla natus: Untersuchungen zu den "hausgebornen" Sklaven und Sklavinnen im Westen des römischen Kaiserreiches*. Stuttgart.

Hermann-Otto, E. 2001. "Soziale Mobilität in der römischen Gesellschaft: persönliche Freiheit im Spiegel von Statusprozessen." In *Fünfzig Jahre Forschungen zur antiken Sklaverei an der Mainzer Akademie 1950–2000*, edited by H. Bellen and H. Heinen, pp. 171–184. Stuttgart.

Hermann-Otto, E. 2002. "Frauen im Römischen Recht: mit einem Ausblick auf Gender Studies in der Alten Geschichte und der antiken Rechtsgeschichte." In *Gender Studies in den Altertumswissenschaften: Möglichkeiten und Grenzen*, edited by B. Feichtinger and G. Wöhrle, Vol. 1, pp. 25–40. Trier.

Hermann-Otto, E. 2004. "Sklavenkinder in Recht, Ökonomie und Gesellschaft des Römischen Reiches." *Revue internationale des droits de l'antiquité* 51: 167–168.

Hermann-Otto, E. 2009. *Sklaverei und Freilassung in der griechisch-römischen Welt*. Hildesheim.

Hermann-Otto, E. 2013. "Slaves and Freedmen." In Erdkamp, ed., pp. 60–76.

Herzog, R. 1919. *Aus der Geschichte des Bankwesens im Altertum: Tesserae nummulariae*. Giessen.

Hesberg, H. von. 2005. "Die Häuser der Senatoren in Rom: gesellschaftliche und politische Funktion." In *Senatores populi romani: Realität und mediale Präsentation einer Führungsschicht*, edited by W. Eck and M. Heil, pp. 19–41. Stuttgart.

Hezser, C., ed. 2003. *Rabbinic Law in Roman and Near Eastern Context (Texts and Studies in Ancient Judaism)*. Tübingen.

Hicks, J. 1969. *A Theory of Economic History*. Oxford.

Hill, J. 2001. "Romanisation, Gender and Class: Recent Approaches to Identity in Britain and Their Possible Consequences." In *Dialogues in Roman Imperialism. Power, Discourse, and Discrepant Experience in the Roman Empire.* Journal of Roman Archaeology Supplementary Series 23, edited by D. Mattingly, pp. 81–100. Portsmouth, RI.

Hingley, R. 2000. *Roman Officers and English Gentlemen: The Imperial Origins of Roman Archaeology*. London.

Hingley, R. 2005. *Globalizing Roman Culture: Unity, Diversity and Empire*. London.

Hingley, R. 2010. "Cultural Diversity and Unity: Empire and Rome." In *Material Culture and Social Identities in the Ancient World*, edited by S. Hales and T. Hodos, pp. 54–75. Cambridge.

Hitchner, R. 2005. "'The Advantages of Wealth and Luxury': The Case for Economic Growth in the Roman Empire." In *The Ancient Economy: Evidence and Models*, edited by I. Morris and J. Manning, pp. 207–222. Stanford, CA.

Höbenreich, E., and G. Rizzelli. 2003. *Scylla: Fragmente einer juristischen Geschichte der Frauen im antiken Rom*. Vienna.

Hobson, M. 2015a. "The African Boom." In Erdkamp, Verboven, and Zuiderhoek, eds., pp. 207–233.

Hobson, M. 2015b. *The North African Boom: Evaluating Economic Growth in the Roman Province of Africa Proconsularis (146 B.C.–A.D. 439*. Journal of Roman Archaeology Supplementary Series, 100. Portsmouth, RI.

Hodge, A. [1992] 2002. *Roman Aqueducts and Water Supply*. 2nd ed. London.

Hollander, D. 2007. *Money in the Late Republic*. Leiden.

Holleran, C. 2013. "Women and Retail in Roman Italy." In *Women and the Roman City in the Latin West,* edited by E. Hemelrijk and G. Woolf, pp. 313–330. Leiden.

Holleran, C. 2017. "Getting a Job: Finding Work in the City of Rome." In Verboven and Laes, eds., pp. 87–103.

Holly, M. 2002. "Reciprocity and Reception Theory." In *A Companion to Art Theory*, edited by P. Smith and C. Wilde, pp. 448–457. Oxford.

Holman, S. 2001. *The Hungry Are Dying: Beggars and Bishops in Roman Cappadocia*. Oxford.

Holmes, W., and S. Symenoides. 1999. "Representation, Mandate, and Agency: A Kommentar on Louisiana's New Law." *Tulane Law Review* 73: 1097–1159.

Holub, R. 1984. *Reception Theory: A Critical Introduction*. New York.

Honoré, T. 1992. *Emperors and Lawyers: With a Palingenesia of Third-Century Imperial Rescripts 193–305 AD*. Oxford.

Honoré, T. 2004. "Roman Law 200–400 AD: From Cosmopolis to Rechtstaat?" In *Approaching Late Antiquity: The Transformation from Early to Late Empire*, edited by S. Sain and M. Edwards, pp. 109–132. Oxford.

Hopkins, K. 1978. *Conquerors and Slaves*. Cambridge.

Hopkins, K. 1980. "Taxes and Trade in the Roman Empire (200 B.C.–A.D. 400)." *Journal of Roman Studies* 70: 101–125.

Hopkins, K. 1983. "Introduction." In *Trade in the Ancient Economy*, edited by P. Garnsey, K. Hopkins, and C. Whittaker, pp. ix–xxv. London.

Hopkins, K. 1995–1996. "Rome, Taxes, Rents and Trade." *Kodai* 6–7: 41–75.

Hopkins, K., and P. Roscoe. 1978. "Between Slavery and Freedom: On Freeing Slaves at Delphi." In Hopkins, *Conquerors and Slaves*, pp. 134–171.

Horsley, R. 1998. "The Slave Systems of Classical Antiquity and Their Reluctant Recognition by Modern Scholars." In *Slavery in Text and Interpretation*, edited by A. Callaghan, R. Horsley, and A. Smith, pp. 9–66. Atlanta, GA.

Horsmann, G. 1986. "Die *divi fratres* und die *redemptio servi suis nummis*. Zu den Motiven der epistula ad Urbium Maximum, Dig. 40.1.4." *Historia* 35: 308–321.

Horwitz, M. 1977. *Transformation of American Law, 1780–1860*. Cambridge, MA.

Howgego, C. 1992. "The Supply and Use of Money in the Roman World, 200 B.C. to A.D. 300." *Journal of Roman Studies* 82: 1–31.

Howgego, C. 2009. "Some Numismatic Approaches to Quantifying the Roman Economy." In Bowman and Wilson, eds., pp. 287–295.

Hoyer, D. 2018. *Money, Culture, and Well-Being in Rome's Economic Development, 0–275 CE*. Leiden.

Hübner, S. 2009. "Callirhoe's Dilemma: Remarriage and Stepfathers in the Greco-Roman East." In *Growing Up Fatherless in Antiquity*, edited by S. Hübner and D. Ratzan, pp. 61–82. Cambridge.

Huchthausen, L. 1974. "Herkunft und ökonomische Stellung weiblicher Adressaten von Reskripten des *Codex Iustinianus* (2. und 3. Jh. u.Z.)." *Klio* 56: 199–228.

Huchthausen, L. 1976. "Zu kaiserlichen Reskripten an weibliche Adressaten aus der Zeit Diokletians (284–305 u.Z.)." *Klio* 58: 55–85.

Huchthausen, L. 1992. *Frauen fragen den Kaiser. Eine soziologische Studie über das 3 Jh. n. Chr. Xenia* Vol. 28. Konstanz.

Hulls, J.-M. 2011. "Poetic Monuments: Grief and Consolation in Statius, *Silvae* 3.3." In *Memory and Mourning: Studies on Roman Death*, edited by V. Hope and J. Huskinson, pp. 150–175. Oxford.

Humbert, M. 1964. "La jurisdiction du préfet d'Égypte d'Auguste à Dioclétian." In *Aspects de l'Empire Romain*, edited by F. Burdeau, N. Charbonnel, and M. Humbert, pp. 95–147. Paris.

Humfress, C. 2006. "Poverty and Roman Law." In *Poverty in the Roman World*, edited by M. Atkins and R. Osborne, pp. 183–203. Cambridge.

Humfress, C. 2011. "Law and Custom under Rome." In *Custom in the Middle Ages*, edited by A. Rio, pp. 1–47. London.

Humfress, C. 2013. "Law's Empire: Roman Universalism and Legal Practice." In du Plessis, ed., pp. 73–101.

Humfress, C. 2014. "Thinking through Legal Pluralism: 'Forum Shopping' in the Later Roman Empire." In *Law and Empire: Ideas, Practices, Actors*, edited by J. Duindam et al., eds., pp. 225–250. Leiden.

Humphreys, S. 1985. "Social Relations on Stage: Witnesses in Classical Athens." *History and Anthropology* 1: 313–373.

Humphreys, S. 2007. "Social Relations on Stage: Witnesses in ClassicalAthens." In *Oxford Readings in the Attic Orators*, edited by E. Carawan, pp. 140–213. Oxford.

Hunt, P. 2018. *Ancient Greek and Roman Slavery*. Malden, MA.

Hurst, J. 1956. *Law and the Conditions of Freedom in the Nineteenth Century United States*. Madison, WI.

Huttner, U. 2020. "Latin Law in Greek Cities: Knowledge of Law and Latin in Imperial Asia Minor." In Czajkowski, Eckhardt, and Strothmann, eds., pp. 136–156.

Ibbetson, D. 2015. "Sources of Law from the Republic to the Dominate." In Johnston, ed., pp. 25–44.

Ige, S. 2003. "Rhetoric and the Feminine Character: Cicero's Portrayal of Sassia, Clodia and Fulvia." *Akroterion* 48: 45–57.

Inglebert, H. 2002. "Citoyenneté romaine, romanités et identités romaines sous l'Empire." In *Idéologies et valeurs civiques dans le monde romaine: Hommage à Claude Lepelley*, edited by H. Inglebert, pp. 241–260. Paris.

Ioannatou, M. 2006. *Affairs d'argent dans la correspondance de Cicéron: L'aristocratie sénatoriale face à ses dettes*. Paris.

Isaac, B. 1992. *The Limits of Empire: The Roman Army in the East*, 2nd ed. Oxford.

Iser, W. 1974. *The Implied Reader: Patterns of Communication in Prose Fiction from Bunyan to Beckett*. Baltimore, MD.

Jacota, M. 1966. "Les pactes de l'esclavage en son nom propre." *Revue internationale des droits de l'antiquité* 13: 205–230.

Jakab, E. 2009. *Risikomanagement beim Weinkauf. Periculum und Praxis im Imperium Romanum (Münchener Beiträge zur Papuyrusforschung und Antiken Rechtsgeschichte, 99. Heft)*. Munich.

Jakab, E. 2013. "Financial Transactions by Women in Puteoli." In du Plessis, ed., pp. 123–150.

Jakab, E. 2016. "Inheritance." In du Plessis, Ando, and Tuori, eds., pp. 498–509.

Jauss, H. 1982. *Toward an Aesthetic of Reception*. Minneapolis, MN.

Jerrard, M. 2000. *Organization of the Roman Clothing and Textile Industry: Skill, Occupation, and the Gender-Segmented Workforce*. Caulfield East Vic, Australia.

Jhering, R. von. 1852–1865. *Geist des römischen Rechts, auf den erschiedenen Stufen seiner Entwicklung*. 4 Vols. Leipzig.

Johnson, L. 1979. "Manumission in Colonial Buenos Aires, 1776–1810." *Hispanic American Historical Review* 59.2: 258–279.

Johnston, D. 1995. "Limiting Liability: Roman Law and the Civil Law Tradition." *Chicago-Kent Law Review* 70: 1515–1538.

Johnston, D. 1999. *Roman Law in Context*. Cambridge.

Johnston, D. 2002. "Peculiar Questions." In McKechnie, ed., pp. 1–13.

Johnston, D. 2007. "Suing the Paterfamilias: Theory and Practice." In Cairns and du Plessis, eds., pp. 173–184.

Johnston, D., ed. 2015. *The Cambridge Companion to Roman Law*. Cambridge.

Johnston, S. 1998. "Cracking the Code of Silence: Athenian Legal Oratory and the Histories of Slaves and Women." In Joshel and Murnaghan, eds., pp. 221–235.

Jones, A. 1950. "The Aerarium and the Fiscus." *Journal of Roman Studies* 40: 22–29.

Jones, B. 1992. *The Emperor Domitian*. London.

Jones, C. 2007. "Juristes romains dans l'Orient grec." *Comptes Rendus de l'Académie des Inscriptions et Belles-lettres* 151: 1331–59.

Jones, D. 2006. *The Bankers of Puteoli: Finance, Trade and Industry in the Roman World*. Stroud, UK.

Jones, D. 2014. *Economic Theory and the Ancient Mediterranean*. Oxford.

Jones, W. 1940. *Historical Introduction to the Theory of Law*. Oxford.

Jongman, W. 2002. "The Roman Economy: From Cities to Empire." In de Blois and Rich, eds., pp. 28–47.

Jongman, W. 2007. "Gibbon Was Right: The Decline and Fall of the Roman Economy." In *Crises and the Roman Empire*, edited by O. Hekster, G. de Kleijn, and D. Slootjes, pp. 183–199. Leiden.

Jongman, W. 2008. "Poverty in the Roman World." *EH.NET* (July 2008).

Jongman, W. 2009. "Archaeology, Demography, and Growth." In Bowman and Wilson, eds., pp. 115–126.

Jördens, A. 2012(a). "Government, Taxation, and Law." In Riggs, ed., pp. 56–67.

Jördens, A. 2012(b). "Status and Citizenship." In Riggs, ed., pp. 247–260.

Jördens, A. 2020. "Aequum et iustum: On Dealing with the Law in the Province of Egypt." In Czajkowski, Eckhardt, and Strothmann, eds., pp. 18–30.

Joshel, S. 1992. *Work, Identity, and Legal Status at Rome: A Study of the Occupational Inscriptions*. Norman, OK.

Joshel, S. 2010. *Slavery in the Roman World*. Cambridge.

Joshel, S. 2011. "Slavery in Roman Literary Culture." In Bradley and Cartledge, eds., pp. 214–240.

Joshel, S. and S. Murnaghan, eds. 1998. *Women and Slaves in Greco-Roman Culture*. London.

Joshel, S., and C. Peterson. 2014. *The Material Life of Roman Slaves*. Cambridge.

Juglar, L. 1894. *Du rôle des esclaves et des affranchis dans le commerce*. Paris.

Just, R. 1985. "Freedom, Slavery and the Female Psyche." In *Crux: Essays in Greek History presented to G.E.M. de Ste. Croix*, edited by P. Cartledge and F. Harvey, pp. 169–188. London.

Kaiser, W. 2015. "Justinian and the *Corpus Iuris Civilis*." In Johnston, ed., pp. 119–148.

Kampen, N. 1981. *Image and Status: Roman Working Women in Ostia*. Berlin.

Kantor, G. 2009. "Knowledge of Law in Roman Asia Minor." In *Kommunikation und Selbstdarstellung: Die Veröffentlichung staatlicher Urkunden auf Stein und Bronze in der römischen Welt*, edited by R. Haensch, pp. 249–265. Munich.

Kantor, G. 2013. "Law in Roman Phrygia: Rules and Jurisdictions." In *Roman Phrygia: Culture and Society*, edited by P. Thonemann, pp. 143–167. Cambridge.

Kantor, G. 2015. "Greek Law under the Romans." In *Oxford Handbook ofAncient Greek Law*, edited by E. Harris and M. Canevaro. Published online August 2015 in Oxford Handbooks Online (www.oxfordhandbooks.com).

Kantor, G. 2016. "Local Law in Asia Minor after the Constitutio Antoniniana." In Ando, ed., pp. 45–62.

Kantor, G. 2020. "Navigating Roman Law and Local Privileges in Pontus-Bithynia." In Czajkowski, Eckhardt, and Strothmann, eds., pp. 184–209.

Karabélias, E. 1997. "L'arbitrage privé dans Athènes classique." In *Symposion 1995 (Akten der Gesellschaft für Griechische und Hellenistische Rechtsgeschichte)*, edited by G. Thür and J. Vélissaropoulos-Kakakostas, pp. 135–149. Cologne.

Kaser, M. 1938. "Die Geschichte der Patronatsgewalt über Freigelassene."*Zeitschrift der Savigny-Stiftung für Rechtsgeschichte* (Romanist. Abt.) 58: 88–135.

Kaser, M. 1962. "Typisierter *Dolus* im altrömischer Recht." *Bullettino dell'Istituto di Diritto Romano* 4 (N.S.): 79–104.

Kaser, M. 1970. "Zum Wesen der römischen Stellvertretung." *Romanitas* 9: 333–355.

Kaser, M. 1971, 1975. *Das römische Privatrecht*. Vols I, II, 2nd ed. Munich.

Kaser, M. 1974. "Stellvertretung und 'notwendige Entgeltlichkeit." *Zeitschriftder Savigny-Stiftung für Rechtsgeschichte* (Romanist. Abt.) 94: 146–204.

Kaser, M. 1986. "Nochmals zu 'in bonis habere.'" In *Römische Rechtsquellen und angewandte Juristenmethode*, pp. 363–368. Vienna.

Kaser, M., and K. Hackl. 1996. *Das römische Zivilprozeßrercht*, 2nd ed. Munich.

Kaser, M., and R. Knütel. 2014. *Römisches Privatrecht*. Munich.

Kay, P. 2014. *Rome's Economic Revolution*. Oxford.

Kay, P. 2018. "Financial Institutions and Structures in the Last Century of the Roman Republic." In Bowman and Wilson, eds., pp. 133–174.

Kehoe, D. 1997. *Investment, Profit, and Tenancy: The Jurists and the Roman Agrarian Economy*. Ann Arbor, MI.

Kehoe, D. 2006a. "Review of *Mentalités et choix économiques des romains*, edited by J. Andreau, J. France, and S. Pittia, Bordeaux 2004." *Classical Review* 56.1: 181–183.

Kehoe, D. 2006b. "Landlords and Tenants." In Potter, ed., pp. 298–311.

Kehoe, D. 2011. "Law and Social Formation in the Roman Empire." In Peachin, ed., pp. 144–163.

Kehoe, D. 2012a. "Roman Economic Policy and the Law of Contracts." In *Obligations in Roman Law: Past, Present, and Future*, edited by T. McGinn, pp. 189–214. Ann Arbor, MI.

Kehoe, D. 2012b. "Contract Labor." In Scheidel, ed., pp. 114–130.

Kehoe, D. 2015a. "Property Rights over Land and Economic Growth in the Roman Empire." In Erdkamp, Verboven, and Zuiderhoek, eds., pp. 88–106.

Kehoe, D. 2015b. "Contracts, Agency, and Transaction Costs in the Roman Economy." In Kehoe, Ratzan, and Yiftach, eds., pp. 231–252.

Kehoe, D. 2017. "Agency, Roman Law, and Roman Social Values." In Kehoe and McGinn, eds., pp. 105–132.

Kehoe, D. 2020. "Mandate and the Management of Business in the Roman Empire." In Dari-Mattiacci and Kehoe, eds., Vol. 1, pp. 307–337.

Kehoe, D., and T. McGinn, eds. 2017. *Ancient Law, Ancient Society*. Ann Arbor, MI.

Kehoe, D., D. Ratzan, and U. Yiftach. 2015. "Introduction: Transaction, Costs, Ancient History, and the Law." In Kehoe, Ratzan, and Yiftach, eds., pp. 1–35.

Kehoe, D., D. Ratzan, and U. Yiftach, eds. 2015. *Law and Transaction Costs in the Ancient Economy*. Ann Arbor, MI.

Kelly, C. 2004. *Ruling the Later Roman Empire*. Cambridge, MA.

Kelly, J. 1966. *Roman Litigation*. Oxford.

Kemp, W. 1998. "The Work of Art and Its Beholder: The Methodology of the Aesthetic of Reception." In *The Subject of Art History: Historical Objects in Contemporary Perspectives*, edited by M. Cheetham, M. Holly, and K. Moxey, pp. 180–196. Cambridge.

Kerremans, B. 2016. "Metus Gallicus, Tumultus Cimbricus? The Possible Promulgation of a Tumulus in the Cimbrian War (105–101 BCE)." *Mnemosyne* 69.4: 822–841.

Kessler, D., and P. Temin. 2008. "Money and Prices in the Early Roman Empire." In W. Harris, ed., pp. 137–159.

Keuls, E. 1985. *The Reign of the Phallus: Sexual Politics in Ancient Athens*. New York.

Kirschenbaum, A. 1987. *Sons, Slaves and Freedmen in Roman Commerce*. Jerusalem.

Kiser, E., and D. Kane. 2007. "The Perils of Privatization." *Social Science History* 31: 191–212.

Klees, H. 1998. *Sklavenleben im klassischen Griechenland* (= Vol. 30 of *Forschungen zur antiken Sklaverei*, edited by H. Bellen). Stuttgart.

Klees, H. 2002. "Die römische Einbürgerung der Freigelassenen und ihre naturrechtliche Begründung bei Dionysios von Halikarnassos." *Laverna* 13: 91–117.

Kleijwegt, M. 2002. "Cum vicensimariis magnam mantissam habet (Petronius *Satyricon* 65.10)." *American Journal of Philology* 123: 275–286.

Kleijwegt, M. 2011. "Deciphering Freedwomen in the Roman Empire." In Bell and Ramsby, eds., pp. 110–129.

Klingenberg, G. 1983. "Die Frau im römischen Abgaben- und Fiskalrecht." *Revue internationale des droits de l'antiquité*, 3rd ser., 30: 141–150.

Klodzinski, K. 2017. "The Office of *a rationibus* in the Roman Administration during the Early Empire." *Eos* 104: 159–167.

Knapp, R. 2011. *Invisible Romans*. Cambridge, MA.

Knapp, R. 2016. "Legally Marginalised Groups: The Empire." In du Plessis, Ando, and Tuori, eds., pp. 362–373.

Knoch, S. 2005. *Sklavenfürsorge im Römischen Reich, Formen und Motive*. Hildesheim.

Knütel, R. 1993. "Das Mandat zum Freikauf." In *Mandatum und Verwantes: Beiträge zum römischen und modernen* Recht, edited by D. Nörr and S. Nishimura, pp. 353–374. Berlin.

Kokkinos, N. 2002. *Antonia Augusta: Portrait of a Great Roman Lady*. London.

Kolendo, J. 1978. "Les esclaves dans l'art antique: la stèle funéraire d'un marchand d'esclaves thrace découverte à Amphipolis." *Archeologia* 29: 24–34.

Kolendo, J. 1979. "Intellectuels et couches serviles: le cas des grammairiens chez Suétone." *Index* 8: 214–226.

Kolendo, J. 1981. "L'esclavage et la vie sexuelle des hommes libres à Rome." *Index* 10: 288–297.

Könczöl, M. 2017. "The Relevance of Roman Law: A Look at Its Roles and Ideologies." *Revista Crítica de Ciências Sociais* 112: 99–114.

Koops, E. 2020. "The Practice of Manumission through Negotiated Conditions in Imperial Rome." In Dari-Mattiacci and Kehoe, eds., Vol. 2, pp. 35–77.

Kopytoff, I., and S. Miers. 1977. "African 'Slavery' as an Institution of Marginality." In *Slavery in Africa: Historical and Anthropological Perspectives*, edited by S. Miers and I. Kopytoff, pp. 3–81. Madison, WI.

Kornemann, E. 1900. "*Colonia*." In Pauly-Wissowa, eds., 4: 511–588. Stuttgart.

Korporowicz, L. 2011. "Buying a Slave in Roman Britain: The Evidence from the Tabulae." *Revue internationale des droits de l'antiquité* 58: 211–224.

Kremer, D. 2006. *Ius latinum: Le concept de droit latin sous la république et l'empire*. Paris.

Kron, G. 2014. "Comparative Evidence and the Reconstruction of the Ancient Economy: Greco-Roman Housing and the Level and Distribution of Wealth and Income." In De Callataÿ, ed., pp. 123–146.

Kron, G. (forthcoming) "Growth and Decline: Forms of Growth. Estimating Growth in the Roman and Byzantine Empires." In Lo Cascio, Bresson, and Velde, eds., pp. XX–XX.

Krugman, P. 2014. "Why We're in a New Gilded Age." *New York Review of Books* 61.8.

Kuhrt, A. 1998. "The Old Assyrian Merchants." In Parkins and Smith, eds., pp. 16–30.

Kunkel, W. 1930. "*Mater familias*." In Pauly-Wissowa, eds., 14: 2183–2184.

Kunkel, W. 1967. *Herkunft und soziale Stellung der römischen Juristen*. Weimar.

Kunkel, W. 1973. *An Introduction to Roman Legal and Constitutional History*, 2nd ed. Oxford.

Labruna, L. 1994. "Il diritto mercantile dei romani e l'espansionismo." In *Le Strade del Potere: Maiestas populi romani, Imperium, Coercitio, Commercium*, edited by A. Corbino, pp. 115–137. Catania.

Laes, C. 2008. "Child Slaves at Work in Roman Antiquity." *Ancient Society* 38: 235–283.

Laffi, U. 1975. *Storia di Ascoli Piceno nell'età antica*. Ascoli Piceno.

Lamberti, F. 2011. "La condizione giuridica della donna romana: ancora una riflessione." *Teoreia e Storia del Diritto* Privato 4: 23–35. http://www.teoriaestoriadeldirittoprivato.com/index.php?com=statics&option=index&cID=248.

Lamberti, F. 2012. "'Mulieres' e vicende processuali fra repubblica e principato: Ruoli attivi e 'presenze silenziose.'" *Index* 40: 244–256.

Lamberti, F. 2014. "Donne romane fra Idealtypus e realtà sociale: Dal 'domum servare' e 'lanam facere' al 'meretricio more vivere.'" *Quaderni Lupiensi di Storia e Diritto* 4: 61–84.

Lamberti, F. 2018. "Ius Latii e leges municipii di epoca Flavia." *Gerión* 36.2: 463–479.

Lanni, A. 2004. "Arguing from 'Precedent': Modern Perspectives on Athenian Practice." In *The Law and the Courts in Ancient Greece,* edited by E. Harris and L. Rubinstein, pp. 159–171. London.

Lanni, A. 2016. *Law and Order in Ancient Athens*. Cambridge.

Lanni, A., and R. Wallace. 2018. "Introduction." In Perlman, ed., pp. 1–9.

Latham, R. 1965. *Revised Medieval Latin Word-List from British and Irish Sources*. London.

Launaro, A. 2011. *Peasants and Slaves: The Rural Population of Roman Italy (200 BC to AD 100)*. Cambridge.

Lavan, M. 2013. *Slaves to Rome: Paradigms of Empire in Roman Culture*. Cambridge.

Lavan, M. 2019. "The Foundation of Empire? The Spread of Roman Citizenship from the Fourth Century BCE to the Third Century CE." In *The Crucible of Empire: The Impact of Roman Citizenship upon Greeks, Jews and Christians*, edited by K. Berthelot and J. Price, pp. 21–54. Leuven.

Lavan, M. 2020. "Beyond Romans and Others: Identities in the Long Second Century." In *Literature and Culture in the Roman Empire, 96–235: Cross-Cultural Interactions*, edited by A. König, R. Langlands, and J. Uden, pp. 37–57. Cambridge.

Lázaros Guillamón, C. 2010. "El depósito irregular como herramienta para la prática cotidiana de negocios crediticios entre mujeres en la antigüeda romana. In *Experiencias jurídicas e identidades femeninas*, edited by R. Rodríguez López and M. Bravo Bosch, pp. 259–267. Madrid.

Lefèvre, E. 2014. "Plautus und die Techniken des Improvisationstheaters." In *Ancient Comedy and Reception: Essays in Honor of Jeffrey Henderson*, edited by S. Olson, pp. 223–234. Berlin.

Lefèvre, E., E. Stärk, and G. Vogt-Spira, eds. 1991. *Plautus barbarus: Sechs Kapitel zur Originalität des Plautus*. Tübingen.

Lefkowitz, J. 2016. "Grand Allusions: Vergil In Phaedrus." *American Journal of Philology* 137: 487–509.

Le Glay, M. 1990. "La place des affranchis dans la vie municipale et dans la vie religieuse." *Mélanges de l'École française de Rome–Antiquité* 102.2: 621–638.

Legrand, P. 2001. *Fragments on Law-as-Culture*. Deventer.

Lemercier, C. 2015. "Une histoire sans sciences sociales?" *Annales: Histoire, Sciences Sociales* 70.2: 271–283.

Lemosse, M. 1998. "Le procès provincial classique." In *Mélanges de droit romain et d'histoire ancienne: Hommage à la mémoire de André Magdelain,* edited by M. Humbert and Y. Thomas, pp. 239–246. Paris.

Lenski, N. 2005. "Review of Weiss 2004." *Bryn Mawr Classical Review* 2005.07.24.

Lenski, N. 2006. "Servi Publici in Late Antiquity." In *Die Stadt in der Spätantike—Niedergang oder Wandel?*, edited by J.-U. Krause and C. Witschel, pp. 335–357. Stuttgart.

Lenski, N. 2018. "Framing the Question: 'What Is a Slave Society?'" In Lenski and Cameron, eds., pp. 15–57.

Lenski, N. and C. Cameron, eds. 2018. *What Is a Slave Society?* Cambridge.

Lerouxel, F. 2006. "Les femmes sur le marché du credit en Egypte romaine (30 avant J.-C.–284 après J.-C.): Une approche néo-institutionnaliste." *Les Cahiers du Centre de Recherches Historiques*: 121–136.

Levine, R. 1997. "Financial Development and Economic Growth: Views and Agenda." *Journal of Economic Literature* 35 (June): 688–726.

Lewis, A. 2015. "Slavery, Family, and Status." In Johnston, ed., pp. 151–174.

Lewis, B. 1995. *The Middle East: A Brief History of the Last 2,000 Years*. New York.

Lewis, N. 1981. "The Prefect's *Conventus*: Proceedings and Procedures." *Bulletin of the American Society of Papyrologists* 18: 119–129.

Lewis, S. 2002. *The Athenian Woman: An Iconographic Handbook*. London.

Libby, B. 2010. "The Intersection of Poetic and Imperial Authority in Phaedrus' Fables." *Classical Quarterly* 60: 545–558.

Liebs, D. 1989. "Sogennante Fragmenta de iure fisci." In *Handbuch der lateinischen Literatur der Antike*, edited by R. Herzog, VIII.5: 69. Munich.

Liebs, D. 2000. "Das testament des Antonius Silvanus, römischer Kavallerist imAlexandria bei Ägypten, aus dem Jahr 142 n. Chr." In *Festschrift für Weddig Fricke zum 70. Geburtstag*, edited by K. Märker, pp. 113–128. Freiburg.

Liebs, D. 2002. "Rechtskunde im römischen Kaiserreich. Rom und die Provinzen." In *Iurisprudentia universalis: Festschrift für Theo Mayer-Maly zum 70. Geburtstag*, edited by M. Schermaier, J. Rainer, and O. Winkel, pp. 383–407. Cologne.

Liebs, D. 2007. *Vor den Richtern Roms: Berühmte Prozesse der Antike*. Munich.

Liebs, D. 2009. "Zur Geschichte der Volksrechte im römischen Reich." In *Studi in onore di Remo Martini*, Vol. 2, pp. 449–472. Milan.

Liebs, D. 2015. "Review of Heinemeyer 2013." *Klio* 97.2: 788–792.

Ligios, M. 2015. "Le banche fallivano anche a Roma: Il *crack* di Callisto all'epoca di Commodo." *Il nuovo diritto delle società* 13.1: 11–52.

Ligt, L. de. 1999. "Legal History and Economic History: The Case of the "*Actiones Adiecticiae Qualitatis*." *Tijdschrift voor Rechtsgeschiedenis* 67: 205–226.

Ligt, L. de. 2002a. "D. 15.1.1.1 and the Early History of the Actio Quod Iussu." In *Viva Vox Iuris Romani: Essays in Honour of J. E. Spruit*, edited by L. de Ligt, pp. 197–204. Amsterdam.

Ligt, L. de. 2002b. "Restraining the Rich, Protecting the Poor: Symbolic Aspects of Roman Legislation." In *After the Past: Essays in Ancient History in Honour of H. W. Pleket*, edited by W. Jongman and M. Kleijwegt, pp. 1–47. Leiden.

Ligt, L. de. 2002c. "Tax Transfers in the Roman Empire." In de Blois and Rich, eds., pp. 48–66. Amsterdam.

Ligt, L. de. 2007. "Roman Law and the Roman Economy: Three Case Studies." *Latomus* 66: 10–25.

Ligt, L. de. 2020, "Law-Making and Economic Change during the Republic and Early Empire." In Dari-Mattiacci and Kehoe, eds., Vol. 1, pp. 85–108.

Lindert, P., and J. Williamson. 2016. *Unequal Gains: American Growth and Inequality since 1700*. Princeton, NJ.

Lintott, A. 1993. *Imperium Romanum: Politics and Administration*. New York.

Litwack, L. 1961. *North of Slavery: The Negro in the Free States.* Chicago.

Lo Cascio, E. 2000. *Il princeps e il suo impero: Studi di storia amministrativa e finanziaria romana*. Bari.

Lo Cascio, E. 2003a. "Introduzione." In *Credito e moneta nel mondo romano*, edited by E. Lo Cascio, pp. 5–15. Bari.

Lo Cascio, E. 2003b. "Il *denarius* e gli scambi intermediterranei." In *Moneta mercanti banchieri*, edited by G. Urso, pp. 147–165. Pisa.

Lo Cascio, E. 2007. "The Early Roman Empire: The State and the Economy." In Scheidel, Morris, and Saller, eds., pp. 619–647.

Lo Cascio, E. 2008. In W. Harris, ed., pp. 160–173.

Lo Cascio,, E. 2009. "Urbanization as a Proxy of Demographic and Economic Growth." In Bowman and Wilson, eds., pp. 87–106.

Lo Cascio, E. 2020. "Setting the Rules of the Game: The Market and Its Working in the Roman Empire." In Dari-Mattiacci and Kehoe, eds., Vol. 1, pp. 111–136.

Lo Cascio, E., A. Bresson, and F. Velde, eds. (forthcoming). *The Oxford Handbook of Economies in the Classical World*. Oxford.

Lokin, J. 1995. "The End of an Epoch." In *Collatio Iuris Romani: Études dédiées à Hans Ankum à l'occasion de son 65e anniversaire*, edited by R. Feenstra, A. Hartkamp, and J. Spruit, I: 261–273. Amsterdam.

Loraux, N. [1984] 1993. *The Children of Athena: Athenian Ideas about Citizenship and the Division between the* Sexes. Translated by C. Levine. Princeton, NJ (originally published as *Les enfants d'Athéna: Idées athéniennes sur la citoyenneté et la division des sexes*, Paris).

Los, A. 1995. "La condition sociale des affranchis privés au 1er siècle aprés J.-C." *Annales: Histoire, Sciences Sociales* 50: 1011–1043.

Lovejoy, P. 2000. *Transformations in Slavery: A History of Slavery in Africa*. 2nd ed. Cambridge.

Lubet, S. 2010. *Fugitive Justice: Runaways, Rescuers, and Slavery on Trial.* Cambridge.

Lübtow, U. von. 1952. *Beiträge zur Lehre von der Condictio nach römischen und geltendem Recht*. Berlin.

Luciani, F. 2017. "Cittadini come *domini,* cittadini come *patroni*. Rapporti tra *serui publici* e città prima e dopo la manomissione." In *Esclaves et maîtres dans le monde romain: Expressions épigraphiques de leurs relations*, edited by M. Dondin-Payre and N. Tran, pp. 45–64. Rome.

Luna, F., and H. Klein. 2003. *Slavery and the Economy of São Paulo*. Stanford, CA.

MacCormack, G. [1985] 1999. "Translation of Book Two." In Watson, ed., pp. 40–78.

MacGaw, C. 2014. "Esclavage et système économique à Rome." In *Les affaires de Monsieur Andreau: Économie et société du monde romain*, edited by C. Apicella, M.-L. Haack, and F. Lerouxel, pp. 77–87. Bordeaux.

MacLean, R. 2018. *Freed Slaves and Roman Imperial Culture: Social Integration and the Transformation of Values*. Cambridge.

MacMullen, R. [1984] 1990. "The Legion as a Society." *Historia* 33: 440–456 (reprinted in R. MacMullen, *Changes in the Roman Empire: Essays in the Ordinary*, pp. 225–235, Princeton, 1990).

MacMullen, R. 1987. *Roman Social Relations 50 B.C. to A.D. 284*. New Haven, CT.

Madden, J. 1996. "Slavery in the Roman Empire: Numbers and Origins." *Classics Ireland* 3: 109–128.

Maddison, A. 2007. *Contours of the World Economy 1–2030 AD: Essays in Macroeconomic History*. Oxford.

Maehler, H. 2005. "Greek, Egyptian and Roman Law." *Journal of Juristic Papyrology* 35: 121–140.

Maffi, A. 2008. "Economia e diritto nell'Atene del IV secolo." In *Symposion 2007 (Akten der Gesellschaft für Griechische und Hellenistische Rechtsgeschichte)*, edited by E. Harris and G. Thür, pp. 203–222. Vienna.

Maffi, A. 2018. "Toward a New Shape of the Relationship between Public and Private Law in Ancient Greece." In Perlman, ed., pp. 70–84.

Magalhães, M. 2009. "Review of Reduzzi Merola 1990." *Phoînix* 15.2: 131–132.

Maiuro, M. 2012. *Res Caesaris: ricerche sulla proprietà imperiale nel principato*. Bari.

Malinowski, M., and J. Van Zanden. 2017. "Income and Its Distribution in Preindustrial Poland." *Cliometrica* 11: 375–404.

Malmendier, U. 2002. *Societas Publicanorum: Staatliche Wirtschaftsaktivitäten in den Händen privater Unternehmer*. Cologne.

Malmendier, U. 2005. "Roman Shares." In *The Origins of Value: The Financial Innovations That Created Modern Capital Markets*, edited by W. Goetzmann and K. Rouwenhorst, pp. 31–42, 361–365. Oxford.

Malmendier, U. 2009. "Law and Finance 'at the Origin.'" *Journal of Economic Literature* 478: 1076–1108.

Malmendier, U. 2013. "Publicani." In *The Encyclopedia of Ancient History*, edited by R. Bagnall et al. Chichester.

Mandry, G. 1876. *Das Gemeine Familiengüterrecht*. Vol. II. Tubingen.

Mantzilas, D. 2016. "Female Domestic Financial Managers: Turia, Murdia, and Hortensia." In Berg, ed., pp. 169–174. Rome.

Maragno, G. 2017. "I numeri nelle fonti giurisprudenziali: Prospettive di analisi." In *Diritto romano e economia: Due modi di pensare e organizzare il mondo (nei primi tre secoli dell'Impero)*, edited by D. Mantovani, pp. 613–644. Pavia.

Marcone, A. 2016. "La storia degli studi." In Marcone, ed., pp. 17–34.

Marcone, A., ed. 2016. *Storia del laboro in Italia: L'età romana. Liberi, semiliberi e schiavi in una società moderna*. Rome.

Marotta, V. 2016. "Doppia cittadinanza e pluralità degli ordinamenti. La tabula banasitana e le linee 7–9 del papiro di Giessen 40 col. I." *Archivio Giuridico* 236 (fasc. 3–4): 461–491.

Marquardt, J. 1886. *Das Privatleben der Römer*, 2nd ed. Leipzig.

Marshall, C. 2006. *The Stagecraft and Performance of Roman Comedy*. Cambridge.

Martini, R. 1980. "Autonomia negoziale dei servi e 'obligationes naturales.'" *Labeo* 26: 104–109.

Masci, A. 2001. "Iscrizione." In *La collezione epigrafica dell' Antiquarium comunale del Celio. Inventario generale, inediti, revisioni, contributi al riordino*, edited by G. Gregori, pp. 801–1000. Rome.

Masi Doria, C. 2011. "Schutzrechte, Humanität, Grundrechte." *Index* 39: 373–385.

Mason, H. 1974. *Greek Terms for Roman Institutions: A Lexicon and Analysis* (American Studies in Papyrology XIII). Toronto.

Matthews, J. 2006. "Roman Law and Roman History." In Potter, ed., pp. 477–491.

Mattingly, D. 2002. "Vulgar or Weak 'Romanization,' or Time for a Paradigm Shift?" *Journal of Roman Archaeology* 15: 536–540.

Mattingly, D. 2006. *An Imperial Possession: Britain in the Roman Empire 54 BC–AD 409*. London.

Mattingly, D. 2011. *Imperialism, Power, and Identity: Experiencing the Roman Empire*. Princeton, NJ.

Maucourant, J. 2004. "Rationalité économique ou comportements socio-économique?" In *Mentalités et choix économiques des romains*, edited by J. Andreau, J. France, and S. Pittia, pp. 227–240. Bordeaux.

Mayhew, L. 1968. "Society." In *International Encyclopedia of the Social Sciences*, Vol. 14, edited by D. Sills, pp. 577–586. New York.

Mayer, E. 2012. *The Ancient Middle Classes: Urban Life and Aesthetics in the Roman Empire, 100 BCE–250 CE*. Cambridge, MA.

McCarthy K. 2000. *Slaves, Masters, and the Art of Authority in Plautine Comedy*. Princeton, NJ.

McDonnell, M. 2006. *Roman Manliness: "Virtus" and the Roman Republic*. Cambridge.

McGinn, T. 1998. *Prostitution, Sexuality and the Law in Ancient Rome*. Oxford.

McGinn, T. 2004. *The Economy of Prostitution in the Roman World: A Study of Social History and the Brothel*. Ann Arbor, MI.

McGinn, T. 2011. "Roman Prostitutes and Marginalization." In Peachin, ed., pp. 643–659.

McGinn, T. 2017. "*Cui Bono?* The True Beneficiaries of Roman Private Law." In D. Kehoe and T. McGinn, eds., pp. 133–166. Ann Arbor, MI.

McKechnie, P., ed. 2002. *Thinking like a Lawyer: Essays on Legal History and General History for John Crook on his Eightieth Birthday*. Leiden.

McKeown, N. 2007. *The Invention of Ancient Slavery?* London.

Meiggs, R. 1973. *Roman Ostia*, 2nd ed. Oxford.

Mélèze (Modrzejewski), J. 1966. "Chronique papyrologique." *Revue historique de droit français et étranger* (4. sér.) 44: 524–541.

Mélèze (Modrzejewski), J. 1970. "La règle de droit dans l'Égypte romaine (état des questions et perspectives de recherches)." In *Proceedings of the Twelfth International Congress of Papyrology*, edited by D.Samuel, pp. 317–377. Toronto.

Mélèze (Modrzejewski), J. 1976. "Aut nascuntur, aut fiunt . . . sources del'esclavage dans la theorie grecque et dans le droit romain." *Annales litteraires de l'universite de Besancon* 18: 351–377.

Mélèze (Modrzejewski), J. 1993. "Diritto romano e diritti locali." In *Storia di Roma*, edited by A. Schiavone, III/2: 985–1009. Turin.

Mélèze (Modrzejewski), J. 2005. "What Is Hellenistic Law? The Documents of the Judaean Desert in the Light of the Papyri from Egypt." In *Law in the Documents of the Judaean Desert*, edited by R. Katzoff and D. Schaps, pp. 7–21. Leiden.

Mélèze (Modrzejewski), J. 2006. "Greek Law in the Hellenistic Period: Family and Marriage." In *The Cambridge Companion to Ancient Greek Law*, edited by M. Gagarin and D. Cohen, pp. 343–354. Cambridge.

Mélèze (Modrzejewski), J. 2014. *Loi et coutume dans l'Égypte grecque et romaine: Les facteurs de formation du droit en Égypte d'Alexandre le Grand à la conquête arabe.* Journal of Juristic Papyrology Suppl. 21. Warsaw.

Melillo, G. 1981. "Review of Morabito 1981." *Index* 10: 340 ff.

Melluso, M. 2000. *La schiavitù nell'età giustinianea: Disciplina giuridica e rilevanze sociale.* Besançon.

Ménard, C., and M. Shirley, eds. 2005. *Handbook of New Institutional Economics.* Dordrecht.

Mentxaka, R. 1986. *La Pignoración de Colectividades en el Derecho Romano Clásico.* Bilbao.

Mentzou-Meimare, K. 1982. "Η παρουσία της γυναίκας στις ελληνικές επιγραφές από τον Δ' μέχρι τον Ι' μ.Χ. αιώνα." *XVI Internationaler Byzantinistenkongress. Akten, Jahrbuch der Österreichischen Byzantinistik* 322/2, edited by W. Hörandner, pp. 433–444. Vienna.

Mercogliano, F. 2001a. *Actiones ficticiae: Tipologie e datazione.* Naples.

Mercogliano, F. 2001(b). "Deterior est condicio feminarum . . . ." *Index* 29: 209–220.

Mercogliano, F. 2011. "La condizione giuridica della donna romana: Ancora una riflessione." *Teoria e storia del diritto privato* 4: 10 (http://www.teoriaestoriadeldirittoprivato.com/index.php?com=statics&option=index&cID=248#_ftmref32).

Merola, G. 2016. "Le attività commerciali." In A. Marcone, ed., pp. 304–340.

Merola, G. 2020. "Perspectives." In Czajkowski, Eckhardt, and Strothmann, eds., pp. 485–494.

Messeri, G. 2001. "Official and Private Archives in the Papyri." In *First International Symposium of Archivists*, edited by M. Basil, pp. 61–69. Athens.

Metcalf, W. 2016. "Review of Butcher and Ponting 2015." *Journal of Roman Archaeology* 29: 742–746.

Metzger, E. 2014. "Cum servo agere." In *Inter cives necnon peregrinos: Essays in Honour of B. Sirks*, edited by J. Hallebeek et al., pp. 533–543. Göttingen.

Metzger, E. 2016. "Agree to Disagree: Local Jurisdiction in the Lex Irnitana." *Judge and Jurist: Essays in Memory of Lord Rodger of Earlsferry*, edited by A. Burrows, D. Johnston, and R. Zimmermann, pp. 207–225. Oxford.

Meyer, E. 1895. "Die wirtschaftliche Entwicklung des Altertums." *Jahrbücher für Nationalökonomie und Statistik* 9.64: 1–70.

Meyer, E. 2004. *Legitimacy and Law in the Roman World: Tabulae in Roman Belief and Practice*. Cambridge.

Meyer, E. 2007. "Diplomatics, Law and Romanisation in the Documents from the Judaean Desert." In Cairns and du Plessis, eds., pp. 53–82.

Meyer, E. 2012–2013. "New Histories of Slaves and Freed." *Classical Journal* 108: 239–249.

Meyer-Zwiffelhoffer, E. 2002. *Politikos Archein: Zum Regierungsstil der senatorischen Statthalter in den kaiserzeitlichen griechischen Provinzen*. Stuttgart.

Miceli, M. 2008. *Studi sulla rappresentanza in diritto romano*. Milan.

Miceli, T. 2020. "Collective Responsibility." In Dari-Mattiacci and Kehoe, eds., Vol. 2, pp. 379–400.

Michel, J.-H. [1962] 1996. *La Gratuité en droit romain*. Brussels.

Micolier, G. 1932. *Pécule et Capacité patrimoniale: Étude sur le pécule dit profectice, depuis l'édit « de peculio » jusqu'à la fin del'époque classique*. Dissertation, Lyon.

Migeotte, L. 2008. "La comptabilité publique dans les cités grecques: L'exemple de Délos." In Verboven, Chankowski, and Vandorpe, eds., pp. 59–76.

Milailescu-Birliba, L. 2006. *Les affranchis dans les provinces romaines del'Illyricum*. Wiesbaden.

Milanovic, B., P. Lindert, and J. Williamson. 2007. *Measuring Ancient Inequality*. National Bureau of Economic Research Working Paper 13550 (October 2007). Cambridge, MA.

Millar, F. 1963. "The Fiscus in the First Two Centuries." *Journal of Roman Studies* 53.1–2: 29–42.

Millar, F. 1992. *The Emperor in the Roman World*, 2nd ed. London.

Millar, F. 2002. *Rome, the Greek World, and the East. I. The Roman Republic and the Augustan Revolution*, eds. H. Cotton and G. Rogers. Chapel Hill, NC.

Millett, P., and S. Todd. 1990. "Law, Society and Athens." In *Nomos: Essays in Athenian Law, Politics and Society*, edited by P. Cartledge, P. Millett, and S. Todd, pp. 1–18. Cambridge.

Milnor, K. 2011. "Women in Roman Society." In Peachin, ed., pp. 609–622.

Minaud, G. 2005. *La comptabilité à Rome: Essai d'histoire économique sur la pensée comptable commerciale et privée dans le monde antique*. Lausanne.

Mirhady, D. 2004. "Contracts in Athens." In *Law, Rhetoric, and Comedy in Classical Athens: Essays in Honour of Douglas M. MacDowell*, edited by D. Cairns and R. Knox, pp. 51–63. Swansea.

Mitteis, L. 1908. *Römisches Privatrecht bis auf die Zeit Diokletians*, Vol. 1. Leipzig.
Modrzejewski, J. 1974. "A propos de la tutelle dative des femmes dans l'Egypte romain." In *Akten des XIII. Internationalen Papyrologenkongresses*, edited by E. Kiessling and H. Rupprecht, pp. 263–292. Munich.
Mommsen, T. 1878. "Libertini Servi." *Ephemeris Epigraphica* IV: 246–247 (reprinted in *Gesammelte Schriften: Juristische Schriften*, Vol. 3, pp. 21–22, Berlin, 1907).
Montevecchi, O. 1988. "L'amministrazione dell'Egitto sotto i Giulio-Claudi." In *Aufstieg und Niedergang der Römischen Welt* II 10.1, edited by W. Haase and H. Temporini, pp. 412–471. Berlin.
Morabito, M. 1981. *Les réalités de l'esclavage d'après le "Digeste."* Paris.
Morabito, M. 1985. "Les esclaves privilégiés à travers le Digeste, témoins et acteurs d'une société en crise." *Index* 13: 477–490, 638–644.
Morabito, M. 1986. "Droit romain et réalités sociales de la sexualité servile." *Dialogues d'histoire ancienne* 12: 371–387.
Mordine, M. 2013. "*Domus Neroniana*: The Imperial Household in the Age of Nero." In *A Companion to the Neronian Age*, edited by E. Buckley and M. Dinter, pp. 102–117. Malden, MA.
Morley, N. 2006. "The Poor in the City of Rome." In Atkins and Osbornbe, eds., pp. 21–39.
Morley, N. 2011. "Slavery under the Principate." In Bradley and Cartledge, eds., pp. 265–286.
Morley, N. 2013. "Population Size and Social Structure." In Erdkamp, ed., pp. 29–44.
Morris, I., and J. Manning. 2005. "Introduction." In *The Ancient Economy: Evidence and Models*, edited by J. Manning and I. Morris, pp. 1–44. Stanford, CA.
Moskovitz, L. 2003. "Legal Fictions in Rabbinic Law and Roman Law." In *Rabbinic Law in Its Roman and Ancient Near Eastern Context*, edited by C. Heszer, pp. 105–132. Tübingen.
Mouritsen, H. 2004. "Freedmen and Freeborn in the Necropolis of Imperial Ostia." *Zeitschrift für Papyrologie und Epigraphik* 150: 281–304.
Mouritsen, H. 2011. *The Freedman in the Roman World*. Cambridge.
Mouritsen, H. 2013. "Slavery and Manumission in the Roman Elite: A Study of the *Columbaria* of the Volusii and the Statilii." In George, ed., pp. 43–68.
Mouritsen, H. 2016. "Manumission." In du Plessis, Ando, and Tuori, eds., pp. 386–401.
Mrozek, S. 1981. "Quelques remarques sur aere collato et pecunia collata." *Epigraphica* 43: 161–163.
Mrozek, S. 1985. "Zum Kreditgeld in der frühen römischen Kaiserzeit." *Historia* 34: 310–323.
Mrozek, S. 1987. *Les distributions d'argent et de nourriture dans les villes italiennes du Haut-Empire romaine*. Brussels.
Müller, K. 1995. *Petronius: Satyricon Reliquiae*. Munich.
Muñiz Coello, J. 1989. "Officium dispensatoris." *Gerion* 7: 107–119.

Nee, V. 2005. "The New Institutionalisms in Economics and Sociology." In *The Handbook of Economic Sociology*, 2nd ed., edited by N. Smelser and R. Swedberg, pp. 49–76. Princeton, NJ.

Nelis-Clément, J. 2000. *Les beneficiarii: Militaires et administrateurs au service de l'Empire (1er s. a.C.–VIe s. p.C.)*. Paris.

Nelken, D. 1984. "Law in Action or Living Law? Back to the Beginning in Sociology of Law." *Legal Studies* 4: 157–174.

Nelken, D., and J. Feest, eds. 2001. *Adapting Legal Cultures*. Oxford.

Newlands, C. 2002. *Statius'* Silvae *and the Poetics of Empire*. Cambridge.

Nicholas, B. 1962. *An Introduction to Roman Law*. Oxford.

Nicolet, C. 1976. "Le cens senatorial sous la république et sous Auguste." *Journal of Roman Studies* 66: 20–38.

Nicolet, C. 1994. "Economy and Society, 133–43 B.C." In *Cambridge Ancient History* IX, 2nd ed., edited by J. Crook, A. Lintott, and E. Rawson, pp. 599–643. Cambridge.

Nikolaou, K. 1994. "Οι γυναίκες στο Βίο και τα έργα του Θεοφίλου." *Σύμμεικτα* 9: 137–151.

Nikolaou, K. 2005. *Η γυναίκα στη μέση βυζαντινή εποχή. Κοινωνικά πρότυπα και καθημερινός βίος στα αγιολογικά κείμενα*. Athens.

Nishida, M. 1993. "Manumission and Ethnicity in Urban Slavery: Salvador, Brazil, 1808–1888." *Hispanic American Historical Review* 73.3: 361–391.

Nonnis, D. 2003. "Le implicazioni socio-politiche della produzione e della distribuzione nell'Italia repubblicana: per un repertorio prosopografico." In *Mercanti e politica nel mondo antico*, edited by C. Zaccagnini, pp. 241–274. Rome.

Nörr, D. 1965. "Pragmaticus." In Pauly-Wissowa, eds., RE Suppl. 10: 639–651.

Nörr, D. 1981. "Zur Reskriptenpraxis in der hohen Prinzipatszeit." *Zeitschrift der Savigny-Stiftung für Rechtsgeschichte* (Romanist.Abt.) 98: 1–46.

Nörr, D. 2000. "PSI VII 743r fr. E: Fragment einer römischen Prozeßformele. Bemerkungen zum vorhadrianischen Edikt und zu den *Hermeneumata Pseudodositheana*." *Zeitschrift der Savigny-Stiftung für Rechtsgeschichte* (Romanist. Abt.) 117: 179–215.

North, D. 1981. *Structure and Change in Economic History*. New York.

North, D. 1991. "Institutions."' *Journal of Economic Perspectives* 5: 97–112.

North, D., J. Wallis, and B. Weingast. 2009. *Violence and Social Orders: A Conceptual Framework for Interpreting Recorded Human History*. Cambridge.

North, M. 1997. "*Qui Facit Per Alium, Facit Per Se:* Representation, Mandate, and Principles of Agency in Louisiana at the Turn of the Twenty-First Century." *Tulane Law Review* 72: 279–326.

Oliver, J. 1989. *Greek Constitutions of Early Roman Emperors from Inscriptions and Papyri*. Philadelphia.

Oost, S. 1958. "The Career of M. Antonius Pallas." *American Journal of Philology* 79: 113–139.

Ortiz de Urbana, E., ed. 2013. *Magistrados locales de Hispania: Aspectos históricos, jurídicos, lingüísticos*. Vitoria-Gasteiz.

Osaba, E. 2000. *Gordianus rescripsit. Rescriptos de Gordiano III en materia dotal dirigidos a mujeres*. Bilbao.

Osberg, L., and T. Smeeding. 2006. "'Fair' Inequality? Attitudes toward Pay Differentials: The United States in Comparative Perspective." *American Sociological Review* 71: 450–454.

Osborne, M. 1981–1983. *Naturalization in Athens*. 4 Vols. Brussels.

Osborne, R. 1985. "Law in Action in Classical Athens." *Journal of Hellenic Studies* 105: 40–58.

Osborne, R. 2006. "Introduction: Roman Poverty in Context." In Atkins and Osborne eds., pp. 1–20.

Osgood, J. 2011a. *Claudius Caesar: Image and Power in the Early Roman Empire*. Cambridge.

Osgood, J. 2011b. "Making Romans in the Family." In Peachin, ed., pp. 69–83.

Oulhen, J. 2004. "La société athénienne." In *Le monde grec aux temps classiques*, Vol. 2: *Le IVe siècle*, edited by P. Brulé and R. Descat, pp. 251–351. Paris.

Pahud, S. 2013. *Le status de l'esclave et sa capacité à agir dans le domaine contractuel: Étude de droit romain de l'époque classique*. Dissertation, Lausanne.

Pakter, W. 1994. "The Mystery of Cessio Bonorum." *Index* 22: 323–342.

Palme, B. 2014. "Reports of Court Proceedings." In *Law and Legal Practice in Egypt from Alexander to the Arab Conquest*, edited by J. Keenan, J. Manning, and U. Yiftach-Firanko, pp. 482–502. Cambridge.

Panciera, S. 1977. "Saggi d'indagine sull'onomastica romana." In *L'onomastique latine*, edited by Noël Duval, pp. 191–203. Paris.

Panciera, S. 2007. "Servire a Palazzo. Nuove testimonianze di *officiales Augustorum* da Roma." In *Herrschen und Verwalten: Der Altag der römischen Administration in der Hohen Kaiserzeit*, edited by R. Haensch and J. Heinrichs, pp. 60–79. Cologne.

Paoli, U. [1930] 1974. *Studi di diritto attico*. Milan.

Paoli, U. 1976. *Altri studi di diritto Greco e Romano*. Milan.

Parker, H. 1997. "Women Doctors in Greece, Rome, and the Byzantine Empire." In *Women Physicians and Healers: Climbing a Long Hill*, edited by L. Furtst, pp. 131–150. Lexington, KY.

Parkins, H., and C. Smith, eds. 1998. *Trade, Traders and the Ancient City*. London.

Patterson, O. 1991. *Freedom: Freedom in the Making of Western Culture*, Vol. 1. London.

Patterson, O. 2009. "Three Notes of Freedom: The Nature and Consequences of Manumissions." In *Paths to Freedom: Manumission in the Atlantic World*, edited by R. Brana-Shute and R. Sparks, pp. 15–29. Columbia, SC.

Pauly-Wissowa, eds. 1894–1972. *Real-Encyclopädie der klassischen Altertumswissenschaft*, rev. G. Wissowa et al. Stuttgart.

Pavón, P. 2019. "La femme: objet et sujet de la justice romaine." In *The Impact of Justice on the Roman Empire* , edited by O. Hekster and K. Verboven, pp. 196–211. Leiden.

Peachin, M. 1996. *Iudex vice Caesaris: Deputy Emperors and the Administration of Justice during the Principate*. Stuttgart.

Peachin, M. 2002. "Introduction." In Aubert and Sirks, eds., pp. 1–14.

Peachin, M. 2011. "Introduction." In Peachin, ed., pp. 3–36.

Peachin, M., ed. 2011. *The Oxford Handbook of Social Relations in the Roman World*. Oxford.

Penner, L. 2013. *The Epigraphic Habits of the Slaves and Freed Slaves of the Julio-Claudian Households*. Dissertation, Calgary.

Peppe, L. 1984. *Posizione giuridica e ruolo sociale della donna romana in etá repubblicana*. Milan.

Perkins, A. 2006. "'You Do Him No Service': An Exploration of Pagan Almsgiving." In Atkins and Osborne, eds., pp. 60–82.

Perlman, P., ed. 2018. *Crossing Divides: Ancient Greek Law in the 21st Century*. Austin, TX.

Perozzi, S. 1947. *Istituzioni di diritto romano*, 2nd ed. Milan.

Perry, M. 2014. *Gender, Manumission, and the Roman Freedwoman*. Cambridge.

Perry, M. 2016. "Defining Gender." In du Plessis, Ando, and Tuori, eds., pp. 432–442.

Pesaresi, R. 2008. *Ricerche sul peculium imprenditoriale*. Bari.

Pescani, P. 1967. *Le "Operae libertorum": Saggio storico-romanistico*. Trieste.

Petrucci, A. 1991. *Mensam exercere: Studi sull'impresa finanziaria romana*. Naples.

Petrucci, A. 1997. "Prime riflessioni su banca ed interressi nell'esperienza romana." In Tafaro, ed., pp. 63 ff.

Petrucci, A. 1999. "I servi impuberum esercenti attività imprenditoriali nella riflessione della giurisprudenza romana dell'età commerciale." In *Societas - ius. Munuscula di allievi a F. Serra*, pp. 221 ff. Naples.

Petrucci, A. 2002. *Profili giuridici delle attività e dell'organizzazione delle banche romane*. Turin.

Pflaum, H. 1950. *Les Procurateurs équestres sous le haut empire romain*. Paris.

Picard, O. 2008. "L'économie grecque: sources, méthodes et problématique." In *Économies et sociétés en Grèce ancienne (478–88 av. J.-C.)*, edited by O. Picard, pp. 10–44. Paris.

Piketty, T. 2014. *Capital in the Twenty-first Century*. Cambridge, MA (published originally as *Le capital au XXI siècle*, Paris, 2013).

Pitts, M. 2007. "The Emperor's New Clothes? The Utility of Identity in Roman Archaeology." *American Journal of Archaeology* 111.4: 693–713.

Pleket, H. 1969. *Epigraphica*, Vol. II: *Texts on the Social History of the Greek World*. Leiden.

Pleket, H. 1971. "Soziale stratificatie en sociale mobiliteit in de romeinse keizertijd." *Tijdschrift voor Geschiedenis* 84: 215–251.

Pleket, H. 1983. "Urban Elites and Business in the Greek Cities of the Roman Empire" In *Trade in the Ancient Economy*, edited by K. Hopkins and C. Whittaker, pp. 131–141. London.

Pleket, H. 1984. "Urban Elites and Business in the Greek Part of the Roman Empire." *Münsterische Beiträge zur antiken Handelsgeschichte* 3.1: 3–35.

Plescia, J. 1984. "The Development of Agency in Roman Law." *Labeo* 30: 171–190.

Plessis, P. du, ed. 2013. *New Frontiers: Law and Society in the Roman World*. Edinburgh.

Pölönen, J. 2016. "Framing 'Law and Society' in the Roman World." In du Plessis, Ando, and Tuori, eds., pp. 8–20.

Pollard, N. 1996. "The Roman Army as 'Total Institution' in the Near East?" In *The Roman Army in the East*, edited by D. Kennedy, pp. 211–227. Ann Arbor, MI.

Pollard, N. 2000. *Soldiers, Cities and Civilians in Roman Syria*. Ann Arbor, MI.

Pollard, N. 2006. "The Roman Army." In Potter, ed., pp. 206–227.

Polt, C. 2014. "Polity across the Pond: Democracy, Republic, and Empire in Phaedrus Fables 1.2." *Classical Journal* 10: 161–190.

Porto, A. di. 1984. *Impresa collettiva e schiavo "manager" in Roma antica (II sec. a. C.–II sec. d. C.)*. Milan.

Porto, A. di. 1997. "Il diritto commerciale romano: Una 'zona d'ombra'nella storiografia romanistica e nelle riflessioni storico-comparative dei commercialisti." In *Nozione, formazione e interpretazione del diritto dall'età romana alle esperienze moderne*, Vol. 3, edited by M. Marrone, pp. 413–452. Naples.

Posner, E. 1972. *Archives in the Ancient World*. Cambridge.

Potter, D., ed. 2006. *A Companion to the Roman Empire*. Oxford.

Pound, R. 1910. "Law in Books and Law in Action." *American Law Review* 44: 12–36.

Prachner, G. 1980. *Die Sklaven und Freigelassene im arretinischen Sigillatagewerbe*. Wiesbaden.

Prados de la Escosura, L. 2008. "Inequality, Poverty and the Kuznets Curve: Spain, 1850–2000." *European Review of Economic History* 12: 287–324.

Prag, J., and I. Repath, eds. 2013. *Petronius: A Handbook*. Oxford.

Prell, M. 1997. *Sozialökonomische Untersuchungen zur Armut im antiken Rom: Von den Gracchen bis Kaiser Diokletian*. Stuttgart.

Pringsheim, F. 1950. *The Greek Law of Sale*. Weimar.

Pringsheim, F. 1956. "Fiktion in antiken rechten." *Studi De Francisci* 4: 211–236. Naples.

Procchi, F. 2007. "*Dolus e culpa in contrahendo* nella compravendita: Considerazioni in tema di sinallagma genetico." In *La compravendita e l'interdipendenza delle obbligazioni nel diritto romano*, edited by I. Garofalo, I, pp. 183–246. Padua.

Pugliese Carratelli, G., and V. Arangio-Ruiz. 1946–1961. "Tabulae Herculanenses." *La Parola del Passato* 1 (1946): 379–385; 3 (1948): 165–184; 8 (1953): 455–463; 9 (1954): 54–74; 10 (1955): 448–477; 16 (1961): 66–73.

Puglisi, G. 1987. "Il microcosmo di C. Pompeius Trimalchio Maecenatianus. Schiavi e liberti nella casa di un mercante romano (Petr. 27–78)." *Index* 15: 207–226.

Purcell, N. 1994. "The City of Rome and the *Plebs Urbana* in the Late Republic." *Cambridge Ancient History* 9: 644–688. 2nd ed. Cambridge.

Purcell, N. 2005. "Romans in the Roman World." In *Cambridge Companion to the Age of Augustus*, edited by K. Galinsky, pp. 85–105. Cambridge.

Quadrato, R. 1983. *Sulle trace dell'annullabilità: Quasi nullus nella giurisprudenzza Romana*. Naples.

Quadrato, R. [2001] 2010. "'Infirmitas sexus' e 'levitas animi': Il sesso 'debole' nel linguaggio dei giuristi romani." In *"Scientia iuris" e linguaggio nel sistema giuridico romano* (Atti del Convegno di Studi [Sassari 22–23 novembre 1996]), edited by F. Sini and R. Ortu, pp. 155–194. Milan 2001 = [2010] *"Gaius dixit": La voce di un giurista di frontiera*, pp. 137–176. Bari.

Rabel, E. 1913. "Ein Ruhmesblatt Papinians: Die Sogenannte Actio Quasi Institoria." In *Festschrift für Zitelmann zu seinem 60. Geburtstage*, edited by F. Stier-Somlo, pp. 3–28. Gottingen.

Ramin, J., and P. Veyne. 1981. "Droit romain et société: Les hommes libres qui passent pour esclaves et l'esclavage volontaire." *Historia* 30: 472–497 (republished in Veyne 1991, pp. 247–280).

Randall, R. 1953. "The Erechtheum Workmen." *American Journal of Archaeology* 57: 199–210.

Rantz, B. 1982. "Les Droits de la femme romaine tels qu'on peut les apercevoir dans le pro Caecina de Ciceron." *Revue internationale des droits de l'antiquité* 29: 265–280.

Rathbone, D. 1991. *Economic Rationalism and Rural Society in Third-Century A.D. Egypt*. Cambridge.

Rathbone, D. 2003. "The Financing of Martitime Commerce in the Roman Empire (I–II A.D.)." In *Credito e moneta nel mondo romano: Atti degli Incontri capresi di storia dell'economia antica*, edited by E. Lo Cascio, pp. 197–229. Capri.

Rathbone, D. 2009. "Earnings and Costs: Living Standards and the Roman Economy." In Bowman and Wilson, eds., pp. 299–326.

Rathbone, D., and P. Temin. 2008. "Financial Intermediation in Rome and England." In Verboven, Chankowski, and Vandorpe, eds., pp. 371–419.

Rawson, B. 2002. "The Express Route to Hades." In McKechnie, ed., pp. 271–288.

Rawson, B. 2010. "Degrees of Freedom: Vernae and Junian Latins in the Roman Family." In *Children, Memory, and Family Identity in Roman Culture*, edited by V. Dasen and T. Späth, pp. 195–221. Oxford.

Reden, S. von. 2012. "Money and Finance." In Scheidel, ed., pp. 266–286.

Reduzzi Merola, F. 1990. *Servo Parere: Studi sulla condizione giuridica degli schiavi vicari e dei sottoposti a schiavi nelle esperienze greca e romana*. Naples.

Reduzzi Merola, F. 2007. "La puella Fortunata: Un rêve." In *Fides Humanitas Ius. Studii in onore di Luigi Labruna*, edited by C. Cascione and C. Masi Doria, Vol. 7: 4721–4723. Naples.

Reduzzi Merola, F. 2010. *Forme non convenzionali di dipendenza nel mondo antico*, 2nd ed. Naples.

Reduzzi Merola, F. 2012. "Le donne nei documenti della prassi campana." *Index* 40: 380–386.

Reggi, R. 1958. *Liber homo bona fide serviens*. Milan.

Reis, J. 2017. "Deviant Behavior? Inequality in Portugal 1565–1770." *Cliometrica* 11: 297–319.

Renfrew, J. 2004. *Roman Cookery: Recipes and History*. London.

Revell, L. 2009. *Roman Imperialism and Local Identities*. Cambridge.

Revell, L. 2010. "Romanization: A Feminist Critique." In *TRAC 2010: Proceedings of the Nineteenth Annual Theoretical Roman Archaeology Conference*, edited by P. Girdwood et al., pp. 1–10. Oxford.

Revell, L. 2016. *Ways of Being Roman: Discourses of Identity in the Roman West*. Oxford.

Reynolds, P. 2018. "The Supply Networks of the Roman East and West: Interaction, Fragmentation, and the Origins of the Byzantine Economy." In Wilson and Bowman, eds., pp. 353–396.

Richardson, J. 1996. *The Romans in Spain*. Oxford.

Richardson, J. 2001. "Social Mobility in the Hispanic Provinces in the Republican Period." In de Blois, ed., pp. 246–254.

Richardson, J. 2015. "Roman Law in the Provinces." In Johnston, ed., pp. 45–58.

Richardson, J. 2016. "Provincial Administration." In In du Plessis, Ando, and Tuori, eds., pp. 111–123.

Richardson, L. 1992. *A New Topographical Dictionary of Ancient Rome*. Baltimore, MD.

Richlin, A. 2014. "Talking to Slaves in the Plautine Audience." *Classical Antiquity* 33.1: 174–226.

Richlin, A. 2017. *Slave Theater in the Roman Republic: Plautus and Popular Comedy*. Cambridge.

Riccobono, S., G. Baviera, C. Ferrini, G. Furlani, and V. Arangio-Ruiz, eds. [1940–43] 1964. *Fontes iuris Romani anteiustiniani*. 3 Vols. Florence.

Riggs, C., ed. 2012. *The Oxford Handbook of Roman Egypt*. Oxford.

Rihll, E. 2011. "Classical Athens." In Bradley and Cartledge, eds., pp. 48–73.

Rilinger, R. 1997. "*Domus* und *res publica*. Die politisch-soziale Bedeutung des aristokratischen 'Hauses' in der späten römischen Republik." In *Zwischen "Haus" und "Staat." Antike Höfe im Vergleich*, edited by A. Winterling, pp. 73–90. Munich.

Rink, B. 1993. "Sklavenfreilassungen in der späten römischen Republik als Beispiel für soziale Mobilität." *Laverna* 4: 45–54.

Rio, A. 2012. "Self-Sale and Voluntary Entry into Unfreedom, 300–1100." *Journal of Social History* 45.3: 661–685.

Rio, A. 2016. *Slavery after Rome, 500–1100*. Oxford.

Robbe, U. 1978. "La fictio iuris e la finzione di adempimento della condizione nel diritto romano." In *Scritti in onore di S. Pugliatti*, Vol. IV, 25–62. Milano.

Robert, L. 1949. "Le culte de Caligula à Milet et la province d'Asie." *Hellenica* 7: 206–238.

Robert, L. 1960. "Épitaphes d'Eumeneina de Phrygie," *Hellenika* 11–12: 416.

Robert, L. 1968. "Trois oracles de la Théosophie et un prophète d'Apollon." *Comptes rendus / Académie des inscriptions et belles-lettres* 112.4: 568–599.

Robertis, F. de. 1963. *Lavoro e lavoratori nel mondo romano*. Bari.

Robleda, O. 1976. *Il Diritto degli Schiavi nell'antica Roma*. Rome.

Roller, M. 2001. *Constructing Autocracy. Aristocrats and Emperors in Julio-Claudian Rome*. Princeton, NJ.

Roselaar, S. 2016. "Local Administration." In du Plessis, Ando, and Tuori, eds., pp. 124–136.

Rosén, H. 1980. "Die Sprachsituation im römischen Palästina." In *Die Sprachen im römischen Reich der Kaiserzeit (Beiheft der Bonner Jahrbücher 40)*, edited by G. Neumann, pp. 215–239. Heidelberg.

Rostovtzeff, M. 1926. *The Social and Economic History of the Roman Empire*. Oxford.

Roth, U. 2005. "Food, Status, and the *Peculium* of Agricultural Slaves." *Journal of Roman Archaeology* 18: 278–292.

Roth, U. 2007. *Thinking Tools: Agricultural Slavery between Evidence and Models*. London.

Roth, U. 2010. "Peculium, Freedom, Citizenship: Golden Triangle or Vicious Circle? An Act in Two Parts." In Roth, ed., pp. 91–120.

Roth, U., ed. 2010. *By the Sweat of Your Brow: Roman Slavery in Its Socio-Economic Setting*. London.

Rotman, Y. 2004. *La esclave et l'esclavage: De la Méditerranée antique à la Méditerranée médiévale*. Paris.

Rowan, E. 2017. "Bioarchaeological Preservation and Non-Elite Diet in the Bay of Naples: An Analysis of the Food Remains from the Cardo V Sewer at the Roman Site of Herculaneum." *Environmental Archaeology: The Journal of Human Palaeoecology* 22: 318–336.

Rowe, G. 2001. "Trimalchio's World." *Scripta Classica Israelica* 20: 225–245.

Rowlandson, J., and R. Takahashi. 2009. "Brother-Sister Marriage and Inheritance Strategies in Greco-Roman Egypt." *Journal of Roman Studies* 99: 104–139.

Ruffing, K., and H.-J. Drexhage. 2008. "Antike Sklavenpreise." In *Antike Lebenswelten: Konstanz—Wandel—Wirkungsmacht. Festschrift für Ingomar Weiler zum 70. Geburtstag*, edited by P. Mauritsch, pp. 321–351. Wiesbaden.

Rüfner, T. 2016. "Imperial *Cognitio* Procedure." In du Plessis, Ando, and Tuori, eds., pp. 257–269.

Ruggiero, E. de. 1961. *Dizionario epigrafico di Antichità Romane*. Rome.

Rüpke, J. 2006. "Religion in the Lex Ursonensis." In *Religion and Law in Classical and Christian Rome*, edited by C. Ando and J. Rüpke, pp. 34–46. Stuttgart.

Rupprecht, H. 1994. *Kleine Einführung in die Papyruskunde*. Darmstadt.

Russell, B. 2018."Stone Use and the Economy: Demand, Distribution and the State." In Wilson and Bowman, eds., pp. 237–264.

Ste. Croix, G. de. 1974. "Ancient Greek and Roman Maritime Loans." In *Debits, Credits, Finance and Profits* (Essays in Honour of W.T. Baxter), edited by H. Edey and B. Yamey, pp. 41–59. London.

Ste. Croix, G. de. 1981. *The Class Struggle in the Ancient Greek World*. London.

Saito, O. 2015. "Growth and Inequality in the Great and Little Divergence Debate: A Japanese Perspective." *Economic History Review* 68: 399–419.

Salazar Revuelta, M. 1999. *La gratuidad del mutuum en el derecho romano*. Jaén.

Saller, R. 1987. "Slavery and the Roman Family." *Slavery and Abolition* 8.1: 65–87.

Saller, R. 1994. *Patriarchy, Property, and Death in the Roman Family*. Cambridge.

Saller, R. 1998. "Symbols of Gender and Status Hierarchies in the Roman Household." In Joshel and Murnaghan, eds., pp. 85–91.

Saller, R. 1999. "*Pater Familias, Mater Familias*, and the Gendered Semantics of the Roman Household." *Classical Philology* 94: 182–197.

Saller, R. 2000. "Status and Patronage." In *Cambridge Ancient History*, 2nd ed., XI, edited by A. Bowman, P. Garnsey, and D. Rathbone, pp. 817–854. Cambridge.

Saller, R. 2007. "Household and Gender." In Scheidel, Morris, and Saller, eds., pp. 90–91.

Saller, R. 2012. "Human Capital and Economic Growth." In Scheidel, ed., pp. 71–86.

Sanchez-Moreno Ellart, C. 2002. *Professio Liberorum: Los registros y las declaraciones de nacimientos en Derecho romano*. Madrid.

Sanchez-Moreno Ellart, C. 2004. "Notes on Some New Issues Concerning the Birth Certificates of Roman Citizens." *Journal of Juristic Papyrology* 34: 107–119.

Sartre, M. 2007. "Romanisation en Asie Mineur?" In *Tra Oriente Occidente: Indigeni, Greci e Romani in Asia Minore*, edited by G. Urso, pp. 229–245. Pisa.

Satlow, M. 2005. "Marriage Payments and Succession Strategies in the Documents from the Judaean Desert." In *Law in the Documents of the Judaean Desert*, edited by R. Katzoff and D. Schaps, pp. 51–65. Leiden.

Scafuro, A. 1997. *The Forensic Stage*. Cambridge.

Scafuro, A. 2003–2004. "The Rigmarole of the Parasite's Contract for a Prostitute in *Asinaria*: Legal Documents in Plautus and His Predecessors." *Leeds International Classical Studies* 3.4: 1–21. (http://www.leeds.ac.uk/classics/lics/).

Schäfer, C. 1998. *Spitzenmanagement in Republik und Kaiserzeit. Die Prokuratoren von Privatpersonen im Imperium Romanum von 2. Jh. v. Chr. bis zum 3. Jh. N. Chr.* St. Kartharinen.

Schaps, D. 1971. "The Woman Least Mentioned: Etiquette and Women's Names." *Classical Quarterly* 71: 323–360.

Schaps, D. 1979. *Economic Rights of Women in Ancient Greece*. Edinburgh.

Scheid, W. 1999. "Aspects religieux de la municipalization: Quelques réflexions générales." In *Cités, Municipes, Colonies: Les processus de municipalization en Gaule et en Germanie sous le Haut Empire romain*, edited by M. Dondin-Payre and M.-T. Raepsaet-Charlier, pp. 381–423. Paris.

Scheidel, S. 1992. *Work, Identity, and Legal Status at Rome: A Study of the Occupational Inscriptions*. Norman, OK.

Scheidel, W. 1990. "Free-Born and Manumitted Bailiffs in the Graeco-Roman World." *Classical Quarterly* 40 (N.S.): 591–595.

Scheidel, W. 1997. "Quantifying the Sources of Slave in the Early Roman Empire." *Journal of Roman Studies* 87: 159–169.

Scheidel, W. 2003. "Review of L. Schumacher 2001." *Journal of Roman Archaeology* 16: 577–581.

Scheidel, W. 2005. "Human Mobility in Roman Italy, II: The Slave Population." *Journal of Roman Studies* 95: 64–79.

Scheidel, W. 2006. "Stratification, Deprivation and Quality of Life." In Atkins and Osbornbe, eds., pp. 40–59.

Scheidel, W. 2008. "The Comparative Economics of Slavery in the Greco-Roman World." In E. Del Lago and C. Katsari, eds., pp. 105–126.

Scheidel, W. 2009. "New Ways of Studying Incomes in the Roman Economy." In *Quantifying the Roman Economy*, edited by A. Bowman and A. Wilson, pp. 346–352. Oxford.

Scheidel, W. 2010. "Real Wages in Early Economies: Evidence for Living Standards from 1800 BCE to 1300 CE." *Journal of the Economic and Social History of the Orient* 52: 425–462.

Scheidel, W. 2011. "The Roman Slave Supply." In Bradley and Cartledge, eds., pp. 287–310.

Scheidel, W. 2012a. "Approaching the Roman Economy." In Scheidel, ed., pp. 1–21.

Scheidel, W. 2012b. "Slavery." In Scheidel, ed., pp. 89–113.

Scheidel, W. 2015. "State Revenue and Expenditure in the Han and Roman Empires." In *Fiscal Regimes and the Political Economy of Premodern States*, edited by A. Monson and W. Scheidel, pp. 229–257. Cambridge.

Scheidel, W. 2017. *The Great Leveler: Violence and the History of Inequality from the Stone Age to the Twenty-First Century*. Princeton, NJ.

Scheidel, W. 2019. *Escape from Rome: The Failure of Empire and the Road to Prosperity*. Princeton, NJ.

Scheidel, W. 2020. "Roman Wealth and Wealth Inequality in Comparative Perspective." *Journal of Roman Archaeology* 33: 341–353.

Scheidel, W., ed. 2012. *The Cambridge Companion to the Roman Economy*. Cambridge.

Scheidel, W., and S. Friesen. 2009. "The Size of the Economy and the Distribution of Income in the Roman Empire." *Journal of Roman Studies* 99: 61–91.

Scheidel, W., I. Morris, and R. Saller, eds. 2007. *The Cambridge Economic History of the Greco-Roman World*. Cambridge.

Schiavone, A. 2000. *The End of the Past: Ancient Rome and the Modern West*. Cambridge, MA.

Schiavone, A. 2020. "Law, Slaves, and Markets in the Roman Imperial System." In Dari-Mattiacci and Kehoe, eds., Vol. 2, pp. 11–34.

Schiller, A. 1971. *An American Experience in Roman Law: Writings from Publications in the United States*. Göttingen.

Schleich, T. 1984. "Uberlegungen zu Problem senatorischer Handelsaktivitäten, Teil II." *Münsterische Beiträge zur antiken Handelsgeschichte* 3.1: 37–76.

Schleppinghoff, A. 1996. *Actio quod iussu: Die Geheissklage (und ihre Bedeutung für die Entwicklung des Stellvertretungsgedankens im 19. Jahrhundert*. Dissertation, Cologne University.

Schlinkert, D. 1996. *Ordo senatorius und nobilitas: Die Konstitution des Senatsadels in der Spätantike*. Stuttgart.

Schmidt-Ott, J. 1993. *Pauli Quaestiones: Eigenart und Textgeschichte einer spätklassischen Juristenschrift*. Berlin.

Schönbauer, E. 1952. "Deditizier, Doppel-Bürgerschaft und Personalitäts-Prinzip." *Journal of Juristic Papyrology* 6: 17–72.

Schönbauer, E. 1960. "Personalitätsprinzip und Privatrechtsordnung im Römmerreiche." *Anzeiger der Österreichischen Akademie der Wissenschaften. Phil-Hist. Klasse* 25: 182–210.

Schuller, W. 1985. *Frauen in der griechischen Geschichte*. Konstanz.

Schulz, F. 1934. *Prinzipien des römischen Rechts*. Munich.

Schulz, F. 1942, 1943. "Roman Registers of Birth and Birth Certificates." *Journal of Roman Studies*, Part 1, 32: 78–91, Part 2, 33: 55–64.

Schulz, F. 1951. *Classical Roman Law*. Oxford.

Schumacher, L. 2001(a). *Sklaverei in der Antike: Alltag und Schicksal der Unfreien*. Munich.

Schumacher, L. 2001(b). "Hausgesinde: Hofgesinde. Terminologische Überlegungen zur Funktion der *familia Caesaris* im 1. Jh. N. Chr." In *Fünfzig Jahre Forschungen zur antiken Sklaverei an der mainzer Akademie 1950–2000: Miscellanea zum Jubiläum*, edited by H. Bellen and H. Heinen, pp. 331–352. Stuttgart.

Schumacher, L. 2010. "On the Status of Private *Actores*, *Dispensatores* and *Vilici*." In Roth, ed., pp. 31–46.

Schumacher, L. 2011. "Slaves in Roman Society." In Peachin, ed., pp. 589–608.

Schwartz, S. 1974. "The Manumission of Slaves in Colonial Brazil: Bahia, 1684–1745." *Hispanic American Historical Review* 4: 603–635.

Sciarrino, E. 2010. "What 'Lies' behind Phaedrus' Fables?" In *Public and Private Lies: The Discourse of Despotism and Deceit in the Ancient World*, edited by K. Chong-Gossard, A. Turner, and F. Verveat, pp. 231–248. Leiden.

Scott, E. 1995. "Women and Gender Relations in the Roman Empire." In *Theoretical Roman Archaeology: Second Conference Proceedings*, edited by P. Rush, pp. 174–189. Aldershot, UK.

Scott, E. 1996. "Locating Women: Space and Gender." *Cambridge Archaeological Journal* 6.1: 124–126.

Scupin, R., and C. DeCorse. 1992. *Cultural Anthropology: A Global Perspective*, 6th ed. Englewood Cliffs, NJ.

Seidl, E. 1965. "Zur Gerichtverfassung in der Provinz Aegypten bis ca. 250 n. Chr." *Labeo* 11: 316–328.

Seidl, E. 1973. *Rechtsgeschichte Ägyptens als römischer Provinz*. Sankt Augustin.

Seitz, W. 1969. *Studien zur Prosopographie und zur Sozial- und Rechtsgeschichte der grossen kaiserlichen Zentralämter bis hin zu Hadrian*. Ph.D. thesis, University of Munich.

Serrao, F. 1947. *Il procuratore*. Milan.

Serrao, F. 1971. *Enciclopedia del diritto* 21: 827–834, s.v. "institor." Milan.

Serrao, F. 1984. "Minima di Diogneto ed Hesicho: gli affari di due schiavi a Pozzuoli negli anni 30 d. c." *Sodalita* (Scritti Guarino) 7: 3605–3618.

Serrao, F. 1989. *Impresa e responsabilità a Roma nell' età commerciale*. Pisa.

Setälä, P. 1998. "Female Property and Power in Imperial Rome." In *Aspects of Women in Antiquity*, edited by L. Larsson Lovén and A. Strömberg, pp. 96–110. Jonsered.

Seuffert, L. 1907. "Der Loskauf von Sklaven mit ihrem Geld." In *Festschrift für die juristische Fakultät Gießen zum Universitäts-Jubiläum*, edited by R. Frank, pp. 1–20. Giesen.

Sharpe, J. 2003. *Ghosts of Slavery: A Literary Archaeology of Black Women's Lives*. Minneapolis, MN.

Shatzman, I. 1975. *Senatorial Wealth and Roman Politics*. Collections Latomus 142. Brussels.

Shaw, B. 1983. "Soldiers and Society: The Army in Numidia." *Opus* 2: 133–159.

Shaw, B. 2020. "Social Status and Economic Behavior: A Hidden History of the *Equites*?" *Ancient Society* 50: 153–202.

Shaw, B. 2022. "The Company-State Model and the *societates publicanorum*." *Historia* 71: 78–127.

Sherk, R., ed. 1988. *The Roman Empire: Augustus to Hadrian*. Cambridge.

Sherwin-White, A. 1973. *The Roman Citizenship*, 2nd ed. Oxford.

Sicari, A. 1991. *Prostituzione e tutela giuridica della schiava: Un problema di politica legislativa nell'impero romano*. Bari.

Sijpesteijn, P. 1982. *Michigan Papyri XV*. Zutphen, Netherlands.

Silver, M. 1995. *Economic Structures of Antiquity*. Westport, CT.

Silver, M. 2007. "Roman Economic Growth and Living Standards: Perceptions versus Evidence." *Ancient Society* 37: 191–252.

Silver, M. 2009. "Must Frequently Performed Economic Services Have Distinctive Names? A Probe of Finley's Hypothesis." *Historia* 58: 246–256.

Silver, M. 2011. "Contractual Slavery in the Roman Economy." *Ancient History Bulletin* 25: 73–132.

Silver, M. 2014. "Places for Self-Selling in Ulpian, Plautus and Horace: The Role of Vertumnus." *Mnemosyne* 67: 577–587.

Silver, M. 2016a. "At the Base of Rome's Peculium Economy." *Fundamina* 22.1: 67–93.

Silver, M. 2016b. "Public Slaves in The Roman Army: An Exploratory Study." *Ancient Society* 46: 203–240.

Silver, M. 2018. "Bondage by Contract in the Late Roman Empire." *International Review of Law and Economics* 54: 17–29.

Simon, D. 1964. *Studien zur Praxis der Stipulationsklausel* (Münchener Beiträge zur Papyrusforschung und antiken Rechtsgeschichte 43). Munich.

Sirks, A. 1981. "Informal Manumission and the Lex Junia." *Revue internationale des droits de l'antiquité* 28: 247–276.

Sirks, A. 2002. "Conclusion: Some Reflections." In Aubert and Sirks, eds., pp. 169–181.

Sirks, A. 2005. "Der Zweck des Senatus Consultum Claudianum von 52 n. Chr." *Rechtsgeschichte (Zeitschrift des Max-Planck-Institut für europäische Rechtsgeschichte)* 122: 138–149.

Sirks, A. 2012. "Review of Fleckner 2010." *Tijdschrift voor Rechtsgeschiedenis* 80: 211–213.

Sirks, A. 2018. "Law, Commerce, and Finance in the Roman Empire." In Wilson and Bowman, eds., pp. 53–115.

Sitek, B. 2017. "A State and the Protection of its Interests: Advocatus fisci vs State Treasury Solicitors' Office." *Journal of Modern Science* 2.33: 49–60.

Smadja, E. 1999. "L'affranchissement des femmes esclaves à Rome." In *Femmes-esclaves: Modèles d'interprétation anthropologique, économique, juridique. (Atti del XXI Colloquio internazionale del G.I.R.E.A.)*, edited by F. Merola and A. Storchi Marino, pp. 355–368. Naples.

Smallwood, E. 1967. *Documents Illustrating the Principates of Gaius, Claudius and Nero.* London.

Smith, P. 2007. "New Legal Fictions." *Georgetown Law Journal* 95: 1435–1495.

Smuts, W., and T. Stromback, eds. 2001. *The Economics of the Apprentice System.* Cheltenham, UK.

Sokala, A. 1993. "The Effectiveness of the 'Ne Prostituatur' Clauses in Roman Law." *Eos* 81: 97–100.

Solazzi, S. [1941] 1963. "L'età dell' *actio exercitoria.*" In *Scritti di diritto romano* IV, pp. 243–264. Naples (= *Rivista del Diritto della Navigazione* 7: 185–212).

Solazzi, S. 1973. "Tutela e Curatela." In *Novissimo Digesto Italiano*, Vol. 18, s.v., edited by A. Azara and E. Eula. Turin.

Solin, H. 1971. *Beiträge zur Kenntnis der griechischen Personennamen in Rom.* Helsinki.

Solin, H. 1974. "Onomastica ed epigrafia: Riflession sull'esegesi onomastici delle iscrizioni romane." *Quaderni urbinati di cultura classica* 18: 105–132.

Solin, H. 1996. *Die stadtrömischen Sklavennamen I–III (Forschungen zur antiken Sklaverei, Beiheft 2).* Stuttgart.

Söllner, A. 2005. "Bona fides—guter Glaube?" *Zeitschrift der Savigny-Stiftung für Rechtsgeschichte* (Romanist. Abt.) 122: 1–61.

Söllner, A. 2012. "Homo liber bona fide serviens." In *Handwörterbuch der antiken Sklaverei*, edited by H. Heinen et al., s.v. homo liber bona fide serviens., pp. 1447 ff. CD-Rom. Stuttgart.

Sommerstein, A. 2009. *Talking about Laughter and Other Studies in Greek Comedy.* Oxford.

Soricelli, G. 2016. "Le attività finanziarie." In A. Marcone, ed., pp. 341–378.

Sosin, J. 2015. "Manumission with Paramone: Conditional Freedom?" *TAPA* 145: 325–381.

Spagnuolo Vigorito, T. 1993. "Cittadini e sudditi tra II e III secolo." In *Storia di Roma 3. L'età tardoantica 1. Crisi e trasformazioni*, edited by A. Schiavone, pp. 5–50. Turin.

Spagnuolo Vigorito, T. 1996. *Città e impero.* Naples.

Spawforth, A., M. Millett, and S. Mitchell. 2014. "Romanization." In *The Oxford Companion to Classical Civilization*, edited by S. Hornblower and A. Spawforth, doi: 10.1093/acref/9780 198706779.001.0001. Oxford.

Spranger, P. 1961. *Historische Untersuchungen zu den Sklavenfiguren des Plautus und Terenz*. Mainz.

Sutherland, C. 1945. "*Aerarium* and *Fiscus* during the Early Empire." *American Journal of Philology* 66: 151–170.

Steinby, E. 1978. *Pauly-Wissowa* Suppl. 15, Cols. 1489–1531, s.v. Ziegelstempel von Rom und Umgebung.

Steinby, E. 1993. "L'organizzazione produttiva dei laterizi: un modello interpretativo per l'*instrumentum* in genere?" In *The Inscribed Economy: Production and Distribution in the Roman Empire in the Light of instrumentum domesticum*, edited by W. Harris, pp. 139–144. Ann Arbor, MI.

Stelzenberger, B. 2008. *Kapitalmanagement und Kapitaltransfer im Westen des Römischen Reiches*. Rahden.

Stephan, R. 2013. *House Size and Economic Growth: Regional Trajectories in the Roman World*. Dissertation, Stanford University.

Sternberg, T. 1985. "Reskripte des Kaisers Alexander Severus an weibliche Adressaten." *Klio* 67: 507–527.

Stewart, R. 2012. *Plautus and Roman Slavery*. Malden, MA.

Stolte, B. 2001. "The Impact of Roman Law in Egypt and the Near East in the Third Century AD: The Document Evidence (Some Considerations in the Margin of the Euphrates Papyri [P. Euphr.])." In de Blois, ed., pp. 167–179.

Stolte, B. 2009. "Roman Private Law in the Greek East." In *Diritto ed economia in età tardoantica*, edited by A. Polichetti and F. Tucillo, pp. 201–215. Penta di Fisciano.

Stone, L. 1965. *The Crisis of the Aristocracy, 1558–1641*. Oxford.

Storey, G. 2000. "An Economic Cost-Benefit Analysis of Statuses in the Roman Empire." In *Hierarchies in Action: Cui Bono?*, edited by M. Diehl, pp. 340–374. Carbondale, IL.

Strack, M. 1914. "Die Freigelassenen in ihrer Bedeutung für die Gesellschaft der Alten." *Historische Zeitschrift* 112: 1–28.

Straus, J. 2004. *L'achat et la vente des esclaves dans l'Egypte romaine: Contribution papyrologique à l'étude de l'esclavage dans une province orientale de l'empire romain*. Munich.

Strong, A. 2016. *Prostitutes and Matrons in the Roman World*. Cambridge.

Sudi, F. 2013. *Les esclaves et les affranchis publics dans l'occident romain (IIe siècle avant J.-C.–IIIe siècle après J.-C.)*. Dissertation, Université Blaise Pascal–Clermont–Ferrand II.

Swain, S. 1996. *Hellenism and Empire: Language, Classicism, and Power in the Greek World, AD 50–250*. Oxford.

Syme, R. 1958. *Tacitus*. Oxford.

Syme, R. 1968. "People in Pliny." *Journal of Roman Studies* 58: 135–151.

Sypher, W. 1942. *Guinea's Captive Kings: British Anti-Slavery Literature of the XVIIIth Century*. Chapel Hill, NC.

Szaivert, W., and R. Wolters. 2005. *Löhne, Preise, Werte: Quellen zur römischen Geldwirtschaft*. Darmstadt.

Tafaro, S., ed. 1997. *L'usura ieri ed oggi*. Bari.

Talamanca, M. 1971. "Su alcuni passi di Menandro di Laodicea relativi agli effetti della 'constitutio Antoniniana.'" In *Studi in Onore di Edoardo Volterra*, V: 433–560. Milan.

Talamanca, M. 1993–1994. "Review of Petrucci 1991." *Bullettino dell'Istituto di Diritto Romano* 96–97: 828.

Talamanca, M. 2008. "Risposta a A. Maffi: Economia e diritto nell'Atene del IV secolo." In *Symposion 2007 (Akten der Gesellschaft für Griechische und Hellenistische Rechtsgeschichte)*, edited by E. Harris and G. Thür, pp. 223–228. Vienna.

Talbert, R. 1984. *The Senate of Imperial Rome*. Princeton, NJ.

Tamanaha, B. 2001. *A General Jurisprudence of Law and Society*. Oxford.

Tan, J. 2017. *Power and Public Finance at Rome, 264–49 BCE*. Oxford.

Tapio, H. 1975. *Organization of Roman Brick Production*. Helsinki.

Taubenschlag, R. 1916. "Die patria potestas im Recht der Papyri." *Zeitschrift der Savigny-Stiftung für Rechtsgeschichte* (Romanist. Abt.) 37: 177–230.

Taubenschlag, R. [1951] 1959. "The Legal Profession in Greco-Roman Egypt." In *Festschrift F. Schulz*, edited by H. Niedermeyer and W. Flume, Vol. 2, pp. 188–192. Weimar (= *Opera Minora*, Vol. 2, pp. 159–165, Warsaw, 1959).

Taubenaschlag, R. 1955. *The Law of Greco-Roman Egypt in the Light of the Papyri*, 2nd ed. Warsaw.

Taubenschlag, R. 1959. "Die Römischen Behörden und das Volksrecht vor und nach der CA." In *Opera Minora*, Vol. 1, pp. 477–493. Warsaw.

Taylor, L. 1961. "Freedmen and Freeborn in the Epitaphs of Imperial Rome." *American Journal of Philology* 82: 113–32.

Taylor, T. 2016. "Social Status, Legal Status and Legal Privilege." In du Plessis, Ando, and Tuori, eds., pp. 349–361.

Tchernia, A. 2011. *Les Romains et le commerce*. Naples.

Teitler, H. 1985. *Notarii and Exceptores: An Inquiry into Role and Significance of Shorthand Writers in the Imperial and Ecclesiastical Bureaucracy of the Roman Empire: From the Early Principate to c. 450 A.D.* Amsterdam.

Temin, P. 2004. "The Labor Market in the Early Roman Empire." *Journal of Interdisciplinary History* 34: 513–538.

Temin, P. 2012. "The Contribution of Economics." In Scheidel, ed., pp. 45–70.

Temin, P. 2013. *The Roman Market Economy*. Princeton, NJ.

Temin, P., and D. Rathbone. 2008. "Financial Intermediation in First-Century AD Rome and Eighteenth-Century England." In Verboven, Chankowski, and Vandorpe, eds., pp. 371–419.

Terpstra, T. 2008. “Roman Law, Transaction Costs and the Roman Economy: Evidence from the Sulpicii Archive.” In Verboven, Chankowski, and Vandorpe, eds., pp. 345–369.

Terpstra, T. 2013. *Trading Communities in the Roman World: A Micro-Economic and Institutional Perspective*. Leiden.

Thaler, R. 2016. *Misbehaving: The Making of Behavioral Economics*. New York.

Thilo, R. 1980. *Der Codex Accepti et Expensi im römischen Recht: Ein Beitrag zur Lehre von der Litteralobligation*. Göttingen.

Thomas, J. 1975. *The Institutes of Justinian*. Oxford.

Thomas, J. 1976. *Textbook of Roman Law*. Amsterdam.

Thomas, Y. [1995] 2011. “Fictio legis. L’empire de la fiction romaine et ses limites médiévales.” In *Les opérations du droit*, edited by M.-A. Hermitte and P. Napoli, pp. 133–186. Paris (originally published in *Droits. Revue française de théorie juridique* 21: 17–63).

Thompson, F. 2003. *The Archaeology of Greek and Roman Slavery*. London.

Thompson, W. 1988. “Insurance and Banking.” In *Civilization of the Ancient Mediterranean*, edited by M. Grant and R. Kitzinger, 2: 829–836. New York.

Thür, G. 1977. *Beweisführung vor den Schwurgerichtshöfen Athens: die Proklesis zur Basanon*. Vienna.

Thür, G. 2001. “Recht im hellenistischen Athen (Ephebie. Kassel/Austin, Adespota 1152. Basanos.” In *Symposion 1997*, edited by E. Cantarella and G. Thür, pp. 141–164. Cologne.

Thür, G. 2005. “The Role of the Witness in Athenian Law.” In *The Cambridge Companion to Ancient Greek Law*, edited by M. Gagarin and D. Cohen, pp. 144–169. Cambridge.

Thür, G., U. Yiftach, and R. Zelnick-Abramovitz, eds. 2018. *Symposion 2017 (Akten der Gesellschaft für Griechische und Hellenistische Rechtsgeschichte)*. Vienna.

Thurmond, D. 1994. “Some Roman Slave Collars in CIL.” *Athenaeum* 82: 459–493.

Thurn, I. ed. 1973. *Ioannis Skylitzes, Synopsis Historiarum*, Vol. I. Berlin.

Todd, S. 1994. “Status and Contract in Fourth-Century Athens.” In *Symposion 1993 (Akten der Gesellschaft für Griechische und Hellenistische Rechtsgeschichte)*, edited by G. Thür, pp. 125–140. Cologne.

Todd, S. 2002. “Introduction to Against Pancleon.” In *The Oratory of Classical Greece*, edited by M. Gagarin, Vol. 2, pp. 245–247. Austin, TX.

Tomber, R. 2018. “Egypt and Eastern Commerce during the Second Century AD and Later.” In Wilson and Bowman, eds., pp. 531–555.

Tomlin, R. 2003. “The Girl in Question: A New Text from Roman London.” *Britannia* 34: 41–51.

Tondo, S. 1967. *Aspetti simbolici e magici nella struttura giuridica della manumissio vindita*. Milan.

Torelli, M. 1980. “Industria estrattiva, lavoro artigianale, interessi economici, qualche appunto.” *Memoirs of the American Academy at Rome* 36: 313–324.

Torelli, M. 1994. "Per un'eziologia del cambiamento in epoca Claudia. Vicende vicine e vicende lontane." In *Die Regierungszeit des Kaisers Claudius: Umbruch oder Episode?*, edited by V. Strocka, pp. 177–190. Mainz.

Tran, N. 2013–2014. "Les statuts de travail des esclaves et des affranchis dans les grands ports du monde romain." *Annales, Histoire, Sciences Sociales* 68: 999–1025.

Tran, N. 2014. "Un esclave préposé au commerce de l'huile dans le port d'Arles. À propos de *Dig.*, 14.3.13pr (Ulp. 28 *ad ed.*)." In Apicella, Haack, and Lerouixel, eds., pp. 223–232.

Tran, N. 2017. "*Ars* and *Doctrina*: The Socioeconomic Identity of Roman Skilled Workers (First Century BC–Third Century AD)." In Verboven and Laes, eds., pp. 246–261.

Treggiari, S. 1969. *Roman Freedmen during the Late Republic*. Oxford.

Treggiari, S. 1975a. "Family Life among the Staff of the Volusii." *Transactions of the American Philological Association* 105: 393–401.

Treggiari, S. 1975b. "Jobs in the Household of Livia." *Papers of the British School at Rome* 43: 48–77.

Treggiari, S. 1976. "Jobs for Women." *American Journal of Ancient History* 1: 76–104.

Treggiari, S. 1979. "Lower Class Women in the Roman Economy." *Florilegium* 1: 65–86.

Treggiari, S. 1980. "Urban Labour in Rome: Mercennarii and Tabernarii." In *Non-Slave Labour in the Greco-Roman World*, edited by P. Garnsey, pp. 48–64. Cambridge.

Treggiari, S. 1991. *Roman Marriage:* Iusti Coniuges *from the Time of Cicero to the Time of Ulpian*. Oxford.

Trimble, J. 2015. "Reception Theory and Roman Sculpture." In *The Oxford Handbook of Roman Sculpture*, edited by E. Friedland, M. Sobocinski, and E. Gazda, pp. 606–621. Oxford.

Trimble, J. 2016. "The Zonimus Collar and the Archaeology of Roman Slavery." *American Journal of Archaeology* 120.3: 447–472.

Trümper, M. 2009. *Graeco-Roman Slave Markets: Fact or Fiction?* Oxford.

Tuori, K. 2007(a). *Ancient Roman Lawyers and Modern Legal Ideals: Studies on the Impact of Contemporary Concerns in the Interpretation of Ancient Roman Legal History*. Studien zur europaeischen Rechtsgeschichte, Vol. 220. Frankfurt.

Tuori, K. 2007(b). "Legal Pluralism and the Roman Empires." In Cairns and du Plessis eds., pp. 39–52.

Twining, W. 2015. "Preface." In *Legal Fictions in Theory and Practice*, edited by M. Del Mar and W. Twining, pp. v–vii. Heidelberg.

Unger, R. 2015. *The Critical Legal Studies Movement: Another Time, A Greater Task*. London.

Urbanik, J. 2014. "On the Uselessness of It All: The Roman Law of Marriage and Modern Times." *Fundamina* 20.2: 946–960.

Vacca, L. 1988. "Il c.d. duplex dominium e l'actio Publiciana." In *La proprietà e le proprietà*, edited by E. Cortese, pp. 39–74. Milan.

Van Bremen, R. 1983. "Women and Wealth." In *Images of Women in Anitquity*, edited by A. Cameron and A. Kuhrt, pp. 223–242. Detroit.

Van Deburg, W. 1984. *Slavery and Race in American Popular Culture*. Madison, WI.

Van der Veen, M. 1998. "A Life of Luxury in the Desert? The Food and Fodder Supply to Mons Claudianus." *Journal of Roman Archaeology* 11: 101–116.

Veal, R. 2012. "Examining Continuity in Landscape Exploitation: Late Roman Fuel Consumption in Silchester's *Insula* IX." In *Silchester and the Study of Romano-British Urbanism*, edited by M. Fulford, pp. 227–245. Journal of Roman Archaeology Supplementary Series, 90. Portsmouth, RI.

Vélissaropoulos-Karakostas, J. 2002. "Merchants, Prostitutes and the 'New Poor.'" In *Money, Labour and Land: Approaches to the Economies of Ancient Greece*, edited by P. Cartledge, E. Cohen, and L. Foxhall, pp. 130–139. London.

Vélissaropoulos-Karakostas, J. 2011. *Droit Grec d'Alexandre à Auguste (323 av. J.-C.–14 ap. J.-C.)*, Vol. II. Athens.

Vélissaropoulos-Karakostas, J. 2018. "Soft Law in Ancient Greece?" In Perlman, ed., pp. 144–156.

Verboven, K. 2000. "L'organisation des affaires financières des C. Sulpicii de Puozolles (Tabulae Pompeianae Sulpiciorum)." *Cahiers Glotz* II: 161–171.

Verboven, K. 2002. *The Economy of Friends: Economic Aspects of Amicitia and Patronage in the Late Republic*. Brussels.

Verboven, K. 2004. "Mentalité et commerce: Le cas des *negotiatores* et de ceux *qui negotia habent*: Une enquete préliminaire." In *Mentalités et choix économiques des romains*, edited by J. Andreau, J. France, and S. Pittia, pp. 179–200. Bordeaux.

Verboven, K. 2007. "The Associative Order: Status and Ethos among Roman Businessmen in the Late Republic and Early Empire." *Athenaeum* 95: 861–893.

Verboven, K. 2008a. "Reflections on the Papers." In Verboven, Vandorpe, and Chankowski, eds., pp. xxxvii–xlviii.

Verboven, K. 2008b. "Faeneratores, Negotiatores and Financial Inrtermediation in the Roman World (Late Republic and Early Empire)." In Verboven, Vandorpe, and Chankowski., eds., pp. 211–229.

Verboven, K. 2011. "The Freedman Economy of Roman Italy." In Bell and Ramsby, eds., pp. 88–109.

Verboven, K. 2013. "A Funny Thing Happened on My Way to the Market: Reading Petronius to Write Economic History." In Prag and Repath, eds., pp. 125–139.

Verboven, K. 2014. "Attitudes to Work and Workers in Classical Greece and Greece and Rome." *Tijdschrift voor Sociale en Economische Geschiedenis* 11.1: 67–87.

Verboven, K. 2018. "Ancient Cliometrics and Archaeological Proxy-Data: Between the Devil and the Deep Blue Sea." In *Cuantificar las economías antiguas: Problemas y métodos*, edited by J. Remesal Rodríguez, V. Revilla Calvo, and J. Bermúdez Lorenzo, pp. 345–373. Barcelona.

Verboven, K. and P. Erdkamp, eds. 2023. *Law and Economic Performance in the Roman World*. Leiden.

Verboven, K., and C. Laes. 2017. "Work, Labour, Professions: What's in a Name?" In Verboven and Laes, eds., pp. 1–19.

Verboven, K., and C. Laes, eds. 2017. *Work, Labour and Professions in the Roman World.* Leiden.

Verboven, K., K. Vandorpe, and V. Chankowski, eds. 2008. *Pistoi dia ten technen: Bankers, Loans and Archives in the Ancient World.* Leuven.

Vermote, K. 2016. "The *macula servitutis* of Roman Freedmen: Neque enim oboletur turpitudo, quae postea intermissa est?" *Revue Belge de Philologie et d'Histoire* 94: 131–164.

Veyne, P. 1961. "Vie de Trimalcion." *Annales (Economies, Société, Civilisations)* 16: 213–247.

Veyne, P. 1979. "Mythe et réalité de l'autarcie à Rome." *Revue des Etudes anciennes* 81: 261–280.

Veyne, P. 1991. *La Société romaine.* Paris.

Veyne, P. 2000. "La 'plèbe moyenne' sous le Haut-Empire romain." *Annales. Histoire, Scienes Sociales* 55: 1187–1194.

Veyne, P. 2001. *La société romaine.* Paris.

Vidal-Naquet, P. 1986. *The Black Hunter: Forms of Thought and Forms of Society in the Greek World.* Baltimore, MD (translation of *Le Chasseurnoir: Formes de pensées et formes de société dans le monde grec*, Paris, 1981).

Vigneron, R. 1983. "L'antifeministe loi Voconia et les 'Schleichwege des Lebens.'" *Labeo* 29: 140–153.

Visky, K. 1970. "Le operae dei liberti." *Index* 1: 221–229.

Vittinghoff, F. 1952. *Römische Kolonisation und Bürgerrechtspolitik unter Caesar und Augustus.* Wiesbaden.

Vittinghoff, F. 1990. "Gesellschaft." In *Europäische Wirtschafts- und Sozialgeschichte in der römischen Kaiserzeit*, edited by F. Vittinghoff, pp. 161–369. Stuttgart.

Vivenza, G. 2012. "Roman Economic Thought." In Scheidel, ed., pp. 25–44.

Vlassopoulos, K. 2011. "Greek Slavery: From Domination to Property and Back Again." *Journal of Helloenic Studies* 131: 115–130.

Vlassopoulos, K. 2016. "Finley's Slavery." In *M. I. Finley: An Ancient Historian and His Impact*, edited by D. Jew, R. Osborne, and M. Scott, pp. 76–99. Cambridge.

Volterra, E. [1967] 1993. "La base economica della elaborazione sistemica del diritto romano." *Scritti giuridici* 5: 123–155 (originally published in *Rivista italiana per le scienze giuridiche* 94: 239–271). Napoli.

Volterra, E. [1973] 1993. "Les femmes dans les 'inscriptiones' des rescrits impériaux." *Scritti Giuridici* 5: 339 ff. (= *Xenion, Festschrift P. J. Zepos*, Vol. 1, Athens, 1973, pp. 717–724). Napoli.

Volterra, E. 1991. "Matrimonio (diritto romano). In *Enciclopedia del diritto 25* (= 1991 *Scritti giuridici* 3: 22–303). Milan.

Vromen, J. 1995. *Economic Evolution: An Enquiry into the Foundations of New Institutional Economics.* London.

Wacke, A. 1994. "Die adjektizischen Klagen im Überblick." *Zeitschrift der Savigny-Stiftung für Rechtsgeschichte* (Romanist.Abt.) 111: 280–362.

Wacke, A. 2001. "*Manumissio matrimonii causa.* Die Freilassung zwecks Heirat nach den Ehegesetzen des Augustus." In Bellen and Heinen, eds., pp. 133–158.

Wacke, A. 2006. "*Die libera administratio peculii: Zur Verfügungsmacht von Hauskindern und Sklaven über ihr Sondergut.*" In *Sklaverei und Freilassung im römischen Recht. Symposion für H. J. Wieling zum 70. Geburtstag*, edited by T. Finkenauer, pp. 251–316. Berlin.

Wagner, H. 1967. "Zur Freiheitserteilung in den einem Generalpfandnexus unterliegenden Sklaven." *Studia et Documenta Historiae et Iuris* 33: 163–188.

Waldstein, W. 1986. *Operae libertorum: Untersuchungen zur Dienstpflicht freigelassener Sklaven*. Stuttgart.

Wallace-Hadrill, A. 2008. *Rome's Cultural Revolution*. Cambridge.

Wallochny, B. 1992. *Streitszehnen in der griechischen und römischen Komödie*. Tübingen.

Ward, I. 2004. *Introduction to Critical Legal Theory*. New York.

Watson, A. 1961. *Contract of Mandate in Roman Law*. Oxford.

Watson, A. 1965. *The Law of Obligations in the Later Roman Republic.* Oxford.

Watson, A. 1967. *The Law of Persons in the Later Roman Republic.* Oxford.

Watson, A. 1974. *Law Making in the Later Roman Republic.* Oxford.

Watson, A. 1987. *Roman Slave Law*. Baltimore, MD.

Watson, A. 1993. *Legal Transplants: An Approach to Comparative Law*, 2nd ed. Athens, GA.

Watson, A. 1994. "Prolegomena to Establishing Pre-Justinianic Texts." *Tijdschrift voor Rechtsgeschiedenis* 62: 113–125.

Watson, A. 1995. *The Spirit of Roman Law*. Athens, GA.

Watson, A. 2001. *Society and Legal Change*, 2nd ed. Philadelphia.

Watson, A. 2006. *The Shame of American Legal Education*, 2nd ed. Lake Mary, FL.

Watson, A. 2007. "Law and Society." In Cairns and du Plessis, eds., pp. 9–35.

Watson, A., ed. 1985, 1999. *The Digest of Justinian*. Philadelphia.

Weaver, P. 1965. "The Father of Claudius Etruscus: Statius *Silvae* 3.3." *Classical Quarterly* 15: 145–154.

Weaver, P. 1972. *Familia Caesaris: A Social Study of the Emperor's Freedmen and Slaves.* Cambridge.

Weaver, P. 1994. "Epaphroditus, Josephus, and Epictetus." *Classical Quarterly* 44.2: 468–479.

Weaver, P. 1997. "Children of Junian-Latins." In *The Roman Family in Italy: Status, Sentiment, Space*, edited by B. Rawson and P. Weaver, pp. 55–72. Oxford.

Weaver, P. 2001. "Reconstructing Lower-Class Roman Families." In *Childhood, Class and Kin in the Roman World*, edited by S. Dixon, pp. 101–114. London.

Weaver, P. 2005. "Phaon, Freedman of Nero." *Zeitschrift für Papyrologie und Epigraphik* 151: 243–252.

Weber, E. 2008. "Libertus et Coniunx." In *Antike Lebenswelten. Konstanz—Wandels—Wirkungsmacht: Festschrift für Ingomar Weiler zum 70. Geburtstag*, edited by P. Mauritsch, R. Rollinger, and W. Petermandl, pp. 367–381. Wiesbaden.

Webster, J. 2005. "Archaeologies of Slavery and Servitude: Bringing 'New World' Perspectives to Roman Britain." *Journal of Roman Archaeology* 18: 161–179.

Webster, T. 1973. *Potter and Patron in Classical Athens*. London.

Weiler, I. 2001. "Eine Sklavin wird frei. Zur Rolle des Geschlechts bei der Freilassung." In Bellen and Heinen, eds., pp. 113–132.

Weiler, I. 2003. *Die Beendigung des Sklavenstatus im Altertum: Ein Beitrag zur vergleichenden Sozialgeschichte*. Stuttgart.

Weishaupt, A. 1999. *Die Lex Voconia*. Cologne.

Weiss, A. 2001. "*Limocincti* in Irni: Zur Ergänzgung des Duumvirnparagraphen 18 der *lex Irnitana*." *Zeitschrift für Papyrologie und Epigraphik* 135: 284–286.

Weiss, A. 2004. *Sklave der Stadt: Untersuchungen zur öffentlichen Sklaverei in den Städten des römischen Reiches*. Historia Einzelschriften no. 173. Stuttgart.

Welch, K. 1995. "The Office of *Praefectus Fabrum* in the Late Republic." *Chiron* 25: 131–145.

Wellebrouck, G. 2016. *Présence et Ambitions des affranchis dans l'Empire Romain*. Dissertation, Université Paris-IV Sorbonne.

Wenger, L. 1953. *Die Quellen des römischen Rechts*. Vienna.

Whitman, S. 1995. "Diverse Good Causes: Manumission and the Transformation of Urban Slavery." *Social Science History* 19: 333–370.

Whitman, S. 1997. *The Price of Freedom: Slavery and Manumission in Baltimore and Early National Maryland*. Lexington, KY.

Wibier, M. 2020. "Legal Education and Legal Culture in Gaul during the Principate." In Czajkowski, Eckhardt, and Strothmann, eds., pp. 461–485.

Wickham, C. 2005. *Framing the Early Middle Ages: Europe and the Mediterranean, 400–800*. Oxford.

Wieacker, F. 1988. *Römische Rechtsgeschichte*. Munich.

Wiedemann, T. 1985. "The Regularity of Manumission at Rome." *Classical Quarterly* 35: 162–175.

Wiedemann, T. [1987] 1997. *Slavery*. Oxford.

Wieling, H. 1999. *Corpus der Römischen Rechtsquellen zur antiken Sklaverei. 1. Die Begründung des Sklavenstatus nach ius gentium und ius civile*. Stuttgart.

Williamson, J. 2009. *History without Evidence: Latin American Inequality since 1491*. National Bureau of Economic Research Working Paper #w14766. Cambridge, MA.

Williamson, O. 1979. "Transaction-cost Economics: The Governance of Contractual Relations." *Journal of Law and Economics* 22: 233–261.

Williamson, O. 1985. *The Economic Institutions of Capitalism: Firms, Markets, Relational Contracting*. New York.

Williamson, O. 2005. "Transaction Cost Economics." In Ménard and Shirley, eds., pp. 41–65.

Wilson, A. 1966. *Emigration from Italy in the Republican Age*. Manchester.

Wilson, A., and A. Bowman, eds. 2018. *Trade, Commerce, and the State in the Roman World*. Oxford.

Wilson, C. 1994. *Freedom at Risk: The Kidnapping of Free Blacks in America, 1780–1865*. Lexington, KY.

Winterling, A. 1999. *Aula Caesaris: Studien zur Institutionalisierung des römischen Kaiserhofes in der Zeit von Augustus bis Commodus (31 v. Chr.–192 n. Chr.)*. Munich.

Wolf, J. 1988. *Das Senatusconsultum Silanianum und die Senatsrede des C. Cassius Longinus aus dem Jahre 61 n.Chr.* Heidelberg.

Wolf, J. 2010a. *Aus dem neuen pompeianischen Urkundenfund: Gesammelte Aufsätze*. Berlin.

Wolf, J. 2010b. *Neue Rechtsurkunden aus Pompeji: Tabulae Pompeianae Novae*. Darmstadt.

Wolf, J. 2015. "Documents in Roman Practice." In Johnston, ed., pp. 61–84.

Wolf, M. 1965. *Untersuchungen zur Stellung der kaiserlichen Freigelassenen und Sklaven in Italien und den Westpovinzen*. Dissertation, Münster.

Wolff, H. 1956. "Zwei Miszellen." *Eos* 48 (= Symbolae R. Taubenschlag): 355–371.

Wolff, H. 1975. "Juristische Gräzistik—Aufgaben, Probleme, Möglichkeiten." In *Symposion 1975 (Akten der Gesellschaft für Griechische und Hellenistische Rechtsgeschichte)*, edited by H. Wolff, J. Méléze, and D. Norr, pp. 1–22. Cologne.

Wolff, H. 1976. *Die Constitutio Antoniana und Papyrus Gissensis 40.1*. Cologne.

Wolff, H., and H. Rupprecht. 2002. *Das Recht der griechischen Papyri Ëgyptens in der Zeit der Ptolemäer und des Prinzipats*, Vol. I. Munich.

Wolodkiewicz, W. 1983. "Attorno al significato della nozione di *mater familias.*" *Studi in honore di C. Sanfilippo* 3: 735–756. Milan.

Woolf, G. 1995. "The Formation of Roman Provincial Cultures." In *Integration in the Early Roman West: The Role of Culture and Ideology*, edited by J. Metzler, pp. 9–18. Luxembourg.

Woolf, G. 1998. *Becoming Roman: The Origins of Provincial Civilization in Gaul*. Cambridge.

Wright, F. [1923] 1969. *Feminism in Greek Literature: From Homer to Aristotle*. Port Washington, NY.

Yiftach-Firanko, U. 2009. "Law in Graeco-Roman Egypt; Hellenization, Fusion, Romanization." In *The Oxford Handbook of Papyrology*, edited by R. Bagnall, pp. 541–559. Oxford.

Yiftach, U., and M. Faraguna, eds. 2017. *Ancient Guardianship: Legal Incapacities in the Ancient World* (Legal Documents in Ancient Societies 6). Trieste.

Zeber, I. 1981. *A Study of the Peculium of a Slave in Pre-Classical and Classical Roman Law*. Wroclaw.

Zelnick-Abramovitz, R. 2005. *Not Wholly Free: The Concept of Manumission and the Status of Manumitted Slaves in the Ancient Greek World*. Leiden.

Zelnick-Abramovitz, R. 2013. "Manumission, Greek and Roman." In *The Encyclopedia of Ancient History*, edited by R. Bagnall, K. Brodersen, C. Champion, A. Erskine, and S. Huebner, pp. 4267–4270. Oxford (online edition, pp. 1–3).

Zelnick-Abramovitz, R. 2018. "The Status of Slaves Manumitted under *Paramonê*: A Reappraisal." In Thür, Yiftach, and Zelnick-Abramovitz, eds., pp. 377–402.

Zimmerman, R. 1990. *The Law of Obligations: Roman Foundations of the Civilian Tradition*. Cape Town.

Zolnierczuk, M. 1976. "Self-Purchase from Slavery in Classical Roman Law: *Servus suis nummis emptus*." *Annales Universitatis Mariae Curie-Sklodowska* 23.6: 87–121.

Zuiderhoek, A. 2013. "Workers of the Ancient World: Analyzing Labour in Classical Antiquity." *Workers of the World: International Journal on Strikes and Social Conflicts* 1.3: 32–48. http://digitalcommons.ilr.cornell.edu/wotw/3/.

Zuiderhoek, A. 2017. "Sorting Out Labour in the Roman Provinces: Some Reflections on Labour and Institutions in Asia Minor." In Verboven and Laes, eds., pp. 20–35.

Zulueta, F. de. 1953. *The Institutes of Gaius*, Part II. Oxford.

Zwalve, W. 2002. "Callistus' Case: Some Legal Aspects of Roman Business Activities." In de Blois and Rich, eds., pp. 116–127.

Zweigert, K., and H. Kötz. 1996. *Einführung in die Rechtsvergleichung: Auf dem Gebiete des Privatrechts*. Tübingen.

General Index

For the benefit of digital users, indexed terms that span two pages (e.g., 52–53) may, on occasion, appear on only one of those pages.

Index of Passages Cited

For the benefit of digital users, indexed terms that span two pages (e.g., 52–53) may, on occasion, appear on only one of those pages.